NEW DIRECTIONS IN SCANDINAVIAN STUDIES

NEW DIRECTIONS IN SCANDINAVIAN STUDIES

This series offers interdisciplinary approaches to the study of the Nordic region of Scandinavia and the Baltic States and their cultural connections in North America. By redefining the boundaries of Scandinavian studies to include the Baltic States and Scandinavian America, this series presents books that focus on the study of the culture, history, literature, and politics of the North.

Small States in International Relations
Edited by Christine Ingebritsen, Iver Neumann,
Sieglinde Gstöhl, and Jessica Beyer

Small States in International Relations

Edited by

CHRISTINE INGEBRITSEN,

IVER NEUMANN,

SIEGLINDE GSTÖHL,

and JESSICA BEYER

UNIVERSITY OF WASHINGTON PRESS • SEATTLE

UNIVERSITY OF ICELAND PRESS • REYKJAVIK

This publication has been supported by generous grants from the
Scandinavian Studies Publications Fund and the Graduate School
of the University of Washington.

This book also received support from the Jackson School
Publications Fund, established through the generous support of the
Henry M. Jackson Foundation and other donors, in cooperation
with the Henry M. Jackson School of International Studies and the
University of Washington Press.

University of Washington Press
P.O. Box 50096
Seattle, WA 98145–5096, U.S.A.
www.washington.edu/uwpress

University of Iceland Press
Haskolabioi v / Hagatorg
IS-107 Reykjavik
Iceland

Library of Congress Cataloging-in-Publication Data
Small states in international relations / edited by Christine
Ingebritsen . . . [et al.].
    p. cm. — (New directions in Scandinavian studies)
Includes bibliographical references and index.
ISBN 0-295-98524-0 (pbk. : alk. paper)
1. International relations.   2. States, Small.   3. International
organization.   4. World politics—1945–1989.   5. World
politics— 1989–   I. Ingebritsen, Christine.   II. Series.
JZ3900.S63   2006
327.1—dc22   2006002213

This book is printed on New Leaf Ecobook 50, which is
100 percent recycled, containing 50 percent post-consumer
waste, and is processed chlorine free. Ecobook 50 is acid free
and meets the minimum requirements of ANSI/NISO
Z39–49–1992 (R1997) Permanence of paper.♾♻

CONTENTS

Small States
in International
Relations

INTRODUCTION

Lilliputians in Gulliver's World?

IVER B. NEUMANN AND SIEGLINDE GSTÖHL

1. Small States in the International System

International Relations (IR) is a state-centric discipline as well as a power-centered discipline, and this volume will not challenge either of those two foundations. Our aim is rather to draw attention to the importance of studying states in their diversity. More specifically, we want to demonstrate the value of studying small states. Of the currently 191 member states of the largely universal United Nations (UN), all but one or two dozen fall into the category of small states. Hence, even though this group is highly heterogeneous, small states are simply too numerous and—sometimes individually, but certainly collectively—too important to ignore. This volume includes leading contributions to scholarship on small states in international relations that should be of interest not only for inherent reasons, but also as an inspiration for students of International Relations to better them by producing novel and innovative work on this undeservedly neglected topic. Following some historical and conceptual observations on what "smallness" entails and on how small state studies have developed, this introduction suggests three different ways to conduct future research on small states which will also benefit the broader IR discipline.

In making the case for studying small states beyond their sheer number, we should first like to question an (implicit or explicit) assumption that is still basic to a lot of thinking in IR: namely that states having powerful capabilities will inevitably use them and are thus the states most worthy of examination. This assumption can only be made for an international system where the states concerned do not feel bound by responsibility or international norms of appropriate behavior such as, for instance, restrictions on the use of force. Second, from an institutionalist point of view, the great powers are also the powers in charge of the international system, and they may shape international institutions accordingly. The status of great-powerhood means that other actors will take what they consider to be the great power's interests into account, even in its absence. On the one hand, large states may have institutional privileges, such as a permanent seat in the UN Security Council or extra voting power in the Bretton Woods institutions. On the other hand, international institutions make resource-based power effects more visible because norms and rules are formalized and thus require justification—a reason for small states to highly value international law and international regimes. Thirdly, institutions and policies may be investigated not only as the outcome of great-power bargains, but also in terms of the actors' relations. The available case studies in IR heavily concentrate on great powers, and thus look at only one particular sample of states. By taking small states into account, International Relations would profit empirically by gaining new data. Such data would be welcome to firm up, for example, the discussions about how anarchy may have relative degrees of maturity, the importance of international institutions as foci of foreign policy, and the character of constitutive relations among the units of the states system. Studying states in all their diversity may well contribute to the advancement of IR theory. Since the publication of Annette Baker Fox, *The Power of Small States*, theorizing has shifted its spotlight from great power capabilities and interests to the role of ideas and global governance efforts of all kinds of actors.

SMALL STATES AS A CATEGORY IN IR

Small states started life as a residual category and under a different name. Until well into the twentieth century, in all European languages states were routinely referred to as "powers" (French *puissance*, German *Macht*, Russian *derzhava*, Spanish/Portuguese *poder*, etc.). While this noun is still used for a different category of states, namely "great powers" (and, more rarely, also for "middle powers"), "small powers" are nowadays simply referred to as "small states." This usage certainly further underlines their presumed lack of power in a quantitative sense. Following the Napoleonic Wars, "the powers" met at the Congress of Vienna. Those powers that made up the winning quadruple alliance—Great Britain, Prussia, Russia, and the Habsburg Empire—were soon convinced by the spokesman of vanquished France, Talleyrand, that questions of importance would have to be settled between these five powers. In today's parlance, we would say that they were to be settled "at five." However, some of the questions would directly concern powers that were deemed too important to be left out entirely. These powers were given access to certain meetings that were held "at six" or "at seven." As the century wore on, these powers sometimes came to be known, through processes that still await their researcher, as "middle powers" (see Holbraad 1984). Those powers that were deemed too inconsequential to be so included came to be known as "small states."

In this formative period of state categories, the dominant grouping of great powers took on a life in international law by dint of the institutionalizing move made by these five powers themselves. They decided on meeting, as it were, in concert on a regular basis in order to discuss questions of concern, and to draw up agreements and treaties. From this activity, documents with legal force evolved, and since they were underwritten by these five powers and not by others, the category of "great power" became a legal category. It has ever since cohabited uneasily with the principle of the sovereign equality of states. From a legal point of view, all sovereign states, great or small, are equal before the law. From a political stance, however, they are far from equal. From the very beginning, the recognition of the great powers' special position in the international system at the Congress of Vienna coexisted uneasily with the system's major principle of the formal equality of sovereign states, which was to prevent the great powers from formalizing their preponderance. In the narrow sense, what is still known as the Congress is taken to mean the meetings of those powers at Aix-la-Chapelle, Troppau, Laibach, and Verona in the period from 1815 to 1822. In the broader sense, congress diplomacy refers to the continued interaction between great powers with a view to managing the system. Such diplomacy was a dominant feature of European politics up to 1848, and was also highly relevant for the rest of the period up to the First World War (cf. Holbraad 1970).[1] As a result, in the nineteenth century, which to an IR scholar runs from 1815 to 1914, small states were all those states that were not great powers. This was so because European empires had incorporated most other polities worldwide, and because there simply were not enough sovereign states around to make for a viable category of "middle powers." As Hinsley (1963: 250) reminds us, if there were six great powers at this time (Germany, Great Britain, France, Russia, Austria-Hungary, Italy), of the rest, there were only three that could even begin to claim a status as middle powers: Denmark, Sweden and Turkey.[2]

In the twentieth century, as the number of states kept rising (as a result mainly of the break-up of the Habsburg Empire in 1919, then of the British, French, and other European empires through decolonialization in the 1950s and 1960s, and of the Soviet Union in 1991), small states were all those states that were not great powers, and that were not consistently insisting on being referred to as middle powers (Australia, Canada, also regionally dominant powers such as South Africa) (cf. Neumann 1992). We note that this definition is still residual: small states are defined by what they are not. Moreover, smallness is a comparative concept: micro-states are smaller than small states, and small states are smaller than middle or great powers, but with regard to what and how much? Many authors use absolute numbers referring to the size of populations, while others also take a state's territory or gross domestic product into account (cf. Handel 1981: 9–65; Crowards 2002). In the European context, the "bar" for small states has often been set at the population size of the Netherlands (currently 16 million inhabitants), which leaves all European countries as being small states except for Russia, Germany, Turkey, France, Great Britain, Italy, Ukraine, Spain, Poland, and Romania. The European micro-states have frequently been defined as having a population of less than 100,000 inhabitants (Andorra, Liechtenstein, Monaco, San Marino, Vatican) or one million people (thus including Iceland, Cyprus, Malta, and Luxembourg). Yet such classifications have been rather contested, since any precise definition can only be arbitrary. Hence, we need not investigate the questions of which countries are small states or great powers here; neither do we need to dwell on the conceptual history of "superpower" (basically a Cold War term) and the sundry terms for the United States (U.S.) that have recently emerged to categorize what Krauthammer (1991) baptized the "unipolar moment," such as "hyperpower." We may content ourselves with making the observation that certain tensions make themselves felt when it comes to classifying states.

If the small state category on the one hand shades into a gelatinous category of "middle powers," on the other hand it comes up against an equally gelatinous category of "micro-states." The literature on micro-states seems to congeal around issues of sovereignty and action capacity—on how dependence on other polities in formulating and conducting policy impinges on that policy (cf. Reid 1974; Plischke 1977; Harden 1985; Duursma 1996). In line with this, we suggest that it may be useful to think of micro-states as those states whose claim to maintain effective sovereignty on a territory is in some degree questioned by other states, and that cannot maintain what larger states at any one given time define as the minimum required presence in the international society of states (membership in international organizations, embassies in key capitals, etc.) for a perceived lack of resources. For example, in 1920, Liechtenstein's application for membership in the League of Nations was rejected because it had "chosen to depute to others some of the attributes of sovereignty" and maintained no army (Gstöhl 2001: 106). As a result, San Marino and Monaco did not further pursue their applications even though the League offered limited forms of participation. The limited capacities of these states led to their sovereignty being contested. Another example for a lack of capacity could be Costa Rica in the inter-war period. That state decided not to maintain its membership in the League of Nations because it did not think it could afford it, and so it went from being a small state to being a micro-state. By contrast, when, in the same period, the Norwegian state did not think it could afford sending its minister in Buenos Aires to the other three states to which he was side-accredited to present his credentials, this would not have an effect on Norway's standing as a small state, because the larger states did not really expect a small state to have a diplomatic presence in all the other states in the system. Lack of capacity means capacity that is seen to be beyond a minimum; what this minimum is, is a question of continuous negotiation. We stress that, for a state to be micro rather than small, absence from international society alone is not enough. The perceived reason has to be a lack of resources. Consider two small states such Albania and Switzerland during the Cold War; in their various ways, they did not maintain what larger states saw as a minimum presence; their reasons had to do with things other than a lack of resources, and so their standing as a small state was not threatened.

Concern about micro-states rose again considerably in the 1960s and 1970s with the process of decolonization. Many authors pointed to the dilemma that the right to self-determination promoted by the United Nations produced several new (very) small states whose influx into the world organization could cause significant problems (e.g., Blair 1967; Harris 1970; Gunter 1977). A vivid debate took place about how those micro-states would use their collective voting power in the General Assembly, who would finance their decisions dominated by Third World concerns, and whether they should be offered restricted membership. Since neither the anticipated proliferation of micro-states nor their capture of the UN happened, the dispute died off silently (cf. Gstöhl 2001: 104–112). Many tiny colonies had not opted for formal independence and sovereignty, but for other solutions, such as autonomy within a bigger state.[3] Nevertheless, Liechtenstein, Monaco, San Marino, Andorra, and other micro-states joined the UN only in the 1990s, when micro-state claims to equal sovereignty within international society were more readily accepted.

QUESTIONS OF QUANTITY AND QUALITY

In addition to the residual, negative way of defining small states as states that are not middle or great powers, small states have often been confused with weak states. Yet, the distinction between small and great does not co-incide with the distinction between strong and weak.[4] The former is a distinction of quantity, the latter of quality. Durkheim (1992: 75) notes that "societies can have their pride, not in being the greatest or the wealthiest, but in being the most just, the best organized and in possessing the best moral constitution." The implication is that they may be strong in the sense of being a model for others to follow in this regard. Within IR, Keohane and Nye (1977) famously argue that the question of smallness and greatness was not necessarily all that useful on the aggregate level of the states system where we have usually studied it, but that it should rather be treated as a question of clout within what they referred to as specific issue areas, that is, small states possessing great issue-specific power (for example the influence of Switzerland in the financial services sector or of Saudi Arabia and Kuwait in the oil sector).

These are interesting ways of bracketing the issue under discussion here, which is what it entails for a state to think of itself as, and be thought of by others as being, generally "small."[5] Asking such questions has led, and will lead, to new work and new insights, and thus it should be condoned. The states system understood as a whole neither is (nor should it be) the only focus of IR inquiry. Still, it is within this system that we can locate most of the talk about great powers and small states, and where these categories first and foremost are meaningful.[6] Within this system, moral greatness, various kinds of perceived greatness in internal organization, or greatness in resources within one specific issue area have so far not been convertible into great-power status. Indeed, the category of middle power basically seems to serve the function of underlining that some small state has achieved greatness in one specific regard, while remaining hopelessly behind in others. Sweden is doubtless a strong state both in the sense that it has a high degree of internal cohesion, is able to project a persona externally, and (for these and other reasons) has a strong sense of self. But regardless of how strong it is or will become, its resources simply will not allow it to make itself felt in enough arenas and to a high-enough degree for it to be recognized as a systems-wide great power.[7] By the opposite token, Russia is no doubt weak in the sense that state-society relations make for a low administrative capacity. Still, and sustained denigration notwithstanding, it would hardly make sense to refer to Russia as a small state. The same holds true for Japan and Germany, which for a long time have been considered economic giants, and yet political dwarves.

Overall, extant scholarship in the IR discipline has focused almost exclusively on great powers, while small states have been a residual category, defined by the alleged non-greatness of its members. It borders on two even more weakly defined sub-categories: middle powers (who may convincingly argue that they have achieved "greatness" in some other regard than in terms of systems-wide presence), and micro-states (who cannot participate fully in the institutions of that system due to a lack of administrative resources). The lack of an agreed concrete definition of small states has also marked the body of literature that might be termed small state studies. In the following sections, we discuss the advancement of this literature, and what lessons can be drawn from it for IR before the selected classic and modern contributions reprinted in this volume are introduced.

2. The Development of Small State Studies

BEGINNINGS

European and in particular German-speaking scholars have been interested in the study of small states throughout the eighteenth and nineteenth centuries (cf. Sieber 1920; Cappis 1923; Bratt 1951). However, by the mid-nineteenth century, the onward march of the idea of the nation-state made small states look increasingly unattractive. A key example is the debate surrounding the many small German states (*Kleinstaaterei*), which were increasingly perceived as being obstacles to the prospect of a unified Germany (Amstrup 1976: 163). The inter-war period offered the foreign policy of small (European) states novel opportunities, in particular in the newly created League of Nations in Geneva (cf. Rappard 1934). Following the idealist school of thought, international law and multilateral organizations were considered of greatest importance to small states. In support of the idea of collective security, some of them even began to disarm. However, the rise of Fascism in Europe and Japan put a sudden end to such peaceful visions. During the Second World War, security studies were on top of the scholarly agenda, and realism with its focus on power emerged as the dominant theory of International Relations. After 1945, the small states' position in the new international organizations such as the United Nations attracted some discussions (cf. Markus 1946; De Rusett 1954; Fleiner 1966), but in general the social sciences were preoccupied with the emergent bipolarity and the Cold War. "In retrospect it seems surprising that in spite of the growing number of small states only a small number of sociological studies were devoted to this subject in the first two decades after World War II" (Höll 1983b: 15).

Larger academic interest in small states returned with a study of the wartime diplomacy of small states by Annette Baker Fox (1959), which marked the beginning of a genuine school of small state studies. In *The Power of Small States*, she inquired into how the governments of small and militarily weak states resisted the pressure of great powers in times of crisis. Sweden, Spain, Turkey, Switzerland, Ireland, and Portugal all avoided being drawn into the Second World War, while other small states such as Denmark, Norway, Finland, and the Benelux countries failed to avoid the hostilities. Baker Fox examines in more detail the wartime diplomacy of Turkey, Finland, Norway, Sweden, and Spain. She argues that success depended on convincing the power pressing a small state that its neutrality was advantageous to the great power, too. Her study demonstrates the importance of the geostrategic neighborhood of small states and of their diplomatic skills (in terms of bargaining and credible arguing), hence taking into account both external and internal factors.

In the aftermath of the Second World War, the fundamental question remained the survival of small states among the bigger powers. In this context, alignment policy was analyzed as a means to compensate for their incapability to guarantee their own security (e.g., Rothstein 1968; Vital 1971; Schou/Brundtland 1971; Mathisen 1971; Azar 1973; Harden 1985). Höll (1978: 260) identifies three reasons for this renewed attention in the 1960s: first, the bias towards great powers and U.S. American research was increasingly perceived as a deficit of the IR discipline (particularly in the Scandinavian scientific community)[8]; second, the rapid social changes at the end of the 1960s put mainstream political science in question; and third, the increasing interdependence raised the issue of how states with limited capacities coped with the costs of dependence.

CLIMAX

Subsequent research set out to explore possible strategies small states might utilize to mitigate the effects of structural constraints. In fact, a whole branch of research focused on the question of which policies might help prevent or reduce the consequences of smallness and scarcity (cf. Vogel 1979; Frei 1977; Riklin 1975). There are strategies to avoid increasing interdependence in the first place (e.g., "system closure" through autarchy and isolationism in world affairs); strategies to avoid high external dependence either through a selective foreign policy that saves resources but increases one's prestige (e.g., membership in international organizations, good offices) or through a specialization in certain products and a diversification of trading partners; and strategies to avoid foreign determination (e.g., neutrality, integration). The options are not limited to foreign policy choices, but also include domestic strategies such as consoci-ational democracy, corporatism, or federalism. For example, Vogel (1983) provides an analytical framework that distinguishes between structurally determined behavior patterns and voluntary strategies of small states. The structural "causal chain" maintains that scarcity due to physical smallness produces external economic dependence, which may lead to external sen-sitivity, which in turn results in the danger of foreign determination. In order to reduce the effects of this causal mechanism, small states may pur-sue certain policies, and according to Vogel, they tend to concentrate on strategies to prevent external sensitivity (e.g., corporatism, or member-ship in international organizations).[9] As Vogel does, Lindell and Persson (1986) indicate that different levels of analysis, structure, and agency play a role. They provide a literary review on how small states can influence great powers, and identify two groups of explanatory factors. On the one hand, possible explanations comprise systemic factors such as the struc-ture of the international system (e.g., hierarchical, hegemonical, or bal-ance of power), the state of the international system (in terms of the de-gree of tension), international norms (e.g., sovereign equality, or a right to self-determination), and the actors' qualities (such as geography, re-sources, or reputation). On the other hand, the alternative courses of ac-tion open to small states may increase their leverage.

The study of small states as a specific research category reached its peak in the mid-1970s, in parallel to the wave of small states ensuing from the process of decolonialization. Small state theory was thriving both in eco-nomics and political science. Many economists, for example, argued that the size of a small nation determined its wealth due to its small domestic market, a low diversification of its economy, scarcity of natural resources, higher costs of production and lower economies of scale, a lack of com-petition, low research and development expenditure, etc. Small economies were assumed to be more dependent on external trade than bigger states, to tend to have trade deficits, to depend often on a single commodity of export, and to export hardly any industrial goods requiring a high inten-sity of capital or research (cf. Höll 1978: 265–270; Vogel 1979: 32–35; Han-del 1981: 220–229). A similar development took place in political science, where, in particular, neorealists argued that the physical size of a state—or its relative power capabilities—determined its behavior in interna-tional politics. Therefore, small states of similar size were expected to pursue similar foreign policies (cf. Vogel 1979: 23–32). For example, as part of a broad effort to establish a research program on comparative for-eign policy, East (1973) set out to test two competing models using a data set of thousands of foreign policy events initiated by 32 states of different size and economic development in the time period from 1959 to 1968.[10] His findings rejected the assumption that small-state behavior is the result of the same general processes of decision-making that are found in larger states. By contrast, small states try to minimize the costs of conducting foreign policy by initiating more joint actions and by targeting multiple-actor fora. Economic issues were relatively more important to small states, and while they tend to avoid ambiguity in their foreign policy, they engage more in conflictive non-verbal behavior than large states.

STANDSTILL

Most of these hypotheses have subsequently been falsified, and small-state research culminated in Baehr's (1975) conclusion that the concept of small states was not a useful analytical tool for understanding world politics. Consequently, these approaches to small states were not much further developed in the 1980s and early 1990s. The few contributions that were published in this tradition concerned specific problems of European small states and lacked any claim to generating theory (Kramer 1993: 252). The relative standstill of theory-driven research on small states at least spurred some exercises of stock-taking (e.g., Höll 1983a; Lindell/Persson 1986). Kramer (1993: 257) argues that this virtual stagnation was due to the fact that those theoretical approaches were middle-range theories bound in time and (European) context. Research on small states simply neglected the changing international environment. Besides the missing agreed-definition of small states, there was, as Amstrup (1976: 178) put it, an "astonishing lack of cumulation" in small state studies. Another scholar lamented that the study of small states had generally suffered from "benign neglect" in IR (Christmas-Møller 1983: 39).

Against these pessimistic assessments, small states still encountered some academic interest in the 1980s, especially issues of economic development (e.g., Clark/Payne 1987; Butter 1985). On the whole, however, scholars either turned to general IR theories because the size of states was not considered a relevant category anymore, or they developed new approaches to study small states. In the latter category, Katzenstein's (1985) analysis of how small states cope with the forces of an increasingly global economy stands out. Neoliberal institutionalism began to challenge the predominance of neorealist theory with its almost exclusive focus on security matters. Economic issues, international institutions and the significance of absolute, as opposed to relative, gains became more important. The general focus on

international regimes and institutions in the 1980s—a genuine area of interest for small states—helped prepare the ground for bringing small states
back in. Krasner (1981), for instance, deals with the impact of (weak) developing countries on international institutions and in particular with their
quest for a new international economic order in the 1970s. He argues that
these countries—many of them small—have in response to their domestic and international structural weaknesses sought to alter international
regimes to gain some control. They have been able to do so because the
dependency school of thought has forged the South into a unified bloc
opposed to the liberal principles and norms of the international system
at the time; hence weak or small states can take advantage of existing institutional arrangements that had originally been created for other purposes.

REVIVAL

The radical historical changes at the end of the 1980s further diluted, as
Waschkuhn (1991: 154) points out, the theoretical claims about the size of
states and its implications that were popular in the 1960s. The rise of modern information technologies and the gradual elimination of barriers to
trade in the context of globalization and regional integration further questioned the assertions about small states' economies and foreign policies.
The improvements in communication and transportation as well as the
liberalization of the movement of goods, services, capital, and even persons and public procurement, rendered borders less meaningful to the
benefit of small states (e.g., Kindley/Good 1997; Armstrong/Read 1998;
Moses 2000; Salvatore/Svetlicic/Damijan 2001). Moreover, the increasingly
deeper integration of small states in the European Union (EU) as well as
the EU's enlargement to numerous small states, have attracted renewed
attention to the small-state issue (e.g., Dosenrode-Lynge 1993; Goetschel
1998; Thorhallsson 2000). For example, Ólafsson (1998) argues—with a view
to Iceland—that small states might not necessarily obtain larger economic gains from European integration than from free trade on the world
market, and that influence may only be increased if each member enjoys
equal rights regardless of size.

   In addition to processes of globalization and regional integration,
small state theory has been both promoted and challenged by the unpre-
dicted emergence of new small states in Central and Eastern Europe, the
Balkans, and the Baltics after the fall of the Berlin wall (cf. Kirt/Waschkuhn
2001a). The right of self-determination, which marked the period of decolonization, regained prominence after the Cold War as a result of the dis-

integration of several multi-ethnic countries—some of which entailed ethno-political conflicts in small states (e.g., Zahariadis 1994; Jazbec 2001). In addition to internal strife, external security issues regained prominence, in particular because since the mid-1990s many small states in Europe have actively been seeking membership in the EU and in the North Atlantic Treaty Organization (NATO) (cf. Bauwens/Clesse/Knudsen 1996; Gaertner/Reiter 2000). In contrast to the upsurge of regional cooperation in Europe (with the exception of Ex-Yugoslavia), the Americas, and the Asia-Pacific region, many small states in Africa have been facing internal breakdown (cf. Jackson 1990). Robert Jackson and Carl Rosberg (1982) distinguish between empirical and juridical components of statehood. Their article, "Why Africa's Weak States Persist," adds a non-European perspective that is important because the "history of Black Africa challenges more than it supports some of the major postulates of international relations theory" (Jackson/Rosberg 1982: 24). The authors claim that, at the time of their writing, some de jure sub-Saharan African states would de facto not have qualified as states because they did not effectively hold a monopoly of force throughout their territory. Unlike in other regions of the world, self-determination came to a halt in Black Africa at the inherited colonial frontiers. That is, in most cases, a colony simply became a state with its territory unchanged even though these frontiers did not correspond to the traditional cultural borders. "In Europe, empirical statehood preceded juridical statehood or was concurrent with it," whereas in Black Africa and some other developing regions, "external factors are more likely than internal factors to provide an adequate explanation for the formation and persistence of states" (Jackson/Rosberg 1982: 23; also Rotberg 2004). To these authors, Africa's weak states persist as a result of the ideology of Pan-Africanism, the vulnerability of all states in the region and the insecurity of statesmen, the support of the larger international society, and the reluctance of non-African powers to intervene in the affairs of African states. Their contribution anticipates aspects of the current debate about failing, failed, and collapsed states.

Finally, the changes in IR theory that came with the end of the bipolar freeze (and, in some cases, the rise of nationalism) —in particular social constructivism with its focus on international norms, identity, and ideas— may have eased the opening of the field of small state studies again in the 1990s. If not only relative power and/or international institutions matter, but also ideational factors, small states may gain new room to maneuver in their foreign policy. They may, for instance, be able to play the role of norm entrepreneurs influencing world politics (cf. Björkdahl 2002;

Ingebritsen 2002); they may not only engage in bargaining with the other (greater) powers, but also argue with them, pursue framing and discursive politics, and socially construct new, more favorable identities in their relationships. Risse-Kappen (1995), for instance, argues that NATO constitutes a community of liberal democracies that has deeply affected the collective identity of all members, including the superpower. Shared values and norms, domestic pressures, and transnational coalitions helped the "small" West European and Canadian allies influence U.S. American security policies.

In sum, there was no continuous flow of research on small states. Knudsen (2002: 182) observes three rather disconnected streams of literature in the study of small states: a first tradition is concerned with issues of self-determination, a second strand deals with the foreign policy options of neutrality or alliance, and a third thread comprises the comparative literature on politics and policy formation in small states.[11]

Table 1.1 recapitulates the postwar development of small state studies described in this chapter by placing it in the context of major historical events and mainstream IR theory. Both general developments in history (such as the Cold War and its end, or decolonization) and in IR literature significantly impacted the field. The theory of International Relations has largely evolved by debates: when in the wake of World War II realism (and later neorealism) superseded the idealist school of thought, power capabilities and security issues constituted the main concern in small state studies. Ironically, this first (neo)realist period—which basically attributed no relevance to small or weak states—coincided with the heyday of small state studies. The 1980s were dominated by the controversy between neorealism (still stressing security issues and relative gains) and neoliberal institutionalism (focusing more on economic cooperation, international institutions, and absolute gains). This second phase was characterized by a relative standstill in the study of small states, even though a few key contributions were made in the field of International Political Economy. This observation matches well with the neoliberal focus on economic interdependence, but one might have expected more literature on small states in international institutions—a topic that was, again somewhat paradoxically, more prominent during the first phase. In the third period of the 1990s, the rationalist "neo-neo debate"—sharing a systemic perspective and the assumption of the (unitary) state acting according to cost-benefit calculations—has been challenged by new social constructivist and post-positivist approaches emphasizing ideas, norms, and (national) identities. This theoretical progress has led to a revival of small state studies. Recent

TABLE 1.1 Synopsis of small state studies

Historical events	1950s–1970s: heyday Cold War conflict; proliferation of small states through decolonization	1980s: standstill decline of the U.S. hegemon and rise of global inter-dependence	1990s: revival end of Cold War, globalization and regional integration; proliferation of small states through disintegration
Dominant IR theory	realism/neorealism	neorealism vs. neo-liberal institutionalism	rationalism vs. social constructivism
Small state topics	definition of small states, size and foreign policy, security issues, small and micro-states in international organizations	small states and economic interdependence and development issues	small states in European integration in globalization processes, ethno-political conflicts

contributions inter alia pay attention to the role of small states as norm entrepreneurs, actors in regional integration, or as sources of ethno-political conflicts. In the age of globalization, not only have non-state actors acquired new meaning, but small states are also benefiting from taking part in efforts of global governance and from renewed scholarly attention.

Small state studies are still a relatively young discipline occupying a niche position in IR (Kirt/Waschkuhn 2001b: 23–25). This niche holds considerable potential for future research, both on individual small states and on theoretical aspects relevant to IR. The continued existence and even proliferation of small states in spite of the supposedly unfavorable odds must constitute a challenge to social scientists. Small states are not just "mini versions" of great powers but may pursue different goals and policies worth studying. Besides, small state studies have several insights to offer to the broader discipline of International Relations.

3. Small State Lessons for IR

We suggest three ways in which the study of small states may be relevant to IR. There are a number of other reasons why small states may be profitably studied: inherent interest, interest in a particular issue area, region or sequence of events, comparative interest, and so forth. Those are not our primary concerns in this volume, however. While our three approaches have an affinity to (neo)realism, neoliberal institutionalism, and social constructivism, respectively, in order to focus directly on the issues at stake rather than on debates about labels and wider patterns of thought, we list them simply as "capabilities," "institutions," and "relations."

CAPABILITIES

The basic way in which smallness has been studied in IR is in terms of capabilities.[12] And indeed, if smallness is a question of a certain lack in relative capabilities, this might be a good starting point. Already Morgenthau (1972: 129–30) had made clear that "A Great Power is a state which is able to have its will against a small state . . . which in turn is not able to have its will against a Great Power," yet "a Great Power could easily sink to the level of a second-rate or small Power, and a small Power could easily rise to the eminence of a Great Power." Such studies are preoccupied with how to measure capabilities. They assume that having the capability implies pending action. The literally classic reference here is to the so-called Melian dialogue in Thucydides' analysis of the Peloponnesian War. The dialogue concerned what the great city state of Athens should do when attempts to bring the small city state of Melos into its alliance against the other great power in the system—Sparta—failed, and the prospect thereby opened up that Melos and its resources might be taken over by Sparta and used against Athens. The exchange between the Athenians and the Melians about this issue is mainly a prelude to the key dialogue, which is between those Athenians who favor killing all the men and enslaving all the women and children and those Athenians who favor letting Melos go about its own business. The former prevails. The reason why the Melian dialogue is famous is that its emblematic formulation, that we live in a world where the strong do what they want and the weak suffer what they must, has been taken to be representative for politics everywhere. If this holds good, then what there is to be said about small states was basically already said some 2,500 years ago.

The key issue here—that having a capability will automatically entail its indiscriminate use—is one that is still widespread in IR thinking. For example, Kagan (2003) recently received much attention for an argument that hinged on the assumption that the United States would act differently than the European Union in global politics simply because it had superior capabilities. Present-day neorealists still tend to begin their analyses of powers great and small with an analysis of relative capabilities—and some of them even end there. It is interesting to note that neorealists based within states with large capabilities tend to celebrate the importance of large capabilities, thus neglecting small states. Neorealists who work in small states, by contrast, are inclined to study such phenomena as bandwagoning (that is, small state strategies of joining coalitions and alliances of states that are perceived as winning ones) or balancing (that is, strategies of joining weaker coalitions to reach a balance of power). For example, the American scholar Walt (1987) stresses how great powers bring alliances into being and maintain them once they exist, while his Danish student Wivel (2000) stresses how and why small states tend to join or not to join those alliances.

The privileging of capabilities may lead one to be dismissive of small states. Kennedy (1991: 186 n 18 in extenso) notes that "No doubt it is theoretically possible for a small nation to develop a grand strategy, but the latter term is generally understood to imply the endeavors of a power with extensive (i.e., not just local) interests and obligations, to reconcile its means and its ends." A similar sense of priority is on display in the work of the cuddly realists of the English School of International Relations, as Watson (1982: 198) writes in his book on diplomacy:

> I have cited . . . some of the services rendered by Switzerland to the diplomatic dialogue. The contribution of the Netherlands to the development of international law is also impressive. Some states are more acceptable than others when it comes to making up a peacekeeping force. . . . The impact of a group or bloc of smaller states, such as OPEC, may be considerable. Even so, these variations are minor. It is the larger powers that determine the effectiveness of diplomacy. This mechanical fact goes far to explain why in many systems of states special responsibilities for the functioning of international relations, the management of order, and the leadership of the diplomatic dialogue have been entrusted by a general consensus to great powers.

As a residual category, small states are often treated as objects, not as subjects of international relations. The history of international politics then is the history of great powers. Morgenthau's magnum opus *Politics Among Nations* (1948) should more appropriately be called *Politics Among Great Nations*. According to him, "Small nations have always owed their independence either to the balance of power (Belgium and the Balkan countries until the Second World War), or to the preponderance of one protecting power (the small nations of Central and South America, and Portugal), or to their lack of attractiveness for imperialistic aspirations (Switzerland and Spain)" (Morgenthau 1948: 196).

The basic problem with starting an analysis of small states from the question of capabilities is that it identifies one structural precondition—a difference in power that is basically materially conceived and often even restricted to military power—and simply assumes that everything else will wither into irrelevance in the long or even short run. Such a blanket assumption, however, can only be made for situations where there are no ties of any kind binding the parties together, and no feeling of responsibility on behalf of actors that are due to other causes such as international norms. In IR terms, it can only be made in a situation of highly immature anarchy, with predatory actors. For example, the assumption does not prove true for the situation that Thucydides actually describes in the Melian dialogue. Even within the system of Greek city states it was not a foregone conclusion that the strong would do as they could and the weak would suffer what they must. There is no textual evidence for arguing that this specific dialogue had to turn out the way it did. Anarchy may, after all, be more or less mature. The degree of immaturity depends, among other things, on the degree to which the system is institutionalized.

INSTITUTIONS

If one starts not from capabilities but from institutions, then the question of smallness presents itself in a different way. Here we find the view that the great powers are also the great responsibles, that they are, as it were, in charge of the system, and that small states should therefore be studied in the light of great-power negotiations. "As when we say that a cold spell in winter is responsible for the deaths of birds, so we may note that larger states are more responsible for the way in which the diplomatic dialogue is conducted and the way in which the system operates than smaller ones are, without saying anything about the intentions of states or making any moral judgement" (Watson 1982: 195). For example, the UN Security Council has five permanent members that are supposed to work together, as well as with the other members, among which we find many small states. This example brings out how congress diplomacy is nested within a broader multilateral diplomacy, where it may make itself more or less felt depending on specific circumstances. Another and institutionally more clear-cut example is the Contact Group setup among the great powers who took an immediate interest in Balkan politics in the 1990s (cf. Schwegmann 2001).

One particularly poignant branch of theorizing that stresses a managerial great-power role is hegemonic stability theory. Hegemony exists where one power acts as the primus inter pares, first among equals (e.g., Kindleberger 1973; Gilpin 1981).[13] It is alone in being great, and other powers are relegated to graded degrees of smallness. Against the background of the debate about an "American decline" in the 1970s, regime theory showed in the following years that international regimes may assume a hegemon's functions of providing international order and cooperation (e.g. Keohane 1984). All the same, it has recently been argued that the G8 (the informal grouping of the seven leading industrial nations plus Russia) has replaced the single U.S. hegemon and increasingly institutionalized itself as the new "group hegemon." Volgy and Bailin (2003: 91), for instance, speak of institutionalized group hegemony "when the great powers act as a group to mitigate crises and to maintain stability, and they take steps to institutionalize their relationships."

But why should the institutionalization of smallness and greatness matter? There are basically two reasons, where the second reason flows from the first. The first reason has to do with effects of power. The status of being a great power is a prerogative and hence a resource. Being recognized as a great power means that decision-makers in other polities will take what they consider to be your interests into account. The great power is thus present even when absent; it exerts power in settings that it does not even know exist. It governs from afar. In addition, other great powers will, at least in principle, recognize its rightful interests. "The contribution of the great powers to international order derives from the sheer facts of inequality of power as between the states that make up the international system" (Bull 1977: 194). Because states are grossly unequal in power, certain international issues are settled, while others are not. There may also be institutional rewards, such as a position as a guarantor of peace or a permanent seat in the UN Security Council. The second reason is that institutionalization makes the power effects that flow from great powerhood less invisible in the sense that a certain set of norms and rules is being formalized, and so it is open to debate and question. A legal and political language in which to speak about interstate relations emerges more clearly as a new medium and a new resource for states to manipulate. The more resources from which a certain state is cut off, the more important to it are those resources on which it may still draw. It follows that, to small states, whose smallness is seen exactly as a result of them having access to limited material resources, this language is likely to be more important than it is to greater powers. We have here a structural factor that may predispose small states to favor discourses that institutionalize rules and norms, such as international law, international regimes, and international institutions.[14] This insight points to the importance of studying the role of small states in international organizations such as the United Nations or the European Union. According to UN Secretary-General Annan (1998),

> It is easy for small nations to feel daunted by the global forces at work . . . Large countries with enormous labour forces, abundant natural resources, arsenals of high-tech weaponry and fleets of expert technicians and negotiators may seem to have all the advantages. . . . I would like to sound the strongest possible note to the contrary. My long experience at the United Nations has shown me that the small States of the world . . . are more than capable of holding their own. I would even go so far as to say that their contributions are the very glue of progressive international cooperation for the common good.

RELATIONS

A different, and in a number of respects opposing, approach to studying small states via institutions is to investigate them not in terms of outcomes of great-power bargains or as already established arenas where great powers may manage international affairs, but in terms of the relations between states.[15] Small states and great powers are mutually constitutive—if there were no small states, there could be no great powers. In fact, the great powers have always been a minority in the society of states: the vast majority of states have been and are minor powers. Few social analysts working in fields other than IR would rest content with an analysis of social organizations or indeed institutions that looked only at one particular class of entities. When considered from this point of view, IR literature comes up fairly short not only because it often focuses on variation along just one variable, namely differences in capabilities, but also because even this job has not been done satisfactorily since case studies are heavily tilted towards the "giants." This weakness in traditional approaches is even more damning since the number of cases that make up the universe being studied—sovereign states—has in certain periods been very small indeed.[16] One should have thought that, given a number of cases this low, theorizing about international relations in those periods would take all cases into account. This, however, has not been the case.

For a discipline that counts perhaps as many as 10,000 scholars worldwide plus their students, it can hardly be considered an impossible task to establish data sets and conduct research that avails itself of a varied set of cases. So, even if we accept the highly contentious claim that IR should be about the states system, as well as the even more contentious claim that the variable to be given sustained attention is capabilities, we may still argue that the extant literature is worse off for its neglect of small states. How did IR as a discipline end up in this highly embarrassing situation? There are several reasons for this relative neglect of small state studies. First, from the perspective of the sociology of knowledge, it has been argued that IR is an American discipline, the U.S. is a great power, and so a great power perspective came to embed itself in the literature (Wæver 1998). This is not the whole story, however, for before the Second World War, IR was a British discipline, and Britain remains the second most important node. The next two states on the list of where to find IR scholars would probably be Germany and Japan, which also have a great-power history. Second, there are inherent difficulties in studying them, as Holbraad (1971: 77–78) rightly points out:

> Some of the charges of distortion that have been directed at the historians of earlier centuries, who snobbishly were inclined to write only about popes and emperors, kings and generals and to ignore the lower orders of society, may apply also to some modern writers on international politics. On the other hand, those who approach the subject from the point of view of the small nations are at a serious disadvantage. Moving among the pawns of international politics, among the states that, at least in major issues, tend to be objects rather than subjects, they find it hard to come to grips with a process which takes place, so to speak, above their heads.

A third reason for the relative neglect of small states in the English-language literature is that scholars studying small states often work in small states and publish in their national languages.[17] Furthermore, even writing in English often appears in journals such as *Cooperation and Conflict: Nordic Journal of International Relations* and *Journal of International Relations and Development* that are based outside of the key IR countries, the U.S. and the UK. Rather than making a mark in mainstream debates, this work tends to remain unnoticed.[18]

Fourth, we should like to add an analytical point relating to the very widespread idea that important events must have important causes, and that great events must have great causes. Serbia was too small to be the instigator of something as great as the First World War. Sweden and Denmark were too small to be the birthplace of something as grand as military conscription; it would have to be France (or, alternatively, it would have to be stressed that Sweden was not a small but a great power at the time when it initiated conscription), let alone that some micro-states could have contributed "grand" endeavors, as did Malta within the international convention on the law of the sea. Regarding the make-up of peacekeeping operations, it is above all others that small states such as Denmark, Fiji, and Nepal are consistently among the stalwart nations ready to contribute troops, police, and observers. The point here is not whether the empirical supposition holds or not—we would, for example, clearly distance ourselves from the idea that an explanation of the First World War that singled out Serbia as its effective cause would be credible—but rather that there exists such a thing as an analytical bias for "grand" causes and cases.

In the following section, we introduce the eight pieces of work on small states reprinted in this volume. They can loosely be grouped into three major themes: definitional, economic, and political issues. The contributions are drawn from different time periods, reflect different theoretical traditions, and use different methods. Even though all have been written in English, the authors come from both great powers and small states on both sides of the Atlantic. We believe that this compilation is likely to provide students of International Relations with a fresh look at a neglected topic and encourage them to undertake rewarding research which will not only enhance our understanding of small states but also enrich IR theory.

4. About this Book

THE CHALLENGE OF DEFINING SMALL STATES

Annette Baker Fox contributed to the first wave of theorizing on the autonomous effect of small state behavior in international relations. Her work spoke to the puzzles of weak vs. strong, might and right, and provided an opening for other scholars to explore cases previously invisible to core international relations theorizing. For these efforts, the study of small states and the scholarly community recognize Fox as a critical player in the history of this sub-field.

Our second chapter, Robert Keohane's (1969) "Lilliputians' Dilemmas," reviews four books dealing mainly with military alliances (Vital 1967; Liska 1968; Osgood 1968; Rothstein 1968). The author critically discusses their different definitions of "small powers" and recommends that instead of focusing on perceptions of capabilities, scholars should focus on the systemic role that leaders see their countries playing. Keohane (1969: 296) therefore suggests the following definitions: "A Great Power is a state whose leaders consider that it can, alone, exercise a large, perhaps decisive, impact on the international system; . . . a middle power is a state whose leaders consider that it cannot act alone effectively but may be able to have a systemic impact in a small group or through an international institution; a small power is a state whose leaders consider that it can never, acting alone or in a small group, make a significant impact on the system." This characterization draws our attention to the importance of (self-)perceptions and to the fact that small states and middle powers might support international institutions such as alliances in order to promote international attitudes and norms favorable to their survival. "Perception of [one's] systemic role, more than perception of need for external aid in security, seems to shape small powers' distinctive attitudes toward international organizations" (Keohane 1969: 297). As mentioned above, there is a need to focus less exclusively on capabilities and more on international institutions and relations.

Chapter 3 reproduces the key part of one of the books reviewed by Keohane, David Vital's *The Inequality of States* (1967). Vital examines the "disabilities" and "possibilities" of small states in terms of their size and policy options. In order to study the material inequality of formally equal states, he focuses on non-aligned small states having "a) a population of 10–15 million in the case of economically advanced countries; and b) a population of 20–30 million in the case of underdeveloped countries" (Vital 1967: 8). Material resources are thus considered crucial, but these attributes may be modified by factors such as the level of development, the effects of geographical proximity to areas of great power interest, the nature of a state's environment, or the cohesion and support of its population. Vital argues that small states acting alone face high (and rising) costs of independence. They have the choice of three broad policies: a passive strategy of renunciation, an active strategy designed to alter the external environment in their favor (e.g., subversion), or a defensive strategy attempting to preserve the status quo (e.g., traditional diplomacy, deterrence).

Chapter 4 provides two sections of Jorri Duursma's (1996) *Fragmentation and the International Relations of Micro-states*, in which she discusses the criteria for statehood and the question of micro-states in international organizations.[19] Her summary of the historical debate shows that the legal status of small states in the international system could in the past not be taken for granted. In general, statehood requires a territory, a population, and a government. Two additional criteria, international recognition and independence, have been more controversial. Today, the effects of recognition by other states are considered purely declaratory (although recognition can have a constitutive effect in case of entities which under the general criteria do not possess statehood). As a practical consequence, however, non-recognized states will have more difficulties in being accepted as members of international organizations. International institutions and international law are of particular importance to micro-states and small states. Their accession may oppose the two principles of the sovereignty equality of states (which favors the decision-making rule "one state, one vote") and of democratic representation according to the relative weight of populations (or "one man, one vote"). In an accentuated form, this problem was highlighted by the UN's "micro-state dilemma." Statehood does not demand a minimum size of territory or population, yet the government criterion expects some degree of effective control over the territory and population. In this context, a certain extent of independence (in terms of the rights an entity has to the exclusion of other states) has often been required, in particular with regard to small states. Besides formal independence, the government should also enjoy some actual independence in internal and external affairs.

SMALL STATE RESPONSES TO THE INTERNATIONAL ECONOMY

Chapter 5 is reprinted from Michael Handel's (1981) *Weak States in the International System*. He starts with the fact that a small state is not necessarily synonymous with a weak state and vice versa. He favors a dynamic, multi-criteria definition of weak states (population, area, economy, military power, interests and influence in the international system) and examines in detail the internal and external sources of states' weakness or strength as well as the power constellations of different international systems.[20] The chapter reprinted in this volume deals with the economic position of weak states in the international system. In light of the oil crises in the 1970s, Handel (1981: 217–256) maintains that the growing reluctance of the great powers to use their superior military might has shifted conflict between states to the economic arena and thus in favor of militarily weak but economically strong states. The OPEC countries, for instance, placed a successful oil embargo on the western industrialized states and could grant or withhold enormous financial aid and investments. Other weak states exporting important raw materials at the time began to consider similar measures.[21] Handel finds that the economic predicament of the weak states may not be so severe as traditional economic theory would suggest, and that the economically weak states can pursue certain strategies to reduce their vulnerability or to react to economic pressures imposed on them by great powers. He concludes that the weakness of states is a continuum, thus requiring evaluation of various types of power such as military and economic power. Weak or small states are not the passive pawns of great powers, for they can obtain, commit, and manipulate the power of other, more powerful states, depending on the conditions of tension and conflict between the powers and the rigidity of their spheres of influence.

Chapter 6 leads us deeper into issues of political economy. Peter Katzenstein's influential book *Small States in World Markets* (1985) explores how national responses to the pressures of the global market might affect the domestic structures of small states.[22] He examines the industrial policies of Sweden, Norway, Denmark, the Netherlands, Belgium, Austria, and Switzerland. Being exposed to the pressures of a liberal international economy over which they cannot exert any influence, these small states have successfully adapted by relying on different variants of democratic corporatism. Whereas the large industrial states have chosen either competition or intervention to respond to adverse economic change, these European states have pursued a strategy of international liberalization and domestic compensation.[23] Katzenstein calls our attention to the historically shaped domestic structures of small states.

In chapter 7, Baldur Thorhallsson (2000) tests several hypotheses based on Katzenstein's observations that the small European economies are more open and more specialized and that their strong corporatism affects their foreign economic policy. He argues that size is a significant explanatory factor for the behavior of small states in the EU's decision-making process, at least in the areas of common agricultural policy and regional policy.[24] Thorhallsson's study confirms the importance of small-state corporatism, but contends that Katzenstein's concept needs to be modified to take into account the size and special characteristics of small administrations in order to be able to explain the small EU members' different negotiation tactics and stronger reliance on Commission officials. In particular, small states are proactive in those sectors of greatest importance to them, while being reactive in other sectors because they do not possess sufficient resources to follow all negotiations.

SMALL STATE SECURITY THREATS
AND POLITICAL OPPORTUNITIES

Chapter 8, Dan Reiter's "Learning, Realism, and Alliances" (1994) compares the predictions of realism and of learning theory about the alliance choices of small states in the twentieth century. His evidence shows that learning is the dominant explanation, while variations in the levels of external threat have only marginal effects on alignment policy.[25] In other words, Reiter argues that small states draw lessons from significant past experiences—they continue a successful policy of neutrality or alliance membership, but replace a failed policy by a new choice. Such a simple alternative is not available to great powers, which are not only concerned with direct threats to their own security, but with broader national interests. This text is of interest not just because it uses quantitative methods of analysis and challenges realism on its own turf, but because it demonstrates that small states are influenced more by their own experiences than by outside threats.

Chapter 9 is a reprint of an article by Christine Ingebritsen (2002) on "Norm Entrepreneurs." She points out that, in contrast to what leading theories of International Relations would have us expect, small states also engage in global agenda-setting. For example, Scandinavia has played a leading role in strengthening appropriate standards, or "norms," in international society. Scandinavia's capacity to influence the international system at particular moments and in specific issue-areas (environment, conflict resolution, etc.) has received little attention and should be explored as another way of exercising what she refers to as "social power" in the international system.

The book is rounded off by Christine Ingebritsen's concluding chapter on the state of the art and on the potential for "Learning from Lilliput." Since a choice had to be made for this volume among decades of writing on small states, many noteworthy pieces of literature have been left out. For the readers who miss certain books or articles, or who long for more, the annotated bibliography by Jessica Beyer at the end of this volume might provide a source of comfort and further inspiration.

5. Conclusion: A Voyage to Lilliput in IR

We have noted a number of reasons why IR as a discipline is paying insufficient attention to the study of small states, and should like to conclude by mentioning a final one, namely the discipline's empirical slant. The idea seems to hold sway that, regardless of their theoretical worth, writings on great-power politics have a certain inherent interest due to the importance of the subject, whereas writings on small states do not. In empirical terms, the study of small states may only be apposite if small states have pertinence for outcomes. Perhaps Keohane (1969: 310) put this argument best when he wrote, "If Lilliputians can tie up Gulliver, or make him do their fighting for them, they must be studied as carefully as the giant." This may indeed be so, but we seem to have here a kind of empirical thinking that may actually hamper the development of IR as a systematic theory-led undertaking, that is, as a social science. Scientifically, analyses should be offered for their theoretical findings rather than for their empirical ones. Let us substantiate this idea by comparing International Relations to another social science, namely social anthropology. As argued by Geertz (1973: 21),

> the anthropologist characteristically approaches such broader interpreta-
> tions and more abstract analyses from the direction of exceedingly
> extended acquaintances with extremely small matters. He confronts the
> same grand realities that others—historians, economists, political scien-
> tists, sociologists—confront in more fateful settings: Power, Change, Faith,
> Oppression, Work, Passion, Authority, Beauty, Violence, Love, Prestige;
> but he confronts them in contexts obscure enough . . . to take the capital
> letters off them.

Social anthropology probably evolved this way of looking at and presenting its findings because it afforded a way to generalize from highly
specific empirical work. In anthropological discussions, material from a
number of different cases is routinely bandied about to substantiate a theoretical argument. Case studies are harnessed to do inductive work that
may result in theories with wide application. In IR, this is not the case to
the same degree. We suggest that one of the reasons for this is that we have
traditionally neglected the study of small states, and so we have also neglected ways to set up a professional dialogue that allows such work to be
relevant across the board. It is simply not the case that studies of Ugandan
warfighting, Malaysian trade, or Portuguese UN policy cannot serve as useful sites from which to investigate the institutions of war and trade, or the
workings of the UN. If, by war, we mean U.S. military history, and by trade
we mean EU external economic relations, then perhaps the discipline of
International Relations should not be considered a social science at all,
but rather a kind of International History *manqué*. A social science worthy of the name takes its entire universe of cases seriously. If the study of
the international system remains central to IR, then there are very clear
theoretical and methodological reasons why studying only a handful of
the system's states is simply not good enough.

Notes

1. It may also be observed at other times and in other places. The Group of
Eight (G8), for instance, has in our days been referred to as a global concert (Penttilä
2003: 20).

2. Latin American powers and Siam did not yet have a global presence at the time.

3. Autonomous territories have not played a big role in international relations. Some of them still serve as military bases (e.g., Guam for the U.S.), while others primarily perform economic functions by providing maritime claims (through the 200 sea-miles Exclusive Economic Zone) or by acting as offshore financial centers (e.g., the Cayman Islands). The latter have recently attracted renewed attention in the context of fighting terrorist financing. Occasionally, remaining overseas dependencies are the object of disputes between states, as in the case of the Falkland Islands (Islas Malvinas) or the Spratly Islands.

4. The debate about so-called "quasi-states," while riddled with other problems, at least has the grace of bringing this out quite clearly—it is a running theme of this literature that weak states may be of any size and even rich in natural resources (cf. Jackson 1990; Grovogui 1996).

5. Geser (2001) distinguishes three kinds of small state notions: first, substantial smallness refers to the "objective," absolute small size of a country's resources such as territory or population (e.g., Monaco); second, the relational concept implies relative smallness in comparison to other countries (e.g., Belgium-France, France-U.S.); and third, attributive smallness refers to the "subjective" small size in the perception of either oneself or others (e.g., Luxembourg).

6. One recent volume on small states concludes that its contributions "leave little doubt that the system level is a key explanatory factor in small state foreign policy" (Hey 2003: 186). Since smallness as a relative phenomenon entails an initial comparison, this is the foundational beginning of the analysis. We must, therefore, take the point to mean that not only is the system level important, but its importance seems to be stronger than other and opposing traits.

7. Three hundred years plus after its demise as a great power, Sweden now seems to be comfortable with this fact. Even within the more limited setting of the European Union, it has had no compunctions about referring to one of the groupings within which it is active as "the seven dwarves."

8. Given the vast non-English literature on small states, Kirt and Waschkuhn (2001b: 25) even argue that one might distinguish two schools of small state studies: an American (or Anglo-Saxon) and a European (or Scandinavian-German). For a similar argument see Christmas-Møller (1983: 36).

9. Vogel (1983) briefly exemplifies his propositions by the case of Switzerland.

10. For a methodological critique see Duval and Thompson (1980), who unsuccessfully tried to reproduce East's results.

11. In order to tie the different parts together, Knudsen (2002) suggests studying the life cycles which small states go through (i.e., state formation, survival, and disappearance).

12. For example, Barston (1973: 15) lists four possible approaches to defining small states: "firstly, arbitrarily delimiting the category by placing an upper limit on, for example, population size; secondly, measuring the 'objective' elements of state capability and placing them on a ranking scale; thirdly, analyzing relative influence; and fourthly, identifying characteristics and formulating hypotheses on what differentiates small states from other classes of states."

13. There is also a second, Gramscian tradition of studying hegemony, where the point of departure is how cultural models of reality mould social interaction (e.g., Cox 1983).

14. General arguments of this kind always rest on a number of assumptions. We assume here that small states will have the capacity to participate (e.g. no lack of international presence due to a shortage of finances or personnel), that they will not see a contradiction between some other, more important goal than participation (e.g., Swiss neutrality vs. UN membership during the Cold War), and that great-power privileges within the organization are not so strong that participation may actually limit small-state room for maneuver rather than widen it.

15. Väyrynen (1983) explores the treatment of small states in different theoretical strands such as realism, world-systems analysis, structuralism, and dependency theory. He argues that the analysis of capabilities alone by the power-based and structural approaches is not satisfactory and requires a focus on the relationships between actors, for instance, as the dependence school does.

16. There are two of many reasons why Baehr's (1975) question: why should we study small states when almost all states are small (or, as he asks, why study black automobiles, when automobiles are black?) is amiss here. Firstly and empirically, small states are not studied when the system does not contain all that many of them either, and secondly, and theoretically, generalizations are usually made through cumulative studies of representative cases. This is exactly not the case where the study of the international system is concerned.

17. As a drawback, much of the work has been rather ethnocentric and largely descriptive. Hence, there are also some lessons for small state studies to be learned from IR theory.

18. According to Knudsen (2002: 182), the study of small states has also remained a field with little visible coherence in IR due to its rather detached branches of literature.

19. The remainder of the book examines the international legal standing of the five European micro-states Liechtenstein, San Marino, Monaco, Andorra, and the state of the Vatican City.

20. Among the domestic sources are the geographic and material conditions, human resources and organizational capabilities, while the external sources comprise both formal (international organizations, alliances) and informal factors (benefits of collective goods, patron-client relationships). These external sources must be understood in the context of the different types of international systems (e.g., bipolar or balance-of-power system) and the changing international norms of conduct (e.g., regarding the use of force).

21. However, many primary commodities have effective substitutes and the demand for them is more flexible than in the case of oil.

22. For an in-depth review of his book, see Katzenstein (2003).

23. Likewise, Ahnlid (1992) argues that, against the expectations of hegemonic stability theory, small industrialized states are not free riding (i.e., implementing protection at home, while enjoying free trade abroad) but are forced to pursue liberal policies mainly by systemic constraints. They thus contribute to an open international economic order, while larger states and developing countries—at

least before the establishment of the World Trade Organization—could sometimes act against the trade regime.

24. He compares seven small EU member states (Luxembourg, the Netherlands, Denmark, Ireland, Belgium, Portugal, and Greece) to five larger states (Germany, France, the United Kingdom, Spain, and Italy). In a similar way, Baillie (1998) identifies three explanatory variables for the influence of a small EU member such as Luxembourg: its particular historical context (e.g., date of accession, strategic location), the European and national institutional frameworks (e.g., voting rules, small administration) and the generally conflict-avoiding negotiation behavior of small states (e.g., coalition-building, low-profile approach, honest broker).

25. In addition, Fendius Elman (1995) argues that it is an empirical question whether external and internal constraints matter more to account for the behavior of small or weak states—which are usually supposed to be more preoccupied with survival than great powers.

References

Ahnlid, Anders (1992). "Free Riders or Forced Riders? Small States in the International Political Economy: The Example of Sweden." *Cooperation and Conflict*, 27(3): 241–276.

Amstrup, Niels (1976). "The Perennial Problem of Small States: A Survey of Research Efforts." *Cooperation and Conflict*, 11(3): 163–182.

Annan, Kofi (1998). "Secretary-General Lauds Role of Small Countries in Work of United Nations, Noting Crucial Contributions." Press Release SG/SM/6639, 15 July 1998.

Armstrong, Harvey W. & Robert Read (1998). "Trade and Growth in Small States: The Impact of Global Trade Liberalisation." *The World Economy*, 21(4): 563–585.

Azar, Edward E. (1973). *Probe for Peace: Small State Hostilities*. Minneapolis: Burgess Publishing Company.

Baehr, Peter R. (1975). "Small States: A Tool for Analysis?" *World Politics*, 27(3): 456–466.

Baillie, Sasha (1998). "A Theory of Small State Influence in the European Union." *Journal of International Relations and Development*, 1(3/4): 195–219.

Baker Fox, Annette (1959). *The Power of Small States: Diplomacy in World War II*. Chicago: Chicago University Press.

Barston, R[onald] P. (1973). "Introduction," in R. P. Barston ed., *The Other Powers: Studies in the Foreign Policies of Small States*. London: George Allen & Unwin Ltd., 13–28.

Bauwens, Werner, Armand Clesse & Olav F. Knudsen, eds. (1996). *Small States and the Security Challenge in the New Europe*. London: Brassey's.

Björkdahl, Annika (2002). *From Idea to Norm: Promoting Conflict Prevention*. Lund Political Studies, 125. Lund: Lund University, Department of Political Science.

Blair, Patricia W. (1967). *The Ministate Dilemma*. New York: Carnegie Endowment for International Peace, Occasional Paper 6.

Bratt, Eyvind (1951). *Småstaterna i idéhistorien. En studie i äldre statsdoktriner*. Uppsala: Almqvist & Wiksell.

Bull, Hedley (1977). *The Anarchical Society: A Study of Order in World Society*. London: Macmillan.

Butter, Anton J. (1985). *An Introduction to Mini-Economics*. Amsterdam: B. R. Grüner Publishing.

Cappis, Oscar Bernhard (1923). *Die Idee des Kleinstaats im Deutschland des 19. Jahrhunderts*. Säckingen: Buchdruckerei Fr. Mehr.

Christmas-Møller, Wilhelm (1983). "Some Thoughts on the Scientific Applicability of the Small State Concept: A Research History and a Discussion," in Otmar Höll, ed., *Small States in Europe and Dependence*. Vienna: Braumüller, 35–53.

Clark, Colin & Tony Payne (1987). *Politics, Security and Development in Small States*. London: Allen/Unwin.

Cox, Robert (1983). "Gramsci, Hegemony and International Relations: An Essay in Method." *Millennium*, 12(2): 162–175.

Crowards, T. (2002). "Defining the Category of 'Small States.'" *Journal of International Development*, 14(2): 143–179.

De Rusett, Alan (1954). "Large and Small States in International Organization: Present Attitudes to the Problem of Weighted Voting." *International Affairs*, 30(4): 463–474.

Dosenrode-Lynge, von, Sören Z. (1993). *Westeuropäische Kleinstaaten in der EG und EPZ*. Chur/Zürich: Rüegger.

Durkheim, Emile ([1950] 1992). *Professional Ethics and Civic Morals*. London: Routledge.

Duursma, Jorri (1996). *Fragmentation and the International Relations of Micro-states: Self-Determination and Statehood*. Cambridge: Cambridge University Press.

Duval, Robert D. & William R. Thompson (1980). "Reconsidering the Aggregate Relationship Between Size, Economic Development, and Some Types of Foreign Policy Behavior." *American Journal of Political Science*, 24(3): 511–525.

East, Maurice A. (1973). "Size and Foreign Policy Behavior: A Test of Two Models." *World Politics*, 25(4): 556–576.

Fendius Elman, Miriam (1995). "The Foreign Policies of Small States: Challenging Neorealism in Its Own Backyard." *British Journal of Political Science*, 25(2): 171–217.

Fleiner, Thomas (1966). *Die Kleinstaaten in den Staatenverbindungen des zwanzigsten Jahrhunderts*. Zürich: Polygraphischer Verlag.

Frei, Daniel (1977). "Kleinstaatliche Aussenpolitik als Umgang mit Abhängigkeit," in Karl Zemanek et al., eds., *Die Schweiz in einer sich wandelnden Welt*. Zürich: Schulthess Polygraphischer Verlag, 201–225.

Gaertner, Heinz & Erich Reiter, eds. (2000). *Small States and Alliances*. The Hague: Kluwer.

Geertz, Clifford (1973). *The Interpretation of Cultures: Selected Essays*. New York: Basic Books.

Geser, Hans (2001). "Was ist eigentlich ein Kleinstaat?" in Romain Kirt & Arno

Waschkuhn, eds., *Kleinstaaten-Kontinent Europa: Probleme und Perspektiven*. Baden-Baden: Nomos, 89–100.

Gilpin, Robert (1981). *War and Change in World Politics*. Cambridge: Cambridge University Press.

Goetschel, Laurent, ed. (1998). *Small States Inside and Outside the European Union: Interests and Policies*. Boston: Kluwer Academic Publishers.

Grovogui, Siba N'Zatioula (1996). *Sovereigns, Quasi-Sovereigns, and Africans: Race and Self-Determination in International Law*. Minneapolis: University of Minnesota Press.

Gstöhl, Sieglinde (2001). "Der Mikrostaat als Variante des Kleinstaats? Erfahrungen mit UNO und EU," in Romain Kirt & Arno Waschkuhn, eds., *Kleinstaaten-Kontinent Europa: Probleme und Perspektiven*. Baden-Baden: Nomos, 101–124.

Gunter, Michael M. (1977). "What Happened to the United Nations Ministate Problem?" *American Journal of International Law*, 71: 110–124.

Handel, Michael (1981). *Weak States in the International System*. London: Frank Cass.

Harden, Sheila, ed. (1985). *Small Is Dangerous: Microstates in a Macro World*. London: Francis Pinter Publishers.

Harris, William L. (1970). "Microstates in the United Nations: A Broader Purpose." *Columbia Journal of Transnational Law*, 9: 23–53.

Hey, Jeanne A. K., ed. (2003). *Small States in World Politics: Explaining Foreign Policy Behavior*. Boulder: Lynne Rienner.

Hinsley, F. H. (1963). *Power and the Pursuit of Peace: Theory and Practice in the History of International Relations*. Cambridge: Cambridge University Press.

Holbraad, Carsten (1970). *The Concert of Europe: A Study in German and British International Theory 1815–1914*. London: Longman.

Holbraad, Carsten (1971). "The Role of Middle Powers." *Cooperation and Conflict*, 2(6), 77–90.

Holbraad, Carsten (1984). *Middle Powers in International Politics*. London: Macmillan.

Höll, Otmar (1978). "Kritische Anmerkungen zur Kleinstaaten-Theorie." *Österreichische Zeitschrift für Politikwissenschaft*, 7(3): 259–273.

Höll, Otmar, ed. (1983a). *Small States in Europe and Dependence*. Vienna: Braumüller.

Höll, Otmar (1983b). "Introduction: Towards a Broadening of the Small States Perspective," in Otmar Höll, ed., *Small States in Europe and Dependence*. Vienna: Braumüller, 13–31.

Ingebritsen, Christine (2002). "Norm Entrepreneurs: Scandinavia's Role in World Politics." *Cooperation and Conflict*, 37(1): 11–23.

Jackson, Robert H. (1990). *Quasi-States: Sovereignty, International Relations, and the Third World*. Cambridge: Cambridge University Press.

Jackson, Robert H. & Carl G. Rosberg (1982). "Why Africa's Weak States Persist: The Empirical and Juridical in Statehood." *World Politics*, 35(1): 1–24.

Jazbec, Milan (2001). *The Diplomacies of New Small States: The Case of Slovenia with Some Comparison from the Baltics*. Aldershot: Ashgate.

Kagan, Robert (2003). *Of Paradise and Power: America and Europe in the New World Order*. New York: Knopf.

Katzenstein, Peter J. (1985). *Small States in World Markets: Industrial Policy in Europe*. Ithaca: Cornell University Press.

Katzenstein, Peter J. (2003). "Small States and Small States Revisited." *New Political Economy*, 8(1): 9–30.

Kennedy, Paul (1991). "Grand Strategy in War and Peace: Toward a Broader Definition," in Paul Kennedy, ed., *Grand Strategies in War and Peace*. New Haven: Yale University Press, 1–7.

Keohane, Robert O. (1969). "Lilliputians' Dilemmas: Small States in International Politics." *International Organization*, 23(2): 291–310.

Keohane, Robert O. & Joseph S. Nye (1977). *Power and Interdependence: World Politics in Transition*. Toronto: Little, Brown and Co.

Keohane, Robert O. (1984). *After Hegemony: Cooperation and Discord in the World Political Economy*. Princeton: Princeton University Press.

Kindleberger, Charles P. (1973). *The World in Depression 1929–1939*. London: Penguin.

Kindley, Randall W. & David F. Good, eds. (1997). *The Challenge of Globalization and Institutions Building: Lessons from Small European States*. Boulder/Oxford: Westview Press.

Kirt, Romain & Arno Waschkuhn, eds. (2001a). *Kleinstaaten-Kontinent Europa: Probleme und Perspektiven*. Baden-Baden: Nomos.

Kirt, Romain & Arno Waschkuhn (2001b). "Was ist und zu welchem Zweck betreibt man Kleinstaaten-Forschung? Ein Plädoyer für die wissenschaftliche Beschäftigung mit kleinen Nationen," in Romain Kirt & Arno Waschkuhn, eds., *Kleinstaaten-Kontinent Europa: Probleme und Perspektiven*. Baden-Baden: Nomos, 23–46.

Knudsen, Olav F. (2002). "Small States, Latent and Extant: Towards a General Perspective." *Journal of International Relations and Development*, 5(2): 182–198.

Kramer, Helmut (1993). "Kleinstaaten-Theorie und Kleinstaaten-Aussenpolitik in Europa," in Arno Waschkuhn, ed., *Kleinstaat: Grundsätzliche und aktuelle Probleme*. Vaduz: LAG, 247–259.

Krasner, Stephen D. (1981). "Transforming International Regimes: What the Third World Wants and Why." *International Studies Quarterly*, 25(1): 119–148.

Krauthammer, Charles (1991). "The Unipolar Moment." *Foreign Affairs*, 70(1): 23–33.

Lindell, Ulf & Stefan Persson (1986). "The Paradox of Weak State Power: A Research and Literature Overview." *Cooperation and Conflict*, 21(2): 79–97.

Liska, George (1968). "Alliances and the Third World." *Studies in International Affairs*, 5. Baltimore: Johns Hopkins Press.

Markus, Joseph (1946). *Grandes puissances, petites nations et le problème de l'organisation internationale*. Geneva: Graduate Institute of International Studies.

Mathisen, Trygve (1971). *The Functions of Small States in the Strategies of the Great Powers*. Oslo: Universitetsforlaget.

Morgenthau, Hans J. (1948). *Politics Among Nations: The Struggle for Power and Peace*. New York: Knopf.

Morgenthau, Hans J. (1972). *Science: Servant or Master?* New York: New American Library.

Moses, Jonathan W. (2000). *Open States in the Global Economy: The Political Economy of Small-State Macroeconomic Management*. New York: Macmillan.

Neumann, Iver B. (ed.) (1992). *Regional Great Powers in International Relations.* London: Macmillan.

Ólafsson, Björn G. (1998). *Small States in the Global System: Analysis and Illustrations from the Case of Iceland.* Aldershot: Ashgate.

Osgood, Robert E. (1968). *Alliances and American Foreign Policy.* Baltimore: Johns Hopkins Press.

Penttilä, Risto E. J. (2003). *The Role of the G8 in International Peace and Security.* Oxford: Oxford University Press for The International Institute for Strategic Studies, Adelphi Papers 355.

Plischke, Elmer (1977). *Microstates in World Affairs: Policy Problems and Options.* Washington: American Enterprise Institute for Public Policy Research, AEI Studies 144.

Rappard, William E. (1934). "Small States in the League of Nations." *Political Science Quarterly,* 49: 544–575.

Reid, George L. (1974). *The Impact of Very Small Size on the International Relations Behavior of Microstates.* London: Sage.

Reiter, Dan (1994). "Learning, Realism, and Alliances: The Weight of the Shadow of the Past." *World Politics,* 46(4): 490–526.

Riklin, Alois (1975). "Ziele, Mittel und Strategien der schweizerischen Aussenpolitik," in Alois Riklin, Hans Haug & Raymond Probst, eds., *Handbuch der schweizerischen Aussenpolitik.* Bern: Haupt, 21–56.

Risse-Kappen, Thomas (1995). *Cooperation Among Democracies: The European Influence on U.S. Foreign Policy.* Princeton: Princeton University Press.

Rotberg, Robert I., ed. (2004). *When States Fail: Causes and Consequences.* Princeton: Princeton University Press.

Rothstein, Robert L. (1968). *Alliances and Small Powers.* New York: Columbia University Press.

Salvatore, Dominick, Marjan Svetlicic & Joze P. Damijan, eds. (2001). *Small Countries in a Global Economy: New Challenges and Opportunities.* Basingstoke: Palgrave Macmillan.

Schou, August & Arne Olav Brundtland, eds. (1971). *Small States in International Relations.* Stockholm: Almqvist & Wiksell.

Schwegmann, Christoph (2001). "Modern Concert Diplomacy: The Contact Group and the G7/8 in Crisis Management," in John J. Kirton, Joseph P. Daniels & Andreas Freytag, eds., *Guiding Global Order: G8 Governance in the Twenty-First Century.* Aldershot: Ashgate, 93–121.

Sieber, Eduard (1920). *Die Idee des Kleinstaates bei den Denkern des 18. Jahrhunderts in Frankreich und Deutschland.* Basel: Verlag der Basler Bücherstube, Kobers Buch- und Kunsthandlung.

Thorhallsson, Baldur (2000). *The Role of Small States in the European Union.* Aldershot: Ashgate.

Väyrynen, Raimo (1971). "On the Definition and Measurement of Small Power Status." *Cooperation and Conflict,* 6(2): 91–102.

Väyrynen, Raimo (1983). "Small States in Different Theoretical Traditions of International Relations Research," in Otmar Höll, ed., *Small States in Europe and Dependence.* Vienna: Braumüller, 83–107.

Vital, David (1967). *The Inequality of States: A Study of the Small Power in International Relations*. Oxford: Clarendon Press.

Vital, David (1971). *The Survival of Small States: Studies in Small Power/Great Power Conflict*. Oxford: Oxford University Press

Vogel, Hans (1979). *Der Kleinstaat in der Weltpolitik: Aspekte der schweizerischen Aussenbeziehungen im internationalen Vergleich*. Frauenfeld: Huber.

Vogel, Hans (1983). "Small States' Efforts in International Relations: Enlarging the Scope," in Otmar Höll, ed., *Small States in Europe and Dependence*. Vienna: Braumüller, 54–68.

Volgy, Thomas J. & Alison Bailin (2003). *International Politics and State Strength*. Boulder: Lynne Rienner.

Wæver, Ole (1998). "The Sociology of a Not So International Discipline: American and European Developments in International Relations." *International Organization*, 52(4): 687–727.

Walt, Stephen (1987). *The Origins of Alliances*. Ithaca: Cornell University Press.

Waschkuhn, Arno (1991). "Strukturbedingungen und Entwicklungsprobleme des Kleinstaates," in *Schweizerisches Jahrbuch für Politische Wissenschaft 1990*, 30. Bern: Haupt, 137–155.

Watson, Adam (1982). *Diplomacy: The Dialogue Between States*. London: Methuen.

Wivel, Anders (2000). "Stephen M. Walt: Back to the Future of Realist Theory?" Arbejdspapir 2000/18. Copenhagen: Institut for Statskundskab.

Zahariadis, Nikolaos (1994). "Nationalism and Small State Foreign Policy: The Greek Response to the Macedonian Issue." *Political Science Quarterly*, 109(4): 647–667.

PART I

Defining Contributions
to the Literature

I

THE POWER OF SMALL STATES

Diplomacy in World War II

ANNETTE BAKER FOX

Introduction

*A prince ought never to make common cause with one more powerful than him-
self to injure another, unless necessity forces him to it . . . for if he wins you rest
in his power, and princes must avoid as much as possible being under the will
and pleasure of others. . . . One never tries to avoid one difficulty without running into another, but prudence consists in being able to know the nature of
the difficulties, and taking the least harmful as good.*[1]

During World War II it was widely asserted that the day of the small power
was over. Not only could such a state have no security under modern conditions of war; it could have no future in the peace that presumably one
day would follow. This was a belief shared by respected students of world
politics and by advocates of *Lebensraum* for the thousand-year Reich.
Striking evidence that this view was exaggerated is found in the European
theater of conflict; Sweden, Spain, Turkey, Switzerland, Eire, and Portugal
all avoided being drawn into the war and emerged from it unwounded
and, if anything, stronger than before. How could such relatively weak states
survive while "total" war swept around them? Other small states were drawn
into the war. What was it about these six that enabled them to succeed
where the others had failed?

A traditional great-power stereotype of the small state was that of a helpless pawn in world politics. The governments of the great powers frequently
regarded the small states simply as objects, to be moved around at will in

From Annette Baker Fox, *The Power of Small States: Diplomacy in World War II*
(Chicago: Chicago University Press, 1959). Reprinted with permission of the University of Chicago Press. Cross references to pages and notes refer to the original publication.

their own struggle for dominance over other great powers. From the small-power point of view, on the other hand, the great states were perceived as cynical manipulators of power and the small states as virtuous and law-abiding countries.

Of course, neither the great states nor the small ones have generally behaved in accordance with these stereotypes.[2] Most great powers have continued to treat small powers on a basis of legal equality even when it was inconvenient. They have tended to shy away from anything which would be portrayed as an intimidation of a small power. Likewise, small states have frequently made unwelcome demands on great powers, with surprising success if one considers only the relative military potentials of the two sides. Thus in recent times Nasser, Syngman Rhee, Sukarno, and Mossadegh, all leaders of small powers, have defied the will of some of the greatest powers and come off well. But the general belief still exists that the great powers determine the course of world politics and that the small powers can do little but acquiesce in their decisions.

The distinctive power of great states flows from their military strength. However, the ability of a state to secure what it wants through the use of violence is only one mark of political power. There are other means which may under certain circumstances be effective in exercising influence or resisting coercion. Both great and small states can employ economic, ide-ological, and diplomatic methods as well as military measures. They may buy consent with goods and services, win friends and influence people with psychological maneuvers, bargain for the exchange of advantages, and gain strength through appropriate alliances.

For the small state, diplomacy is the tool of statecraft in whose use it can on occasion hope to excel. The representatives of great powers have more than once been outmatched at the conference table by the diplo-mats from the small states. But this is often tied in with other means of gaining support. For example, small states may have at their command the capacity to appeal to world opinion, operating from a "rectitude" base, or their fighting qualities may gain them a reputation for being likely to resist violence with violence.

Success or failure in securing its own demands or in resisting the demands of other states is the test of the power position of any state. In the case of the small powers, it has historically been the latter, the capac-ity to resist great-power demands, which has been the more important in defining their power status.[3]

What are the kinds of claims which great powers have made upon small states? In the past, those have often had to do with such things as concessions for the exploitation of natural resources or the control over strategic passageways. Demands of this nature have usually been made upon states falling in the class now known as "underdeveloped states." Today we are witnessing the reverse process as these states struggle to achieve a political independence commensurate with their conception of sovereignty.[4]

There is another kind of claim, however, which both underdeveloped and industrialized states have had to meet in the past and continue to face today. This demand, or complex of demands, is likely to be made whenever there is a war or threat of war between the great powers. Small states which could add to the military capabilities of either side are bound to be under heavy pressure to yield this aid or to forbid it to the opposing camp.

War among the great powers is only one situation in which small-power diplomacy may be observed to advantage. In a world of peace a small power's freedom from encroachment by a great power often depends upon the great power's unwillingness to fritter away its strength, which has to be conserved for inter-great-power competition. The small state may run the gamut from being unheeded to being the arbiter of its own fate in a deadlock struggle between giants. It is in the crises of inter-great-power war that one sees the most active and most intense phase of the relationships between the small powers and the great.

A knowledge of the relations between certain strategically located small European states and the major belligerents during World War II should provide some clues leading to a clearer understanding of the more general question: How can the small state exercise power in international politics? Here one may watch under the microscope the behavior of various small states struggling in the web of great-power diplomacy to preserve their independence and to save their territories from becoming battlegrounds for the great powers. The observations made in this study could later be compared with the experience of other small states in World War II, of small states in earlier periods, and of small states in the era following World War II.

The states chosen for the present study were Turkey, Finland, Norway, Sweden, and Spain. In all five there was national unity as to the main purpose of wartime diplomacy—non-participation in the hostilities.[5] None of them was surrounded by hated or hostile neighbors; each possessed geographical advantages giving it some chance to remain non-belligerent through self-defense. For reasons to be stated later, two of these states were eventually drawn into the war.

The three northern states were culturally very similar and presented marked political contrasts to both Spain and Turkey, but only one of them, Sweden, succeeded in staying out of the war. Finland and Turkey bordered in part on Russia, their mutually most feared antagonist. Spain and Turkey in many respects mirrored each other's experience, located as they were at the eastern and western ends of the Mediterranean and showing marked leanings at the beginning of the war toward opposing sides in the struggle. Spain, Sweden, and Norway had been successful in maintaining their neutrality in World War I. That period also witnessed the birth of Finland as an independent nation and the rebirth of Turkey as a republic.

There were numerous other similarities and contrasts among the selected states which will be considered later, but all five had a common geographical asset. Unlike the Low Countries, for example, none of them lay on the direct path of invasion of the great-power belligerents. The location of each could sustain the hope that the war might not come their way, or might at least shift its course before involving them. That such seemingly disparate countries as Sweden and Turkey had a common interest was recognized by their governments, which kept each other informed during the war.

Switzerland, most famous neutral of all, was excluded from this study, partly because legal and political recognition of Switzerland's neutrality goes so far back into history and has become so fixed a feature in the thinking of European diplomats that there was a psychological obstacle to invasion possessed by no other neutral. In addition, the physical barrier of the Alps helped to make the Swiss relatively secure in the midst of the conflict. Not only would Switzerland have refused to participate in the war, but its participation would probably have been of much less value to any of the belligerents than that of the other states considered here. Further, the basis of the Swiss Confederation is a union of three nationality groups, making a choice of sides quite impracticable. The combination of these features makes Switzerland unique among European small states, and in fact among small states anywhere. Hence the contribution of the Swiss experience to the understanding of how small states can resist pressure for participation in a great-power conflict would not be very significant.

In certain ways, of course, Switzerland resembles the other European state most renowned for its neutrality policy over a long period: Sweden. Each has, for example, a formidable militia-type army and a highly skilled labor group, together with an industrialized economy. During the war each provided humanitarian and diplomatic services as well as valuable war matériel to both sides. If invaded, the Swiss could have destroyed the tunnels and passes in the Alps so useful to Germany's communication with its Italian partner, just as the Swedes controlled a similarly useful and destructible facility in their iron mines. When surrounded by German might, both countries made concessions worth far more to Germany than any advantage it could have gained through an obviously costly use of force.[6] To the extent that Swiss experience duplicated that of Sweden, investigation of the latter should be sufficient for the purposes of this analysis.

All these states differ in important respects from the countries outside western European civilization which, since World War II, have posed important problems in United States foreign policy. The general perspectives of the leaders and their followers on what is valuable and how it is to be obtained vary greatly between the two worlds. Nevertheless, for many situations of great-power pressure on a small state, the accomplishments of the European neutrals in this study probably represent the limit of success which any small state could hope to reach under similar circumstances.

We may also learn lessons of value to the great powers. Many of the factors that prevented a belligerent, during World War II, from achieving its total objectives with respect to a particular small state are equally present in postwar relations between the great and small powers, whether European or not. By including Spain and Turkey, elements can be weighed which are also characteristic of the non-European world.

Periods of crisis in the wartime experience of the five selected states will be analyzed separately. These were the periods when the small power was being subjected to heavy pressure from one or more belligerents and the actions and reactions of the parties to the conflict resulted in some lowering of the tension. In this way, the power of each of the small states at each particular moment of crisis can be appraised, and then a more generalized picture of the great-power-small-power confrontation can be attempted.[7]

To facilitate the comparison among the five states here studied and to permit generalization based on their combined experience, the chapters dealing with the individual countries have a common pattern of organization. There will be a brief treatment of the distinctive characteristics of the country relevant to the question of power. The analysis of each successive crisis will be made in terms of (1) the political and military relationships between the pertinent states at the moment, (2) the expectations of the participants, (3) the demands upon the small state, (4) the techniques employed by each side, and (5) the resultant effect on the power position of the small state concerned. Following a brief summary of the pertinent events in the crisis, a number of hypotheses about the potentialities of the small state will be outlined. These will be based on the experience of the particular state under examination and will relate to the special circumstances of the crisis. Although the total experience of each of the five states was unique, they will be found to have had many features in common at particular points in their wartime history.

The timing of the events is of great importance to their proper assessment. At the end of the book will be found a chronology of major war events interpolated with the specific experiences of the small states studied. The footnotes are especially important in this study, because they have to bear much of the burden of factual confirmation for statements made in the historical portions of the work. The narrative has had to be so drastically compressed that the bases for many hypotheses cannot be fully described in the text.

While a number of writers have contributed to a knowledge of the diplomatic history during World War II of the five countries chosen for this analysis—as the appended bibliography amply demonstrates—there is no study which gives an account of their diplomacy during this period in such a way as to permit comparison. Previous narratives have usually been *ex parte*, providing no depth of understanding about what went on except from the point of view of a single participant. The study of the foreign policies of small powers is a relatively unworked field, and gathering together the histories of these five may suggest other themes to be pursued. For each country the crises of great-power-belligerent-small-power-neutral relations have had to be dealt with chronologically. Otherwise the account would have been deficient in at least two respects. It could not have shown how experience in early crises had a cumulative effect on the diplomacy of later crises, nor could the power of the small states have been portrayed in the light of the changing fortunes of World War II. With the chapters dealing with individual countries organized in parallel form and with each crisis in the wartime diplomacy of each country treated according to a common pattern, comparison of and generalization about the small states become possible.

What is impressive is the variety of circumstances under which the power of a small state, when confronted with an unwelcome great-power demand, turns out to be much greater than any inventory of its internal resources would suggest. The leaders often had some genuine choice of action, and even though this was only in the form of a selection of the lesser of two evils, the choice had an effect on their subsequent experience. Their ability to choose was, however, derived largely from the existence of competition among the great states. The main external source of a small state's strength in dealing with one great power was the knowledge, open to both parties, that there were behind the small state one or more other great powers, despite the customary absence of alignment. This strength of the small state was thus "other-conditioned" and therefore inherently unstable, depending as it did upon the existing relationships between the great powers. The question for the small-state leaders was how they could best draw on such power, and the possibility of choice lay chiefly in the ways the small powers could influence the expectations of the interested great powers. Geography was often an important element in the calculations of the great and small powers, but it could not be said to *determine* their course. The expectations of the leaders, sometimes influenced by geographical considerations, to be sure, were the crucial factor.[8]

For the particular time-segment and the particular kind of pressure— aid to one or more belligerents during World War II—the operational question for the government of each of these small states was how to wait out a crisis while making its neutrality desirable to both sides. Their power of choice lay in their capacity to convince the great-power belligerents that the costs of using coercion against them would more than offset the gains. The great-power leaders were not likely to press too hard for a concession if one or more of the following undesirable consequences appeared probable: (1) the demanding great power would be deprived of valued goods or services over which the neutral had control; (2) the enemy would retaliate directly or indirectly so severely as to outbalance any conceivable advantage; (3) the neutral would go over to the enemy side.

Not all the would-be neutrals could avail themselves of these possibilities, and even those who remained out of the war could not do so all the time. The chapters to come will suggest the conditions for success in resisting the pressures of the great-power belligerents during wartime. They should also illustrate some aspects of the power of small states in world polities.

Notes

1. Machiavelli's advice to the head of the principality of Florence (*The Prince*, chap. xxi). (Full bibliographical details of sources cited in footnotes will be found in the Bibliography).

2. A more realistic appraisal may be found in George Liska, *International Equilibrium*, pp. 24–33, and Arnold Wolfers, "In Defense of Small Countries."

3. Small powers are almost by definition "local" powers whose demands are restricted to their own and immediately adjacent areas, while great powers exert their influence over wide areas. In the terminology of Harold D. Lasswell and Abraham Kaplan (*Power and Society*, p. 77) the power of the small state is narrow in "domain," however much or little may be its "weight."

4. For a consideration of the power of the newer kind of small state which has constituted a post-World War II problem in international relations, see the author's "Small Power Diplomacy in a Changing World," in Stephen D. Kertesz (ed.), *Diplomacy in a Changing World* (Notre Dame, IN: University of Notre Dame Press, 1959).

5. In the case of Spain, unity existed because of a combination of all-pervasive war fatigue and the coercive power of the victorious dictatorship.

6. See, for the Swiss experience, Edgar Bonjour, *Swiss Neutrality*; Edgar Bonjour et al., *A Short History of Switzerland*, pp. 365 ff.; Nils Ørvik, *The Decline of Neutrality*; Ernst Weizsäcker, *Memoirs*, pp. 243–44; Constance Howard, "Switzerland," in Royal Institute of International Affairs, *The War and the Neutrals*, pp. 199–230; and Georg Schwarzenberger, *Power Politics*, pp. 105, 108–9.

7. Although Norway and Finland failed to stay out of the war, in some crises they succeeded in resisting a great-power demand; on the other hand, the "successful" wartime neutrals in certain crises had to yield. Thus the analysis will draw on the total experience of all five.

8. See Harold and Margaret Sprout, "Man-Milieu Relationship Hypotheses in the Context of International Politics."

The Influence of Small Powers

The one who is not your friend will want you to remain neutral, and the one who is your friend will require you to declare yourself by taking arms.[1]

It is not wise to form an alliance with a Prince that has more reputation than power.[2]

The twenty-five situations examined in the foregoing pages illustrate ways in which five small states sought to resist the demands of great-power belligerents in wartime crises without themselves being drawn into war. They indicate that success depended on convincing the power pressing the small state that its continued neutrality was advantageous to the great power too. The small state's leaders had to make clear that the belligerents' major requirements could be satisfied without the use of force or that the use of force would be too expensive in terms of the benefits sought and the larger dividends available if applied elsewhere

Not all the states studied had equal opportunities for diplomatic maneuver, and the involuntary entrance of Finland and Norway into war came at crises when they had little chance to modify in their favor the expectations of the leaders of the great power or powers involved. Yet even these small states were able to avoid capitulation in some crises. Furthermore, both Finland and Norway emerged from the war as completely independent countries. The others survived not only without the devastation of war but with increased military strength. They had achieved their purpose of non-participation, even if it required some payment in pride and self-respect.

The problem of influencing the great-power leaders was complicated by the vast and very significant differences in perspectives between the great powers and the small powers. This gap existed regardless of ideology or any other factor linking the interests of a particular small state with one or another of the great belligerents. The primary difference—and it generally holds true regardless of time, situation, or states involved—was the scope of their attention. Great-power leaders had to broaden their gaze to sweep the whole international arena, and thus their focus upon a particular small power tended to be fleeting and not especially directed to the particular interests of that state. The leaders in the latter, on the contrary, were primarily concerned with their own fate, regardless of the larger constellations of power over which they could have no control. The diplomatic task of the small-power leaders was thus much easier than that of the great powers in one respect. Whether or not they believed that their behavior could alter the outcome of the war, their practical objective was simple and clear: to stay out of the hostilities. And they could attend to this task with great concentration and intensity.

Great-power pressure on a small power to take some action which would make it a belligerent was always justified by an assertion of some distinctive shared interest; like every other great-power move, however, such pressure was only one element in the great power's necessarily wide and shifting set of maneuvers. For the small-state leaders, the prospect of a long-term victory of commonly held values was outweighed by the immediate likelihood that their regime—if not their nation—might not survive to enjoy the triumph. The government of the small state had to concentrate on the short-run possibilities. Its own estimate of the effects of participation could not easily be impressed upon the great-power leaders, who had a large number of other intermeshed interests to claim their attention. While the great power might be almost the whole concern of the small state, the latter was only a small part of the concern of the great power. There were times when this difference was advantageous to the small state, for example, when the great power was unwilling to concentrate its power on one little country. The more extensive range of great-power interests also provided the opportunity so necessary to the small state of holding on until the attention of a demanding belligerent shifted.

Another difference in perspectives between the great and the small powers was the acute sensitivity of the small to possible encroachments on their independence. Characteristically, small-state leaders strive to compensate for their military inferiority by emphasizing respect for their dignity. The great powers regularly overlooked this need even in such matters as requiring public declarations of policy from the small.

In World War II, when the small states' leaders did examine their position in the balance of power, their perspectives on Germany and Russia almost without exception differed from those of the West and not primarily for ideological reasons. For them Germany was a valuable counterweight against the equally threatening Russians, and they were quite unable to obtain acceptance of this idea in the West, even as they failed every time in their several efforts at mediation to shorten the war. The longer the war lasted, the more precarious did they view their position, for they regarded the threatened extinction of Germany and the expansion of Communist Russia as two sides of a single catastrophe. Because of their views on the dual character of the war, they could not share the Western Allies' preference for final, unconditional, and total victory over Germany.

Once a state, great or small, became involved in the war, the perspectives in that country changed very rapidly. Caution also tended to be thrown aside. But for the leaders of a small state still outside the battle, participation seemed more likely to destroy their regime than to preserve it by assisting in the ultimate victory of the side they favored. Perhaps only a small percentage of all the states participating would face disaster, but for them the tragedy could be 100 percent. This attitude was another barrier to the great powers' understanding of the neutrals' course of action.

Despite basic differences in perspectives, the small-state diplomats had to exert every effort to insure that the great power at least entertained accurate expectations of the likely course of events. Miscalculations within a great power could be very costly both to that power and to the small state involved. The small state had to sound credible when arguing that a proposed action was likely to lead to an enemy attack or at least to the small state's overdependence upon the opposing side.

There were times when the small state had very little chance to participate in a decision affecting its status. Thus one great power sometimes made a demand relating to a neutral, not on the neutral directly but on another great power. Whether or not the demand was then made upon the small state, and with what pressure, were questions determined outside the sphere in which the small state could operate. Furthermore, demands upon a small state often varied according to changes in the belligerents' relations with one another rather than with their direct interest in the small state.

Other states than the one pressing a small country hardest might also enter into a situation decisively. When a great state had occupied a particular neutral's neighbor and then stopped short of the neutral, the latter, while not helpless, might come within the orbit of the great power without force being used upon the neutral. For it could no longer draw much strength from an opposing great power to balance the pressure of the dominant belligerent.

In such situations, where the locus of the decision-making was outside the sphere of the small state, the range of action available to it was minimal if not completely nonexistent. We have already seen that in other types of situations this was not always or even usually true. But in general the main boundaries of action for the small state were set by the relative military strength of the belligerents.

Within the limits set by inter-great-power relations, leaders in the small states employed tactics which did not vary greatly despite the differences among the countries involved. Their main hope was to ride out the storm represented by a particular crisis, rolling and pitching but not slipping their moorings. Eventually the pressure of any given great power would diminish because its great-power opponents were creating larger or more urgent problems elsewhere. The experience of the five states in this study indicates that the would-be neutral's chance of successfully resisting the pressures from the belligerents increased with the following circumstances:

The more numerous the great powers with conflicting demands who were concerned about the small power and who could give effect to their concern; i.e., the more complex the balance

The more equal the balance of military strength among the contending great powers in the region of the small state

The greater the range of competing interests elsewhere on which the demanding great power needed to focus

The greater the distance the small state was located from a direct line between belligerents

The more massive the physical barriers to invasion of the small state

The larger the quantity of scarce commodities or services useful for war purposes which the small state controlled and the more critical the scarcity to one or both sides

The more self-contained the small state's economy

The less unified the side making the demand

The greater the moral inhibition in the demanding power to the use of force when there was an alternative

The more influential the groups in the demanding power identifying themselves with the small state

The longer the small state had been a member of the family of nations, an independent country with which the great powers had had to negotiate

The larger the number of neutrals

In these cases the small state could not determine the circumstances, although its government could often exploit them to its own advantage. The following conditions were much more likely to be decided within the small state, and the more they prevailed, the better for the small state:

The capacity and will to employ force to resist violently an act of violence, and the great power's realization of these facts

A conciliatory approach, making concessions where the great power's dominance is unquestionable without giving up the principal means of protecting the small state's independence, which in wartime usually meant no foreign troops within the small state's territory and outside its control

Unity in the government, a constitutional consensus, and self-control among the people despite the activities of subversives in their midst

Friendly relations with neighboring small states

The ability to concentrate on the main goal at the expense of other values, e.g., the capacity to ignore irredentist temptations and internal demands for peace-time economic welfare

Possession and use of accurate political and military intelligence regarding the great powers and the ability to calculate correctly their dispositions

Negotiators with experience, imagination, flexibility, nerve, and capacity to conceal intentions disadvantageous to the demanding state

The capacity to set off the demands of one side against those of the other while extracting concessions from each[3]

Readiness to exploit each great power's interest in the small state's ability to resist the other side by securing from them the economic and military supplies permitting the small state to build up its defense against any side

The ability to practice the art of procrastination by such means as the following: holding out the possibility of concessions at some price and then making the price exorbitant, distracting the demanding state by such means as reference to cheaper alternatives, increasing the demanding power's fear of retaliation from the other side, trading off individually trivial concessions to avoid making vital ones, taking advantage of conflicts within the demanding side, giving "informal" and secret understandings to avoid open declarations fixing policy and to counteract favors to the other side, insisting that compensation be tangible and immediately receivable, and otherwise avoiding a decision until its timeliness disappears[4]

The foregoing factors, both those subject to choice within the small state and the others, were particularly useful in making it possible for the small state to draw on the strength of a great power to supplement its own. Correct timing was of the greatest importance in view of the shifting interests of the belligerents. Drawing upon the power of one side to oppose the other took the form of an outright alliance in only one of the cases studied; yet under particular circumstances such an alignment could have been more of a protection than the danger most of the neutrals regarded it to be. On the other hand, attempts to add to the power of the small state by combining with other small and presumably disinterested states regularly failed, for the sum of their power was weakness and the combinations were too insubstantial. None of the small states studied here dared to go so far in using the strength of one side to oppose another as to threaten joining the enemy, but the possibility of such a move was frequently in the minds of the great-power leaders.

This study has dealt with the demands which were actually made upon the small states. There has been hardly any discussion concerning desires which did not reach this state of concreteness because the great-power leaders' expectations changed sometimes because of lessons learned from negotiations here described. Where the military use of neutral territory was at issue, the great power converting such a desire into a demand did so only at the expense of its long-run interests. Careful consideration would have shown such a demand to be completely incompatible with a small state's views of its interests and likely to be resisted by arms.

When the leaders in the great power recognized accurately the pattern of demands, identifications, and expectations of the small state, they saved their negotiating energy for securing concessions more relevant to their war effort than military co-operation; thus they could also avoid fully mobilizing the small state's powers of resistance. The small state's need for strength to resist would also have decreased in some cases had its leaders acknowledged the substantial identity of their value position with that of the Western great powers and the rationality of these great powers' perspectives, given this shared value position.

The evidence in this study pertains only to a particular period of armed conflict and to a persistent small-power objective of non-participation. Even though it was drawn from the pre-atomic era, it should continue to be applicable to many situations today. The H-bomb is an unsuitable instrument for dealing with small states. A thermonuclear war would be too short for the small state to play any role at all. But in a cold-war period or a period of any kind of limited war the conditions still exist for the kind of great-power-small-power relations described in this study.[5] Furthermore, the horrors of a two-way atomic war are so great that those possessing the bombs have been giving recalcitrant small states much leeway in order to avoid a conflict leading possibly to the destruction of civilization. Paradoxically the small states in the 1950s seem to have found a greater freedom of maneuverability at the very time their military inequality vastly increased.

This study is perhaps least applicable to understanding the great-power-small-power relationship within coalitions such as NATO. Once committed, the small power moves into a wholly different set of relationships, although its skill in maintaining its particular interests may remain very great. Before World War II the small states were not offered such an alternative—membership in an integrated mobilized defense organization and one in which they could participate as decision-makers. The experience of World War II was a prerequisite for the acceptance of this idea among the great and the small alike.

The data in this study, though limited in time and situation, do suggest some general conclusions about the power of small states in international affairs. Postwar changes in the orientation of the countries studied here, as well as the small state's "benevolent neutrality" toward the dominant side during the war, indicate that the decisions of small states are likely to increase the imbalance between two power constellations. Instead of moving to the side of the less powerful and thereby helping to restore the balance, they tended to comply with the demands of the more powerful and thus to accentuate any shifts in the balance of forces caused by changing fortunes of war or prospects of ultimate victory. Viewed in this way, the small state's characteristic behavior may be described as "anti-balance of power" while that of a great power is characteristically "pro-balance of power." Where the margin between a self-righting balance and the complete overturn of the balance is very close, this behavior pattern may conceivably be decisive. Ordinarily, however, the small state's weight is unimportant in determining the distribution of power among the great, because the small state follows a pattern already being set and only accents it. In the large decisions marking out the configuration of power in world politics, the small state has little influence in the sense that it does not participate directly. Yet its own leaders may modify decisions of the great powers indirectly by affecting the expectations of great-power governments in the competition which involves the small. In this manner the small state may be said to be influential.

World War II was settled in favor of the West and the Soviet Union without the active aid or opposition of the small states of Spain, Turkey, and Sweden, while the roles played by Norway and Finland were very small in the total drama. Nevertheless, the battle would have been waged differently at different times had not the governments of the small states exerted their efforts to maintain an independent policy. In retrospect, the benefits to themselves and to the Western democracies of their independent policies have demonstrated that their diplomats were frequently wiser than those pressing them to take opposing courses. Virtue was no monopoly of the small powers, but wisdom was not an exclusive attribute of the great.

CHRONOLOGY

Highlights of World War II combined with important events concerning Turkey, Finland, Norway, Sweden, and Spain

September, 1939: Germans invade Poland and war begins. Self-governing Dominions except Eire join British and French. Declaration of Panama. All states in Western Hemisphere except Canada announce neutrality zone 300 miles out. Finland, Norway, Sweden, and Spain declare neutrality.

October, 1939: Poland partitioned by Germans and Russians. Turkey signs Tripartite Mutual Assistance Pact with Britain and France after failing to agree with Soviet Union on a pact. Finns begin futile two-month negotiations with Russians over Soviet demands for territory.

November, 1939: Soviet Union attacks Finland. Norwegians conclude shipping agreement with British.

December, 1939: League of Nations expels Soviet Union. Sweden concludes war trade agreements with Britain and Germany.

January, 1940: Allies warn Norway and Sweden regarding German use of the Leads for transport of iron ore and hint direct action. British agree to pre-empt Turkish chrome for two years.

February, 1940: Allies press Norway and Sweden to permit expeditionary force through to Finland. Anglo-Norwegian war trade agreement concluded; also trade agreement between Norway and Germany. "Altmark" captured by British in Norwegian waters. Balkan Conference high point in Turkish efforts to consolidate Balkan resistance.

March, 1940: Sweden and Norway refuse Allies permission for transit to Finland. Finland signs Moscow Peace ending Winter War. Anglo-Spanish war trade, payments, and loan agreements signed.

April, 1940: Germany invades Norway and Denmark. Abortive Allied mine-laying operation in the Leads. British come to aid of Norway. Sweden observes strict neutrality toward all sides.

Notes

1. Machiavelli, *The Prince*, chap. xxi.
2. *Discourses*, Book II, chap. xi.
3. The deliberate balancing by the small-state leaders was not always necessary. There were times when the great powers balanced each other without the small "playing off one against the other."
4. While many of the factors enumerated above would in most cases be of peripheral importance to the great power, supplementing its military strength, they may be essential to the small state, substituting for the military power which it lacks.
5. To take just one example, many of the experiences of the great powers dealing with Spain during World War II have since been duplicated in the case of Yugoslavia. A clearer understanding of the effects upon small-power-great-power relations caused by post-World War II technological changes in communications and warfare requires further research. The author is currently engaged in such a study.

2

LILLIPUTIANS' DILEMMAS

Small States in International Politics

ROBERT O. KEOHANE

One of the most striking features of contemporary international politics has been the conspicuousness of small states in an era marked by increasing military disparity between Great and Small. Using the United Nations as a forum and a force and claiming "nonalignment" as an important diplomatic innovation, small states have risen to prominence if not to power. With their emergence nonalignment has become a serious focus of scholarly research; some writers have considered it an institution of great importance.[1] Yet with the exception of Annette Baker Fox's pioneering work on five small states in World War II,[2] very little systematic work has been done on small states' foreign policies. The discussion of nonalignment has sometimes seemed to be a substitute for the comparative analysis of specific policies and dilemmas of small powers.

If the books here reviewed do not provide the systematic comparative analysis for which we may eventually hope, they have escaped from the "nonalignment trap"—the tendency to study a vague category, used by policymakers for their own purposes, rather than to analyze the policies and decisions themselves.[3] Not only have these authors studied problems rather than a cliché; they have often considered the same problems. All are interested in alliances and nonalignment as foreign policy alternatives; all deal with nuclear proliferation, three of them at length. Vital and Rothstein contend with the problem of defining small states and determining whether they behave in distinctive ways; Osgood, Liska, and Rothstein all write extensively on the functions of alliances. This convergence of concerns makes a topically organized review article possible. We will begin with the problem of definition.

Robert O. Keohane (1969), "Lilliputians' Dilemmas: Small States in International Politics." *International Organization* 23(2): 291–310. Reprinted with permission of the World Peace Foundation.

I

Robert Rothstein is concerned only with a limited category of small powers: those that "feel that they are potentially or actually threatened by the policies of the Great Powers" (p. 4). For these states he seeks to establish "one central proposition: that Small Powers are something more than or different from Great Powers writ small" (p. 1). This leads him (p. 23) to reject a definition of "small power" based purely on "objective or tangible criteria" since such a definition

> ends by aligning states along an extended power spectrum so that it can only be said that B is stronger than A but weaker than C. The result is that the significance of the categories "Great" and "Small" is effectually denied.

Yet,

> if there is a unique category of states called Small Powers, which possess distinct patterns of behavior, then it is clearly inadequate to describe them merely in terms of being less powerful (p. 23).

Thus, Rothstein is quite aware that if he is to argue (pp. 23–24) that Great Powers and small powers "develop behavioral patterns which decisively separate them from non-group members," he must provide a clear definition by which states can be categorized. Rothstein therefore develops a definition (p. 29) with a psychological as well as a material dimension:

> *A Small Power is a state which recognizes that it can not obtain security primarily by use of its own capabilities, and that it must rely fundamentally on the aid of other states, institutions, processes, or developments to do so; the Small Power's belief in its inability to rely on its own means must also be recognized by the other states involved in international politics.*

Rothstein illustrates the distinction he is drawing by contrasting the situations of Great Powers and small powers in otherwise similar situations of threat. Rothstein points to three unique aspects of the small power's situation: 1) Outside help is required; 2) the state has a narrow margin of safety, with little time for correcting mistakes; 3) the state's leaders see its weakness as essentially unalterable.

Rothstein does not specify which states in the contemporary world would *not* be small powers under this definition, but it would seem that only the United States, the Union of Soviet Socialist Republics, and the People's Republic of China could possibly qualify. Certainly, the Federal Republic of Germany, France, the United Kingdom, and Japan all rely primarily on American protection for their security; for all four outside help is required when they are threatened by a Great Power and the margin of safety is narrow. And except for proponents of nuclear egalitarianism such as General Pierre Gallois few believe that any but the superpowers could alter a situation of military inferiority vis-à-vis the strongest power.

Yet Rothstein elsewhere mentions that "very few would deny" that West Germany and France are Great Powers; presumably, he would consider the United Kingdom to be one as well (p. 21). Rothstein has constructed a psychological-material definition taking into account the national "state of mind"; yet he continues throughout his book to rely implicitly on a conventional division between "small" and "great." The explicit definition regards almost all states in the current international system as "small," although it may serve well for earlier periods; the implicit definition rests either on traditional judgments or on simple material-strength calculations that Rothstein has himself shown to be unsatisfactory in such an argument. Rothstein's explicit definition is anachronistic in that it serves well only for those periods in the past in which obtaining "security primarily by use of its [a state's] own capabilities" was a live option for five to ten states in a system of limited scope. When only two or three states qualify for great-power status, with 130—from West Germany (or at least Italy) to Lesotho—categorized as "small," the definition becomes useless for analysis.

The source of Rothstein's difficulties is clear: In a nuclear age in which "defense" is impossible for all states and effective deterrence possible only for a few a definition based on capacity to obtain security must collapse. Where insecurity is constant and all-pervasive, it cannot serve as a significant distinguishing variable.

The inapplicability of Rothstein's definition to contemporary world politics may indicate that we should categorize states into size-groups along intuitively acceptable lines without defining the categories in conceptually useful terms. In *The Inequality of States*, David Vital takes this approach. With apparent diffidence he argues that "we recognize, *or find it convenient to posit*, that the world community is divided into certain, admittedly loose, groups" (p. 7). He then distinguishes three groups, great, middle, and small states, drawing the "rough upper limits" for the latter as "a) a population of 10–15 million in the case of economically advanced countries; and b) a population of 20–30 million in the case of underdeveloped countries" (p. 8). Admitting (p. 8) that such a categorization is "frankly subjective, if not arbitrary," Vital concludes (p. 9) that

it should, perhaps, be stressed that these definitions are put forward to make
clear the identity of the subject of this study, not with a view to the creation
of a precise concept for manipulative analytical purposes.

He thus eschews Rothstein's objective.

We must then ask whether the objective is worthwhile. Should we
attempt to develop a conceptually based definition of a term such as "small
power" that is relevant to the nuclear age? This author's view is that precise analytical definitions are more likely than arbitrary or intuitive delin-
eations to point out conceptually significant differences between categories
of states and therefore to facilitate behavioral comparison. Thus a definition
should be judged not only on the relevance of its categories but also on
the power of the explanations that it suggests. An intuitive definition that
makes clear and relevant distinctions is better than any definition that does
not; but a clearly categorizing definition based on concepts that suggest
valid explanations is best of all. The question then arises whether Rothstein's
definition directs us toward effective explanations of behavior for the period
in which it does create relevant categories.

Rothstein deals at length with two types of small-state behavior that
demand explanation: attitudes toward international organizations and
actions taken in "balance-of-power" situations. In explaining small states'
support of international organizations, particularly between the wars,
Rothstein mentions three attributes of international organizations that may
appeal to these countries: their formal equality; the potential security of
membership; and the possible capacity of the organizations to restrain Great
Powers. The stress on security as a small-power motivation is clear. Yet,
having cited these supposed virtues, Rothstein undertakes a trenchant critical analysis of recent and present international organizations arguing that
the "defects [of collective security] submerged its virtues" (pp. 44–45). Thus,
we are left less with an explanation of small-power support for international organizations than with a judgment that such support has often been
misguided; if security is not achieved and Great Powers often not effectively
restrained, is the pursuit of formal equality of status sufficient explanation
for the energies small powers have devoted to these institutions? The reader
is left to wonder at the dubious perspicacity of small-state leadership.

Rothstein repeatedly writes of the "vaunted irresponsibility" of small
powers which he attempts partially to explain on the basis of the temptations of appearing insignificant (p. 27) and the "imperatives of immediate security" which may preclude consideration of long-range problems.
Thus, in discussing Rumania before World War I, Rothstein says (p. 215),

Rumania chose to ally with what clearly seemed to be the stronger side. It was a tactic which, though sanctioned by all the canons of traditional diplomacy, merely increased the imbalance of power, a condition detrimental to Rumania's long-range interests. The Rumanians were too preoccupied with immediate problems to consider the long-range. However, even if they had, the imperatives of immediate security would probably have prevailed.

Yet weak Great Powers may also face such imperatives; if they behave differently, is their obvious inability to become insignificant sufficient reason for the differentiation? Perhaps a different set of criteria for grouping states by size, replacing the small-great dichotomy with a fourfold division, could contribute to more convincing explanations.

I suggest that instead of focusing on perceptions of whether security can be maintained primarily with one's own resources we should focus on the *systemic role* that states' leaders see their countries playing. Systems theorists have on occasion been criticized for assuming that a particular international system rigidly dictates the behavior of states within it. However cogent this objection may be to the work of particular authors, the critics have emphasized the valid point that state behavior determines the nature of international systems as well as vice versa. Going further, analysts have argued that systems themselves can be classified as "system-dominant" or "subsystem-dominant" depending on the extent to which the system determines state behavior.

But if such classifications are useful for systems, they may also be useful for states. A "system-determining" state plays a critical role in shaping the system: The "imperial power" in a unipolar system and the two Great Powers in a bipolar system are examples. In a second category are "system-influencing" states which cannot expect individually to dominate a system but may nevertheless be able significantly to influence its nature through unilateral as well as multilateral actions. Thirdly, some states that cannot hope to affect the system acting alone can nevertheless exert significant impact on the system by working through small groups or alliances or through universal or regional international organizations. These may be labeled "system-affecting" states. Finally, most international systems contain some states that can do little to influence the system-wide forces that affect them, except in groups which are so large that each state has minimal influence and which may themselves be dominated by larger powers. For these small, "system-ineffectual" states foreign policy is adjustment to reality, not rearrangement of it. These four types of states can be referred to briefly, in conformity with traditional usage, as "great," "secondary," "middle," and "small" powers.

Thus in the contemporary international system the United States and the Soviet Union can be considered "system-determining"; the United Kingdom, France, West Germany, Japan, Communist China, and perhaps India "system-influencing"; Canada, Sweden, Pakistan, Brazil, Argentina, and comparable states "system-affecting"; and an array of other states— most of which would fall into Vital's population/development categories for small states—"system-ineffectual."

Yet if we rely purely on objective criteria, we will again encounter the spectrum that can only be divided arbitrarily, as Rothstein has so cogently shown for power-based analysis. A psychological dimension must therefore be added for the sake of clarity as well as in recognition of the fact that "objective reality" does not determine statesmen's behavior directly. I therefore suggest the following definition with the caveat that in all cases statesmen's attitudes must have considerable basis in reality:

> *A Great Power is a state whose leaders consider that it can, alone, exercise a large, perhaps decisive, impact on the international system; a secondary power is a state whose leaders consider that alone it can exercise some impact, although never in itself decisive, on that system; a middle power is a state whose leaders consider that it cannot act alone effectively but may be able to have a systemic impact in a small group or through an international institution; a small power is a state whose leaders consider that it can never, acting alone or in a small group, make a significant impact on the system.*

How does this categorization contribute to an understanding of the behavior of small powers (or, in the above schema, small and middle powers) toward international organizations or balance-of-power politics? With respect to international organizations it draws our attention immediately to the fact that small states may promote international organizations quite rationally without believing that these institutions will promote their security in specific ways or restrain Great Powers from particular actions. The small and middle powers' leaders realize that although they may be able to do little together, they can do virtually nothing separately. Through an international organization they can attempt to promote attitudes favorable to their survival—to develop, as it were, an "international political culture" shaped largely by themselves. Rothstein, for instance, holds (p. 20) that in the twentieth century

> the less tangible elements of strength have become progressively more important, ranging from a good historical "record" to belief in the correct vision

of the good life or merely to an unusual ability to foresee the opportunities in passing events.

This author would argue that this is true and significant and that a major function of international organizations—perceived by many small and middle powers—is to allow these states acting collectively to help shape developing international attitudes, dogmas, and codes of proper behavior.[4] Perception of systemic role, more than perception of need for external aid in security, seems to shape small powers' distinctive attitudes toward international organizations.

With respect to balance-of-power politics the issue seems simpler: As Rothstein mentions, "fearing risks, the Small Powers assert 'nothing we do matters very much'" (p. 28). Mancur Olson has shown that actors with large capabilities relative to a system are more likely than smaller ones to try to influence outcomes that may affect them, not because they have more at stake but because their contributions are more likely to be decisive.[5] Olson and Richard Zeckhauser have pointed out how this discrepancy may work to the benefit of the small in a discussion of burden sharing in NATO: In such a situation the large states have an interest in providing the "public good" (in this case, defense) regardless of what the small do.[6] This phenomenon is clearly crucial for balance-of-power politics: Since Rumania could not redress the imbalance of power in the years before World War I, there was no point in attempting to do so. Perception of inability to influence the system was more important in differentiating Rumanian behavior from that of, say, the United Kingdom, than was perception of ability to rely on its own resources for defense. Using the latter criterion, in fact, we might have erroneously predicted that Britain, more self-sufficient defensively, would remain neutral whereas Rumania would be forced to involve itself early in the fighting. Compared with a definition based on perceived security-capability, a definition in terms of perceptions of systemic role both differentiates more clearly between contemporary states and points to more cogent explanations of some important and distinctive facets of small-state behavior in international organizations and balance-of-power systems.

II

The Inequality of States fulfills the expectations engendered by its title: David Vital spares no effort to show the great disparities in political, economic, and military power and potential between the Great and the Small. In examining the small state's situation he self-consciously chooses (p. 5) to consider the nonaligned state:

> It is only when acting alone—rather than in concert with other, greater states—that the small power can be said to be pursuing an external policy which is in any sense of a class with the external policies of great powers and capable of being compared with them. And it is only when the small power is unaligned and unprotected that the full implications of, say, maintaining or failing to maintain a modern defense establishment can be seen. In short, it is when the state is *alone*—not necessarily in all its affairs, but at least in the great and crucial ones—and is thrown back on its own resources that the limitations and, indeed, the possibilities inherent in its condition are best seen.

Vital is studying the small state that to Rothstein is by definition not a "Small Power." But he goes further in the next paragraph (p. 6):

> Nevertheless, if the rough limits of the isolated small power's strength can be delineated and its characteristic disabilities outlined, something that is typical of all small states will have been shown. For the unaligned state can best be regarded as a limiting case for the class of small states, one from which all other small states shade off, in varying and progressively lessening degrees of political and military isolation. What can be said of the limiting case is likely to be applicable *mutatis mutandis* to the others. It is of the unaligned power as the paradigm for all small powers that the present study is conceived.

Whereas Vital considers the nonaligned state as paradigm, Rothstein regards it as aberration: "It seems fair to conclude that neutrality or nonalignment is a dangerous security policy for Small Powers which are exposed to a Great Power threat" (p. 34). Even if one is not fully prepared to accept Rothstein's view, it is hard to know what to make of Vital's "limiting case" argument. One suspects that the deck has been stacked against the small state from the outset: If alignment is not to be considered, the small state's two most effective weapons—maneuver and exploitation of position—have been severely restricted. Clearly if one is bent on comparing the power of small states with that of any possible great-power opponent, it will be easy to show the small state's weakness. Yet this misses the point, for security and independence can be protected by situation as well as by sheer military or economic strength.

If Vital and Rothstein disagree on definition, categorization, and the analytical significance of nonalignment, they share some common ground regarding attributes of the small state. Both agree that advancing technology has reduced the relative military power of small states; Vital argues this convincingly and in detail (Chapter 4) whereas Rothstein refers to it at several points (for example, p. 20). Both argue that small states perceive themselves differently from Great Powers: Rothstein, consistent with his emphasis on alliances, focuses on needs for external assistance, Vital on *weakness* as "the most common, natural and pervasive view of self in the small state" (p. 33). Vital also considers the small power at a disadvantage due to its smaller foreign policy machinery, which Americans, appalled by the unwieldiness of the United State government, often envy! Vital also stresses the efficacy of economic coercion, using his own country, Israel, as an example of vulnerability; the American reader, remembering Cuba, Southern Rhodesia, and, earlier, Mussolini's Italy, may wonder about the emphasis placed on this argument.

A crucial difference between these two "realistic" and analytical authors lies in their conceptions of the role of intangible factors in international politics: attitudes summarized in phrases such as "liberalism" and "national self-determination"; international law; the importance to a Great Power of its image; and other culturally based factors that may smooth the path of the small state. Rothstein has a sophisticated view of the importance of these intangible elements; Vital, by contrast, persists in describing too narrowly only the stark essentials of power. But if clothes do not "make the man" in international politics any more than in personal life, neither does the skeleton alone. Rothstein contends that "the status and prestige of Small Powers has risen, while their relative strength in the traditional elements of power has actually declined" (p. 3) and that their influence has also increased since 1919 (p. 267). Vital's emphasis on the "traditional elements of power" limits his analysis to strength and therefore restricts the usefulness of his well-written and often cogently argued study.

One of Rothstein's most interesting theoretical arguments is his effort to describe the effects of various types of international systems on small-power situation and behavior. With the disdain for clichés and platitudes that marks his writing the author criticizes the proposition that the balance of power assured, in the past, the survival of small powers. Rothstein distinguishes three variants of the balance of power: the "conservative" balance-of-power system, occurring immediately after 1815 and 1919, wherein the Great Powers were most concerned with maintaining what they had; a fluid and competitive balance-of-power system, as in the 1850s and 1860s; and the bipolar bloc-balance system epitomized by the European system after 1871, and particularly after 1890 or 1905. In Rothstein's view the "conservative" balance protects small-power security at the expense of influence or opportunities for advancement; it is best suited to the satisfied small states and least to the revisionist ones. The fluid, competitive system presents the small powers with more room for maneuver, whereas the two-bloc system presents opportunities for maneuver and influence—due to the scramble for allies—but at the expense of security (pp. 186–191). Thus, in opening his chapter on contemporary small-power politics and alignment (p. 237) Rothstein can say:

> A functioning balance of power system, comparable to the one which existed throughout the first half of the nineteenth century, limits the ability of Small Powers to achieve their own goals. However, in compensation, it provides more real security for them—in terms of the maintenance of independence— than any other historical system, all of which offered the Small Power some elements of maneuverability, but to the detriment of long-range security.

In less systematic terms Vital seems to agree that great-power competition is the condition for small-power influence, if not security (pp. 190–191). In a brief comment Liska also argues that "small-state subsystems would enjoy a maximum of practically attainable autonomy in a multipower global system combining competition with concert" (p. 44). But only Rothstein carries out the analysis—supported by studies of Belgian-French relations, the Little Entente, and small states between 1815 and the present—needed to substantiate the argument.

In a fluid international system, however, the small state must still maneuver in order to prosper, if not to survive. Maneuvering involves making alliances—or finding an appropriate alternative policy. It is to the alliance decision that we now turn.

III

The imprecision of international relations terminology is nowhere more obvious or painful than in discussions of *alliances*. Although the three authors here considered who deal extensively with alliances (Liska, Osgood, and Rothstein) all teach at the same university (Johns Hopkins) and are in general agreement on most substantive issues, they differ on problems of definition. Osgood (p. 17) defines an alliance as a

> formal agreement that pledges states to cooperate in using their military resources against a specific state or states and usually obligates one or more

of the signatories to use force, or to consider (unilaterally or in consultation with allies) the use of force, in specified circumstances.

Liska is less explicit although he notes that his "discussion will adhere to an extensive conception of 'alliance,' going beyond the hard core of an explicit, contractual pledge of military assistance" (p. 3). Despite his usual analytical care—as in his definition of a small power—Rothstein is even less precise: He seems to define alliances as formal ties (p. 49) but not to impose such strict conditions as Osgood does. But since Osgood himself acknowledges that "an alliance may be difficult to distinguish from other kinds of military contracts such as military subsidies, military assistance agreements or military base agreements" (p. 19) his definition seems to serve more as a point of reference (the "pure" alliance) than as a comprehensive delineation of the subject. Yet we are clearer on what constitutes an alliance than we are about a "small power" or "small state." Each author agrees that a special tie must be agreed to by both parties; they merely disagree on how formal or explicit that tie must be to be considered an "alliance." Thus, the problem is chiefly semantic, in contrast to the small-power definitional dilemma, which was of substantive significance as well.

Osgood and Liska, both of whom list functions of alliances, agree on three: aggregation of power, interallied control or restraint of allies, and promotion of international order. Osgood adds a fourth, internal security, which he considers especially important for small states.[7] Rothstein, with small states particularly in mind, cites the bargaining advantages that may accrue from offering to dismantle a new alliance and the political and psychological advantages of allying with a prestigious and powerful state (p. 50). Liska takes account both of Osgood's "internal security" function and the political-psychological advantages when he characterizes special small-state interests in alliances under the headings of security, stability, and status (pp. 27–29). Thus there is general agreement on function, with Liska and Rothstein more sensitive to particular purposes of small states than Osgood, who writes from a great-power and alliance-wide perspective. Vital does not discuss alliances extensively, but whereas he might agree with these lists of functions, he would surely warn that the price of alignment is the loss of real independence and effective sovereignty (pp. 184–186, especially).

What policy toward alliances, then, makes sense for the small state? Of these authors only Rothstein considers this issue systematically. Using the case studies of the Franco-Belgian Military Accord of 1920 and the Little Entente, Rothstein devotes over 100 pages to the question of what types of alliances are most beneficial to small powers. Contending that (p. 170) "in theory, Small Power alliances are condemned; in practice, they remain popular," his most novel conclusion is his defense of these arrangements. He concludes (p. 177):

> Small Powers *ought* to prefer mixed, multilateral alliances. They provide the most benefits in terms of security and political influence. If unavailable, they probably should choose a Small Power alliance in preference to an unequal, bilateral alliance, particularly if the Small Powers do not fear an immediate threat to their security, and if their goals in allying are primarily political. An alliance with a single Great Power ought to be chosen only if all the other alternatives are proscribed, and if the Small Powers fear an imminent attack—and even then only in hopes of improving their deterrent stance.

Rothstein's dim view of alliances with a single Great Power applies not only to bilateral ties but also to alliances between several small powers and one Great Power (p. 127). The careful historical discussion and the convincing argument by which Rothstein supports these conclusions constitute highly recommended reading for all students of international politics.

This author's only major quarrel with the analysis is that its abstract quality blurs inter-great-power distinctions that may be highly relevant to the small state. The Southeast Asia Treaty Organization (SEATO) and the Central Treaty Organization (CENTO) may be highly deficient unequal alliances, but they do not operate like the Warsaw Treaty Organization (WTO). The special case of such an alliance—that is, unequal alliance with a *contiguous, imperialistic* Great Power—does not receive adequate consideration. The Warsaw Treaty Organization, which Osgood discusses in straightforward fashion, might well be labeled an "Al Capone alliance" in which remaining a faithful ally protects one not against the mythical outside threat but rather against the great-power ally itself, just as, by paying "protection money" to Capone's gang in Chicago, businessmen protected themselves not against other gangs but against Capone's own thugs. What happened in August 1968 to Czechoslovakia is not so different from what would have happened to a recalcitrant Chicago bootlegger in the 1920s.

From the perspective of contemporary international policies the most interesting questions about the future of alliances concern the policies of African and Asian states, on which Liska, Osgood, and Rothstein all focus their attention. All three men agree that the zenith of nonalignment has been reached. Liska points to the danger that "a free hand might come to mean an empty and unarmed hand" (p. 20); Osgood writes of the decline of superpower ardor in courting the nonaligned (p. 91); and Rothstein, in an extensive discussion, concludes that "it is doubtful that nonalignment can ever be very much more than a tactical principle" (p. 254). As we have seen, Vital, although favorable to a policy of independence where power realities can be reconciled with it, emphasizes that "the price is rising" (p. 186).

Does the decline of nonalignment therefore presage a rise in alignment policies for states in the so-called "third world"? Vital, despite his pessimism about the power of small states, gives the most emphatically negative answer. In his view (p. 186)

> the coalition or alliance is not an effective unit of foreign policy and strategy at all, except in the narrow, if extremely important, respect that it can from time to time marshal great strength.

Thus he denies a significant political role for alliances. Their liabilities are such that many small states will continue to refuse to join available combinations.

Liska, Osgood, and Rothstein all give this question more extensive consideration, and each of them differentiates between small-state alliances and ties between a Great Power and small states. In contrast to Vital Rothstein argues that "from the point of view of Small Powers, alliances have increasingly become instruments designed to achieve nonmilitary goals" although this holds, in his view, less for bilateral great-power/small-power alliances than for other forms (pp. 262–263). Small powers, he implies, will normally agree to unequal alliances only where a military threat is perceived. By contrast, in his view "an argument for the increased utility of alliances composed solely of Small Powers can be made" (p. 263). Admitting that "the record of the few regional groups which have been formed scarcely justifies optimism," he does not argue that the significance of small-power alliances is increasing, only that they should not necessarily be considered worthless (pp. 263–264).

Liska and Osgood both envisage the possibility of alliances between small states and what we have called "secondary powers"; both appear favorably disposed toward such a development. As Liska puts it (p. 29):

> To an increasing number of less developed countries, selectively disengaged ex-metropolitan powers may be more efficient and more tolerable great-power allies in the search for post-independence stability than superpowers without colonial antecedents, as long as the ex-metropoles retain the capacity and will for instant but limited re-engagement.

Osgood is quite skeptical that this will take place. Liska, who is more critical than Osgood of American "overinvolvement" (p. 35), seems to regard such secondary-power action as a more realistic possibility, citing Japan's relations with the Republic of Korea as well as British and French connections with Africa (pp. 49, 54).

Liska takes a dim view of pure small-power alliances, arguing that "the less-developed countries of today and tomorrow are unlikely to transcend the limitations inherent in small-state alliances as a category" (p. 57). Yet he argues (p. 49) that where combined with a great-power (or "secondary-power") tie, most desirably to an ex-metropole, and supplementing larger organizations such as the United Nations, such alliances could be useful:

> The alliances might bring latent conflicts among lesser states into the open, but they would not actually generate them; they might serve to contain and adjust these conflicts rather than treat them as nonexistent or illegitimate. They would thus lay the bases of an embryonic order for the less developed segment of the international system. If they proved workable, small-state alliances would be preferable to grand designs of regional or continental unity.

Osgood is once again more skeptical of the possibilities for change although he argues (p. 131) that

> In the long run, in two or three decades, this political introversion [of new states] might lead to loose regional and subregional groupings, which would provide the framework within which more coherent patterns of international polices and semiautonomous balance-of-power systems could emerge.

Liska's enthusiasm for small-state alliances when combined with a tie to a larger state and Osgood's emphasis on "coherence" raise the question of whether clearly defined *structure* is necessary to insure *order*. One is reminded of some Marxists' inability to understand capitalist economic successes because of the assumption that the apparent confusion of decentralized market decision-making (Marx's "anarchy") must lead eventually to chaos. A considerable measure of regulation and control was essential to the survival of capitalism, but the imposition of centralized planning structures was not. It is not entirely clear that alliance structures are any more necessary (or even conducive) to order for international politics among the new states. There are, however, strong historical and analytical grounds—cited by Rothstein and Liska particularly—for believing that patterns of alignment will necessarily emerge in the competitive international subsystems to be expected in Africa as well as Asia. The degree to which they promote international order or disorder may depend as much on great-power as on small-power policies.

IV

Apart from future problems of nuclear proliferation, what policy should a Great Power such as the United States follow in an area of small-power confrontation, for which the Middle East may serve as a prototype? This problem is touched upon by Osgood and Liska but not given, in this author's view, the attention it deserves. Osgood states the problem as it relates to the Middle East without discussing it extensively. After describing a likely situation of Israeli military strength, an approximate balance of American and Soviet assistance, and superpower diplomatic intervention, preserving an uneasy peace, Osgood states (p. 131):

> Under these conditions the United States will be drawn, perforce, into more active intervention by one means or another in the internal and international politics of the area. Thus the United States and the Soviet Union will be major competitors in an international subsystem that will be neither independent of, nor determined by, the global sphere of politics. For this reason the Middle East will present the greatest danger of an American-Soviet crisis or war growing out of commitments to local states over which neither state has much control.

Osgood thus projects present (potentially disastrous) trends into the future with the air of a man who believes them to be inevitable. The reader is left to wonder about the fatalism of this paragraph which may be prudent as forecasting but which cries out for policy analysis. Why will the United States allow itself to be drawn into more active intervention? In the service of what national interests will this country become committed to supporting a state over whose policies it has little control? If the consequences of present policy are so hazardous, should the sources of that policy, and its moral and political justification, remain unexamined?

Broadly speaking, a Great Power can take one of three attitudes toward an area in which it has less than absolutely critical interests. It can actively *support* one power or set of powers in the politics which *those states* decide to pursue; it can intervene in order to *control* the international politics of the area, usually at the price of supporting one state or another up to a point; or it can *withdraw* partially from the region in the hope that a regional conflagration could thus be contained.[8] None of these policies is a priori either prudent or unwise, slogans about the "indivisibility of peace" and the evils of "appeasement" notwithstanding. The analyst must consider the gains and cost associated with support, against the costs of commitment in case of war; the likely efficacy of attempts at control; and the feasibility of limiting a conflict to the region.

If postwar American foreign policy has had one salient characteristic, it has been to regard the withdrawal-containment approach as unfeasible where important interests are at stake. We have followed a policy, in Asia particularly, that may have sought control and limitation of violence but which, failing that, furnished massive support for an uncontrollable client and increased the scale of violence manyfold. We have also supported the United Nations, as in the Congo, in more successful policies of control-by-intervention. Liska, aware of the positive functions of conflict in some situations, argues that "relatively uninhibited foreign relations encompassing conflicts and alliances may be the primary necessity in political development" (p. 47); he is also conscious of American overcommitment. Yet (p. 40) he sees limited support rather than withdrawal-containment as the solution:

> An outside power can often best influence the negotiations for peaceful settlement if it has previously guaranteed the lesser state against total defeat and obliteration even if not against all setbacks or against failure to satisfy maximum goals. Holding the ring for a lesser ally is to render him, and the alliance, better service on occasion than would be the case if he were held back at all costs. In the long run, this may prove to be a vital point for America's relationship with Israel.

This is dangerous counsel. It may be extremely difficult to limit one's commitment to a client state if one renounces control over the circumstances, nature, and timing of *its* initiative. Neither Liska nor Osgood considers whether a more restrained American policy, breaking the potential links between a fourth Middle Eastern war and a Third World War by reducing American involvement in the area, should be seriously considered. If grand visions of a *Pax Americana* were renounced, it might become clearer not only that the American interest in preventing a world war far outweighs our interest in preventing local fighting but also that pursuit of the two objectives may at times be contradictory. "Keeping the lid on" is an appropriate metaphor. If the lid flies off, the force of the explosion may be roughly proportional to the effort expended in keeping it on. The lack of an activist American policy toward Africa probably represents less an experiment with restraint than it reflects disinterest and preoccupation elsewhere. In the Middle East the current commitments of both superpowers would probably require an explicit agreement to become more disinterested; in Africa tacit consent to remain only marginally involved could be sufficient.

Yet it is unlikely that the United States will, in the next few years, limit its commitments in the Middle East or significantly alter its stance toward Israel.[9] Both major presidential candidates promised continued support for Israel during the 1968 campaign. The chief explanation for this phenomenon—Israeli political power in the United States—is well known. But, remarkably enough, neither Liska nor Osgood mentions this. They both write on the apparent assumption that Great Powers are the masters of their own policies: that (except for small, "penetrated" or satellite countries) modern states can be regarded as discrete decision-making entities. This conventional assumption has by now become an inconvenient fiction that hinders our understanding of great-power/small-power relations.

Contrary to this discrete-entity assumption "informal penetration" is a pervasive phenomenon in contemporary international politics which works in both directions. Small states can penetrate large ones as well as vice versa. Of the books under review, however, only Vital considers this tool of statecraft—which he designates as "subversion" —and he discusses it only in the context of small-state politics. Yet it is clear that a small power holding potential political assets in a Great Power, particularly if the Great Power has an open political system, may be able to exercise influence on that state's policy that could not be explained by the discrete-entity model. Furthermore, membership in an alliance with a "penetrated" Great Power may provide the small state with much more than "access" or "the right to be consulted."[10] It may increase already substantial influence by widening and deepening ties that contribute to the small power's political leverage. In the extreme case the small power may be able to exercise the function of "interallied control" with a vengeance by putting severe restraints on the Great Power's policy options.

This is true to some extent vis-à-vis the United States for a number of relatively small states although Israel is the most obvious example. Nationalist China, Spain, Portugal, and the Philippines, for instance, have all undertaken significant public relations and lobbying activities in this country with substantial if varying degrees of success. Where the small state's influence derives from the conjunction of low intensity of American interests and high intensity of small-state interests, it may be beneficial to the small state without seriously hampering United States policy. But where, as in the cases of Nationalist China and Israel, it virtually forbids

official reconsideration of established policy in an area of critical importance and danger, the results may be disastrous and should certainly not
be ignored.[11]

V

Osgood, Rothstein, and Vital all discuss nuclear proliferation at length;
Liska refers to it only in a passing comment which indicates that he believes
"orderly" acquisition of nuclear weapons by major industrial powers to
be possible (p. 45). Of the three authors devoting attention to the problem only Rothstein seems particularly concerned. He regards proliferation as likely and dangerous, whereas Osgood views it as likely but not
particularly perilous. Vital, interested in small-power policy rather than
systemic effects, hardly considers the global results of proliferation.

Vital argues that although acquisition of nuclear weapons would be feasible for a number of states, it would "not automatically 'equalize' small
and great nor even, necessarily, reduce the gap between them" (p. 166).
Nuclear weapons would, in his view, have an "extremely limited" deter-
rent value against Great Powers (p. 173). Rothstein agrees: "It is not very
difficult to explode a nuclear device, but it is extremely difficult to become
an *effective* nuclear power" (p. 274). Osgood, consistent with his great-
power emphasis, does not consider the advantages and disadvantages of
acquiring nuclear weapons for the small state but rather assumes that "the
balance of incentives and disincentives, unlike that in France, Britain and
China, will be complex and delicate" (p. 144) and that it is likely that proliferation will proceed in limited and moderate fashion.

Vital, always ready to emphasize, even to overstate, small-state weakness, contends that for defensive small states nuclear capability may be
effective in rare but conceivable circumstances but that for active or aggressive small states "the acquisition of nuclear capability is likely to narrow
their field of political maneuver and intensify their sensitivity to pressure. . . . The effect may be capital" (p. 180). Rothstein agrees that acquisition of nuclear weapons "may actually make Small Powers more, not
less, dependent on the actions of the Great Powers" (p. 295) but he also
argues that "a very rudimentary nuclear force can be an extremely persuasive military instrument against a very wide range of states" (p. 284)
as long as the small power "stays out of trouble with the Soviet Union and
the United States" (pp. 283–284).

In response Vital would contend (p. 178) that a nuclear small state with
an activist policy could not "stay out of trouble" with the superpowers:

In so far as there can be a concerted effort on the part of the great powers to prevent the proliferation of nuclear weapons among the minor ones, it is here that it is most likely to be effective and straightforward.

The contrast of views is somewhat more apparent than real: Vital expects superpower policies for which Rothstein argues. Beyond this Rothstein is explicitly skeptical of the ability of small states to calculate their interests on nuclear-weapons questions rationally, taking into account reactions from the Great Powers and other states. Although he does not believe that small states will gain by acquiring nuclear weapons, he sadly concludes that "it is unfortunate, but undoubtedly true, that few if any Small Powers are likely to evaluate the decision" as he does (p. 293). He expects the siren call of great possibilities to outweigh listings of disadvantages unless explicit and forceful measures are taken by the Great Powers to prevent proliferation.

Rothstein's and Vital's analyses are therefore quite similar in essentials. Their differences arise because both men are pessimists, yet pessimistic from different perspectives. Rothstein sees great obstacles to the attainment of his desired objective, which is nuclear nonproliferation; Vital sees huge barriers in the way of attaining his objective, small-power independence, through proliferation or in any other way. Thus the "Cassandra syndrome" of the analyst!

Lacking a systemic orientation, Vital does not suggest what the Great Powers should do about proliferation; only Rothstein and Osgood consider that question. And here the differences are wide indeed. Rothstein does consider the possibility that in a nuclear-armed world Great Powers might take the option of "loosening the alliance commitment" (p. 288) although he considers the opposite alternative of quick, decisive intervention equally likely (p. 291). Yet Rothstein, despite his pessimism about stopping proliferation, believes that except in limited instances "the United States ought to try to prevent proliferation at all costs" (p. 323). Toward this end he proposes a policy that would combine nuclear guarantees to states promising not to develop nuclear weapons with military and economic aid to those states. He also suggests that the United States might, in certain circumstances, *give* nuclear weapons to a state suddenly threatened by a major nuclear power, arguing that "this promise might inhibit the whole process of proliferation."

> Any state intent on developing its own nuclear forces for security, prestige, to steal a march on its enemies, or whatever would presumably be extremely reluctant to do so if it knew that its competitors would simultaneously receive a nuclear force of its [sic] own, and a more effective one at no cost (p. 316).

Osgood reveals a concern about overcommitments when analyzing nuclear weapons that is not evident in his discussion of nonnuclear problems. He attacks the solution of guarantees, arguing first that the protégé state might not accept a guarantee from a superpower in *lieu* of developing its own weapons and second that superpowers might be quite reluctant to guarantee states with which they were not allied. But further, in his view (p. 146):

> Countervailing guarantees by the United States and the Soviet Union to competing protégés might involve the superpowers too deeply in minor power polities and could even lead to a direct confrontation, which a more detached position might avoid.

Thus Osgood wonders

> whether the American interest in containing China may not be better served in the long run by encouraging, rather than trying to discourage, the creation of a nuclear multipolar balance of power in which American power is supplemented, and American commitments are somewhat relieved, by the power and commitments of others (p. 149).

He makes it explicit that he has Japan and India in mind.

Through their disagreement Osgood and Rothstein clarify a central issue of American policy for the next decade or more: whether to deal with situations of local conflict through a policy of intervention, commitment, and control, as in the past, or through a new policy of restraint, partial withdrawal, and containment of such quarrels as arise. How much reliance can be placed on other states, and how much latitude should they be allowed? How high a price should be paid for control?

This review article is hardly the place to attempt resolution of the question although the point that restraint-withdrawal-containment should be seriously considered has already been made clear. But the question deserves extensive thought by analysts as well as vague if repeated mention in a Presidential nominating campaign. We will be lucky if the issue is not resolved by the bureaucracy or the public without regard to the requirements of a rational foreign policy (out of inertia on the one hand or impatience on the other). Specialists, through failure to confront the issue, should not allow such an outcome to occur by default.

VI

All four books under review deserve to be read by serious students of international relations. Rothstein's work, despite a certain lack of organizational coherence and a complex style, is clearly the most important of the four. It is the most systematic theoretically and based on the most extensive research. Liska's brief work should be particularly appreciated for its conciseness as well as for the author's illuminating use of historical events of current relevance. Here we find references to fifteenth-century Venice, or to Anglo-Dutch union in the seventeenth century, that enhance our understanding of contemporary world politics rather than merely creating respect for the author's erudition.

The works by Vital and Osgood are well written and often cogently argued, yet they contain more serious deficiencies which have been touched upon above. Vital overemphasizes the weaknesses of small states largely by considering their worst possible situations. He also reduces the value of his argument by excessive reliance on tangible power and influence factors. Much of Osgood's book covers rather familiar ground in a somewhat conventional way, as in his discussion of contemporary alliance systems; only in the last chapter, on "the future of alliances," do his imagination and insight lead us down interesting and original paths.

These books perform valuable service to students of small states and alliances as much for the problems they raise but leave unsolved as for the solutions they offer. Critical issues of policy, as well as significant theoretical problems, remain unresolved and unexplored. Future work in this area, while building on these analyses, must go considerably beyond them. If Lilliputians can tie up Gulliver, or make him do their fighting for them, they must be studied as carefully as the giant.[12]

Notes

1. J. W. Burton, *International Relations: A General Theory* (Cambridge: Cambridge University Press, 1965) constitutes the most enthusiastic long discussion of nonalignment. See also, for more critical commentary, Cecil V. Crabb, Jr., *The Elephants and the Grass: A Study of Nonalignment* (New York: Frederick A. Praeger, 1965); and Laurence W. Martin (ed.), *Neutralism and Nonalignment: The New States in World Affairs* (New York: Frederick A. Praeger [for the Washington Center of Foreign Policy Research, School of Advanced International Studies, Johns Hopkins University], 1962).

2. Annette Baker Fox, *The Power of Small States: Diplomacy in World War II* (Chicago: Chicago University Press, 1959).

3. For a very critical view of nonalignment as a policy see Francis Low-Beer, "The Concept of Neutralism," *American Political Science Review*, June 1964 (Vol. 58, No. 2), pp. 383–391.

4. Consider, for example, the discussions and resolutions on "nonintervention" at the twentieth session of the General Assembly. Inis L. Claude has com-

mented on one aspect of this phenomenon in his discussion of "collective legitimization." ("Collective Legitimization as a Political Function of the United Nations," *International Organization*, Summer 1966 [Vol. 20, No. 3], pp. 367–379.) The discussions and resolutions on "nonintervention" at the twentieth session of the General Assembly provide further examples of collective dogma creation.

5. Mancur Olson, Jr., *The Logic of Collective Action: Public Goods and the Theory of Groups* (Cambridge, Mass: Harvard University Press, 1965).

6. Mancur Olson, Jr., and Richard Zeckhauser, "An Economic Theory of Alliances," *Review of Economics and Statistics*, August 1966 (Vol. 48, No. 3), pp. 266–279.

7. See Osgood, pp. 21–22; Liska, pp. 23–25.

8. Great Powers need not pursue any of these policies unilaterally. International organizations can often be used in the service of any of the three alternatives or, as in peacekeeping operations, in an attempt to combine policies of involvement and withdrawal.

9. This sentence may be taken to imply skepticism that the comments on "evenhandedness" by William Scranton, then President-elect Richard M. Nixon's foreign policy envoy, foreshadow significant policy changes.

10. These phrases are used by Rothstein, p. 49.

11. This emphasis on small-state influence on Great Powers' decisions may perhaps be explained by the fact that the author is currently working on a study of that problem and by authors' natural tendencies to assume the importance of questions that interest them.

12. For an excellent example of "giant study" see Stanley Hoffmann, *Gulliver's Troubles, Or the Setting of American Foreign Policy* (New York: McGraw-Hill [for the Council on Foreign Relations], 1968) which also provided inspiration for the title of this essay.

3

THE INEQUALITY OF STATES

A Study of the Small Power in International Relations

DAVID VITAL

Introduction

This study is an attempt to spell out some of the practical political implications of the material inequality of states. While the formal equality of
states is a valuable and, on the whole, valued convention of international
relations, it is evident that in peace, no less than in war, differences of size
have political consequences for both large and small nations. All things
being equal, the state with great economic resources and a large population has more influence on events outside its frontiers, greater security from
pressure and attack, more prestige, and a larger element of choice in respect
of the national policy it pursues. A small state is more vulnerable to pressure, more likely to give way under stress, more limited in respect of the
political options open to it, and subject to a tighter connection between
domestic and external affairs. In other words, the smaller the human and
material resources of a state, the greater are the difficulties it must sur-
mount if it is to maintain any valid political options at all and, in consequence, the smaller the state, the less viable it is as a genuinely independent
member of the international community. Of course, sheer physical
(human and material) size is not the only factor. The level of economic
and social development that has been attained, the chance effects of geographical proximity to areas of conflict and importance between and to
the great powers, the nature of the environment in which the state is placed,
the cohesion of the population, and the degree of internal support given
the government of the day—these are some of the factors that modify the
ability of the state to perform as a resistant rather than vulnerable, and

David Vital, *The Inequality of States: A Study of the Small Power in International
Relations* (London, UK: Clarendon Press, Oxford, 1967). Cross references to pages
and notes refer to the original publication.

active rather than passive, member of the international community. But material size is the factor which is least of all given to modification through the deliberate efforts of governments. It sets the limit to what can be attained and fixes the international role and status of the nation more securely than any other.

Since the Second World War the economic and military power available to the great states has vastly increased. It is true that for reasons which are beyond the scope of this book (but of which the most important are the acquisition of nuclear power and the strategic deadlock that has ensued), the great powers have been reluctant to employ their power to the full. Some very great states have, in effect, abdicated from positions of influence; in other cases there is uncertainty as to whether and how available power can be safely and effectively exploited in the national interest. One consequence of this has been that the post-war proliferation of small states has occurred in an atmosphere peculiarly conducive to illusions about national strength and to a corresponding emphasis and reliance on the formal, *legal*, equality of nations. This may be a good or a bad thing; what is uncertain is whether it will last. But the fact that great states have, from time to time, broken through their inhibitions to exert some part at least of the vast economic and military power available to them in order to impose their will on others suggests that reliance on these inhibitions would be misplaced and that the operative factors in crisis remain the national interest as seen at the time and the material bars, if any, to its pursuit.

The strength and weakness of states and their long-term viability must therefore be examined not in terms of current, typical international practice, still less in terms of legal and moral rights. It is the capacity of the state to withstand stress, on the one hand, and its ability to pursue a policy of its own devising, on the other, that are the key criteria. And these can best be explored in terms of limiting cases, exposed positions, and barriers which cannot, possibly, be surmounted.

In alternative terms, this study attempts to answer three questions:

(a) What are the practical consequences for the small power of the material inequality of states?

(b) What are the limits of the small power's strength and, in particular, its capacity to withstand great external stresses?

(c) Given its limited resources and the ease with which overwhelming strength can be marshaled against it, what national policies are open to the small power to pursue?

Of course, some small powers can—and in very many cases do—seek to offset their weaknesses by association or alliance with other powers, great and small. But where the quest for protection and insurance is successful a price must normally be paid in terms of sacrifice of autonomy in the control of national resources and loss of freedom of political maneuver and choice. For such states the answers to the first and third questions posed above are largely pre-determined. As for the second question, the task of unraveling what fraction or aspect of national power[1] it owes to its own resources and what to its partners, apart from being extremely complex in itself, would teach little about the general problems of the small state as an independent international entity. Furthermore, it is only when acting alone—rather than in concert with other, greater states—that the small power can be said to be pursuing an external policy which is in any sense of a class with the external policies of great powers and capable of being compared with them. And it is only when the small power is unaligned and unprotected that the full implications of, say, maintaining or failing to maintain a modern defense establishment can be seen. In short, it is when the state is *alone*—not necessarily in all its affairs, but at least in the great and crucial ones—and is thrown back on its own resources that the limitations and, indeed, the possibilities inherent in its condition are best seen.

Nevertheless, if the rough limits of the isolated small power's strength can be delineated and its characteristic disabilities outlined, something that is typical of all small states will have been shown. For the unaligned state can best be regarded as a limiting case for the class of small states, one from which all other small states shade off in varying and progressively lessening degrees of political and military isolation. What can be said of the limiting case is likely to be applicable *mutatis mutandis* to the others. It is of the unaligned power as the paradigm for all small powers that the present study is conceived.

For this reason the present attempt at an analysis of the political viability of the small state has been cast in terms of the isolated, maverick, unaligned power, the small power *alone*—the state which can rely least on outside help and sympathy and which, by virtue of its situation, is compelled to make its own decisions on the basis of its own understanding of that situation and such resources as are available to it.

There is no simple term which adequately expresses this condition. The term used most frequently here—"non-alignment"—is not entirely satisfactory because it has special political, not to mention emotive, connotations. But I have found none better. At any rate, it is used here in its simplest sense, the negative one of implying that there are no clear, effective, and mutually binding ties with other powers. Nothing of the legal or ideological significance that attaches to such terms as "neutrality" and "neutralism" is intended. The test of "non-alignment" is seen as whether the state in question must rely ultimately on its own political and material resources in the pursuit of an external policy of its own devising—or not. In consequence, a formal commitment which is ignored in practice, or which has fallen into desuetude, or which has been explicitly or implicitly denounced will be given no weight. It is the actual state of political affairs which is thought to matter, not the legal one. And it follows that such formal obligations as, say, France bore towards Czechoslovakia in 1938 or which the members of the Arab League bear towards each other today are not taken as invalidating an *ex post facto* view of Czechoslovakia then and a contemporary view of Egypt or Syria now as *unaligned* states in substantially the same sense that Sweden and Burma are of this category, whatever differences there may be on historical and other scores.

Some clarification on the term "small state"[2] is clearly necessary, but there is the difficulty that if an objective definition is attempted it will be circular: along the lines of "those powers which lack/possess the resources and ability to maintain an independent international role are true small powers, those that do/do not are pseudo small powers" when it is the intention of this study to explore the circumstances under which a small state can maintain such a role. A frankly subjective, if not arbitrary, definition has therefore been chosen. But it is one which is supported by common usage.

We recognize, or find it convenient to posit, that the world community is divided into certain, admittedly loose, groups. The formal equality of states notwithstanding, these groups have from time to time been given a degree of overt and even legal recognition.[3] The fundamental test has almost invariably been that of actual or potential military power, modified, to be sure, by historical and contemporary political circumstances. However, it is only the top of the pyramid that is normally defined with any clarity, while it is important to distinguish between at least two more broad classes among the lesser states. Some of these, while outside the generally accepted category of great powers, are nevertheless so populous (Indonesia and Pakistan, for example) that their cases cannot reasonably be compared with those of their small neighbors (say, Malaysia and Sri Lanka). Similarly, certain less heavily populated, but more highly developed states (such as Argentina, Canada, and Poland) are properly distinguished from smaller states of a roughly equivalent level of development (such as Uruguay and Finland). The present study is concerned with the latter class of smaller states to the exclusion of such middle powers.

The dividing line between the two groups may be drawn by defining the rough upper limits of the class of small states as being:

(a) a population of 10–15 million in the case of economically advanced countries; and

(b) a population of 20–30 million in the case of underdeveloped countries.

The first group would therefore include Sweden, Australia, Belgium, and Switzerland, for example, but not Italy; the second group would include most of the South and Central American states, but not Mexico or Brazil, all the Arab states, and all the African states except Nigeria.[4]

This is, of necessity, very imperfect. Certainly, no pretense is made that the 2:1 relationship between developed and underdeveloped populations is anything but rough and convenient. It has been argued by some economists that the term "underdeveloped" is excessively crude in any case. But while this point is important to economists concerned with the origins of underdevelopment and its cure, here the interest is solely with the brute fact of underdevelopment and its general, but nevertheless plain, limiting effect on military and economic potential.

No lower limit has been set; it seems evident that the disabilities that are a consequence of size where the population is ten million will clearly be intensified where it is five or ten times smaller. However, such "micro-powers" as Western Samoa have not been seriously considered at all. They surely constitute yet another class of states with reasonably distinct and characteristic problems of their own.

Finally, it should, perhaps, be stressed that these definitions are put forward to make clear the identity of the subject of this study, not with a view to the creation of a precise concept for manipulative analytical purposes.

Conclusions

The general question with which this study has been concerned is whether a small and independent state is viable in the world of contemporary international politics and to what degree and under what circumstances. It is clear that there are, in practice, a number of states in this category whose viability is not in question at the present time because they are spared having to sustain any serious opposition to their purposes—including the fundamental one of political survival. Yet for that reason little of general

significance about the small states as a class can be learned from examining their affairs. The question whether, say, El Salvador is internationally
viable cannot be divorced from the fortunate circumstance that its external relations present it with few problems of any gravity. It is under no
military threat; it chooses not to oppose the paramount power in Central
America in any of the latter's major purposes; and it is assured of that
power's support should it find itself under threat from either its neighbors or another major power. There is thus no apparent, *structural* reason why it should not maintain its political identity for as far as the
prophetic eye can see. Of course, the tranquility of El Salvador's external
affairs is conditional upon the pursuit of what might be termed a non-
policy, one of passivity in the international arena. Should the United States
require something of the El Salvador Government that the latter finds excessively disagreeable or should El Salvador itself embark on a political course
which the United States, for its part, finds discordant with its policy for
the region, the material inequality between the two states, the vast disparity
in economic, military, and organizational resources would soon be felt.
Moreover, these disparities could be brought to bear by the stronger party
on the weaker long before the conflict emerged into the public light, to
say nothing of its assuming violent form. In brief, the cornerstone of any
Central American republic's foreign policy is its relations with the United
States—as Guatemala's conflict with the United States in the early fifties
and Cuba's today so amply illustrate. Whether, in such circumstances, these
and other small states which are similarly placed can be described as fully
sovereign and politically independent is largely a matter of definition and
opinion. But it is worth noting that the conventions of sovereignty and
legal equality and of inter-international behavior generally are such that
it remains possible, even for a small client state, to rebel against the paramount power without violating international practice and habits of
thought and, possibly, with some prospect of receiving support from other
major states. The ability *in principle* to alter course and reconsider political and economic arrangements entered into in past times is a fair test of
political independence at an elementary level. The capacity to carry out
such a decision in the face of opposition is a test of political independence
at a second level, a more important one. It is at this latter level that the
viability of the state is tested, (i.e., by its capacity to withstand opposition
and stick to purposes thought commensurate with the national interest).
But whereas the great powers are, ultimately, impervious to coercion, the
degree of opposition that small states can reasonably be expected to withstand will vary from case to case and be amenable, in the final analysis,

only to subjective evaluation. Viability, in consequence, is a relative quality fluctuating with circumstances, possessed by different states in a different degree, but in no case absolutely and finally as it is by the major powers. Furthermore, where the opposition is very great and the capacity of the state to overcome it is doubtful, it is the national interest itself that must be reconsidered. It may lie, quite simply, in passivity—a condition in which most small states are placed, some by choice, some by dint of circumstances, and others (many of the new states in Africa, for example) because, while they have been spared the full blast of major opposition thus far, they are still chiefly concerned with internal affairs. To dismiss all these—the majority of the members of the class that has been discussed here—as states that are sovereign only in form and not in any of the real implications of the term would be absurd. They retain important options, of which the greatest, as has been said, is that of changing course. But because of their present passivity it is impossible to say how they would fare except by analogy with the cases of those states which, given roughly equivalent resources, have ventured further. It is therefore on the Guatemalas—and Finlands and Hungarys—of the world that this study has dwelt and also on those, such as Cambodia, Egypt, Ghana, Guinea, and Israel, which face heavy opposition from lesser powers, but which have this in common with those directly confronted by the great states that they are alone and must rely, in the last resort, on their own political and material resources. By analogy and by extension, such cases are instructive even for states, such as Australia and Malaysia, which at present have the benefit of the political encouragement and material support of the great powers, but which need to consider how far they can, in fact, manage on their own in the event of such support slackening or lapsing totally.

On the whole, the picture that emerges is a somber one. The price of independence and effective sovereignty at the second level mentioned here may be extremely heavy both in human and material terms. Where the external opposition is very great it may be quite beyond the power of the small state to withstand it even where it is both socially and economically feasible for the government in question to lead its subjects to heavy and unusual sacrifices and exertions. At the same time, since it is the combination of physical resources with human determination that matters in any given case, it is impossible to say flatly where the breaking point may be. The imponderables are at least as important as those resources which are measurable in terms of arms, supplies, money, and manpower.

What does seem clear is that the price is rising and that the effort that is required of governments and peoples is likely to increase with time rather than diminish. And further, that the condition of ultimate reliance on autonomous strength—which for the sake of brevity has been termed non-alignment throughout this study—is one which increases and multiplies the difficulties that are common to all small states regardless of the character of their relations with others.

Yet it does not therefore follow that the small and unaligned state is an anachronism in the sense that the struggle to maintain political autonomy with meager resources is one which cannot be maintained in the contemporary world, nor that the somewhat patronizing and impatient view held of small states by leaders, officials, and many scholars of great nations is essentially a true one. Admittedly, it is easy to fit the pattern of spiraling difficulties which has been described here into the larger, familiar notion that there is, generally, a trend away from the independent state towards larger units and that these alone are truly viable. Thus Lester Pearson:

> In this new era on which we have entered, the effective unit of foreign policy and strategy is no longer the nation state, however large, but the coalition of such states brought together and held together for certain purposes.[5]

But in fact this view, however agreeable to contemplate, is open to serious objections. The weight of recent evidence is all to the effect that the coalition or alliance is not an effective unit of foreign policy and strategy at all, except in the narrow, if extremely important, respect that it can from time to time marshal great strength. So long as it is a true *coalition* of equal partners it is unwieldy and subject to the weakness that apart from the "certain purposes" which hold it together there are almost invariably other purposes which are held separately and which are mutually incompatible. In consequence, a coalition requires collective leadership and the sinking of national interests as individually defined by each member. In war-time and in great international crises this may be acceptable. In other periods, leadership is likely to lapse into domination by the senior partner and the willing sinking of interests be replaced by resentment and resistance. No two states are alike and no two states can arrive at an identical appreciation of their national interest. Unless the coalition is replaced by a *confederation* that is, unless the political and institutional relations that subsist between the member states and between each one of the member states and other states which are external to the system are thoroughly re-ordered, the coalition is unlikely to survive the crisis in which it was born for very long. At all events, the attempt to keep it in being beyond the point where interests seriously diverge can be disastrous for the state which is obliged to make the major concessions. And it is, of course, the small state which is called upon to make sacrifices, as Munich illustrates in classic manner. It would therefore be misleading to argue that the solution to the small state's problems lies in alliance and other forms of semi-permanent association with more powerful states without taking these dangers into account—unless, indeed, the association or coalition is intended as no more than a stage preliminary to full integration. Naturally, if the small state loses its political identity by merger with other states, its problems as such are solved. It may be that as a *program* the amalgamation of states has a great deal to recommend it, even though the difficulties in the way of its execution are only too familiar. But this is a question of a different order and certainly one that is beyond the bounds of a study that is concerned with the *de facto* world of states.

But over and above the question of a voluntary or involuntary change in the contemporary state system the temptation to argue from the difficulties that beset the small state to the proposition that it is an anachronism is only justified if states so placed have a reasonably free choice to make. In fact, only a few have one. Non-alignment is by no means exclusively a political posture, freely adopted because of its international uses. In many cases it is as much a symptom of the situation in which the state finds itself as a recipe for dealing with it. For Cambodia, Finland, and Israel, for example, there is no alternative today to their admittedly precarious condition of non-alignment because the only states with which they can conceivably merge or even ally themselves with are either those with which they are in conflict or are states which demonstrably have nothing to gain by such a merger and a great deal to lose. Where non-alignment is a consequence of conflict and the conflict itself is due to a fundamental incompatibility between states and societies, abandonment of sovereignty would mean the sacrifice of social and national issues of the first importance. Once again, certainty would only be purchased at very heavy cost, probably heavier than that which must be borne in the effort to maintain independence. It is natural that it be rejected.

For yet another group, those unaligned states which pursue an aggressive or active policy, merger on a basis of equality may be possible, but it would mean a radical change in the political purposes of the state and resignation to the prospect of a transfer of domestic power. Neither of these are likely to be acceptable to the ambitious, power-hungry leaders who are so often an essential element of the driving force behind an aggressive national policy.

All these appear valid reasons for thinking that there is very little prospect of the small and politically autarchic states with which most of the continents are studded gently withering away by dissolving into larger units as a straightforward consequence of the difficulties and disabilities inherent in their situation. Some may succumb in time, but other small states, disappointed in the coalitions of which they are now members, may choose a propitious moment to escape from the orbit of a great power and take the place of those who could not stay the course.

Broadly speaking, it would seem that the contradictions between the pursuit of political independence and national security on the one hand and the consequences of limited human and material resources on the other can only be resolved in two ways. One is by a fall in the value attached to political independence and to the nation state as such; the other is by the great powers applying overwhelming force against their weaker, isolated opponents. There are no signs of this occurring in the near future, but it is not impossible or even difficult to envisage.

The implications of the acquisition of nuclear power—if thought out to the end—come close to indicating limits to which the impulsion to maintain and fortify national independence can reasonably be allowed to lead. From recognition of these limits doubts about the logic which impels states to approach them may gradually emerge. This may well be true of all states, irrespective of size, but, as in so many other aspects of national power, the implications of nuclear warfare are harshest for the small nation. To that extent critical re-thinking of the moral and ideological bases of political nationalism is likely to carry more weight and to be informed by greater urgency in a small community than in a large one.

Whether the great powers will ever again proceed to employ the tremendous force that is available to them to the fullest is a great question in itself, well beyond the scope of this study. But it is a question which is reasonable to ask, even though no clear answer is now apparent. The inhibitions to which the great states are subject at the present time derive, in the first instance, from the strategic and political relationship which has arisen between them in the last two decades, though the broad political philosophies of those who lead the powers and residual memories of the Second World War are also factors of no small relevance and importance. However, should the character and purposes of great-power leaders change and should the emergence of China as a major nuclear power alter this strategic relationship very substantially, as indeed it might, it is not impossible that the behavior of the United States and the Soviet Union towards third parties may acquire an asperity that, up to now, has been reserved for special problems such as those of Cuba and Hungary. Equally, if the United States were to withdraw its presence from Southeast Asia it is likely that the character of the relations between China and the many small states on its periphery will change and that the full implications of the latter's weakness and exposure to China's great strength be felt very rapidly.

All in all, a clear appreciation of the small states' condition is made difficult by the fortunate circumstance that the great powers operate today in a climate of thought which promotes caution and hesitation, particularly where the use of force is in question. This too may change. The conception of what is politically permissible and what can safely be done by one great power without fear of retaliation or counteraction by another, or, indeed, any significant reaction at all, may alter. The practice of pursuing great-power rivalry through minor intermediaries so as to avoid direct confrontation between the major states may take on new forms. Russia might respond to the arming of West Germany with nuclear weapons by the occupation of Finland, or even Sweden. A really effective penetration of Africa or the Middle East by China might impel both Russia and America to abandon all restraint in their dealings with those regions, imposing rigid spheres of influence and tight control of regional affairs. There is no reason not to take such possibilities into account.

The survival of small, politically isolated states as independent powers is thus precarious, depending on a multitude of factors over many of which they themselves have little influence. Long-term considerations in all major fields—the economic, the military, and the political—are disquieting. And yet, what has been said of the economic sphere is largely true of the political and military: in an imperfect world a great many short- and middle-term tactics can be adopted to keep the machinery of state running and to keep a measure of autonomous control over the national destiny. Some states will be more successful in this than others, either because they are better placed in terms of resources or else because they are more fortunate in their opponents. Still, the crucial factor in almost every case is the human one and where the society coheres and is strongly led very great obstacles can often be overcome. This, at any rate, is the evidence of the past. So although it is fairly plain that survival will require an ever increasing effort, it is unlikely that the effort be lightly abandoned, at any rate by strong societies, until an entirely unassailable obstacle has actually been reached. And for some that may not occur for a very considerable period.

Notes

1. In the sense that "political power is a psychological relation between those who exercise it and those over whom it is exercised." Hans J. Morgenthau, *Politics Among Nations*, 3rd ed. New York, 1962, p. 29.

2. "State" and "power" are used throughout as interchangeable terms.

3. At the Paris Peace Conference (1919) "Great Powers" were entitled to five delegates, "Lesser Powers" to three, "New States" to two, "States in process of formation" to one and "Neutrals" to one. The League of Nations and the United Nations have perpetuated (and somewhat modified) this tradition, which may be said to have been formally initiated for the modern period at the Congress of Vienna.

4. At the time of writing the future of Nigeria as a great federal state is unclear.

5. Lester Pearson, *Democracy in World Politics*. Princeton, 1956, p. 40.

4

MICRO-STATES

The Principality of Liechtenstein

JORRI DUURSMA

Territory, Population, and Economy

The Principality of Liechtenstein has a total land area of 160 square kilo-meters.[1] It has 30,310 inhabitants of whom 61.4 percent are of Liechten-steinese nationality, the rest being of foreign origin.[2] In 1993, Liechtenstein had an export surplus of 1,024 million Swiss francs.[3] Of the exports of the products of Liechtenstein industry, 13.8 percent go to Switzerland, 6.2 per-cent to the other EFTA countries, 41.6 percent to the European Community, and 38.4 percent to other countries.[4] The Liechtenstein economy is based on a small agricultural sector, a strongly export-oriented industrial sector, and a highly developed service sector comprising banking and tourism.[5]

The State budget for 1994 showed surplus receipts of 16.99 million Swiss francs.[6] Liechtenstein's budget is mainly financed by taxes and fees which cover 80.5 percent of the State receipts.[7] Liechtenstein has a moderate tax system comprising twelve main categories of taxes with relatively low levies.[8] Due to the limited possibilities of internal trade, the Liechtenstein economy is highly dependent on exports and the inflow of foreign capi-tal. Consequently, the economy is more exposed to external influences than those of larger countries.

History

The area which is now Liechtenstein was part of the ancient Roman prov-ince of Rhaetia. This province was turned into a county by Charlemagne.[9] The territory of Liechtenstein is composed of the "Oberland," which used

From Jorri Duursma, *Fragmentation and the International Relations of Micro-States: Self-determination and Statehood* (Cambridge, UK: Cambridge University Press, 1996). Reprinted with permission of Cambridge University Press.

to be the county of Vaduz, and the "Unterland," which was the seignory of Schellenberg. Both territories were united in 1434 and were "reichsfrei," which meant that the Count of Vaduz and Seignor of Schellenberg was placed under the immediate authority of the Emperor without the intermediary of another liege lord. The inhabitants were poor and came through a difficult time in the seventeenth century. Their lands were used for battlefields in the Austrian war against the Three Federations, and their lives were endangered by the plague and by witch-hunting. The then-ruling Count von Hohenems was deep in debt, and after complaints by his subjects about his mismanagement, the Emperor divested him of his functions. An imperial Commissioner was appointed who decided to sell the county and seignory. Prince Johann von Liechtenstein bought the seignory of Schellenberg in 1699 and the county of Vaduz in 1712.[10] The Liechtenstein family had held high offices in Austria and had acquired the title of Prince in 1608, without however possessing a Principality.[11] The purchase of both territories permitted the Prince to become Elector or "Reichsfürst" in the Council of Electors or "Reichsfürstentag" with a seat and right to vote. In order to be seated in this high Council, the Prince von Liechtenstein needed a minimum possession of "reichsfrei" territory. The acquired territories were raised to an Immediate Imperial Principality and named Principality of Liechtenstein after its Prince.[12]

In 1799, Liechtenstein was briefly occupied by Napoleon's troops and the Austrian army. Napoleon had met General Prince Johann I of Liechtenstein as the Austrian peace negotiator, and it is said that, out of esteem for the Prince, Napoleon had included Liechtenstein in his Rhine Confederation as a sovereign State in 1806.[13] The Prince's signature does not appear on the founding document of the Confederation, and the inhabitants of Liechtenstein were not informed of the new status.[14] The Principality of Liechtenstein became formally a sovereign State even though it had to accept Napoleon as a protector. After the Congress of Vienna, Liechtenstein was admitted to the new German Federation ("Deutsche Bund") which comprised thirty-nine sovereign German States. The Federation was dissolved in 1866, due to the Austro-Prussian war, which freed Liechtenstein of any alliance. In 1852, Liechtenstein concluded a customs union treaty with Austria, followed by a postal union treaty in 1912.

During the First World War the Principality of Liechtenstein remained neutral but was nevertheless severely affected. Its textile industry lacked raw material, and the savings of the Liechtenstein people were lost after the strong devaluation of the Austrian currency. After the war, Liechtenstein severed its links with Austria, seeking a rapprochement with

Switzerland. It concluded a postal union convention with Switzerland in 1920, gradually introduced the Swiss Franc as legal currency, and signed a customs union treaty with Switzerland in 1923.

The Liechtenstein population demanded a greater influence in the administration of their country. In 1918 the first direct, male elections of Liechtenstein's Parliament, the "Landtag," were held. A new Constitution was drafted in 1921. In the Second World War Liechtenstein remained neutral, and due to its rapprochement with Switzerland it was not afflicted with famine. After the war, there was a strong growth of the economy due to the development of high-tech industry. Liechtenstein had a friendly tax and trade legislation which attracted foreign enterprises, despite its unfavorable location. Moreover, the country possessed a large labor reserve coming from the agricultural sector, which could be deployed in the industries. Liechtenstein has managed to attain a higher degree of prosperity than most other European countries in the same period.

Constitutional and Legal Order

FORM OF GOVERNMENT

The State structure of the Principality of Liechtenstein can be described as a constitutional hereditary monarchy upon a democratic and parliamentary basis, according to which the power of the State is vested in the Prince and in the people.[15] The Constitution of Liechtenstein sets forth a complete system of checks and balances between the powers of the Prince, the Government, the Diet (Liechtenstein's Parliament), the people, and the judiciary.

The Prince is the Head of State and exercises his authority in conformity with the provisions of the Constitution and of other laws.[16] He represents the State in all its relations with foreign countries.[17] Every law requires the sanction of the Prince in order to acquire validity.[18] The Prince takes care of the execution and administration of the laws through the Government.[19] Every law, decree, or ordinance issued by the Prince has to be countersigned by the Head of the Government.[20] The only exception to this rule concerns the appointment and dismissal of the Head of the Government.[21] Furthermore, the Prince may take the necessary measures in urgent cases for the security and welfare of the State, subject to the countersignature, but without the cooperation of the Diet.[22] The succession to the throne is determined by the law of the Princely House, which also provides for an internal control over the Prince Regnant in the family council.[23] Since 1989, the Prince Regnant has been Prince Hans-Adam

II von und zu Liechtenstein, who had been charged with the Princely sovereign rights as a representative of the Prince in 1984.[24] In his address of 12 May 1993 from the throne, the Prince Regnant announced his intention to propose an amendment of the Constitution which would make it possible to discharge a Prince Regnant from office and/or to abolish the monarchy.[25] According to this draft amendment, which has not been submitted to the Diet so far, the Liechtenstein nationals could adopt a motion of no-confidence against the Prince by way of referendum. The Princely House would then have to decide on the Prince's deposition, or the Diet could submit a new Constitution to the people, to be approved by referendum, installing a Republic.

The Government of Liechtenstein consists of the Head of the Government and four Government Councilors who are appointed by the Prince with the concurrence of the Diet and on the proposal of the latter for a period of four years.[26] The Government conducts the national administration and is responsible both to the Prince and to the Diet.[27] The Prince can dismiss the Government on his own initiative or at the request of the Diet.[28] The Government members must have been born with Liechtenstein nationality.[29] Each member of the Government has one or more portfolios. The Head of the Government is, generally, in charge of internal and external affairs and finance, while his deputy has the responsibility for, among other things, economy and justice.[30] The Constitution does not preclude combined membership of the Government and of the Diet. Juridically, the two functions are not incompatible, which is rather logical in a country with a very small population. Nowadays, the combination of both functions is considered politically undesirable in consideration of a greater control and objectivity. Only the Head of the Government and the Government Councilor acting as his deputy are fully employed, whereas the other three Councilors have additional functions.[31]

Liechtenstein's Parliament, the Diet, consists of twenty-five members elected by universal and direct suffrage for a period of four years.[32] All Liechtenstein citizens who are at least twenty years old and legally residing in the Principality at least one month before the elections are entitled to vote and are eligible for election.[33] The Diet can be convened or dissolved by the Prince, or by the people subject to a referendum.[34] The Diet participates in the work of legislation and in the conclusion of certain treaties, and establishes the annual budget.[35] It has the right of interpellation, of petition, and of budgetary control. Moreover, it can initiate a parliamentary inquiry.[36] The right of initiative with regard to legislation appertains to the Prince, through the procedure of Government bills, the Diet, and the citizens by means of a referendum.[37] Decisions are taken by an absolute majority or, in the case of constitutional amendments, by a majority of at least three-quarters at two successive sittings.[38] A law cannot enter into force without the approval of the Diet, the Prince, and the Head of the Government. In addition, under certain conditions a law has to be approved by referendum. This constitutional system necessitates a close cooperation between the Prince, the Government, and the Diet.

The citizens of Liechtenstein have substantial political rights of which, besides the right to elect the members of the Diet, the right of referendum occupies a substantial place. A referendum may be held in the following cases:

1. At the initiative of 1,000 Liechtensteinese or three communes a draft law can be submitted to a referendum. An initiative aimed at amending the Constitution needs the support of 1,500 citizens or four communes.[39]

2. A law or a financial resolution, if it is not declared to be urgent, may be submitted to a referendum if the Diet so decides or at the request of 1,000 citizens or three communes (1,500 citizens or four communes for issues affecting the Constitution).[40] The Diet may also call for a referendum on certain principles embodied in a law.

3. Treaties which need the approval of the Diet under Article 8 of the Constitution can be submitted to a referendum by the Diet or at the request of 1,500 citizens or four communes.[41] This possibility further democratizes Liechtenstein's foreign policy and gives the people a say in external affairs. This provision was especially drafted with a view to the ratification of the EC-EFTA Agreement relating to the creation of the European Economic Area (hereafter, EEA Agreement). Nevertheless, if a request for a referendum is in contravention of the Constitution or of an existing treaty which has already been ratified, the Diet may declare the initiative invalid.[42]

JUDICIAL SYSTEM

The system of law regarding the civil and criminal code is based on the Austrian example. Before the entry into force of the 1921 Constitution, the Liechtensteinese could in second instance appeal only to a High Court in Vienna and in last instance to a Supreme Court in Innsbruck.[43] At present, all Liechtenstein's courts are established in the Principality. The judicial organization is based on the principle of independence of the Government, and the administration of justice is carried out in the name of the Prince.[44] If the court is composed of a Sole Judge, he will be a professional magistrate appointed by the Prince for life. At present, there are eight Sole Judges of whom three are Austrians and five are Liechtensteinese. If the court consists of more than one judge, the majority will be laymen, whereas foreign judges (i.e., non-Liechtensteinese) may never constitute a majority.[45] Every citizen can be appointed as judge for a period of four years.[46]

In civil procedures, the Lower Court of Vaduz ("Landgericht") will be competent to decide the dispute in first instance. A Sole Judge ("Einzelrichter") will hear the case. In second instance, appeal is possible to the civil chamber of the High Court ("Obergericht"), which is composed of five judges appointed by the Prince on the proposal of the Diet.[47] A third instance is possible by appealing to the Supreme Court of Justice ("Oberster Gerichtshof").[48] Lastly, a case may be brought before the State Tribunal ("Staatsgerichtshof") if a violation of a constitutional right or a breach of a right set forth in the European Convention for the Protection of Human Rights and Fundamental Freedoms is claimed.[49]

In criminal procedures, the course of proceedings is the same as in civil procedures. In first instance, however, there are four different courts which are competent to hear criminal cases depending on the seriousness of the offense.[50] If it concerns an imposed imprisonment of not more than six months, the prison sentence will in general be served in the prison of Vaduz.[51] For punishments exceeding six months of imprisonment, the sentence will be served in a Swiss prison under the agreements concluded with certain Swiss cantons.[52] The Prince possesses the prerogative of remitting, mitigating, or commuting pronounced sentences and of quashing initiated prosecutions.[53]

All decisions and orders of the Government are subject to appeal before the Administrative Tribunal ("Verwaltungsbeschwerdeinstanz").[54] The Administrative Tribunal consists of a chairman trained in the law and four appeal judges who are appointed by the Prince on the proposal of the Diet.[55] In this administrative judicial process, the Administrative Tribunal examines the formal validity of a Government order and considers objections against an unreasonable course of action, a refusal, or slowing-down of administrative action.[56] The Administrative Tribunal has executive power in the sense that it may replace a Government order with its own decision.[57] If one of the parties in civil, penal, or administrative proceedings claims that a law or a Government order is contrary to the Constitution, the court or tribunal may request an opinion on this incompatibility from the State Tribunal.[58]

The State Tribunal occupies a special place in Liechtenstein's judicial system.[59] The State Tribunal has different areas of competence, *inter alia*:

1. It examines the constitutionality of (draft) laws and of administrative orders.[60] The Government or the Diet may request an interpretation of a constitutional provision.[61]

2. It is competent to judge claims by the Diet against a member of the Government concerning a violation of the Constitution or other laws.[62]

3. It decides certain administrative cases attributed to it by law in first and last instance.[63] Thus, the law on political rights permits appeal to the State Tribunal if the Diet has declared invalid a people's initiative for a referendum on a treaty.[64]

HUMAN RIGHTS SITUATION

The Principality of Liechtenstein has ratified the European Convention for the Protection of Human Rights and Fundamental Freedoms of 1950 (hereafter, ECHR).[65] It is also a party to the UN Convention against Torture and Other Cruel, Inhuman or Degrading Treatment or Punishment of 1984[66] and the Convention on the Prevention and Punishment of the Crime of Genocide of 1948.[67]

Liechtenstein's Constitution guarantees the exercise of several human rights.[68] The most important reform in the field of human rights was initiated in 1984, when Liechtenstein women were granted the right to vote and to be elected.[69] The equality of men and women in the eyes of the law has always been a sensitive subject in Liechtenstein. On 16 June 1992, the Diet approved the introduction of a new paragraph to Article 31 of the Constitution guaranteeing equal rights to men and women.[70] The introduction of this provision was deemed especially necessary as the principle of equality of men and women was laid down in Articles 69 and 70 of the EEA Agreement.[71] The Government has listed fourteen laws which have to be adapted to the new principle of equality, among which are the law on nationality and the legislation on social security.[72]

At the ratification of the ECHR, Liechtenstein made three reservations, of which two were withdrawn in 1991, due to a revision of its penal code.[73] The new criminal code also abolished the death penalty in Liechtenstein. It therefore acceded to Protocol No. 6 to the ECHR.

Liechtenstein has recognized the competence of the European Commission of Human Rights to receive petitions from individuals. So far, nine applications against Liechtenstein have been received and decided by the European Commission of Human Rights; all of them were either declared inadmissible or struck off the list of cases.[74] Two applications are considered here: The first application, introduced by a Liechtenstein national on 6 July 1988, concerned the alleged violation of Article 6 of the ECHR and Article 1 of Protocol No. 1 to the Convention.[75] The applicant, who was the former director of a Liechtenstein company which had been declared bankrupt, complained that the civil proceedings before the Liechtenstein courts, instituted against him by the official liquidator for unlawful financial transactions, had been too lengthy, incorrect, and unfair. With regard to Article 6 of the Convention, the Commission concluded that the application was manifestly ill-founded. The application in respect of Article 1 of Protocol No. 1 was declared incompatible *ratione personae*, as Liechtenstein was not a party to Protocol No. 1.[76] The second application concerned a Swiss businessman convicted for aggravated fraud under the Liechtenstein Penal Code. The applicant claimed that his conviction for aggravated fraud had been contrary to Article 7, paragraph 1 of the ECHR as the notion "particularly serious damage" used under the Liechtenstein Penal Code was too vague to define the fraud and constituted therefore a violation of the principle of *nulla poena sine lege*. The Commission declared the application manifestly ill-founded as it believed the Liechtenstein Penal Code had not been unreasonably applied.[77]

Lastly, the differentiation between foreigners and Liechtenstein nationals should be noted in Article 31 of the Constitution. By virtue of this stipulation all nationals ("Landesangehörigen") are equal before the law.[78] This right is not guaranteed to the foreign inhabitants of Liechtenstein, for their rights are determined in the first instance by treaties, or, in the absence of such, on the basis of reciprocity.[79] This difference will have to disappear for the nationals of EU and EFTA countries in consequence of the EEA Agreement. Chapter IV of the Constitution sets forth in its heading the "allgemeinen Rechten und Pflichten der Landesangehörigen," which implies that the human rights set forth in this Chapter do not apply to aliens. For them the ratification of the ECHR is of special value, as it constitutes the source of their legally protected human rights in Liechtenstein. The place that a micro-state like Liechtenstein reserves for foreigners in its legal system is of particular interest, as usually a relatively high percentage of micro-states' inhabitants are aliens. Due to internal efforts and to the ratification of the ECHR and the EEA Agreement, the protection of human rights and its national development has been strengthened.

Relations with States

FOREIGN POLICY

Liechtenstein's foreign policy is characterized by the following elements:

Recognition of statehood: The main purpose of Liechtenstein's foreign policy is the maintenance and protection of its independence and its statehood.[80] It therefore strove for membership in certain international organizations such as the Council of Europe and the United Nations. This was also a means of making diplomatic contacts with a great number of States without going to great expense.[81] In general, it can be concluded that Liechtenstein aims at combining effective steps towards more political or juridical acceptance by the international community with a careful management of its limited financial and human resources.

Neutrality: Liechtenstein managed to remain neutral during the First and Second World Wars.[82] Independently of other political factors which might have influenced Liechtenstein's survival as a neutral State during both World Wars, it is evident that its neutrality was indispensable in order to stay outside the conflict. In peacetime, the Principality's neutrality takes on a different practical meaning of non-alignment. It should not be forgotten that Liechtenstein's neighboring countries are traditionally neutral as well. Liechtenstein's neutrality is not necessarily identical with that of its neighbors and at present lacks a specific definition. A practical result of its neutrality policy can be seen in Liechtenstein's behavior in international organizations. When voting or speaking in the assembly of an international organization such as the OSCE*, the Council of Europe, or the United Nations, Liechtenstein does not act according to a certain political ideology or "bloc," but according to what it considers the general interest, where national interests are not prominent. This also implies that Liechtenstein does not necessarily adjust its vote to that of its neighboring countries.

RELATIONS WITH SWITZERLAND

Diplomatic representation. When after the First World War the Diet decided to terminate the customs treaty with Austria, thus announcing the withdrawal from Austrian influence and the rapprochement with

---

*Organization on Security Cooperation in Europe (later formalized into the Conference on Security Cooperation in Europe)

Switzerland, the Liechtenstein Government sought to secure its international interests through the diplomatic channels of Switzerland.[83] On 21 October 1919 the Liechtenstein Head of Government requested from the Swiss Federal Council "die Vertretung der Liechtensteinischen Interessen in den Ländern zu übernehmen, wo das Fürstentum keine Vertretung hat, während die Schweiz eine solche besitzt."[84] The request explained that although only a very small number of Liechtensteinese lived outside the Principality, Liechtenstein attached great value to the representation of its interests in other countries. It should be borne in mind that after the First World War Liechtenstein's State budget did not permit the establishment of a costly diplomatic service. The Swiss Federal Council accepted the mandate and informed the States with which it maintained diplomatic relations of its entrusted agency. Most States accepted Liechtenstein's representation by Switzerland, but Czechoslovakia refused to accept it in 1946.[85]

In the instructions to its embassies and consulates, Switzerland explained that the representation of Liechtenstein consisted of the exercise of diplomatic or consular protection of the Liechtensteinese, their registration, delivering travel documents, and assisting Liechtensteinese in distress.[86] General diplomatic relations between the Principality and third States will only be attended to by Switzerland on a case-by-case basis, after having received specific orders from Liechtenstein.[87] Actions on behalf of Liechtenstein nationals will, in general, only be instituted at Liechtenstein's request, except in case of emergency.[88] Switzerland is not obliged to give effect to all Liechtenstein orders, and Liechtenstein always has the freedom to establish its own diplomatic missions or to negotiate directly with a third State.[89]

Since the Second World War, Liechtenstein has increasingly taken care of its own representation, especially in international organizations and at conferences.[90] At present, Liechtenstein has accredited ambassadors to four countries (Austria, Belgium, the Holy See, and Switzerland). It maintains diplomatic or consular relations with fifty-three States.[91] In addition, Liechtenstein has a permanent representative mission in Strasbourg for the Council of Europe, a permanent mission in New York to the United Nations, an EFTA-UN mission in Geneva, a mission to the European Union, and a permanent representation to the OSCE in Vienna. Considering Liechtenstein's limited human resources it is evident that not all international posts can be held by Liechtenstein nationals. In 1980, for instance, a Canadian was appointed as the "Liechtenstein" judge of the European Court of Human Rights.[92] Young Liechtensteinese are however given the opportunity to train in the Swiss or Austrian diplomatic services.[93]

Postal union. On 10 November 1920, Liechtenstein and Switzerland signed a convention relating to the maintenance of postal, telegraph, and telephone services in Liechtenstein by the Swiss postal, telegraph, and telephone administration.[94] This convention has been replaced by a treaty of 9 January 1978,[95] which now includes provisions on radio and television, and which in turn has been amended and supplemented by a treaty and agreement of 2 November 1994, for the purpose of Liechtenstein's entry into the EEA.[96] After having specified that the postal and telecommunications regalia belong to Liechtenstein,[97] the treaty sets forth that the postal and telecommunications services will be maintained by the Swiss postal and telecommunications office.[98] All Swiss legal and administrative regulations relating to the postal and telecommunications services are applicable in Liechtenstein,[99] though EEA law takes precedence in relation to the EEA States.[100] Conventions which have been or shall be concluded by Switzerland with third States with regard to postal and telecommunications services are equally valid in Liechtenstein.[101] To this end, Liechtenstein has authorized Switzerland to represent it during negotiations with third States on the conclusion of postal and telecommunications treaties, and to conclude such treaties with effect in Liechtenstein.[102] The postal union treaty does not prevent Liechtenstein from concluding international conventions or from becoming a member of an international organization itself.[103] If Switzerland has not adhered to such a convention or organization, a special agreement between the two States has to be concluded.[104] The treaty can be terminated by either State subject to one year's notice.[105]

Customs union. After the termination of the customs relations with Austria, Liechtenstein signed a customs union treaty with Switzerland on 29 March 1923.[106] Under Article 1, the territory of the Principality is attached to the Swiss customs territory and no restrictions on imports and exports can be accepted, unless they are permitted for the commerce between cantons. The Swiss authorities appoint, pay, and dismiss the customs officers and border guards in Liechtenstein.[107] As a basic rule, all present and future Swiss customs legislation and regulations on industrial and intellectual property are applicable in Liechtenstein.[108] Treaties relating to these subjects concluded by Switzerland with third States are equally valid for Liechtenstein.[109] Since 1991, Liechtenstein can become a party to an international convention or a member of an international organization to which Switzerland has also adhered.[110] Because of Switzerland's non-ratification of the EEA Agreement, the customs union treaty was amended so as to permit Liechtenstein's accession to this Agreement while upholding the customs union with Switzerland.[111] Special agreements have been concluded to this end, under which, in Liechtenstein, the EEA law takes precedence over the Swiss customs regulations in relation to EEA States.[112] The Swiss customs officers in Liechtenstein have to apply EEA law in relation to products originating from EEA States.[113] A joint commission is established, charged with the supervision of the correct implementation of the agreements.[114] Liechtenstein makes sure that no products are illegally imported into Switzerland through an internal surveillance and control system.[115] It has created its own customs department to that end.[116] Switzerland pays annually Liechtenstein's share of customs receipts.[117] In case of a conflict relating to the interpretation of the customs union treaty, the dispute can be brought before an arbitral tribunal.[118] Both States' parties can terminate the treaty subject to one year's notice.[119]

Following the example of Switzerland, Liechtenstein introduced a VAT (value-added tax) system on 1 January 1995. It concluded a treaty and a supplementary accord with Switzerland under which it committed itself to taking the Swiss VAT law into its own legislation.[120] The Swiss Federal Court will act as the highest court in VAT matters,[121] and a mixed commission has been established in which Liechtenstein can defend its interests, subject to an arbitral procedure.[122] For VAT purposes, Liechtenstein and Switzerland will constitute one territory. Their common receipts will be apportioned on the basis of a distribution code, making border control on goods unnecessary.[123]

Monetary union. Due to the strong devaluation of the Austrian currency after the First World War and the financial losses which this implied for the Liechtensteinese inhabitants, Liechtenstein decided to introduce the Swiss Franc as legal tender in its territory.[124] By virtue of a 1980 currency treaty,[125] the Swiss legislation relating to money, credit, and foreign-exchange policy and to the protection of Swiss coins and banknotes is applicable in Liechtenstein.[126] Liechtenstein's sovereignty in currency matters remains untouched.[127] Switzerland's National Bank exercises its rights over banks and companies in Liechtenstein in the same manner as in Switzerland.[128] A violation of the applicable Swiss currency legislation is, in general, judged by the Liechtenstein courts in first and second instance. An appeal for nullification of a sentence of the Liechtenstein High Court can only be lodged with the Swiss Court of Cassation.[129]

A mixed commission is charged with the consideration of interpretation and implementation questions relating to the currency treaty.[130] If a dispute cannot be solved by the mixed commission, an arbitral tribunal can be established.[131] The treaty can be terminated subject to six months' notice. In addition, Liechtenstein can withdraw from the treaty within one month of the enactment of a new Swiss currency law.[132] Under the currency treaty, Liechtenstein cannot develop its own independent monetary policy. The monetary union with Switzerland facilitates and supplements the postal and customs unions. Liechtenstein retains, however, the possibility of adopting any other legal tender within a relatively short time.

Aliens office. By virtue of Article 33 of the customs union treaty of 1923, Liechtenstein and Switzerland cooperate in the maintenance of the aliens police and border control. Two treaties with Switzerland were concluded on 6 November 1963, which are corollaries of the customs union treaty.[133]

The first treaty regulates the treatment of Swiss and Liechtenstein nationals in Liechtenstein and Switzerland respectively. There are no border controls between Liechtenstein and Switzerland.[134] Liechtenstein and Swiss nationals receive a residence permit and a work permit in the other country upon request.[135] This stipulation has been suspended since 19 October 1981 on the initiative of Liechtenstein which endeavored to maintain a well-balanced relation between Liechtenstein nationals and aliens in Liechtenstein.[136] Nevertheless, Liechtenstein reserves a preferential treatment for Swiss nationals. In certain cases, Swiss residents may exercise a liberal profession[137] and be put on an equal footing with EEA nationals.[138]

The second treaty of 1963 lays down the general legislation on the sojourn of aliens in Liechtenstein. The Swiss legislation concerning the sojourn and residence of aliens is applicable in Liechtenstein to third-State nationals and, since the suspension of Article 3 of the first treaty, also to Swiss nationals.[139] Liechtenstein can fix its own regulations regarding the expulsion of aliens, which have no effect in Switzerland.[140] Conversely, an expulsion from Swiss territory also applies to Liechtenstein territory, unless the Swiss aliens police expressly exclude this territorial effect for Liechtenstein.[141]

In 1977, the European Commission of Human Rights considered a joint application by X and Y against Switzerland, which had prohibited the entry of X onto Swiss and Liechtenstein territory for two years.[142] X, a third-State national, had stayed in Liechtenstein with Y without a residence permit for more than the ninety days which are allowed under the Swiss legislation. The question was raised whether X had been within Switzerland's jurisdiction within the meaning of Article 1 of the ECHR. Switzerland maintained that it was not responsible for the prohibition of entry. The plaintiffs alleged that Liechtenstein had renounced its sovereignty in this matter, for it could not undo Switzerland's decision. The Commission stated that the acts with effect in Liechtenstein brought all those on whom they were applicable within Switzerland's jurisdiction, for "the Swiss authorities when acting for Liechtenstein do not act in distinction from their national competences. In fact on the basis of the treaty [on third nationals of 1963] they act exclusively in conformity with Swiss law and it is only the effect of this act that extended to Liechtenstein territory."[143]

If Swiss and EEA laws on the establishment and sojourn of aliens do not coincide, only the EEA law will be applicable in Liechtenstein.[144] In this context, Liechtenstein's restrictive legislation on foreign ownership of immovable properties and on foreign land investments will be adapted for EEA nationals.[145] Both 1963 agreements on the sojourn of aliens can be terminated subject to one year's notice.

Defense. Since the dissolution of the German Federation in 1866, Liechtenstein has not had an army. The Constitution however sets forth the civic duty of every man fit to bear arms, up to the completion of his sixtieth year, to serve in the defense of his country in the event of emergency.[146] Apart from this contingent, no armed units may be organized or maintained, except for the provision of the police service.[147] In line with the traditional neutrality of the two countries, Switzerland and Liechtenstein have not concluded a defense treaty with each other. Neither has the Liechtenstein territory been included in the Swiss defense system.[148]

RELATIONS WITH AUSTRIA

Apart from its proximity, Liechtenstein's ties with Austria are related to the Austrian origins of the Princely House. In the nineteenth century the Austrian postal services extended to Liechtenstein. On 5 June 1852 a customs union treaty was concluded with Austria.[149] The commerce between the two countries was free.[150] Austria undertook to extend existing customs treaties to Liechtenstein and to conclude new customs treaties also in the name of Liechtenstein if the Prince approved.[151] The Austrian customs officers swore an oath of allegiance to the Prince and were subject, in first instance, to the Liechtenstein judiciary. This customs union treaty was terminated by the Diet on 2 August 1919, and its termination was approved by Austria on 30 August 1919.[152] The breach with Austria was prompted on the one hand by the financial losses which Liechtenstein had suffered due to the devaluation of the Austrian currency after the First World War and on the other hand by Liechtenstein's desire to accentuate its independence from Austria so as to receive a more favorable political and economic treatment from the Allied Powers.[153]

Until the coming into force of the postal and customs union treaties with Switzerland, Liechtenstein concluded new, transitional agreements with Austria. On 22 April 1920 an exchange of letters with Austria regulated the new customs regime.[154] A postal agreement was concluded on 1 May 1920 which remained valid until 31 January 1921.[155]

At present, Liechtenstein has concluded certain treaties with Austria in matters of judicial cooperation,[156] education,[157] social security,[158] double taxation,[159] and border demarcation.[160] Even if the relations with Austria are not regulated in the same manner as the legal relations with Switzerland, the Government of Liechtenstein has noted an intensification of Austro-Liechtenstein cooperation.[161] Thus, like Switzerland, Austria has supported Liechtenstein's candidature for membership in the Council of Europe and the United Nations.

Relations with International Organizations

LEAGUE OF NATIONS

On 28 August 1919, not long after the conclusion of the Covenant of the League of Nations, which would enter into force on 10 January 1920, the Diet discussed the question of whether it was opportune to apply for membership of the League of Nations.[162] Questions were raised concerning the financial and military obligations flowing from League membership, especially under Article 1, paragraph 2 of the Covenant of the League of Nations. Moreover, Liechtenstein wondered whether the League of Nations would accept the maintenance of its neutrality, which it had officially declared in the First World War. As, on 11 May 1920, Switzerland had agreed to become a member of the League of Nations, Liechtenstein decided to prepare its application for membership too. On 15 July 1920, Liechtenstein submitted its application through the Swiss Minister in London.[163] In its letter, Liechtenstein recalled its neutrality during the last war and the absence of military forces since 1866.

The request for admission was discussed in the first instance by the second Sub-Committee of Committee No. 5 of the Assembly.[164] The French member of the second Sub-Committee was opposed to granting such a small State as Liechtenstein the same right to vote as a large State.[165] The Sub-Committee considered five questions in order to determine the acceptance or refusal of Liechtenstein's application.[166] After having concluded that the application for admission was in order, the Sub-Committee observed that the Government of the Principality of Liechtenstein was recognized *de jure* by many States. Liechtenstein possessed a stable Government and fixed frontiers with a population between 10,000 and 11,000. Nevertheless, the Sub-Committee's findings under questions 4 and 5 led to the conclusion "that the Principality of Liechtenstein could not discharge all the international obligations which would be imposed on her by the Covenant."[167] The Sub-Committee based its conclusion on two arguments, namely that Liechtenstein had deputed to others some of the attributes of sovereignty and that it had no army.[168]

The second Sub-Committee's report was endorsed by Committee No. 5 on 6 December 1920.[169] On 17 December 1920, the Assembly voted against the admission of Liechtenstein to the League of Nations by twenty-eight votes to one (Switzerland) and thirteen abstentions.[170] The stated reasons for the League of Nations' refusal to admit Liechtenstein as a full member were however not the real reasons. At the time of the discussions on Liechtenstein's admission to the League of Nations, between 25 November 1920 and 17 December 1920, it could hardly be maintained that Liechtenstein had delegated many attributes of its sovereignty to other Powers. In this period the scarcely restrictive transitional customs agreement with Austria of 22 April 1920 was in force, as well as a provisional postal agreement, leaving Liechtenstein considerable freedom. The customs union treaty with Switzerland had not yet been concluded, although negotiations had started on this subject in May 1920.[171] As we have seen, the diplomatic and consular representation by Switzerland could only be exercised *ad hoc* and subject to Liechtenstein's orders. Moreover, the same second Sub-Committee had approved Austria's request for membership even though under Article 88 of the Treaty of Saint-Germain of 1919 Austria had restricted its sovereign rights to choose those economic relations which it desired.[172] At that time, Liechtenstein's obligations under its agreements with Austria and Switzerland were less burdensome than Austria's renouncements under the Treaty of Saint-Germain.

It is furthermore doubtful whether the possession of military forces was obligatory under Article 1, paragraph 2 of the Covenant of the League of Nations. This article regulates the deployment of military forces of Member States, but does not necessarily impose the existence of an army in a Member State. It would however have raised considerable political and juridical criticism if the Assembly had officially refused to admit Liechtenstein to the League of Nations on grounds of its small size. The Covenant of the League of Nations did not provide for such an exclusion. In addition, the question of smallness was also discussed at the admission of Luxembourg. The Czechoslovakian delegate declared that "in practice, the smallness of a State does not prevent its being admitted into the League."[173] He explained Liechtenstein's non-admission by reason of "its close connection with another State which is able to defend the interests of Liechtenstein and thus ensure that this little State is not left outside the League of Nations."[174]

Liechtenstein had weakened its position and had provided the League of Nations with an excuse for non-admission by applying for membership through the mediation of Switzerland. In Committee No. 5, the Swiss President of the Federal Council, Motta, had admitted that "Liechtenstein est un trop petit État pour être admis dans les conditions actuelles"[175] and therefore suggested that the Swiss representative might be allowed to represent Liechtenstein interests in the League.[176] This procedure could have shown a certain dependence of Liechtenstein on another Power, which was immediately emphasized by the League of Nations and given more importance than the real juridical relations with Switzerland or Austria at the time revealed. Nevertheless, the Assembly of the League of Nations did not doubt Liechtenstein's sovereign statehood, although it did not expressly mention the criteria according to which it had tested Liechtenstein's statehood. The true reason for the non-admission of Liechtenstein was its smallness, not its deputation of some sovereign attributes by reason of its smallness.[177] It was thought unacceptable to grant Liechtenstein, or any other micro-state, the same right to vote, and even a veto right when unanimity was required, as larger States.

INTERNATIONAL COURTS

Permanent Court of International Justice. On 17 May 1922, the Council of the League of Nations adopted a resolution which permitted all non-Member States of the League of Nations to become a party to the Statute of the Permanent Court of International Justice.[178] It was left to the Court to decide to which States it would send a letter offering them this option.

Liechtenstein was among the States to receive the Court's communication. It did not respond to the Court's letter until 22 March 1939, when it accepted the Statute of the Court and submitted a declaration to the registry of the Permanent Court of International Justice accepting its general and compulsory jurisdiction under Article 36, paragraph 2, of the Statute for five years.[179] On 17 June 1939, the registrar of the Court received an application from the Government of Liechtenstein instituting proceedings against Hungary, which had also accepted the compulsory jurisdiction of the Permanent Court of International Justice.[180] The case concerned a Liechtenstein national, Gerliczy, who had been ordered by a Hungarian court to pay a considerable amount of money to some Hungarian nationals. Liechtenstein alleged that the court's decision had ruined Gerliczy financially and was contrary to the Hungaro-Romanian Convention of 16 April 1924, which regulated the payment of debts in ancient Austrian or Hungarian crowns. At the time of the entry into force of this Convention, Gerliczy had been a Romanian national. By reason of the invasion of the Netherlands by Germany the proceedings before the Court were discontinued.[181] On 3 September 1945, the registrar of the Court asked the Government of Liechtenstein what its intentions were with regard to the *Gerliczy* case. The letter remained without answer.

International Court of Justice. On 24 March 1949, the Swiss Office for Liaison with the United Nations submitted to the Secretary General a letter from the Liechtenstein Head of Government concerning Liechtenstein's request to become a party to the Statute of the International Court of Justice.[182] The application was first submitted to the Security Council which referred it to its Committee of Experts. The Soviet delegate did not approve of this procedure, as he did not consider Liechtenstein a "free and independent" State.[183] On 16 June 1949, the Committee of Experts decided to advise the Security Council to admit Liechtenstein as a party to the Statute of the International Court of Justice.[184] The Soviet and Ukrainian members of the Committee of Experts had stated that "[i]t was apparent that Liechtenstein had yielded important parts of its sovereignty to another State. Liechtenstein was not, therefore, a sovereign and independent State and there was no need to admit it to become a party to the Statute of the International Court of Justice."[185] The majority of the members of the Committee, however, maintained that Liechtenstein was a State in the sense of Article 93, paragraph 2 of the Charter, "since it possessed all the qualifications of a State," and added that the jurisdiction of the Court "should be extended as far as possible."[186] Moreover, this was considered "all the more useful for Liechtenstein since it was a small State, and the protection of law was most necessary in such a case."[187] The Soviet and Ukrainian delegates in the Security Council abstained from voting, and the Soviet Union did not exercise its veto against Liechtenstein's admission.[188]

On 26 October 1949, Liechtenstein's application was discussed in the Sixth Committee of the General Assembly.[189] The Australian delegate emphasized that Liechtenstein was "a State possessing all the necessary qualifications for admission to the Statute of the International Court" and advocated "the greatest possible use of the International Court."[190] There are no indications that the Sixth Committee applied a more flexible definition of statehood in this case, so as to encourage the use of the International Court of Justice, than is adopted in general international law. Yugoslavia emphasized that "[o]nly independent sovereign States could become parties to the Statute of the International Court" and that "[t]aking into account the particular conditions of the union between Liechtenstein and Switzerland, he was satisfied that Liechtenstein was an independent State."[191] The Egyptian representative "believed that the United Nations should apply the principle of universality" and that Liechtenstein satisfied all requirements "although it was a small State. Moreover, the small States were the ones that most needed the protection of the Court."[192] The Byelorussian delegate, however, declared: "A review of the economic and political situation of Liechtenstein would show that it had never been an independent State . . . It had formed a customs union with Switzerland, which country took care of Liechtenstein's post and telegraph service and its diplomatic representation . . . it must be considered a dependent State," and therefore it could not be a party to the Statute of the International Court of Justice.[193] Under these requirements the Byelorussian delegate should have concluded that the Byelorussian Soviet Socialist Republic was not an independent State either.

The opposition of the Soviet Republics and the Soviet Union is to be understood in the "cold war" context. The communist countries, in general, did not favor the participation of the European micro-states which were Western-orientated in international fora. The Egyptian representative defended the opinion of the majority who believed that the fact that Liechtenstein "had formed a customs union with another State and that Switzerland represented it diplomatically did not make it a dependent State. There were several countries which were represented by other countries in international affairs, and that did not affect their independence."[194] On 1 December 1950, the General Assembly adopted a resolution enabling Liechtenstein to become a party to the Statute of the International Court of Justice.[195]

Not long after having been admitted as a party to the Statute of the International Court of Justice, Liechtenstein filed an application in 1951, instituting proceedings against Guatemala. In what was to become the well-known *Nottebohm* case, the Court did not doubt Liechtenstein's statehood either, for it stated: "It is for Liechtenstein, *as it is for every sovereign State* [emphasis added], to settle by its own legislation the rules relating to the acquisition of its nationality."[196] Nottebohm had obtained Liechtenstein nationality on 13 October 1939, only four days after his request for naturalization and a few brief visits to Vaduz.[197] The Liechtenstein law on nationality of 1 January 1934 provided for the possibility of naturalization after three years' residence in the territory of the Principality, but this requirement could be dispensed with in circumstances deserving special consideration and by way of exception.[198] The Court concluded in 1955 that Nottebohm had no "genuine connection" with Liechtenstein, which could therefore not extend its protection to Nottebohm vis-à-vis Guatemala.[199] Interestingly enough, Liechtenstein amended its law on nationality in 1960 so that naturalization is only possible after five years of residence in the Principality, without any possibility of dispensation with this requirement.[200]

OSCE

Liechtenstein participated in the very first conference of the CSCE organized in Helsinki in 1972. The reasons for inviting Liechtenstein to the conferences and the preparatory talks may have been diverse. Von Ledebur suggests that the interest which the Holy See had shown in promoting peace, the right of self-determination, and religious freedom had been a motive for including the other European micro-states in the CSCE negotiations.[201] Prince Regnant Hans-Adam II of Liechtenstein explained that Liechtenstein was invited to the first preparatory talks organized by the Eastern European countries in Romania because they had invited all existing European States which had participated in the Congress of Vienna of 1815.[202] Liechtenstein, which joined the group of neutral and non-aligned States, had several interests in its participation in the CSCE.

In the first place, it allowed Liechtenstein to stand on terms of sovereign equality with other European States, the United States, and Canada. The Helsinki Declaration of 1975 could not come into being without the cooperation and consensus of Liechtenstein. This fact was furthermore accepted by the other participating States. In contrast with the Soviet Union's position in the United Nations on Liechtenstein's application to become a party to the Statute of the International Court of Justice, the Eastern European States did not question Liechtenstein's statehood in the CSCE. Despite the small size of its delegation, Liechtenstein could make certain contributions to the work of the Helsinki Conference. Thus, Liechtenstein endeavored to secure respect for the procedural rules of the conference. In critical phases of the negotiations certain larger States wished to close the list of speakers or to vote by majority rule instead of by consensus. In order to still exert a certain influence, Liechtenstein defended the principle of consensus and its right to speak.[203]

In the second place, Liechtenstein's interest in participating in the CSCE lay in the strengthening of the solidarity between the European States.[204] By reason of its small size and of its sensitivity to external economic and military influences, Liechtenstein attaches great importance to a stable security in Europe.

In the third place, Liechtenstein participated actively in the so-called third Basket, that is, the Helsinki negotiations on cooperation in humanitarian and other fields. In this domain, Liechtenstein's neutrality and wish for security made it a supporter of human rights and the exchange of information.[205]

It is represented in the OSCE Parliamentary Assembly by two members of the Diet[206] and bears 0.20 percent of the cost of the OSCE institutions.[207] The OSCE has also served as a forum to draw international attention to Liechtenstein's claims against another participating State. Thus it has repeatedly recalled its claims against the Czech and Slovak Republics with respect to the confiscation by the communist Government of certain lands in Czechoslovakia owned by Liechtenstein nationals.[208]

COUNCIL OF EUROPE

In May 1948, a conference was organized by the coordination committee of the European movement in the Hague in which Liechtenstein participated. The recommendations of this conference have strongly influenced the establishment of the Council of Europe,[209] yet Liechtenstein did not become a founding member of the Council of Europe. It only entered into contact with the Council of Europe in 1969, when it became a party to the first five European conventions.[210] On 27 November 1974, Liechtenstein was given official permanent observer status at the Parliamentary Assembly.[211] In fact, by becoming an observer, Liechtenstein was able to familiarize itself with the work of the Council of Europe while at the same time gaining the confidence of the Member States of the Council.

Thus, in 1977, exploratory talks began with the Member States and the Secretary-General on the feasibility of Liechtenstein becoming a member of the Council of Europe. At the beginning certain objections were raised concerning the advisability of admitting more small Member States to the Council of Europe, which would toughen the decision-making process. Liechtenstein promised that it would respect the justified wishes of the larger States.[212] As a consequence, Liechtenstein deposited its request for admission on 4 November 1977. On 17 March 1978, the Committee of Ministers invited the Consultative Assembly (now called the Parliamentary Assembly) to express its opinion on the matter.[213] The Assembly's Political Affairs Committee and the Committee on European Non-Member Countries both prepared a report on the admission of Liechtenstein and concluded that Liechtenstein fulfilled the conditions for accession to the

Council of Europe as laid down in Article 4 of the Statute.[214] The first study, by the Political Affairs Committee, inquired into three main issues:

Does the Principality of Liechtenstein have all the attributes of a sovereign State? After having examined Liechtenstein's history and relations with Switzerland, the rapporteur concluded that "[t]here can therefore be no doubt about Liechtenstein's independence."[215] Although he gave no general norms according to which Liechtenstein's independence was evaluated, the rapporteur emphasized Liechtenstein's freedom to set up its own diplomatic missions, the Swiss position that the customs union treaty did not prejudice Liechtenstein's sovereignty, and the fact that Liechtenstein had proved its capacity to sustain international relations.[216] Special attention was given to Liechtenstein's adherence to the Statute of the International Court of Justice and to the Final Act of the CSCE. It should be noted that the rapporteur did not explicitly examine whether Liechtenstein had been recognized by other States according to the constitutive theory of recognition. Rather, he sought confirmation of Liechtenstein's statehood by proving that it had been accepted by certain international fora that are only open to States.[217]

Does Liechtenstein recognize its citizens' fundamental freedoms and respect them in practice? The rapporteur concluded that the crucial basic human rights were guaranteed and manifestly observed, that the economic and social rights were in certain respects superior to those of some Member States of the Council of Europe, and that the equality of rights of women had not yet become law to the extent considered necessary by the Parliamentary Assembly.[218]

Is Liechtenstein, despite its relatively small population, able to fulfill all the obligations and duties arising from the Statute? Liechtenstein's financial position was considered very healthy. Furthermore, the Liechtenstein Government had declared its willingness to respect all obligations flowing from the Statute.[219]

The second report, prepared by a rapporteur of the Committee on European Non-Member Countries, was based on a fact-finding visit to Liechtenstein.[220] Three major points were raised:

Sovereignty and independence: As all bilateral agreements with Switzerland could be revoked at short notice and as Switzerland could only represent

Liechtenstein diplomatically on specific instructions of the latter, the rapporteur reaffirmed Liechtenstein's statehood.[221]

Specific problems which had raised discussion in the Council of Europe: In the first place, the absence of women's voting rights was not considered a determining factor for the rejection of Liechtenstein's entry into the Council of Europe.[222] In the second place, Liechtenstein had declared its willingness to cooperate with the Member States of the Council of Europe to combat tax offenses and evasion.[223] In the third place, Liechtenstein's size and implications for its behavior in the Council of Europe were considered. It was feared that it would use its vote in such a way as to frustrate the will of other members, although there is no unanimity rule in the Council of Europe as there used to be in the League of Nations. The Government of Liechtenstein had therefore declared that "in the decision-making of the Council of Europe, Liechtenstein would exercise the vote as a member in a manner appropriate to her size."[224] The Member States wanted to ascertain that Liechtenstein would not toughen the decision-making process or sell its vote and would vote independently of any other State. In practice, however, the Liechtenstein declaration has no legal meaning. After its accession, Liechtenstein has always voted as it deemed right, even if its vote just tipped the balance.[225] The Statute of the Council of Europe does not provide for two categories of votes. The rapporteur furthermore observed that "quantity has never been regarded as a criterion in the Council of Europe."[226]

Liechtenstein's European vocation: It was demonstrated that Liechtenstein already belonged "to the family of advanced democratic European nations, both politically and economically."[227]

On 28 September 1978, the Parliamentary Assembly voted in favor of Liechtenstein's admission to the Council of Europe.[228] It was the first political international organization of which Liechtenstein became a member. The debates in the Parliamentary Assembly can be summarized as follows: A British parliamentarian wanted to re-examine the two reports on Liechtenstein in the Committees and prepare a general study on the problems of the relations between the Council of Europe and European micro-states. He feared that if more micro-states entered the Council of Europe they would have a disproportionate amount of votes.[229] This proposition was rejected as it was thought incorrect after almost one year of discussion to delay a final decision on Liechtenstein's admission. It was also considered contrary to the Statute, which does not distinguish between micro and maxi-states.[230] There was a general consensus that the contractual relations with Switzerland did not prejudice Liechtenstein's independence and therefore its statehood.[231] The delegates who opposed Liechtenstein's admission based their argument on the absence of women's voting rights.[232]

Liechtenstein's conduct in the Council of Europe has in certain ways been an advantage for other European micro-states which wanted to become members of the Council of Europe, because it has shown the other Member States what a micro-state can contribute to the work of a political international organization. Liechtenstein considers that it has often a more responsible voting pattern than other Member States, because it has no important national interests and can vote for the general good.[233]

The advantages of its membership are diverse. On a long-term basis, Liechtenstein wanted to strengthen the international, in this case European, recognition of its independence and its statehood. It was also a means of entering into regular diplomatic relations with other European States without having to establish costly diplomatic missions to each of them. It facilitated the conclusion of multilateral treaties which otherwise had to be drafted separately with the neighboring States. Furthermore, membership in the Council of Europe permits the influencing of the policies of other Member States, self-criticism, and participation in the general construction of Europe.

At the beginning, the Liechtensteinese feared that by acceding to the Council of Europe they would be forced to make important concessions in fiscal and company legislation. In practice, however, this has not been the case. Liechtenstein is at a certain disadvantage in the sense that it cannot man all the committees of experts. It also demands time from the non-professional Liechtenstein parliamentarians to attend the Assembly's sessions.

EUROPEAN INTEGRATION

EFTA. On 4 January 1960, seven European States signed a Convention establishing the European Free Trade Association in Stockholm (hereafter, Stockholm Convention).[234] The problem concerning the legal position Liechtenstein should have in the European Free Trade Association (hereafter, EFTA) when Switzerland ratified the Stockholm Convention was raised. Switzerland maintained that by virtue of Article 7 of the customs union treaty of 1923 with Liechtenstein, the Stockholm Convention would also apply to Liechtenstein, whereas Liechtenstein preferred to become a full member of EFTA.[235] As, however, the field of application of the Stockholm Convention was more extensive than the customs union treaty, Switzerland could not represent Liechtenstein in matters which were not related to customs regulations.[236] Because, at the time, Liechtenstein could not conclude customs-related treaties independently, it was decided to draft a Protocol to the Stockholm Convention extending Switzerland's mandate.[237] This Protocol of 4 January 1960 was ratified by all signatory States of the Stockholm Convention and by Liechtenstein and proposed to give special powers to Switzerland. The Protocol stated: "1. The Convention shall apply to the Principality of Liechtenstein as long as it forms a customs union with Switzerland and Switzerland is a Member of the Association. 2. . . . Liechtenstein shall be represented by Switzerland."[238]

The special powers are only valid for the Stockholm Convention. Thus, when Switzerland signed free trade agreements with the EEC and the ECSC on 22 July 1972, additional Agreements between the European Communities, Switzerland, and Liechtenstein were required in order to make the free trade agreements applicable to Liechtenstein.[239] Liechtenstein could represent its interests through a representative within the Swiss delegation to the Joint Committees.[240] Such Joint Committees were established with the EEC and with the ECSC.[241] When talks between the European Community and EFTA aimed at the creation of a European Economic Area, which would extend well beyond the Swiss mandate under the customs union treaty, Liechtenstein took advantage of this occasion to redefine and strengthen its position vis-à-vis Switzerland, EFTA, and the European Community. In order to avoid exclusive negotiations between the European Community and Switzerland, which legally could have been possible, as in the case of the additional Agreements of 1972, Liechtenstein managed to be accepted as a separate negotiating partner. Considering the wide implications of the draft EEA Agreement, this was believed to be an adequate solution which emphasized Liechtenstein's sovereignty.[242] On 3 April 1990, the EFTA Ministers declared their willingness to accept Liechtenstein as the seventh negotiating partner on the EFTA side in the EEA talks.[243] This declaration was accepted by the European Council on 18 June 1990.[244]

Liechtenstein wanted to become a full party to the EEA Agreement and therefore decided to become a full member of EFTA. This was made possible by the amendment of the Swiss-Liechtenstein customs union treaty of 29 March 1923.[245] The EFTA Council approved Liechtenstein's accession to the Stockholm Convention on 22 May 1991.[246] Liechtenstein's accession to EFTA has not been made conditional upon the maintenance in force of the customs union treaty of 1923.

The question arises whether Liechtenstein may vote independently of

the Swiss position in matters which fall within the regulations of the customs union treaty of 1923. All States Parties have one vote in the EFTA
Council; although normally voting is by consensus, in certain cases a unan-
imous vote is requested.[247] Article 8, first paragraph of the customs union
treaty forbids Liechtenstein to conclude independently customs treaties
with third States. The customs union treaty does not however provide for
the concordance of Liechtenstein and Swiss customs and voting policies
in international organs. Thus Liechtenstein is legally free to vote in the
EFTA Council according to its own policy. This is equally so for the EEA
Council and Common EEA Commission as well as the EFTA and Common
EEA Parliamentary Committee. In addition, through its full membership
in EFTA, Liechtenstein may present at its own initiative a claim against
other EFTA Member States before the EFTA Council.[248]

European Economic Area. The EEA Agreement, in the drafting of
which Liechtenstein had actively participated, was approved by referendum by the Liechtenstein nationals on 13 December 1992.[249] As Switzerland's
referendum on the EEA Agreement held on 6 December 1992 had led to
the non-ratification of the EEA Agreement by Liechtenstein's neighboring State, certain legal questions arose. By virtue of old Article 8 bis of the
customs union treaty between Switzerland and Liechtenstein, Liechtenstein
could only have become a party to a customs convention if Switzerland
was a contracting party itself. In the days following the Liechtenstein referendum, Liechtenstein and Swiss experts met to discuss a solution to the
question. According to the EEA Agreement, the regional union between
Switzerland and Liechtenstein should not be precluded provided that the
good functioning of the Agreement is not impaired.[250] Given the close links
between Switzerland and Liechtenstein, special arrangements were needed
for the entry into force of the EEA Agreement in Liechtenstein, both on the
EC-EFTA side and on the bilateral side. On 17 March 1993, the diplomatic
conference of EC and EFTA countries (except Switzerland) approved the
Protocol adjusting the EEA Agreement.[251] The Protocol stipulates that for
Liechtenstein the EEA Agreement, as adjusted by the Protocol, will come
into force on a date to be determined by the EEA Council, provided that
the EEA Council has not only decided that the good functioning of the
Agreement is not impaired, but has also taken the appropriate decisions
in particular as to the application to Liechtenstein of measures already
adopted by the EEA Council or the EEA Joint Committee.[252] In addition,
the protocols of the EEA Agreement which referred to both Switzerland
and Liechtenstein will only apply for Liechtenstein.[253] Certain joint declarations of Switzerland and Liechtenstein are declared void.[254] The EFTA

States referendum held on 11–13 Dec. 1992 showed 55.81 percent in favor of and 44.19 percent against the EEA Agreement. BA No. 147/1992 adjusted their "internal EFTA Agreements" so as to regulate the number of seats reserved for Liechtenstein in the Court of Justice, the EFTA Standing Committee, and the EFTA Parliamentary Committee.[255]

On 2 November 1994, a number of treaties and accords were signed by Switzerland and Liechtenstein, permitting the entry into force of the EEA Agreement in the Principality, without the establishment of borders between the two countries. On 20 December 1994, the EEA Council declared that these arrangements fulfilled the conditions set in Article 121 (b) of the EEA Agreement.[256] The EEA Agreement entered into force for Liechtenstein on 1 May 1995.[257]

The ratification of the EEA Agreement constitutes a considerable economic and political advantage for Liechtenstein even if it has to make certain concessions on its traditional policies. Liechtenstein's industrial sector is strongly export-oriented,[258] and since 1987 the export to EC countries has risen proportionately.[259] The Liechtenstein Government believed that long-term economic advantages could only be guaranteed if Liechtenstein's "Eigenstaatlichkeit" was maintained and strengthened.[260] This necessitated a cooperation in the process of European integration and not a marginalization. The fundamental consequences of the EEA Agreement for Liechtenstein are as follows:

Free movement of persons:[261] Traditionally, Liechtenstein has a restrictive system where the entry and sojourn of foreigners is concerned. Under the EEA Agreement the Liechtenstein labor market will be open to all EEA nationals. New regulations, depending on their subject, will have to be introduced within two to five years. The States Parties will then re-examine the results of the transitional period and possibly extend it.[262] The States Parties have declared that when deciding on a request for an extension, they will take into account Liechtenstein's special geographical situation,[263] that is, its smallness and the problems which that entails. Furthermore, Liechtenstein plans to take protective measures under the general protection clause of the EEA Agreement in the event of an exceptional increase in the number of foreigners.[264] To this end, Liechtenstein issued a unilateral declaration explaining in which cases it understood that it was justified to take protective measures.[265]

Freedom of establishment:[266] This freedom permits the establishment of foreign enterprises, foreign banks, and self-employed workers in Liechtenstein. Traditionally, Liechtenstein's laws did not allow the establishment of foreign enterprises with large foreign capital in their territory; only enterprises under Liechtenstein law could be founded in the Principality. Likewise, a branch of a foreign bank could not be established in Liechtenstein. Doctors, engineers, and architects exercising their profession in Liechtenstein had to possess Liechtenstein nationality.[267] After the transitional period of three to five years, Liechtenstein may take protective measures if the inflow of foreign enterprises becomes disproportionate.[268] The bilateral currency treaty is the only agreement which has not been adapted to Liechtenstein's ratification of the EEA Agreement, as it was believed highly unlikely that Swiss currency legislation would become contrary to an EEA regulation.[269]

Free movement of services:[270] This is of particular importance for the Liechtenstein banks which, although they will have to accept more internal competition, will now be able to offer their services in the other EEA States.[271]

Free movement of capital:[272] Foreign investment in Liechtenstein must be permitted on the basis of non-discrimination vis-à-vis Liechtenstein citizens. The implications for Liechtenstein are especially felt in the ownership of land. Traditionally the ownership of Liechtenstein land could only be acquired after permission from the Liechtenstein authorities. Foreigners could only own land in certain restricted cases. This stipulation was designed to prevent speculation and the concentration of land ownership in the hands of a few persons.[273] By unilateral declaration, Liechtenstein can provide for the establishment of protective measures under Article 112 of the EEA Agreement if the access to the land market for Liechtenstein's inhabitants is jeopardized.[274]

The EU as well as EFTA countries have treated Liechtenstein as a full negotiating partner and, instead of using Liechtenstein's smallness against it, have accepted its special characteristics. Such an understanding will be especially necessary when Liechtenstein requests an extension of the transitional period concerning the free movement of persons and when it unilaterally takes protective measures. It remains to be seen for how long the EEA States will accept these protective measures, especially as they do not have reciprocal effect.[275]

European Union. All EFTA States, except for Iceland, Liechtenstein, and Norway, have joined the EU. The Liechtenstein Government, as a result of the discussions in the Diet on the EEA Agreement, took the position that a request for admission should only be made if there existed a true political will to accede and to accept the complete *acquis communautaire*.[276] The Government nevertheless keeps close contacts with the EU and Switzerland on possible options for Liechtenstein. The Liechtenstein Government believes that its smallness cannot be a reason for not admitting Liechtenstein to the EU, although some problems could be raised with regard to its participation in the EU institutions.[277] From Liechtenstein's point of view, membership in the EU would cause certain financial problems. The Government expects that Liechtenstein would be a net contributor to the EU.[278] Thus it would lose most of its customs revenue and possibly be confronted with higher customs tariffs on imports of raw materials from third States on which Liechtenstein's processing industry is dependent.[279] The EU could doubt, according to the Liechtenstein Government, whether Liechtenstein had the work capacity to participate in its institutions.[280] Moreover, the EEA Agreement sets forth a more extensive protection clause than the EC Treaty.[281] The issue is therefore whether the EU would be willing to make certain concessions in favor of Liechtenstein as was done in the EEA negotiations. Liechtenstein must also be assured that no EC regulation will force it to abandon its moderate tax system, though the Principality has already introduced a VAT system.

As Liechtenstein has become a State Party to the EEA Agreement independently of Switzerland, it has abandoned an absolute assimilation with the Swiss customs regime. When considering an EU membership for Liechtenstein, the question of whether or not Switzerland will become a member of the EU is irrelevant, though Switzerland would have to agree to a special bilateral arrangement or face the termination of the customs union with Liechtenstein.[282]

International Responsibility. Does Liechtenstein have international responsibility for the non-observance of a treaty obligation that is applicable in Liechtenstein by virtue of the postal or customs union treaty with Switzerland? It must first be determined whether Liechtenstein becomes a State Party to the treaties which Switzerland concludes under Article 4 of the postal union treaty and Articles 7 and 8 of the customs union treaty. Special Rapporteur Waldock of the International Law Commission prepared a draft Article 59 to be included in the Vienna Convention on the Law of Treaties. This article, which was specially drafted to cover the Swiss-Liechtenstein relations, ran as follows:

> The application of a treaty extends to the territory of a State which is not itself a contracting party if:

(a) the State authorized one of the parties to bind its territory by concluding the treaty;

(b) the other parties were aware that the party in question was so authorized; and

(c) the party in question intended to bind the territory of that State by concluding the treaty.[283]

The Special Rapporteur emphasized that Liechtenstein did not itself become a party to those treaties and that in case of a violation of the treaty a third State "would not be able to bring that complaint directly against Liechtenstein, but would have to lodge it through Switzerland."[284] This position was severely criticized by the members of the International Law Commission. The Chairman thought that "since Liechtenstein was an autonomous subject of international law, it was the State of Liechtenstein that was bound by a treaty of that kind and not its territory," and that "if Liechtenstein failed to observe the treaty it was still Liechtenstein that was failing to meet its obligations; consequently Liechtenstein . . . must be regarded as a party to the treaty."[285] These arguments were generally endorsed by the other members. Draft Article 59 was believed to deal with a very special and rare case that need not be generalized into a rule.[286] The International Law Commission did not retain the article.

Article 2, paragraph 1 (g) of the Vienna Convention on the Law of Treaties describes a "party" as "a State which has consented to be bound by the treaty and for which the treaty is in force." Liechtenstein has, admittedly, expressed its general consent to be bound by postal and customs treaties that are concluded by Switzerland, by accepting their application in its territory. In this sense one could call Liechtenstein a State Party to the treaties. Nevertheless, the postal and customs union treaties themselves stipulate that Liechtenstein has the right to become a State Party itself to international conventions if Switzerland has ratified these conventions too.[287] This implies that if Liechtenstein does not ratify a convention itself, it is not considered a State Party. As we have seen, the Protocol of 4 January 1960 which made the Stockholm Convention applicable in Liechtenstein did not make Liechtenstein a State Party to the Convention. It only became a full member of EFTA after it had ratified the Stockholm Convention in its own name. Likewise, the free trade Agreements with the European Communities of 22 July 1972 were applied in Liechtenstein, but Liechtenstein had no seat or voting power of its own in the Joint Committees. In fact, only States Parties had the right to vote and have their own representation in the Joint Committees. Liechtenstein could not terminate a treaty, suspend it, or invoke any international principle likely to terminate or invalidate the treaty. It must be concluded that Liechtenstein has never been considered or treated as a State Party to the international conventions concluded by Switzerland and applicable in the Principality.

Can Liechtenstein be considered a third State with rights and obligations from a treaty concluded by two or more other States, within the meaning of Articles 35 and 36 of the Vienna Convention on the Law of Treaties?[288] Third States which are not States Parties to a treaty may have certain obligations arising from this treaty if they accept these obligations in writing. It does not seem incompatible with this provision that a third State gives its general consent to be bound by obligations of a treaty without expressly mentioning this or that obligation. In the case of Liechtenstein, such a general consent can be withdrawn by denouncing the postal and customs union treaties. In this respect Liechtenstein could be classified as a third State within the meaning of Article 35 of the Vienna Convention on the Law of Treaties.

It is more controversial whether the parties to a treaty had the intention to accord all the rights of the treaty provisions to Liechtenstein, when they declared that the treaty would apply to the Principality. Considering that under the postal and customs union treaties Liechtenstein has no freedom of action because Swiss authorities are charged with their implementation, the rights flowing from a treaty will not apply to Liechtenstein insofar as they permit a State action. Such actions can only be performed by Switzerland. Conversely, if the right does not imply an action of the holder of the right but a direct obligation of the other State Party, such as a most-favored-nation provision, the right will apply to Liechtenstein. It seems therefore logical that if a State Party does not respect its obligations, Liechtenstein has the right to invoke that State's international responsibility. In this sense, Liechtenstein is also a third State within the meaning of Article 36 of the Vienna Convention on the Law of Treaties.

It should be borne in mind that the applicability in Liechtenstein of postal and commercial treaties concluded by Switzerland and the fact that Switzerland does not sign the treaties *in the name of* Liechtenstein are closely related to the execution of those treaties by Swiss authorities. If the Liechtenstein-located Swiss authorities violate a provision of a postal or customs treaty concluded with a third State, they do not act in distinction from the Swiss-located authorities. As they are not put at Liechtenstein's disposal, Liechtenstein cannot be held internationally responsible for the acts of the Swiss postal and customs offices in Liechtenstein territory.[289] This situation will change if Liechtenstein installs its own postal and customs services. Liechtenstein remains internationally responsible for breaches of commercial agreements that do not require an implementation by the Swiss authorities or for the acts of the Swiss customs officers under the express authority of Liechtenstein by virtue of the EEA Agreement.[290]

UNITED NATIONS

Liechtenstein envisaged United Nations membership at a rather early stage. Preliminary unofficial talks with certain delegations in New York had already begun in the sixties, but the admission of Liechtenstein seemed, as yet, impossible. At that time the United States and the United Kingdom in particular were against admitting a great number of micro-states to the United Nations. By 1988, discussions with the permanent representatives of the Security Council, other Security Council members, and the representatives of the regional groups showed that all delegations were in favor of Liechtenstein's admission by reason of the principle of universality underlined in the United Nations.[291]

The problems arising from Liechtenstein's application for membership in the United Nations were not so much of an international order as of a national order; in general, the application for membership lacked popular support. In March 1986, a Swiss people's referendum resulted in a 75 percent refusal of Switzerland's membership in the United Nations. It was also known that the Liechtenstein population tended to vote in a similar way to the nearby Swiss cantons which had rejected Switzerland's membership in the United Nations with an even higher percentage.[292] It was eventually decided not to consult the Liechtenstein people by way of referendum.[293] On 14 December 1989, the Diet unanimously approved the application for membership in the United Nations.[294] The main argument against United Nations membership focused on the costs which a United Nations membership would entail and on the fact that the United Nations would not bring anything new or substantial to Liechtenstein.[295]

The reasons for seeking admission to the United Nations were diverse. They included:[296] the reinforcement of Liechtenstein's independence and statehood through an active foreign policy at an international level; a global cooperation and international solidarity on the basis of an international order ruled by international law; the establishment of diplomatic contacts with virtually all States of the world without having to run into disproportionate costs; and participation in the finding of international solutions for environmental, health, and food problems.[297]

By letter of 10 August 1990, Liechtenstein applied for membership in the United Nations.[298] On 13 August 1990, the Security Council referred the request for examination to its Committee on the Admission of New Members,[299] which issued its report the following day and recommended that Liechtenstein be admitted.[300] On 14 August 1990, the Security Council unanimously recommended the admission of Liechtenstein to membership in the United Nations.[301] Most Security Council members declared that they had no doubt that Liechtenstein was fully capable of carrying out the obligations of a Member State, as it had already effectively participated in several agencies of the United Nations, the CSCE, and the Council of Europe.[302] China emphasized that Liechtenstein was a peace-loving country which met the requirements for United Nations membership.[303] Romania believed that Liechtenstein would "help to strengthen the quantitative dimension of the universality of [the] Organization."[304] The Soviet delegate, whose country was previously opposed to Liechtenstein's admission to the Statute of the International Court of Justice, declared that Liechtenstein would "make a positive contribution to the multifaceted work of the Organization" and that "all States, large and small, can and should make their contribution to the process of strengthening security and expanding mutual understanding between peoples."[305]

On 18 September 1990, the General Assembly accepted Liechtenstein's admission by acclamation.[306] The President of the General Assembly stated that "Liechtenstein brings to the United Nations a rich experience in the ways and means open to small States to foster their well-being and independence. There is much here, I am sure, that other States can learn from."[307] In general, the delegates declared that "all members of the international community, even if they are small in terms of geography and population, can contribute decisively to the . . . work of the General Assembly and the Organization as a whole."[308] Thus Liechtenstein became the 160th Member State of the United Nations.[309]

It is remarkable that Liechtenstein's application was not submitted to a thorough investigation into its statehood. Due to the active role which it had played in the CSCE and the Council of Europe there was no room left for doubt about its statehood, nor on its capacity to fulfill the membership obligations. This international attitude stands in glaring contrast to the international reactions which arose in the League of Nations when Liechtenstein applied for membership. Apart from the institutional objections which prompted the League's attitude, the difference in reaction can be explained by the success of Liechtenstein's foreign policy in emphasizing its "Eigenstaatlichkeit" and in proving that it can provide a valuable contribution to the work of international fora despite its smallness.

During the forty-eighth session of the General Assembly, Liechtenstein requested the inclusion of a sub-item entitled "Effective realization of the right of self-determination through autonomy" in the existing item "Right of peoples to self-determination." This initiative sought to promote a broader and more flexible application of the right to self-determination, by *inter alia* providing different levels of autonomy for communities living within States and at least a certain initial and very basic level of autonomy for communities with a sufficient degree of distinctive identity.[310] After a lively debate in the Third Committee, some States feared that the initiative would lead to disintegration of existing States, to interference in internal affairs, and to difficult discussions on the definition of "communities."[311] Armenia and Ecuador were among the States supporting Liechtenstein's ideas, and they even envisaged the creation of an impartial organ which would be charged with examining claims for self-determination.[312] It was however decided to defer the consideration of this matter to one of the Committee's future sessions.[313]

The United Nations gives Liechtenstein the opportunity to make its voice heard on a universal political level. The wide range of topics dealt with by this Organization makes it necessary for small delegations such as Liechtenstein's to define clear priority areas.[314]

OTHER INTERNATIONAL ORGANIZATIONS

Liechtenstein participates in other governmental organizations or conferences, besides the ones we have discussed in the preceding paragraphs, of which we can mention the following:

UPU: On 17 January 1950 the Liechtenstein Head of Government declared to the UPU that by virtue of Article 2 of the postal union treaty of 1920 with Switzerland, Liechtenstein was a member within the meaning of Article 10 of the Universal Postal Convention. On 13 April 1962, Liechtenstein became a full and independent member of the UPU and therefore was no longer represented by Switzerland.[315]

ITU: Liechtenstein became a member of the ITU on 25 July 1963. Liechtenstein was granted a reserved radio frequency, which it started using in 1995.[316]

UNCTAD: Liechtenstein was invited to the first world conference of UNCTAD held on 23 March 1964. As a member of two United Nations specialized organizations, the UPU and the ITU, Liechtenstein was always invited to United Nations conferences. When on 30 December 1964 UNC-TAD became a permanent organ of the United Nations, Liechtenstein remained a Member State.[317]

IAEA: Liechtenstein has been a member of the IAEA since 13 December 1968.[318] The Board of Governors of the IAEA[319] and the General Conference[320] had approved Liechtenstein's application without discussion. The Liechtenstein representative explained thereupon his State's interests in the Organization, declaring that "[c]lose cooperation with Switzerland had enabled Liechtenstein to carry out useful research work in the field of atomic energy, to develop new materials for reactors, and to train nuclear energy experts."[321]

WIPO: Liechtenstein adhered to the WIPO on 17 February 1972.[322]

GATT: When Switzerland ratified GATT on 1 April 1966, it declared that the customs territory of Switzerland included the Principality of Liechtenstein as long as it formed a customs union with Switzerland.[323] Liechtenstein was seen as a part of the "metropolitan customs territory" of Switzerland within the meaning of Article XXIV, paragraph 1 of the General Agreement. On 29 March 1994, the Liechtenstein Government decided to accede to GATT 1947. It has also signed GATT 1994 and the WTO Agreement, thus enabling it to become an original Member of the new World Trade Organization.[324]

European Bank for Reconstruction and Development: Liechtenstein signed the Convention establishing the European Bank for Reconstruction and Development on 29 May 1990. Liechtenstein pays 0.02 percent of the Bank's total capital.[325] Liechtenstein's participation in the Bank shows its solidarity in the European economic construction and the role it wants to play therein.[326]

Application of the Criteria for Statehood

Combining our findings, the following can be concluded with regard to the examination of Liechtenstein's statehood:

Territory: The relative smallness of Liechtenstein's territory has not precluded its statehood. In addition, it has formally been maintained that its smallness was no reason to exclude it from an international organization or conference. This international position was phrased as a general rule.

Population: Liechtenstein possesses a permanent population of which 38.6 percent are foreigners. This proportion of foreign inhabitants has never led to the international denial of the existence of a State population in Liechtenstein.

Government: As we have found, Liechtenstein has an elaborate system of government on a highly democratic basis. There can be no doubt about the effective power which the governmental institutions wield in the territory of Liechtenstein.

Independence: It should be noted that, although prompted by political reasons, the Soviet Union argued that Liechtenstein was not a State only because it lacked independence, and not because it was too small. The most examined and most sensitive aspect of Liechtenstein's legal position has always been its independence from Switzerland and Austria. The following foreign elements are present in Liechtenstein's governmental organization:

1. *Certain Swiss or Austrian judges in the judicial system*: They do not comprise the majority of a court's judges. They are independent and therefore by definition not under Swiss or Austrian control.
2. *Some diplomatic relations are maintained by Switzerland*: Switzerland can only act under Liechtenstein's orders and is not as such in charge of Liechtenstein's diplomatic missions. Liechtenstein is free to set up its own diplomatic representations. This has been underlined by the Council of Europe. Since Liechtenstein became a member of the Council of Europe, EFTA, and the United Nations, Switzerland's political representation on behalf of Liechtenstein has lost much of its value.
3. *Swiss control over postal and customs services*: The postal and customs officers in Liechtenstein are under Swiss authority. Swiss postal and customs legislation is applicable in Liechtenstein as well as the treaties concluded by Switzerland with third States. Liechtenstein cannot, in general, oppose the application of a customs treaty in its territory. These restrictions on its independence can however be lifted within one year on denunciation of the postal and customs treaties. Moreover, as a result of its independent ratification of the EEA Agreement, Liechtenstein will have its own specific customs control and can take a different legal course from

Switzerland. It has the freedom to act independently of Switzerland within the institutional bodies set up by the EFTA and EEA Agreements.

4. *Swiss monetary control*: Liechtenstein cannot develop its own monetary policy, and the Swiss National Bank exercises its authority over Liechtenstein-based banks, persons, and companies virtually as in Switzerland. Liechtenstein's treaty obligations in this matter can be revoked within six months.

5. *Swiss legislation on the residence and sojourn of aliens*: Switzerland can expel an alien with effect for Liechtenstein without the latter's cooperation or influence. Liechtenstein maintains its own aliens office and still has a certain freedom to apply the Swiss aliens legislation. The implementation of the EEA Agreement will lead to a disparity in the application of the aliens legislation in Switzerland and Liechtenstein. The ratification of the EEA Agreement by Liechtenstein has thus accentuated Liechtenstein's freedom of action in its relations with Switzerland.

The delegation of certain powers to Switzerland has not prejudiced Liechtenstein's formal independence. The treaty obligations and functions delegated to Switzerland have not been considered by the international community as precluding Liechtenstein's statehood.

Does Liechtenstein also have actual independence from Switzerland? Given its small size, Liechtenstein has, in practice, managed to keep a high degree of real independence. Its actual freedom of political action is for instance reinforced by the fact that Liechtenstein provides for its own water consumption and electricity supply through a hydroelectric power station supplemented by solar energy installations. Liechtenstein can sever its links with Switzerland on twelve months' notice by terminating the postal, customs, and monetary union treaties. The effects of such an action would not be dramatic, as 86.2 percent of industrial exports go to countries other than Switzerland.[327] The Swiss Franc could be replaced by any other currency and the postal services could be privatized. Even if the Liechtensteinese prefer to keep their present friendly relations with Switzerland, it is this factual situation that places Liechtenstein in a better negotiating position and makes it less prone to external pressures. It is evident that Liechtenstein possesses actual independence and is not submitted to substantial external control by Switzerland.

Recognition: Liechtenstein's international recognition seems to have a purely declaratory nature. The League of Nations had "no doubt" that juridically the Principality was a sovereign State. A clear distinction should nevertheless be made between the recognition of Liechtenstein's statehood and the admission of Liechtenstein to an international organization, as the former does not guarantee the latter. The League of Nations' refusal to admit Liechtenstein as a full member was not based on the rejection of its statehood, as we have seen. The first postwar recognition came from the Member States of the United Nations, when they approved Liechtenstein's accession to the Statute of the International Court of Justice. The Principality was said to possess "all the qualifications of a State." This position was confirmed by the International Court of Justice.[328] The non-recognition by the Soviet, Byelorussian, and Ukrainian Republics, though based on legal arguments, seemed to have been mainly inspired by political reasons. The Soviet Union did not object to Liechtenstein's admission in the CSCE.

Liechtenstein's foreign policy aimed at consolidating even further its international recognition by adhering to the Council of Europe and the United Nations. In practice, Liechtenstein's problems were not, at that stage, linked to the recognition of its statehood, but to the reluctance of the international community to admit the Principality with open arms in political organizations. The Council of Europe took more care to examine the statehood of Liechtenstein than it usually did for larger States. It was, in general, concluded that Liechtenstein had enough independence to be qualified as a State. Therefore, Liechtenstein's recognition was not meant to be reparative of a lack of independence. It was nevertheless examined and thought important whether Liechtenstein had been previously admitted to certain international conferences or organizations. This was considered especially by the Council of Europe and to a lesser degree by the United Nations in 1991. The United Nations, when deciding on Liechtenstein's application for membership, did not show any doubts as to Liechtenstein's statehood. The object of these investigations was not so much to search for proof of Liechtenstein's statehood and recognition thereof, but to ascertain the Principality's ability to fulfill its international obligations and to participate in the work of the organization in question.

We can conclude that Liechtenstein is a State in international law and that its degree of formal and actual independence falls within the generally demanded criterion of independence.

Self-determination of the Liechtenstein People

The inhabitants of a State, that is, independent peoples, have the right of self-determination with force of *jus cogens*. Now that Liechtenstein's statehood has been ascertained, the Liechtenstein inhabitants undoubtedly have the right of self-determination, provided that they constitute a "people" or "fraction of a people" within the meaning of international law. As we have seen, objective and subjective criteria should be taken into account as well as an attachment to the territory. It is noticeable that a small population like that of Liechtenstein cannot clearly distinguish itself on strictly objective criteria from its surrounding populations due to the social "openness" of its society and frequent interrelations with the neighboring populations. The objective characteristics of the Liechtenstein inhabitants are therefore especially combined in the historical and traditional togetherness. The origins of their national character can be retraced to the beginning of the eighteenth century when the territory was bought by the Prince of Liechtenstein, who gave his name to the Principality and its people. The Liechtenstein nationals are to a great extent the descendants of families which are long established in the Liechtenstein territory. Even if the Liechtenstein inhabitants do not have their own Liechtenstein language and clearly distinct culture, they do have a subjective we-consciousness.[329] The Liechtenstein nationals, to the exclusion of the foreign inhabitants, are also anxious to preserve their own identity so as not to be overwhelmed by foreigners.

It can therefore be sustained that the Liechtenstein nationals possess the objective and subjective characteristics required to be a people and have an attachment to their territory. If the objective criteria are taken more restrictively, or if less importance is given to the subjective criteria, the Liechtenstein people could be considered a part of a people. This would however not prejudice their right of self-determination, because they constitute a State.

Conclusions

We have set out to investigate the legal consequences of Liechtenstein's smallness, on the basis of which the following can be concluded:

1. Liechtenstein's statehood is well established and recognized.
2. Liechtenstein's foreign policy, which aimed at consolidating its sovereignty in the long term through membership in several international political organizations, does not as such have any legal consequences for Liechtenstein's international status. Its statehood was juridically unquestionable before its admission to the Council of Europe, and especially fortified by its adherence to the Statute of the International Court of Justice. Liechtenstein's membership in the Council of Europe, the United Nations,

EFTA, and the OSCE, as well as its adherence to the EEA, have however the effect of proving its political existence, thus preventing a marginalization and an assimilation with Switzerland. It also emphasized Liechtenstein's capacity to cooperate in the work of international organizations and to take an active part in their results.

3. Liechtenstein's international behavior has been in a certain sense a pioneer work for the other European micro-states, because it was the first European micro-state to enter actively into the Council of Europe and the United Nations. In general, its activities inspired confidence from the international community and influenced the behavior of the international community towards micro-states in general.

4. Liechtenstein's degree of independence is not only due to legal efforts but has also been determined by its historical development, internal facilities, and the political structure of its neighboring States. It thus seems probable that (and this is not a legal but a political conclusion) Liechtenstein's international actions were facilitated by the fact that Switzerland is, by its very nature, used to small decentralized political units. This could have been different if Liechtenstein had been confronted with a more centralized neighboring State.[330]

5. In general it can be observed that Liechtenstein's legal and political status over the years have been fortified to a degree which has lessened the effects of dependence due to its small territory and restricted human and natural resources. In view of these achievements, Liechtenstein has managed to compensate for the inherent disadvantages of being a micro-state.

Notes

1. Fürstentum Liechtenstein Amt für Volkswirtschaft, *Statistisches Jahrbuch 1994*, p. 3.

2. Ibid., p. 21: status as of 31 Dec. 1993, percentages calculated on the basis of the figures represented. Of the total population, 15.7 percent are Swiss, 7.4 percent Austrian, 3.7 percent German, 2.9 percent Italian, and 8.3 percent of other nationality, forming a foreign population of 38.6 percent.

3. Ibid., pp. 188–189. This figure does not take into account imports to and exports from Switzerland.

4. Ibid., p. 192: status as of 31 Dec. 1993, percentages calculated on the basis of the figures represented.

5. Liechtenstein has five banks, of which two were established in 1992 and 1993 respectively. In 1994, the balance sheet total of these banks amounted to 23,477.9 million Swiss francs. The main export products are machines, including means of transport and products from the metal industry, comprising 44.6 percent and 16.6 percent of exports respectively, excluding the trade with Switzerland:

Statistisches Jahrbuch 1994, p. 189 (percentages calculated on the basis of the figures represented). See also "Der internationale Erfolg der Liechtensteinischen Wirtschaft ist kein Zufall," *VN Magazin Extra* (1986); 2.6 percent of the working population in Liechtenstein was employed in the agricultural sector, against 52.8 percent in the industrial sector and 44.6 percent in the service sector; and F. Kneschaurek, "Entwicklungsperspektiven der liechtensteinischen Volkswirtschaft in den neunziger Jahren," 17 *Liechtenstein Wirtschaftsfragen* (1990) p. 15.

6. "Voranschlag 1996," Annex to BA No. 71/1995, p. 2. For 1995, a surplus of 16.05 million Swiss francs was foreseen.

7. Predictions for 1995, "Voranschlag 1995," Annex to BA No. 66/1994, pp. 81–84. Company taxes cover 15 percent, property and income taxes 9.9 percent, and indirect tax on the sale of goods 11.0 percent of total receipts.

8. Property tax is about 0.07 percent, income tax 1.4 percent, and company taxes vary between 7.5 and 15 percent. See W. Kranz, ed., *The Principality of Liechtenstein: A Documentary Handbook*, 5th ed. (1981) pp. 97–102 and P. Marxer et al., *Companies and Taxes in Liechtenstein*, 4th ed. (1988).

9. O. Seger, *Überblick über die Liechtensteinische Geschichte* (1974) pp. 5–6. For further reading, see P. Kaiser, *Geschichte des Fürstentums Liechtenstein*, 1847 ed. (1983).

10. For 115,000 and 290,000 gulden respectively: P. Raton. *Liechtenstein: History and Institutions of the Principality* (1970) p. 20.

11. Before 1608 the family held the title of Seignors von Liechtenstein. Seger, *Überblick*, p.27.

12. This is in contrast to the usual practice according to which the Prince takes over the name of the territory. Ibid., pp. 9–10.

13. Ibid., p. 12.

14. Ibid.

15. Art. 2 of the 1862 Constitution as amended by the 1921 reform. Text in LGBl (1921) No. 15. pp. 69 ff. English text in A. P. Blaustein and G. H. Flanz, eds. *Constitutions of the Countries of the World* (1987): Liechtenstein.

16. Art. 7 of the Constitution.

17. Art. 8, 1st para. of the Constitution.

18. Art. 9 of the Constitution.

19. Art. 10 of the Constitution.

20. Art. 85 of the Constitution.

21. T. Allgäuer, *Die parlamentarische Kontrolle über die Regierung im Fürstentum Liechtenstein*, Diss. No. 1097 (1989) p. 36 at n. 23.

22. Art. 10, last sentence of the Constitution. This possibility was used for instance in 1943, when the Prince prolonged the period of session of the Diet to prevent elections and the entrance of a national socialist party; in 1982, in order to declare the Swiss law on narcotics of 1951 applicable in Liechtenstein; and on 10 Aug. 1990 to take economic sanctions against Iraq.

23. Art. 3 of the Constitution and Art. 12 (1) of the law of the Princely House, LGBl (1993) No. 100. The succession to the throne is assured for the male descendants, with priority over the female descendants, of the Prince Regnant. The family council is composed of three members and three substitutes chosen for a period

of five years by the members of the Princely House who are allowed to vote: Art. 10 of the law of the Princely House. The law of the Princely House creates an autonomous legal regime, which in certain domains (nationality legislation, political rights) derogates from the common legislation.

24. Art. 13 of the Constitution was amended in 1984 so as to permit the delegation of powers to the hereditary Prince in case of temporary incapacity of the reigning Prince or in preparation for governmental succession. LGBl (1984) Nos. 28 and 32.

25. *Protokoll über die Eröffnungssitzung des Landtages* (12 May 1993) pp. 4–6.

26. Art. 79 of the Constitution.

27. Art. 78, 1st para. of the Constitution.

28. Art. 80 of the Constitution. This power was used for the first time in 1993. See also Allgäuer, *Die parlamentarische Kontrolle*, p. 82.

29. Art. 79. 4th para. of the Constitution. On 17 Jun. 1992 the Diet approved an initiative to amend the Constitution aimed at eliminating the discrimination between born Liechtensteinese and non-born Liechtensteinese in public functions. *Postulat* of 14 May 1992. *Protokoll über die öffentliche Landtagssitzung* (16/17 Jun. 1992) pp. 1131–1132. The Constitution has not yet been amended to this end.

30. See the table in Allgäuer, *Die parlamentarische Kontrolle*, p. 74.

31. Ibid., pp. 78–79.

32. Arts. 46 and 47 of the Constitution. Before the constitutional amendment of 20 Oct. 1987, LGBl (1988) No. 11, the Diet consisted of fifteen members. There are fifteen seats reserved for the "Oberland" and ten for the "Unterland."

33. LGBl (1985) No. 4. para. 1. On 15 Apr. 1992, the Diet approved an amendment of the law on political rights and of the Constitution, lowering the age of eligibility to vote and to be elected to eighteen years. *Protokoll über die Oeffentliche Landtagssitzung* (15/16 April 1992) pp. 362–363 and BA No. 50/1991. The amendment was however rejected in a referendum of 26/28 Jun. 1992.

34. Art. 48 of the Constitution. At least 1,000 Liechtenstein citizens or three communes may request the Diet to convene. A referendum initiated by at least 1,500 citizens or four communes must be held in order to dissolve the Diet. In order to prorogue the Diet for three months or to dissolve it, the Prince must prove warrantable grounds.

35. Art. 62 of the Constitution. Under Art. 8 only those treaties which cede national territory, alienate national property, dispose of rights of sovereignty or State prerogatives, assume any new burden for the Principality or its citizens, or contract any obligation to the detriment of the rights of the people of the Principality have to be approved by the Diet.

36. Allgäuer, *Die parlamentarische Kontrolle*, p. 83.

37. Art. 64 of the Constitution.

38. Arts. 58 and 111 of the Constitution.

39. Art. 64 of the Constitution.

40. Art. 66 of the Constitution.

41. Art. 66 bis of the Constitution. An initiative of the people to introduce this new article in the Constitution was submitted on 18 Sept. 1991 and approved by referendum on 13/15 March 1992, BA No. 87/1991. The Diet criticized the initiative

because it would make Liechtenstein's foreign policy less flexible and endanger its position in the EEA, if amendments to the EEA Agreement could be rejected, *Protokoll über die Oeffentliche Landtagssitzung* (11/12 Dec. 1991) pp. 1796–1804.

42. Art. 70 (b) (2) of the law on political rights, LGBl (1973) No. 50. Art. 70 (b) (3) permits appeal to the State Tribunal ("Staatsgerichtshof") against the decision on invalidity. This law has been amended following the adoption of new Art. 66 bis of the Constitution, BA No. 48/1992.

43. A. Oehry, "Fürst und Volk bei der Bestellung der liechtensteinischen ordentlichen Gerichte," 7 *Liechtensteinische Juristen Zeitung* (1986) p. 145.

44. Art. 99 of the Constitution.

45. Art. 2 of the law on judicial organization ("Gerichtsorganisationsgesetz"), LGBl (1922), No. 16. See also Allgäuer, *Die parlamentarische Kontrolle*, p. 87. By virtue of Art. II of a treaty with Austria signed on 19 Jan. 1884, Austria has promised to place its judges at Liechtenstein's disposal to serve as judges in the Principality, LGBl (1884) No. 8. See also K. Kohlegger, "Als österreichischer Richter in Liechtenstein," in *Herbert Battliner Festgabe zum 60. Geburtstag* (1988) pp. 281–290.

46. Art. 21 of the law on judicial organization.

47. Art. 2 of the law on judicial organization.

48. Art. 101 of the Constitution.

49. Art. 104 of the Constitution and Art. 23 of the law on the State Tribunal ("Staatsgerichtshof-Gesetz"), LGBl (1925) No. 8 as amended by LGBl (1982) No. 57. A new law on the State Tribunal, expected to be promulgated in 1996, will enable claims against rights set forth in any convention (Art. 14 (1) of the draft law).

50. A Sole Judge is competent to deal with all offenses punishable by a maximum of six months' imprisonment, a Court of Aldermen judges indictable offenses, a Criminal Court more serious crimes, and a Juvenile Court all juvenile offenses. See Oehry, "Fürst und Volk," p. 146 and Anon., "Die Organisation der Strafgerichte und der Strafvollzug im Fürstentum Liechtenstein," 4 *Der Strafvollzug in der Schweiz* (1980) No. 112, pp. 204–206.

51. The Court may decide the execution of the sentence in a foreign prison in case of an imposed imprisonment of at least one month. Anon., "Die Organisation," pp. 205–206.

52. Ibid., p. 206.

53. Art. 12, 1st para. of the Constitution. If it concerns a member of the Government the prerogative of remission or mitigation can only be exercised at the instigation of the Diet: Art. 12, 2nd para. of the Constitution. The prerogative may not be used in contravention of basic rules and rights laid down in the Constitution and penal code. See Allgäuer, *Die parlamentarische Kontrolle*, p. 91.

54. Art. 97 of the Constitution.

55. All members of the Tribunal have a substitute. The chairman and his deputy (substitute) must be of Liechtenstein nationality. Art. 97 of the Constitution.

56. Allgäuer, *Die parlamentarische Kontrolle*, p. 88 at n. 9.

57. Ibid., p. 88.

58. Art. 28, 2nd para. of the law on the State Tribunal.

59. The Tribunal consists of five judges appointed by the Diet for a period of

five years. The President of the Tribunal is appointed with the approval of the Prince. The Tribunal must include at least two jurists. The President of the Tribunal and at least two other members must be of Liechtenstein nationality: Arts. 2 and 4 of the law on the State Tribunal.

60. Art. 11 (2) of the law on the State Tribunal.

61. Arts. 11 (3) and 29 of the law on the State Tribunal.

62. Arts. 14 and 44 of the law on the State Tribunal.

63. Art. 13 of the law on the State Tribunal.

64. Art. 70 (b) (3) of the law on political rights.

65. It has also signed Protocols Nos. 1, 9, 10, and 11 to this Convention. Only Protocol No. 6 was ratified on 15 Nov. 1990. The others are expected to be ratified soon.

66. Ratified on 2 Nov. 1990.

67. Ratified on 22 Jun. 1994. It has signed the UN Convention on the Rights of the Child and the European Framework Convention for the Protection of National Minorities.

68. Chapter IV of the Constitution entitled "General Rights and Obligations of the Citizens of the Principality," which applies only to Liechtensteinese.

69. Introduction of universal suffrage in Art. 29 (2) of the Constitution, LGBl (1985) No. 4. Communes could grant the right to vote or to take part in elections to Liechtenstein women under Art. 110 bis of the Constitution introduced in 1976, LGBl (1976) No. 50.

70. LGBl (1992) No. 81.

71. Art. 69 (1) of the EEA Agreement guarantees equal pay for men and women for the same work, whereas Art. 70 and Annex XVIII lay down the general equal treatment of men and women in labor and Social Security legislation.

72. BA No. 58/1994. Until the approval of the amendments, the State Tribunal may not examine the constitutionality of these laws in respect of Art. 31 (2) of the Constitution: Part II of the law amending the Constitution, LGBl (1992) No. 81. Liechtenstein nationality is passed onto the legitimate children of a Liechtenstein father, whereas the legitimate children of a Liechtenstein mother can only acquire Liechtenstein citizenship through naturalization. The foreign spouse of a Liechtenstein man has the right to acquire her husband's nationality through a simple procedure, whereas the foreign husband of a Liechtenstein woman has to apply for citizenship through a more complicated procedure of naturalization: Arts. 4, 5 and 5 bis of the law on nationality, LGBl (1960) No. 23 with subsequent amendments in LGBl (1976) No. 41, LGBl (1984) No. 23, and LGBl (1986) No. 104. As soon as Liechtenstein has adhered to the EEA Agreement, new laws on Social Security will eliminate the differentiation between men and women, especially with regard to the imposed contributions and the calculation of the Social Security benefits.

73. BA No. 11/1991, approved by the Diet on 26 Mar. 1991, *Protokoll über die Oeffentliche Landtagssitzung* (25/26 March 1991) p. 253. The penal code of 24 Jun. 1987, entered into force on 1 Jan. 1989, decriminalized homosexual acts between adults, thus the reservation to Art. 8 of the ECHR could be lifted. The reservation which is still valid affects Art. 6 (1) of the ECHR, as the public nature of the court sessions and of the pronouncement of the judgment are limited by the Liechtenstein

laws on the subject. See also T. Bruha, "Liechtenstein and an All-European System of Human Rights Protection," 1 All-Eur. HR Yearb. (1991) pp. 55–61.

74. Apart from the cases mentioned in nn. 78 and 80 the following applications were considered: Application No. 11399/85 (*A. Laupper v. Switzerland, Liechtenstein and Austria*), decision of the Commission of 6 Oct. 1986 (no appearance of a violation), Application No. 16705/90 (*M. v. Liechtenstein*), decision of the Commission of 10 Febr. 1993 (case struck off list after withdrawal by applicant), Application No. 21139/93 (*L. v. Liechtenstein*), decision of the Commission of 1 Jul. 1993 (non-exhaustion of domestic remedies), Application No. 21657/93 (*X v. Liechtenstein*). decision of the Commission of 14 Oct. 1993 (inadmissible), Application No. 21902/93 (*X v. Liechtenstein*), decision of the Commission of 13 Jan. 1994 (inadmissible), Application No. 26981/95 (*X v. Liechtenstein*), decision of the Commission of 7 Sept. 1995 (inadmissible) and Application No. 27630/95 (*X v. Liechtenstein*), decision of the Commission of 7 Sept. 1995 (inadmissible).

75. Application No. 14245/88 (*W. v. Liechtenstein*), decision of the Commission of 9 Dec. 1991.

76. Ibid., pp. 4–6.

77. Application No. 19570/92 (*H. v. Liechtenstein*). decision of the Commission of 31 Mar. 1993, p. 5.

78. An explanatory law of 1971, LGBl (1971) No. 22, declares: "Unter dem vor der Verfassung verwendeten Begriff 'Landesangehörige' sind alle Personen mit liechtensteinischem Landesbürgerrecht ohne Unterschied des Geschlechts zu verstehen."

79. Art. 31 (3) of the Constitution. As a consequence, old-age pensions and disablement benefits will only be paid to foreigners after they have paid their contributions for ten years. Certain bilateral treaties have provided for a reduced period of five years: treaty on Social Security with Austria of 30 Oct. 1968, LGBl (1969) No. 15, treaty with the Federal Republic of Germany of 7 Apr. 1977, LGBl (1982) No. 32, and treaty with Italy of 11 Nov. 1976, LGBl (1980) No. 29. Swiss nationals are in general treated on the same footing as Liechtensteinese: exchange of letters of 31 Dec. 1932, LGBl (1933) No. 4 and subsequent accords on equalization of Swiss and Liechtenstein Social Security legislation of 3 Sept. 1965, LGBl (1966) No. 13, on family allowances of 26 Febr. 1969, LGBl (1970) No. 16, on disablement benefits of 3 Sept. 1965, LGBl (1966) No. 13, and on unemployment benefits of 11 March 1980, LGBl (1980) No. 19.

80. *Die Aussenpolitik des Fürstentums Liechtenstein: Standort und Zielsetzungen*, Schriftenreihe der Regierung (1988) No. 1, p. 13; D. J. Niedermann, *Liechtenstein und die Schweiz: Eine völkerrechtliche Untersuchung* (1976) p. 60.

81. The expected expenditure in 1995 for foreign affairs activities constitutes 1.8 percent of total expenditure: "Voranschlag 1995," Annex to BA No. 66/1994, calculated on the basis of foreign affairs expenditures of the department of foreign affairs, the costs of participation in the Council of Europe, the United Nations, the EEA, the expenditures for the EFTA-UN representation in Geneva, the missions to the EU, and the OSCE and the embassy in Berne.

82. On 20 Sept. 1914 it officially declared its neutrality to the Austro-Hungarian Empire. Later other belligerent parties were also informed of its neutrality. Niedermann, *Liechtenstein und die Schweiz*, pp. 63–67.

83. P. Raton, *Staat und Geschichte* (1969) pp. 76–77.

84. G. F. de Martens, *Nouveau Recueil Général de Traités*. 3rd series, vol. XXIII (1930) pp. 543–544.

85. See, for example, the acceptance of Sweden on 18 Nov. 1919: ibid., p. 544. The refusal of Czechoslovakia is mentioned by H. Thévenaz, "La Suisse, Etat mandataire," 6 ASDI (1949) pp. 15–16. This refusal was probably due to claims of the Liechtenstein Princely family to land properties in Czechoslovakia.

86. "Instruktionen des Politischen Departements betreffend die Vertretung der liechtensteinischen Interessen vom 20 Februar 1948 an die schweizerischen Gesandtschaften und Konsulate," full text in P. Guggenheim, "Völkerrecht," 7 ASDI (1950) pp. 176–184.

87. Ibid., p. 176.

88. The Swiss representatives in their dealings with foreign governments will have to specify that in a specific case they represent the Principality of Liechtenstein. Diplomatic or consular protection may be refused to a Liechtenstein national if he has prejudiced Switzerland's interests so that his protection cannot reasonably be demanded: ibid., pp. 177–178.

89. A Swiss note of 10 March 1920 makes clear that Switzerland's representation of Liechtenstein does not prejudice the Principality's sovereignty and does not entail that the Prince cannot appoint his own delegations: cited by V. Lanfranconi, *Die Staatsverträge und Verwaltungsabkommen zwischen der Schweiz und dem Fürstentum Liechtenstein unter besonderer Berücksichtigung der daraus entstandenen völkerrechtlichen Konsequenzen* (1969) p. 65 and n. 19.

90. Until Liechtenstein became a member of the United Nations, a member of the Swiss delegation in United Nations conferences was often mandated by the Prince and voted as a Liechtensteinese: Raton, *Staat und Geschichte*, p. 85.

91. Status as of Jan. 1996. The Liechtenstein ambassador to Switzerland is also accredited to the Holy See. There are no foreign resident ambassadors, and thirteen of the forty-one consular representatives have their consulate in Liechtenstein. Diplomatic relations will soon be established with Andorra and Monaco. Information from the Liechtenstein Office for Foreign Affairs.

92. Council of Europe, *The Protection of Human Rights in Europe* (1981) p. 7.

93. Interview with HH Prince Hans-Adam II von and zu Liechtenstein of 5 Apr. 1991.

94. Text in de Martens, *Nouveau Recueil Général de Traités*, vol. xv, pp. 707 ff.

95. LGBl (1978) No. 37. French text in SWRO (1979) No. 2, pp. 25 ff.

96. Treaty revising the 1978 postal union treaty and agreement to the 1978 postal union treaty of 2 Nov. 1994, LGBl (1995) Nos. 81 and 82.

97. Arts. 1 and 2 (1) of the postal union treaty.

98. Art. 3 of the postal union treaty. The expenses are borne by Liechtenstein which also receives the benefits.

99. Art. 4 (1) of the postal union treaty, for both present and future regulation.

100. Art. 3 (2) of the 1994 agreement to the 1978 postal union treaty.

101. Art. 4 (2) of the postal union treaty, which states that those treaties "haben im Fürstentum Liechtenstein in gleicher Weise Geltung wie in der Schweiz."

102. Art. 4 (3) of the postal union treaty, under which treaties are concluded

by Switzerland "mit Wirksamkeit für das Fürstentum Liechtenstein." Liechtenstein has the right to oppose the inclusion of a new treaty concluded by Switzerland in the annex on applicable regulations of the postal union treaty. In that case recourse to an arbitral tribunal is foreseen: Arts. 4 (4) and 30 of the postal union treaty.

103. Art. 6 (1) of the postal union treaty.

104. Art. 6 (2) of the postal union treaty as amended by treaty of 2 Nov. 1994. Thus a special agreement was needed for the accession of Liechtenstein to the EEA. This agreement of 2 Nov. 1994 determines the relation between EEA and Swiss PTT law and establishes a joint commission to ascertain the proper functioning of the agreement (Arts. 5–6 of the 1994 agreement to the 1978 postal union treaty).

105. Art. 33 (2) of the postal union treaty. After 1989, the treaty is tacitly renewed each time for a period of five years at the end of which, subject to one year's notice, the treaty can be terminated.

106. For relations with Austria see pp. 169–170 below. Text of the 1923 customs union treaty with Switzerland in 21 LNTS (1924) No. 545. pp. 232 ff. and LGBl (1923) No. 24.

107. Art. 19 of the customs union treaty.

108. Arts. 4 and 5 (1) of the customs union treaty.

109. Arts. 5 (2) and 7 of the customs union treaty.

110. Art. 8 bis (1) of the customs union treaty, permitting Liechtenstein's full membership in EFTA.

111. New Art. 8 bis (2) of the customs union treaty, as amended by treaty of 2 Nov. 1994, permits the accession of Liechtenstein to conventions or organizations to which Switzerland has not adhered, subject to a special agreement, LGBl (1995) No. 76.

112. Art. 3 of the 1994 agreement to the 1923 customs union treaty, LGBl (1995) No. 77. This agreement is supplemented by an additional protocol on product liability, an agreement on the recognition of civil judicial judgments, an exchange of letters on the control of medicines, and an accord amending the 1978 treaty on patent protection, LGBl (1995) Nos. 78–80 and BA No. 1994/93, Annexes.

113. Art. 7 and Annex III of the 1994 agreement to the 1923 customs union treaty.

114. Arts. 9–10 of the 1994 agreement to the 1923 customs union treaty.

115. Art. 4 and Annex I of the 1994 agreement to the 1923 customs union treaty.

116. Arts. 6–7 of the law on customs, LGBl (1995) No. 92.

117. Art. 37 of the customs union treaty as amended in 1994. For 1994, Liechtenstein's share amounted to 26.9 million Swiss francs, which accounted for 5.3 percent of Liechtenstein's State revenues. See "Voranschlag 1996," Annex to BA No. 71/1995.

118. Art. 43 of the customs union treaty.

119. Art. 41 of the customs union treaty.

120. Art. 1 (1) of the treaty on VAT of 28 Oct. 1994 and Art. 1 (1) of the agreement to the treaty on VAT of 28 Nov. 1994, LGBl (1995) Nos. 30–31. It is the first time that Swiss law is not automatically made applicable in Liechtenstein, but needs to be transformed into Liechtenstein law. Law on VAT, LGBl (1994) No. 84.

121. Art. 1 (3) of the treaty on VAT.

122. Arts. 2 and 3 of the treaty on VAT and Arts. 12 and 13 of the agreement to the treaty on VAT.

123. Art. 8 of the agreement to the treaty on VAT.

124. This decision was based on a verbal agreement with Switzerland and on Liechtenstein laws: LGBl (1920) No. 8 and LGBl (1924) No. 8; see also Raton, *Staat und Geschichte*, p. 79.

125. LGBl (1981) No. 52. The currency treaty came into force on 25 Nov. 1981.

126. Art. 1 (1) of the currency treaty. Liechtenstein may oppose the inclusion of a new Swiss regulation in the annex. The currency treaty does not provide for the application of a treaty concluded by Switzerland with third States: Art. 1 (3).

127. Art. 2 (1) of the currency treaty reads: "Die liechtensteinische Währungshoheit bleibt unberührt."

128. Art. 3 (1) of the currency treaty.

129. Art. 6 (1) and (5) of the currency treaty. The Swiss National Bank may request the Liechtenstein authorities to institute criminal proceedings against Liechtenstein banks, persons, or companies: Art. 6 (2).

130. Art. 13 (1) of the currency treaty. The mixed commission is composed of three Liechtenstein and three Swiss members: Art. 13 (2).

131. Art. 14 of the currency treaty. If the parties do not appoint their arbitrators within two months or if the arbitrators fail to appoint the umpire within three months, the parties may ask the President of the European Court of Human Rights to designate the members of the arbitral tribunal.

132. Art. 15 of the currency treaty.

133. Both agreements replace an earlier treaty of 20 Dec. 1923. The first treaty relates to the sojourn of Swiss and Liechtenstein nationals, LGBl (1963) No. 38, and the second treaty concerns third-State nationals, LGBl (1963) No. 39. The two treaties terminate as soon as the customs union treaty has been terminated: Art. 10 (2) of the treaty on Swiss/Liechtenstein nationals and Art. 11 (2) of the treaty on third-State nationals.

134. Art. 1 (1) of the treaty on Swiss/Liechtenstein nationals. Liechtenstein and Swiss nationals can cross the border with Switzerland without travel documents.

135. Art. 3 (1) of the treaty on Swiss/Liechtenstein nationals. Naturalized Liechtensteinese only receive Swiss residence and work permits if they no longer fall under the Swiss aliens police control or ten years after the naturalization: Art. 3 (2).

136. Exchange of letters between Liechtenstein and Switzerland of 19 Oct. 1981, LGBl (1981) No. 49. The suspension applies reciprocally, but does not affect, *inter alia*, students, cross-border workers, persons working for certain public services, and patients in hospitals and clinics.

137. Art. 3 bis of the treaty on Swiss/Liechtenstein nationals as amended by agreement of 2 Nov. 1994, LGBl (1995) No. 84 (to the exception of police, lawyers, notaries, trustees, and medical professions). See also "Can Liechtenstein's Lawyers Survive the EEA?", 11 *Int'l Fin. Law Review* (1992) pp. 21–24.

138. Joint Swiss/Liechtenstein declaration on the question of equal treatment of 2 Nov. 1994, BA No. 1994/93. The equal treatment applies only once Liechtenstein has decided on extra liberalization after the end of the EEA transitional period.

139. Art. 1 (1) of the treaty on third-State nationals.

140. Art. 2 (b) of the treaty on third-State nationals.

141. Art. 3 of the treaty on third-State nationals.

142. Applications No. 7289/75 and 7349/76, *X and Y v. Switzerland*, D & R 9, pp. 57 ff.

143. Ibid., p. 73.

144. Art. 2 (e) of the treaty on third-State nationals as amended by agreement of 2 Nov. 1994, LGBl (1995) No. 83.

145. Art. 6 of the draft law on land acquisition provides for ownership permits of land, which are granted to Liechtenstein and other EEA nationals if they prove a valid interest in the acquisition, such as the establishment of an enterprise, the exercise of a profession, or for residential purposes, BA No. 118/1992.

146. Art. 44, para. 1 of the Constitution.

147. Art. 44, para. 2 of the Constitution.

148. Raton, *Staat und Geschichte*, p. 165.

149. H. Neumann, *Recueil des Traités et Conventions conclus par l'Autriche*, vol. v, pp. 686–700.

150. Art. IX of the Austro-Liechtenstein customs union treaty.

151. Art. XII of the Austro-Liechtenstein customs union treaty.

152. Raton, *Staat und Geschichte*, p. 177.

153. See also for a further elaboration E. von und zu Liechtenstein, *Liechtensteins Weg von Oesterreich zur Schweiz: eine Rückschau auf meine Arbeit in der Nachkriegszeit 1918–1921* (1945) pp. 169–243.

154. De Martens, *Nouveau Recueil Général de Traités*, vol. xv, p. 630. Liechtenstein promised not to impose customs tariffs on imports to and exports from Austria, whereas Austria applied a most-favored-nation clause to Liechtenstein. As this arrangement proved to be too burdensome for Liechtenstein's exports, it unilaterally introduced its own customs tariffs on 1 Dec. 1921: LGBl (1921) No. 25. The customs agreement with Austria was amended on 30 Dec. 1921 so that the most-favored-nation clause would be used both by Liechtenstein and by Austria: ibid., p. 634.

155. Raton, *Staat und Geschichte*, pp. 80–81. Under this agreement Liechtenstein issued and sold its own stamps and covered the costs of its postal services.

156. Treaty of 19 Jan. 1884, LGBl (1884) No. 8 on the use of Austrian judges in Liechtenstein; treaty of 1 Apr. 1955, LGBl (1956) No. 10 and subsequent treaties on legal cooperation, LGBl (1968) No. 14, LGBl (1983) Nos. 40 and 41.

157. See, for example, on post-doctoral education for Liechtenstein doctors, treaty of 31 Oct. 1980, LGBl (1980) No. 74.

158. Treaties on Social Security of 26 Sept. 1968, LGBl (1969) Nos. 14 and 15, and further LGBl (1974) No. 34, LGBl (1977) Nos. 48 and 63 and LGBl (1987) No. 73.

159. Treaties of 7 Dec. 1955, LGBl (1956) No. 12 and of 5 Nov. 1969, LGBl (1970) No. 37.

160. Border treaty of 1 Sept. 1960, LGBl (1960) No. 19 as amended on 1 March 1991, LGBl (1991) No. 11.

161. *Die Aussenpolitik*, p. 22.

162. N. Jansen, "Liechtenstein und die Vereinte Nationen," 18 *Liechtenstein Wirtschaftsfragen* (1991) p. 18.

163. League of Nations, *Documents of the Assembly* (1920) No. 18.

164. League of Nations, *Reports of the First Assembly, 4th-6th Committee* (1920), Report of the Sub-Committee on the admission of Albania, Austria, Bulgaria, and Liechtenstein (27 Nov. 1920) Annex 2, p. 217.

165. Jansen, "Liechtenstein und die Vereinte Nationen," p. 22.

166. These questions were:

1. Is the application for admission to the League of Nations in order?

2. Is the Government recognized "de jure" or "de facto," and by which States?

3. Does the country possess a stable government and settled frontiers? What are its size and population?

4. Is the country fully self-governing?

5. What has been the conduct of the government including both acts and assurances with regard to:

(1) Its international obligations?

(2) The prescriptions of the League as to armaments?

League of Nations, *Reports of the First Assembly* (1920) p. 217.

167. Ibid.

168. Ibid. It stated: "There can be no doubt that juridically the Principality of Liechtenstein is a sovereign State, but by reason of her very limited area, small population, and her geographical position, she had chosen to depute to others some of the attributes of sovereignty. For instance, she has contracted with other Powers for the control of her Customs, the administration of her Posts, Telegraphs and Telephone Services, for the diplomatic representation of her subjects in foreign countries, other than Switzerland and Austria, and for final decisions in certain judicial cases. Liechtenstein has no army."

169. League of Nations, *Records of the First Assembly, Plenary Meetings* (1920), Annex C, pp. 667–668.

170. Ibid., p. 652.

171. Lanfranconi, *Die Staatsverträge*, p. 77.

172. See also M. M. Gunter. "Liechtenstein and the League of Nations: A Precedent for the United Nations' Ministate Problem?", 28 AJIL (1974) p. 499.

173. League of Nations, *Records of the First Assembly, Plenary Meetings* (1920) p. 563.

174. Ibid.

175. League of Nations, *Records of the First Assembly, 4th-6th Committee* (1920) No. 12, p. 11.

176. Ibid.. p. 217.

177. See also Gunter, "Liechtenstein and the League of Nations," pp. 496–501. *Contra*, defending the juridical validity of the non-independence and lack-of-army arguments: A. Rougier, "La première Assemblée de la Société des Nations (Genève, novembre-décembre 1920)," 28 RGDIP (1921) pp. 230–231 and G. Scelle, "L'Admission des nouveaux Membres de la Société des Nations par l'Assemblée de Genève," 28 RGDIP (1921) pp. 136–137.

178. *Rapport Annuel de la Cour Permanente de Justice Internationale* (1 Jan. 1922–15 Jun. 1925) series E, No. 1, p. 139.

179. *Seizième Rapport de la Cour Permanente de Justice Internationale* (15 Jun. 1939–31 Dec. 1945) series E, No. 16, p. 348.

180. *Gerliczy* case: ibid., pp. 144–148.

181. On 18 Oct. 1939, the President of the Permanent Court of International Justice had fixed the time limits within which the memorials had to be submitted. This term had been extended on 17 Mar. 1940.

182. UN Doc. S/1298 & Corr. 1 (1949) p. 6.

183. UN Doc. S/PV.423 (1949) No. 26, pp. 16–17. The Soviet and Ukrainian delegates abstained from voting.

184. By nine votes to nil with two abstentions (USSR and Ukrainian Soviet Socialist Republic). Report of the Committee of Experts, UN Doc. S/1342 (1949) pp. 2–3.

185. Ibid., p. 3.

186. Ibid.

187. Ibid.

188. UN Doc. S/PV.432 (1949) and UN Doc. A/967 (1949).

189. UN Doc. A/C.6/L47 (1949), also report of the Sixth Committee, UN Doc. A/1054 (1949). Australia and Belgium had submitted a draft resolution in favor of Liechtenstein's application, which was approved by forty-two votes to four with one abstention: UN Doc. A/C.6/5/PV.174 (1949) p. 215.

190. Ibid., p. 214.

191. Ibid.

192. Ibid.

193. Ibid.

194. Ibid., pp. 214–215.

195. GA Res. 363 (IV) of 1 Dec. 1949. Liechtenstein has recognized as compulsory *ipso facto* and without special agreement, in relation to any other State accepting the same obligation, the jurisdiction of the International Court of Justice. Declaration of 29 Mar. 1950 under Art. 36 (2) of the Statute of the ICJ.

196. ICJ Reports (1955) p. 20.

197. Ibid., pp. 13–16.

198. Art. 6 (d) of the 1934 law on nationality, LGBl (1934) No. 1. After having made certain financial contributions, Nottebohm was given dispensation from the condition of three years' residence: ibid., p. 15.

199. Ibid., pp. 25–26.

200. New Art. 6 (d) as amended on 2 Nov. 1960, LGBl (1960) No. 23.

201. M. von Ledebur, "Licht und Schatten über der KSZE," 10 *Liechtenstein Politische Schriften* (1984) p. 183.

202. Liechtenstein was not invited to the second preparatory negotiations organized by the Western European countries. As Liechtenstein objected to this exclusion, it was allowed to re-enter the conferences and thus participated in the Helsinki talks between 1972 and 1975. Interview with HH Prince Hans-Adam II von and zu Liechtenstein of 5 Apr. 1991.

203. Von Ledebur, "Licht und Schatten," pp. 187–188.

204. Ibid., pp. 184–185.

205. As von Ledebur put it: "In Liechtenstein kann man das kleine Modell einer politischen Gemeinschaft erkennen, die ohne Ideologie Arbeiter und Unternehmer, Bürger mit ihren Familien und einem Monarchen in lebendiger Gemeinschaft vereint. Diese Gemeinschaft strahlt, obwohl sie klein ist, wegen ihrer Menschlichkeit und Würde über ihre Grenzen hinaus": ibid., p. 189.

206. Art. 1 (I) of the final resolution of the Madrid Conference concerning the establishment of the CSCE Parliamentary Assembly, 3 Apr. 1991, 30 ILM (1991) pp. 1344 ff.

207. Part III (2) of the Supplementary Document to give effect to certain provisions contained in the Charter of Paris for a New Europe, 30 ILM (1991) p. 220.

208. At the admission of the Czech and Slovak Republics to the CSCE during the Stockholm Council Meeting of Dec. 1992, Liechtenstein made an interpretative statement reminding them that "outstanding issues between the Czech and Slovak Federal Republics and the Czech and the Slovak Republic do encompass nationalization of property of Liechtenstein nationals seized without compensation in the years 1945 and thereafter," in A. Bloed, ed., *The Conference on Security and Co-operation in Europe: Analysis and Basic Documents* (1993) p. 896. At the signing of the free trade agreement between the EFTA countries and Czechoslovakia in Mar. 1992, Liechtenstein expressed its reservations to ratifying the agreement as long as the Czechoslovakian Government refused to modify its position. Liechtenstein's proposals to refer the matter to the ICJ and to make major investments in the Czech and Slovak Republics were rejected: Liechtenstein press release No. 118 of 26 Mar. 1992.

209. N. von Liechtenstein, "Liechtensteins Mitgliedschaft im Europarat," 10 *Liechtenstein Politische Schriften* (1984) p. 197.

210. Ibid., p. 205.

211. At the first parliamentary session as an official observer, Liechtenstein explained its difficulties in collaborating seriously with the Council, as it had such a small delegation. Liechtenstein was allowed to have two parliamentary observers, which was extended to four on 7 Mar. 1975 by adding two substitute members. Council of Europe, *Parliamentary Assembly, Official Report* (22–29 Jan. 1975), vol. III, 23rd Session (3rd part), 16th mtg (22 Jan. 1975) p. 495.

212. Von Liechtenstein, "Liechtensteins Mitgliedschaft," p. 207.

213. Council of Europe Doc. 4139, Res. 78 (23) of 17 Mar. 1978, in Council of Europe, *Parliamentary Assembly, Documents: Working Papers* (24–28 Apr. 1978) vol. I, p. 1.

214. Council of Europe Docs. 4193 and 4211, ibid., vol. III and vol. IV respectively.

215. Council of Europe Doc. 4193, p. 13, adopted by the Committee on 6 Jul. 1978.

216. Ibid., pp. 8 and 10.

217. The rapporteur emphasized, for example, that "[c]olonies, protectorates or other territories which are not independent states are excluded from membership of the ICJ . . . the United Nations recognised Liechtenstein's sovereignty." Ibid. pp. 12–13.

218. Ibid., p. 17.

219. The rapporteur rejected the Status of Associate Member of Article 5 of

the Statute for Liechtenstein, as this membership "implies denial, or at least doubt that an area has the character of a state": ibid., p. 20.

220. Council of Europe Doc. 4211, approved by the Committee on 8 Sept. 1978, and amendments of Doc. 4193.

221. Ibid., pp. 2–6.

222. Ibid., pp. 6–7. Switzerland had also been admitted to the Council at a time when women's right to vote had not yet been introduced in all cantons. Furthermore, excluding Liechtenstein could be counterproductive and could disappoint or discourage Liechtenstein's only women's political organization, which had declared itself in favor of accession.

223. Ibid., pp. 8–9.

224. Letter of 4 Nov. 1977 of the Liechtenstein Head of Government to the Secretary-General of the Council of Europe: ibid., p. 10. See also point 7 of the Assembly's Opinion (28 Sept. 1978), Doc. 4193, p. 2.

225. Interview with HH Prince Hans-Adam II von und zu Liechtenstein of 5 Apr. 1991.

226. Council of Europe Doc. 4211, p. 10.

227. Ibid., p. 12, para. 40.

228. The Committee of Ministers therefore invited Liechtenstein to become a full member of the Council of Europe on 13 Nov. 1978, and its accession to the Council of Europe followed on 23 Nov. 1978. Committee of Ministers Resolution (78) 48 of 13 Nov. 1978. It has two seats on the Parliamentary Assembly.

229. Council of Europe, *Parliamentary Assembly, Official Report* (27 Sept.-5 Oct. 1978) vol. II, 30th Session (2nd part), 11th mtg (28 Sept. 1978) p. 381.

230. Ibid., pp. 382–383.

231. Ibid., pp. 385, 398, and 402.

232. Thus, for example, a British, a Danish, and a Norwegian delegate: ibid., pp. 389, 391, and 396 respectively. In addition, it was argued that Liechtenstein was a tax haven, but this argument was not sustained as an official reason for rejecting its candidature, because Liechtenstein planned to review its fiscal and company laws. This domain was a matter of internal legislation according to the supporters of Liechtenstein's membership: ibid., p. 401.

233. Liechtenstein keeps close contacts with Switzerland and Austria in matters to which it cannot attend itself, due to the smallness of its delegation. Liechtenstein consults with Switzerland or Austria or any other Member State that has particular expertise in the subject concerned. Interview with HH Prince Hans-Adam II von und zu Liechtenstein of 5 Apr. 1991.

234. The founding States of EFTA were Austria, Denmark, Norway, Portugal, Sweden, Switzerland, and the United Kingdom. Text of the Stockholm Convention in EFTA Secretariat, *The European Free Trade Association* (Jun. 1987) pp. 98 ff.

235. Interview with HH Prince Hans-Adam II von und zu Liechtenstein of 5 Apr. 1991.

236. Thus Switzerland lacked the legal power to act for Liechtenstein in certain domains regulated by the Stockholm Convention, such as State subsidies, State enterprises, competition laws, and the establishment of enterprises: Arts. 13–16 of the Stockholm Convention.

237. Art. 8 (1) of the 1923 customs union treaty.

238. Protocol relating to the application of the Convention establishing the European Free Trade Association to the Principality of Liechtenstein: EFTA Secretariat, *The European Free Trade Association* (Jun. 1987) pp. 137–138.

239. European Communities, *Collection of the Agreements concluded by the European Communities*, vol. III (1958–1975) pp. 160–161 for the Additional Agreement between the EEC, Switzerland and Liechtenstein of 22 Jul. 1972, and vol. V (1952–1975) pp. 351–352 for the Additional Agreement between the Members of the ECSC, Switzerland and Liechtenstein of 22 Jul. 1972. Supplementary Protocols with Greece of 17 Jul. 1980, LGBl (1989) No. 23 and with Portugal and Spain of 14 Jul. 1986 extending the ECSC-Switzerland-Liechtenstein free trade Agreement of 22 Jul. 1972 to the new ECSC members. The free trade Agreements with the European Communities were only applicable to Liechtenstein for as long as the customs union treaty with Switzerland of 1923 remained in force: Art. 3 of both additional Agreements of 22 Jul. 1972.

240. Art. 2 of both additional Agreements of 22 Jul. 1972.

241. The Liechtenstein observer within the Swiss delegation to the Joint Committees could not take any initiatives, impose sanctions, or terminate the free trade Agreement, for he had no right to vote. W. B. Gyger, *Das Fürstentum Liechtenstein und die Europäische Gemeinschaft* (1975) part 4, p. 96.

242. BA No. 56/1990, p. 17.

243. Ibid., p. 18.

244. BA No. 81/1990, p. 4.

245. An agreement on Art. 8 bis was signed on 26 Nov. 1990, ratified and entered into force on 28 Aug. 1991.

246. Annex 3 to BA No. 43/91. Liechtenstein officially acceded to the Stockholm Convention on 1 Sept. 1991. As a consequence, the Protocol of 4 Jan. 1960 is no longer valid: Point V of the Council decision of 22 Mar. 1991.

247. Art. 32 (5) of the Stockholm Convention.

248. Art. 31 of the Stockholm Convention.

249. The referendum held on 11–13 Dec. 1992 showed 55.81 percent in favor of and 44.19 percent against the EEA Agreement, BA No. 147/1992.

250. Art. 121 (b) of the EEA Agreement. Text in ECOJ No. L 1 (3.1.94) pp. 3 ff.

251. ECOJ No. L 1 (3.1.94) pp. 572 ff.

252. Art. 1 (2) of the Protocol adjusting the EEA Agreement. Before the entry into force of the EEA Agreement for Liechtenstein, the Principality was already allowed to participate in the decisions of the EEA Council: Art. 1 (3).

253. Protocols Nos. 5, 6, 8, 9, 15, and 16: Arts. 9–14 of the Protocol adjusting the EEA Agreement.

254. Declarations Nos. 2, 14, and 33 to the EEA Agreement: Final Act of the diplomatic conference, EC Doc. AF/EEE/f, ad II.

255. Protocols adjusting the EFTA Agreement on the Establishment of a Surveillance Authority and a Court of Justice, the Agreement on a Standing Committee of the EFTA States and the Agreement on a Committee of Members of Parliament of the EFTA States. See H. Frennered, "The Protocols Adjusting the EEA Agreement and the EFTA Agreements," *EFTA Bulletin* (1993) No. 2, pp. 9–11.

256. Point 4 of the EEA Council decision of 20 Dec. 1994, Press release No. 280–G. EEA 1610/94.

257. After a second referendum of 7–9 Apr. 1995 approving by 55.9 percent Liechtenstein's participation in the EEA, BA No. 14/1995 and pursuant to the decision of the EEA Council No. 1/95 of 10 Mar. 1995, ECOJ No. L 86 (20.4.95) p. 58.

258. Liechtenstein's nominal Gross National Product in 1988 was 1,700 million Swiss francs against total industrial exports of 2,417 million Swiss francs. The latter figure does account for net exports, which explains the gap between Gross National Product and total exports. *Statistisches Jahrbuch 1994*, pp. 110 and 192.

259. In 1987, 39.3 percent of total exports were sent to EC countries against 45.4 percent in 1991 and 41.6 percent in 1993. Exports to Switzerland and other EFTA countries have decreased in percentage terms in the same period. Figures calculated on the basis of *Statistisches Jahrbuch 1994*, p. 192.

260. Commentary to the EEA Agreement, BA No. 46/92, p. 238.

261. Art. 28 (1) of the EEA Agreement.

262. Art. 9 (1) of Protocol 15 to the EEA Agreement.

263. Art. 9 (2) of Protocol 15 to the EEA Agreement. This point has been confirmed by express declaration of the EEA Council of 20 Dec. 1994.

264. Art. 112 (1) of the EEA Agreement.

265. The declaration of 2 May 1992 concerns especially the residence of foreigners and the foreign ownership of lands. Declaration by the Liechtenstein Government on the country's special situation, Annex 1 to BA No. 46/92, p. 1016. There were no objections raised by the other States Parties to this interpretative declaration.

266. Art. 31 (1) of the EEA Agreement.

267. BA No. 46/92, pp. 84 and 94.

268. The indicative factor, according to Liechtenstein's unilateral declaration to Art. 112 of the EEA Agreement, is an exceptional increase in the number of jobs. Ibid., p. 85.

269. BA No. 1994/93, p. 5.

270. Art. 36 (1) of the EEA Agreement.

271. BA No. 46/92, pp. 94–96. By virtue of EC Regulation No. 91/308, ECOJ No. L 166/77 (28 Jun. 1991), which is part of the *acquis communautaire* and has to be taken over by the EFTA countries, a State's financial system should not be used for money laundering. Liechtenstein has therefore provided for the penalization of actions which obstruct inquiry into the legal origins of money. LGBl (1993) No. 6. See also A. Batliner and R. J. Proksch, "Changes on the Way for Liechtenstein Banks?", 10 *Int'l Fin. Law Review* (1991) pp. 28–29.

272. Arts. 40 ff. of the EEA Agreement.

273. BA No. 118/1992, p. 10.

274. BA No. 46/92, p. 125.

275. Art. 113 of the EEA Agreement provides for consultations in the common EEA Commission aimed at withdrawing the protective measures as soon as possible or limiting their effects.

276. BA No. 92/1992, p. 16.

277. Ibid., p. 5.

278. Ibid., p. 13.

279. See Gyger, *Das Fürstentum Liechtenstein*, pp. 112–113.

280. BA No. 92/1992, p. 15.

281. Art. 112 (1) of the EEA Agreement provides for protective measures in case of serious economic, social, or ecological difficulties. Art. 226 of the EC Treaty can be invoked in case of serious economic problems but only in the transitional period, whereas Arts. 223 and 224 are related to national security and war difficulties.

282. Ibid.

283. ILC Yearbook (1964) vol. II, p. 15.

284. ILC Yearbook (1964) vol. I, pp. 53–54, paras. 2 and 8.

285. Ibid., p. 53, para. 6 and p. 54. para. 9.

286. Ibid., p. 63, para. 35 (Conclusion of the Special Rapporteur).

287. "Das Recht des Fürstentums Liechtenstein, *selbst Vertragsstaat* [emphasis added] . . . zu werden." Same formula in Art. 6 (1) of the postal union treaty and Art. 8 bis (1) of the customs union treaty.

288. See C. Chinkin, *Third Parties in International Law* (1993) pp. 32–33 and P. Reuter, *Introduction to the Law of Treaties* (1989) pp. 73–76.

289. This position is confirmed by the European Commission of Human Rights with regard to acts of the Swiss Aliens Office with effect in Liechtenstein: Applications No. 7289/75 and 7349/76, *X and Y v. Switzerland*, D & R 9, pp. 57 ff.

290. By virtue of Art. 7 and Annex III of the 1994 agreement to the 1923 customs union treaty, Switzerland takes certain administrative measures by order of Liechtenstein.

291. BA No. 41/1989, p. 3.

292. Interview with HH Prince Hans-Adam II von and zu Liechtenstein of 5 Apr. 1991. An unofficial student opinion poll showed that in 1988 66.3 percent of the Liechtensteinese were against United Nations membership, with 26.3 percent in favor, and 7.4 percent undecided: M. Beck et al., *Die Vereinten Nationen–Ein Thema für Liechtenstein* (1988) p. 78.

293. The possibility of a referendum on treaties instead of laws was not provided for in the Constitution. Arts. 8 and 66 of the Constitution were examined by two legal experts, an Austrian and a Swiss, who came to opposite conclusions as to whether the Constitution permitted a referendum on a treaty. A people's initiative for a referendum on the United Nations membership was rejected by the Diet. Interview with HH Prince Hans-Adam II von and zu Liechtenstein of 5 Apr. 1991.

294. *Landtags-Protokolle* (1989) vol. V, *Oeffentliche Landtagssitzung* (13/14 Dec. 1989) p. 1589.

295. Arguments cited in the Diet, *Landtags-Protokolle* (1989) vol. V, *Oeffentliche Landtagssitzung* (13/14 Dec. 1989) p. 1575.

296. BA No. 41/1989.

297. Ibid., p. 7.

298. UN Doc. S/21486 (1990).

299. UN Doc. S/PV.2935 (1990).

300. UN Doc. S/21506 (1990).

301. SC Res. 663 (1990) and UN Doc. A/45/419 (1990).

302. UN Doc. S/PV.2936 (1990) pp. 3 and 6, United Kingdom and Finnish delegates respectively.

303. Ibid., p. 7.

304. Ibid., p. 12.

305. UN Doc. S/PV.2936 (1990) pp. 7–8.

306. GA Res. 45/1 and UN Doc. A/45/PV.1 (1990) p. 23.

307. Ibid.

308. Austrian delegate: ibid., p. 33. Also Sri Lanka, p. 27 and Hungary, pp. 28–30.

309. Liechtenstein had been admitted to the ECE in a consultative capacity on 30 Mar. 1976: Decision by the ECE M (XXXI) of 30 Mar. 1976, UN Doc. E/5781, E/ECE/909, ECOSOC OR (25 Apr. 1975–9 Apr. 1976) Suppl. No. 8, pp. 93 and 106. In 1993, total costs of UN membership amounted to 1,784,966 Swiss francs: "Voranschlag 1995," Annex to BA No. 66/1994.

310. UN Doc. A/48/147 and Add.1 (1993), A/50/492 (1995) and Memorandum (not published).

311. In this spirit: Ghana, India, Indonesia, Iraq, Kenya, and Malaysia, UN Doc. A/C.3/48/SR.21–22 (1993).

312. Armenia proposed to charge the Trusteeship Council or a special committee of the Security Council with this matter, whereas Ecuador thought the Sixth Committee would be more competent to formulate legal answers to present-day self-determination questions: ibid., pp. 4–5.

313. Liechtenstein is presently developing the initiative further within an academic rather than political framework. The Prince of Liechtenstein has given a grant to Princeton University's Woodrow Wilson School of Public and International Affairs to establish a research program on self-determination. Information from the Permanent Mission of the Principality of Liechtenstein to the UN.

314. Information from the Permanent Mission of the Principality of Liechtenstein to the UN. It also protested against the violations of humanitarian law in the former Yugoslavia, UN Doc. S/1387 (1994).

315. Jansen, "Liechtenstein und die Vereinte Nationen," p. 29. LGBl (1962) No. 22.

316. The Liechtenstein Government has granted a concession for the establishment of "Radio L": BA No. 63/1994.

317. Jansen, "Liechtenstein und die Vereinte Nationen," pp. 31–32.

318. LGBl (1969) No. 44. It ratified the Treaty on the Non-Proliferation of Nuclear Weapons on 20 Apr. 1978, following Switzerland's ratification of 9 Mar. 1977.

319. IAEA Doc. GOV/1268 (18 Apr. 1968) and IAEA Doc. GOV/OR.404 (13 Jun. 1968) p. 8, paras. 35–36.

320. IAEA Doc. GC (XII) OR.119 (24 Sept. 1968) p. 3, paras. 21–28.

321. Ibid., para. 28.

322. LGBl (1972) No. 25.

323. Point 3 of the Protocol of accession, 570 UNTS (1966) No. 814, p. 276.

324. BA No. 1994/23, p. 4. Acceptance as an "original Member" under Art. XIV of the WTO Agreement, 33 ILM (1994), pp. 1144 ff.

325. This amounts to 3.6 million Swiss francs, of which 70 percent is in the

form of a guarantee. It has one seat in the Council of Governors and one seat in the Executive Board shared with Switzerland and Turkey. BA No. 84/90, p 9.

326. Ibid.

327. Status as of 31 Dec. 1993, calculated on the basis of the figures represented in *Statistisches Jahrbuch 1994*, p. 192.

328. *Nottebohm* case, ICJ Reports (1955) p. 20.

329. Amelunxen notes on this subject that the actual Liechtenstein conscious-ness of its nationhood was born out of the confrontation with Germany in 1939 when the Liechtenstein people became aware that they did not constitute a part of the German nor of the Swiss nation: C. Amelunxen, "Schwierige Vaterländer-Aspekte der liechtensteinisch-deutschen Beziehungen in Vergangenheit und Gegen-wart," 2 *Liechtenstein Politische Schriften* (1973) p. 60.

PART II

Refining the Small State Debate

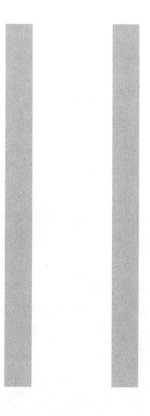

5

WEAK STATES IN THE INTERNATIONAL SYSTEM

MICHAEL HANDEL

Introduction

The studies of modern diplomatic history and the theories of international relations have usually been based on the relations among the great powers: Britain, France, Prussia/Germany, Russia, and the United States. The available works are already exhaustive, but the output continues.[1] The study of the weak states, on the other hand, has been sorely neglected. This work is an attempt to look at the international system through the eyes and experiences of the weak states.

Methodologically, I have focused my attention at the level of analysis referred to by Kenneth Waltz as the "third image"[2] and by Graham Allison as the "rational actor" model (model 1).[3] The "third image" concentrates on the primacy of the international system for determining foreign policy. The "rational actor" model assumes that states are unitary, purposive, value-maximizing calculators.

While most of the existing theories of international relations can be readily applied to the behavior of weak states in the international system, the overall weakness of these states must be taken into account. Although the differences between the constraints which affect weak and powerful states can be overemphasized, several distinctions are important.

Domestic determinants of foreign policy are less salient in weak states. The international system leaves them less room for choice in the decision-making process. Their smaller margin of error and hence greater preoccupation with survival makes the essential interests of weak states less

From Michael Handel, *Weak States in the International System* (London, UK: Frank Cass, 1981). Reprinted with permission of Taylor & Francis Books UK. Cross references to pages and notes refer to the original publication.

ambiguous. Kenneth Waltz's "third image" is therefore a most relevant level of analysis.

Moreover, because of the reduced scale of complexity of bureaucratic and decision-making structures of weak states, there are *usually* fewer bureaucratic influences on foreign policy making, which makes Allison's "rational actor" model more appropriate.

Therefore it has been suggested that "the most obvious fact about small powers is that their foreign policy is governed by the policy of others. It follows that the student of small power policy, even more than the student of great power policy, must concentrate on the environment in which his subject exists."[4]

The available studies of weak states in international relations employ two basic methodological approaches. One is a "horizontal section," namely an attempt to develop general theories for the position and conduct of weak states in the international system. The other is a "vertical section," an in-depth study of the foreign policy of one (or a few) weak state(s) in a given period of history. This work comes closer to the first category, attempting to find some general insights and observations on the behavior and position of the weak states in international relations.

Each method has its advantages and disadvantages. The more general the theory, the greater the number of countries that must be taken into account. But the more countries studied, the less the possibility of achieving a deep and meaningful analysis of each specific case. Whatever is gained on the theoretical level might result in the loss of richness in detail. Samuel Huntington referred to the same problem in *The Soldier and the State* as follows: ". . . understanding requires theory; theory requires abstraction; and abstraction requires the simplification and ordering of reality."[5] On the other hand, even if one were to exhaust the literature on any given country, one would surely reach the point of diminishing returns because so much of the information is repetitive and so little new knowledge can be gained.

In this work, I have attempted to analyze all the available theoretical literature on weak states in international relations, as well as to look into as many case studies as possible. Many of the theories in this growing body of literature can be accepted, but a sizeable number must be rejected, since they generalize too much from unique cases. Too many generalizations are also made for a given historical period and then cavalierly applied to another.

The historical period and the structure of the international system in which the position of weak states is examined are of great importance. The position of the weak European countries for most of the nineteenth century (excluding the Napoleonic wars and Prussia's war with Denmark) was relatively secure, while the weak states *outside* the European system had to face the dangers of European imperialistic policies and very often could not maintain their independence. Although the weak European countries were not recognized as equal until the end of the First World War, and most of the important decisions in international politics were made by the Concert of Europe and later the great powers, the actual existence of the weak states was rarely at stake. During the decade or so that preceded the First World War, the competition among the great powers for the allegiance of the weak states considerably enhanced the bargaining power and maneuverability of the latter. After the First World War the position of the weak states further improved, as they achieved almost complete formal-legal equality in the League of Nations, while at the same time the great powers grew weaker.

The rise of the revisionist powers in the 1930s, however, marked the lowest point in the security of the weak states since the Napoleonic wars. Their security and very survival were directly threatened and many predicted their disappearance. This trend continued after the Second World War and at the beginning of the Cold War as the great powers—especially the USSR—tried to establish control over what they regarded as their spheres of influence. On the other hand, most of the African and Asian states have freed themselves from the grip of the powers and considerably improved their position vis-à-vis the great powers, a process which continues today.

It is therefore possible to distinguish between cycles of security or insecurity, influence or impotence of the weak states in the international system. The position and relative security of any weak state must be gauged in terms of the specific international system in which it is operating.[6]

A further impediment to arriving at more general pronouncements on the position and behavior of weak states in the international system is that, even at the same period in history, weak states located in different areas have different neighbors and thus face different problems. This indicates the central importance of the geographical location of weak states. Therefore, studies of Finland, Czechoslovakia, Belgium, Poland, Hungary, and Israel stress problems of survival and vulnerability, while works on Portugal, New Zealand, Chile, and even Switzerland and Sweden emphasize their relative safety and capacity to hold their own against the powers.

In like manner, two basic approaches are evident in the theoretical discussions on weak states. One stresses their preoccupation with problems of survival and their limited freedom of maneuver. The other approach tends to inflate the influence of the weak states out of proportion to their real power. On the whole, I find myself taking a position somewhere in between the two. Weak states have not disappeared *en masse* as Treitschke and his followers and some social Darwinists predicted in the last quarter of the nineteenth century.[7] But neither can the weak states ever afford to relax their vigilance on matters of security, nor bask in the protection and good will of the powers. Even more than the powerful, the weak must be continuously on the alert. Any error in judgment can be fatal, "as those who are weak hang on a single turn of the scale."[8]

In fact, very few weak states have disappeared from the international scene during the last century. Weak states have demonstrated a remarkable capacity to survive despite all the dangers they faced due to their lack of power. The worst "enemy" of the weak states has been national unifications, such as in Germany and Italy. This process accounts for the "disappearance" of most of the weak states. When Karl Haushofer predicted the disappearance of the small countries, he recommended that they unify with the larger states: ". . . we may say that small states have a constantly decreasing chance of independent survival."[9] During the First and Second World Wars many weak states were temporarily occupied but they re-emerged after the war. Since the end of the First World War, but especially after the Second, the number of weak independent states has grown continuously. In the twentieth century, the only weak states which have disappeared are the Baltic States. Others, such as the East European States after the Second World War, and perhaps Finland, have lost much of their freedom of action in the international system, as well as much of their freedom to determine their own internal affairs. Having retained their national framework and cohesion as separate political entities, however, they can at least maintain the hope of regaining complete independence sometime in the future.

In this book, I have attempted to present a balanced account not only of the weaknesses and vulnerability of weak states, but also of the positive capabilities which they can develop to compensate for their deficiencies, i.e., those conditions under which their security is endangered and those under which it is enhanced. Many of the problems faced by the weak are also, to a lesser extent, shared by the more powerful. It must be remembered that if weakness and strength were *absolute* rather than *relative*, and fixed rather than dynamic qualities, the result of each conflict and collision of interests between weak and powerful states would always end in favor of might. For, as Professor Schelling has observed,

"Bargaining power," "bargaining strength," "bargaining skill" suggest that the advantage goes to the powerful, the strong, or the skillful. It does, of course, if those qualities are defined to mean only that negotiations are won by those who win. But, if the terms imply that it is an advantage to be more intelligent or more skilled in debate, or to have more financial resources, more physical strength, more military potency, or more ability to withstand losses, then the term does a disservice. These qualities are by no means universal advantages in bargaining situations; they often have a contrary value.[10]

Given the broad scope of this book, there were certain subjects in the field which could justify a whole study on their own, such as guerrilla warfare as the weapon of the weak, the position of weak states in regional integration projects, the role of multinational corporations in weak states, etc. Rather than treat them superficially, I preferred to leave them to other times, or other hands.

Notes

1. Italy, Japan, and other states could be added to the list. It is tempting to suggest that the number of books, articles, monographs, and other publications devoted to a given state, at different periods in history, can serve as a quantitative indicator to its power, rank, and position in the international hierarchy and to the impact of a state on the international system.

For example, the literature on the Habsburg Empire's foreign policy during the nineteenth century and up to the outbreak of the First World War is voluminous. The literature on Austrian foreign policy since the end of the First World War is quite limited. The works on Mussolini's foreign policy are quite extensive, whereas the literature on post-Second World War Italian foreign policy is minimal. The research on Germany's foreign policy on the eve of the First World War or on Hitler's foreign policy cannot be read by a single researcher; the literature on the Weimar Republic's foreign policy, a low point in German power, can easily be read by anyone.

2. Kenneth N. Waltz, *Man, the State and War* (New York: Columbia University Press, 1968), pp. 159–186.

3. Graham T. Allison, *Essence of Decision* (Boston: Little, Brown & Co., 1971), pp. 10–38.

4. Quoted in J. E. Spence, *Republic Under Pressure: A Study of South African Foreign Policy* (London: Oxford University Press, 1967), p. 6. See also Richard Kennaway, *New Zealand's Foreign Policy 1951–1971* (Wellington: Hicks Smith, 1972), pp. 153–155.

5. Samuel P. Huntington, *The Soldier and the State* (New York: Vintage Books, 1969), p. vii.

6. For an interesting analysis of historical international systems, see Richard

N. Rosecrance, *Action and Reaction in International Politics* (Boston: Little, Brown & Co., 1963) and Kyung-Won Kim, *Revolution and the International System* (New York: New York University Press, 1970). However, both concentrate mainly on the position and interrelationship of the great powers.

7. See, for example, Gertrude Himmelfarb, *Darwin and the Darwinian Revolution* (New York: Norton, 1968), pp. 412–431; also Richard Hofstadter, *Social Darwinism in American Thought* (Boston: Beacon Press, 1971), pp. 170–200.

8. Thucydides, *The History of the Peloponnesian War* (New York: E. P. Dutton, 1950), p. 405.

9. Karl Haushofer, quoted in Andreas Dorpalen, *The World of General Haushofer: Geopolitics in Action* (Port Washington, N.Y.: Kennikat Press, 1966): "Small Countries have no Right to Exist," p.220.

10. Thomas C. Schelling, *The Strategy of Conflict* (New York: Oxford University Press, 1969), p. 22.

The Economic Position of the Weak
States in the International System

Most theoretical studies of weak states in international relations are strictly political and military.[1] Such economic studies as exist rarely include any political-military analyses. This is not surprising, for to analyze the economic position of the weak states in the context of a basically political-military study is a very difficult task. In addition to the interdisciplinary problems, the enormous amount of existing research on international trade, primary commodities, markets for raw materials, and economic theory would have to be mastered. It would be a mistake, however, to perpetuate the unnatural separation between the economic and the political and military spheres, which are closely interrelated in reality. Without pretending to undertake an exhaustive or innovative analysis, this chapter will summarize some of the economic problems involved in the relations between the weak and strong states, and will relate them to the subject matter of the preceding chapters.

Some of the most important events in international politics in 1973–74 have been based in economics. For example, OAPEC (Organization of Arab Petroleum Exporting Countries) has placed a successful oil embargo on Western Europe, Japan, and the United States. Weak states that export other raw materials, such as copper, tin, bauxite, rubber, and coffee, have been considering similar measures to improve their terms of trade.[2] These activities have demonstrated the growing importance of the economic dimension in the relations between the weak, less developed countries (LDCs) and the economically powerful states, as well as between other states and groups of states, such as the United States and the EEC.

The growing reluctance of the great powers to use their superior military might against the weak states and among themselves has shifted conflict between states to the economic arena and has emphasized, perhaps more than ever before, the economic dimension of international relations.[3] As a result, the question can be raised whether the relative distribution of strength and therefore the relationship between some of the weak states and the great powers has not changed radically in favor of the weak states.

So far in modern history, the great powers in political and military terms have also been the great powers economically. They could take advantage of their military superiority to improve their economic position vis-à-vis the weak states. They did so by directly controlling the economies of the weak states through their imperialistic and colonial policies; by exploiting special trade relations with less developed countries dependent on their markets (examples are Germany's dominant trade position in the Danubian and Balkan states between the two World Wars, and Great Britain's and France's trade relations with their former colonies, often referred to as neo-colonialism); by explicit or veiled threats of military intervention; by raising the specter of economic sanctions, and later by threatening to withhold positive economic rewards such as loans, financial aid, and private investments.

But now a new breed of states seems to be appearing, states that are militarily weak and technologically underdeveloped but economically strong. Saudi Arabia, Libya, Kuwait, and Iran combine enormous capital revenues with relatively small populations and basically "finite," limited domestic economies which cannot absorb the enormous capital revenues accumulated. Because these "capital surpluses" cannot be invested at home, they must be invested abroad.

Between 1974 and 1977 OPEC countries invested 162 billion dollars in foreign countries. See Table 5.1.

For the first time, relatively weak states (in military and political terms) can grant or withhold enormous financial aid and investments, and they can also finance military purchases on the scale of the great powers. For the first time, states which were hitherto considered weak have offered rewards to other countries that will support their causes and have thus carved out their own little spheres of influence.[4]

For the first time, then, the "highest stage of imperialism" is working in reverse. The very large surpluses of capital accumulated by the rich oil-exporting countries are being invested in modern industrialized countries, yielding higher profits. Although Hobson's and Lenin's theories of economic imperialism do not accurately describe the behavior of the industrialized great powers, they may, ironically, prove to be true for some of

TABLE 5.1 OPEC foreign investment 1974–1977

Investment	%	Billion $
Eurodollar and other Banking Deposits	63.82	39.4
Bilateral Lending	46.33	28.6
Investments	24.78	15.3
U.S. Government Securities	15.22	9.4
Lending to International Organizations	9.88	6.1
U.S. Bank Deposits	6.64	4.1
British Government Securities	1.94	1.2

NOTE: Figures are rounded-off; therefore totals exceed 100% and 162 billion dollars.

SOURCE: *The Economist*, June 10, 1978, pp. 87–88.

the *nouveaux riches* countries. A new class of states seems to be emerging in Arabian deserts—"coupon-clipping sheikdoms," to paraphrase Lenin. Such countries will be able to manipulate and disrupt the monetary system of the industrial Western World, and speculate against the currency of any of the great powers.

Can these militarily weak but economically strong states translate their newly acquired economic power into political power? If so, under what conditions? Will their circle be joined by other weak states that do not produce oil, or will it remain an exclusive club of the oil-producing countries? Are the oil-producing countries economically *sui generis*? Under what conditions will their bargaining position be strengthened or weakened? What are the limits to their strength? How vulnerable are they now, in spite of their growing economic might?

Many of the new problems in international economics defy conventional economic wisdom, for they involve highly complicated political, social, and psychological factors. It seems that international economics, at least concerning the relations between the developed and underdeveloped states, has reached a turning point. The definitions of economically weak and strong states are in flux, and it is difficult to predict the focus of future relations between the developed and the underdeveloped states. Therefore the questions raised above can be answered only speculatively. It may well be that many earlier theories of international trade, which were based on the economic relations between the developed and underdeveloped states, will be of little value in understanding international economic developments and may even be misleading. For the present, the best that one can do is to look at the relations between the economically weak and strong states in the light of traditional economic theory.

SOURCES OF ECONOMIC WEAKNESS

According to traditional economic theory, a state's territorial size and the size of its domestic market play important roles in determining its economic strength and viability. Economic logic is based on the assumption that all other things being equal (i.e., all states being on the same general level of economic development), the state with a large area and population has an advantage over the small one. Territorially small states are less likely to have diverse and balanced sources of raw materials, and because of climatic uniformity they tend to have a smaller variety of agricultural products.[5]

> There is . . . the possibility that a large geographical size would, other conditions given, connote a richer supply base, and if the supply base is also rich from a potential point of view so that there is a large gap between the actual levels of utilization of resources and their potential supply, a large population might connote the possibility of higher incomes and hence of a larger-sized market. Other conditions given, if resources are abundant in relation to population, productivity levels can potentially rise, and the economy has considerable scope of expansion, the process having increasing returns.[6]

Economically weak states, which frequently produce only a limited number of products, are sometimes referred to as one-dimensional states.[7] It has been found by economists that the "smaller the country . . . the stronger is the concentration in production and exports."[8] This high concentration on one-commodity production is illustrated by the export patterns of Latin American countries and African states, as summarized in Tables 5.2 and 5.3.

> The developing countries are heavily dependent on primary products for most of their exports: currently 88 percent of their export earnings are derived from primary product sales. Furthermore, these exports are concentrated on a narrow range of products: almost one half of these countries depend on one commodity for more than 50 percent of their total exports and as many as three-quarters derive more than 60 percent of their

total exports from three primary commodities. As a result, the export earnings of the developing countries, with their crucial influence on import capacity and development potential, are heavily dependent on the prices and trading opportunities prevailing in world commodity markets.[9]

Because of this situation, many LDCs are more vulnerable to political pressures from the states that purchase their products (usually the great powers). Their sensitivity to price fluctuations and political pressures varies directly with the demand for their products and the number of countries competing for them in the international markets.

This can be demonstrated by the following table:

TABLE 5.2 Relation between size of country
(population, GNP) and country export concentration

Groups of Countries			
Countries Ranked in Increasing Order of Population Size (Quartiles)	*Number of Countries*	*Average Population (millions)*	*Median Country Export Concentration*
I	20	2.04	55.5
II	20	6.02	42.1
III	20	13.33	40.7
IV	20	74.01	33.1
Countries Ranked in Increasing Order of GNP Size (Quartiles)	*Number of Countries*	*Average GNP ($ billions)*	*Median Country Export Concentration*
I	19	0.405	50.6
II	19	1.35	41.0
III	19	3.48	40.7
IV	20	51.69	31.9

SOURCE: Nadim G. Khalaf, *Economic Implications of the Size of Nations* (Leiden: E. J. Brill, 1971), p. 82.

TABLE 5.3 Percent commodity share
in country total export by value, 1965 (for African states)

Country	Product	Percent	Year (other than 1965)
Algeria	Petroleum (oil)	51.1	
Burundi	Coffee	73.9	
C.A.R. (Central African Republic)	Diamonds	53.8	
Congo (Brazzaville)	Diamonds	42.7	30.1% (1968) registered
	Wood	38.9	50.1% (1968) exports
Ethiopia	Coffee	66.5	
Ghana	Cocoa	61.0	(1970)
Guinea	Bauxite	45.7	(1964)
Ivory Coast	Coffee	37.8	
Kenya	Coffee	22.3	(1970)
	Tea	12.7	(1970)
Liberia	Iron ore	72.5	(1964)
Libya	Petroleum (oil)	99.4	
Malagasy	Coffee	31.5	
Mauritania	Iron ore	95.1	
Nigeria	Petroleum (oil)	57.1	(1970)
	Cocoa	15.0	(1970)
Rwanda	Coffee	50.5	
Senegal	Peanuts	37.3	
	Wood	27.0	
Sierra Leone	Diamonds	60.0	(1970)
Sudan	Cotton	46.5	
UAR	Cotton	44.5	
Uganda	Coffee	59.0	(1970)
Zaire	Copper	60.0	(1968)
Zambia	Copper	97.0	(1970)

SOURCE: Henry L. Bretton, *Power and Politics in Africa* (Chicago: Aldine Publishing Co., 1973), p. 26.

Since their products are less diversified, the economically weak states have little chance to achieve autarky.[10] They depend on foreign trade for many of the goods necessary for their development and improvement in their standard of living. The rich country can with little effort supply a poor country with implements for agriculture or the chase which doubled the

TABLE 5.4 Latin America's exports (1959)

Country	Primary Export	Producing % Export Earnings of Total	Second Export	% by Both
Argentina	Meat	26	Wheat	39
Bolivia	Tin	62	Lead	71
Brazil	Coffee	58	Cacao	64
Chile	Copper	66	Nitrates	76
Colombia	Coffee	77	Oil	92
Costa Rica	Coffee	51	Bananas	86
Cuba	Sugar	77	Tobacco	83
Dominican Rep.	Sugar	48	Cacao	65
Ecuador	Bananas	57	Coffee	75
El Salvador	Coffee	72	Cotton	88
Guatemala	Coffee	72	Bananas	85
Haiti	Coffee	63	Sisal	80
Honduras	Bananas	51	Coffee	70
Mexico	Cotton	25	Coffee	36
Nicaragua	Cotton	39	Coffee	73
Panama	Bananas	69	Cacao	72
Paraguay	Wood pulp	24	Meat	46
Peru	Cotton	23	Sugar	38
Uruguay	Wool	54	Meat	68
Venezuela	Oil	92	Iron ore	98

Latin American Average export earnings:
from one item: 55.3%   from two: 70.3%

SOURCE: John Gerassi, *The Great Fear in Latin America* (New York: Collier Books, 1973), p. 32.

effectiveness of her labor, and which she could not make for herself; while the rich country could without great trouble make for herself most of the things which she purchased from the poor nation or at all events could get fairly good substitutes for them. A stoppage of the trade would therefore generally cause much more real loss to the poor than to the rich nation.[11]

It is not surprising that on the whole the ratio of foreign trade to GNP is higher for the small and economically weak states than for the great powers.

... the smaller is the country the larger is the proportion of its exports to its total output. This renders a small country especially vulnerable to changes in its exports, first, because a given percentage change in exports means a relatively large change in the market for its products; and secondly, because the balance of payments deficit, if one comes into being with a decline in exports, is relatively larger. . . .[12]

The generally high foreign trade (or export) proportions that often characterize small countries are unusually sensitive to fluctuations in their foreign trade. Any shift in demand for their exports will mean, because of the high proportion of exports to national income, a relatively large proportionate change in the demand for the country's total product. . . . The unavailability of abundant and diversified resources and a limited domestic market obstruct a small country's capacity to accommodate sudden changes in demand for its products.[13]

A small state has already been defined economically

. . . as one which, while depending comparatively heavily upon foreign trade both for supplies and sales markets, makes only a modest contribution to the aggregate flow of international trade.[14]

Marshall Singer has suggested that

. . . if more than 20 percent of the G.D.P. of any country is accounted for by foreign trade (as was the case in more than two thirds of all the countries in the world in 1967), at least the monetized sector of that country's economy can be considered dependent on foreign trade.[15]

Not only do the economically weak states produce a narrow range of products and export a high percentage of their GNP, but very frequently they export to relatively few states. This means that they often become dependent on the good will of one great power, and thus a single state can have an extraordinary impact on their economic well-being. Marshall Singer has suggested that

. . . if more than one third of . . . [a] country's total trade is with just one Power . . . then clearly any decisions—public or private—made in the more powerful country that relate to the foreign trade of the weaker could have a profound effect on the economic well-being of the weaker; and thus the weaker could legitimately be considered economically dependent upon the stronger.[16]

Such a situation enables a great power to extract political support (such as votes in the UN or military bases) from an economically weak state in return for continuing economic support. The strong power can also exploit the economic dependence of the weak state to "retard" its economic development. For example, the great power may encourage the weak state to concentrate on the production of primary commodities, or may refuse to import from it anything but primary commodities. Although trade relations between an economically strong and an economically weak, less developed state usually do not reflect a conscious design on the part of the strong state to retard or contain the development of the weak, this is often the result. Many states, especially in Latin America and Africa, fear a "deliberately planned," conspiratorial development of dependency ("Dependencia") on a great power's economy.[17]

In the 1930s, Germany's trade policy toward the Danubian and Balkan states was aimed at limiting production in its weak trading partners to primary commodities.[18] Later, it was Nazi Germany's deliberate policy to gain an economically dominant position in southeastern Europe and finally to use its economic bargaining position to exact political and economic concessions. The Germans achieved this by offering higher prices for primary commodities than other states. Though the weak states were aware of the dangers involved, they decided to opt for economic gain rather than economic security.[19]

> ... Germany was ready to trade with Hungary and Yugoslavia and Roumania; and to countries still wallowing in the wake of the Depression, a Great Power which was prepared to modify its economic policy to their benefit was a more attractive partner than a Great Power which talked only of security and the need to preserve the European Order [France]. A secret commercial treaty between Germany and Hungary was signed in February 1934, and the Germans thereafter began to receive almost a quarter of Hungary's total exports, mostly livestock, bauxite and raw materials for industry; and Hungary, in turn, imported from Germany manufactured products and coal and coke, or their derivatives. The economies of the two countries became so interlocked that had there been an interruption in the supply of machinery or spare parts from Germany, the Hungarian factories would once more have faced disaster ... and when the Second World War began Germany was receiving more than half of Yugoslavia's exports and was supplying almost as large a proportion of her imported requirements.
>
> Naturally the Germans did not help the Danubian States to solve their economic problems out of sheer kindness of heart. A German Foreign Office memorandum of June 1934 ... records that both the Hungarian and Yugoslav agreements "had political significance above their actual commercial content" and were "designed to create in Hungary and Yugoslavia two points of support for German policy in the Danube region, and above all to coun-

teract French and Italian policy directed against German policy there." It is significant that when, only three weeks after the Yugoslavs had struck their bargain, the Roumanians sought a commercial agreement, they were told by the German Foreign Minister that Germany "could make sacrifices only in favor of those states which did not support our opponents politically, as was the case with Roumania."[20]

The extent of German economic penetration into southeastern Europe within a period of four years is shown on Table 5.5.

In trade relations between unequal partners,

> If a nation with an absolutely large volume of trade imports from, or exports to, a small trading nation, the trade they conduct together will inevitably result in a much higher percentage for the small than for the large trading nation. German-Bulgarian trade in 1938, for example, represented 52 and 59 percent of Bulgarian imports and exports respectively, but only 1.5 and 1.1 percent of the German imports and exports. These figures indicate that although the same absolute amount is involved, it will be much more difficult for Bulgaria to shift her trade with Germany to other countries than it will be for Germany to replace Bulgaria as a selling market and a source of supplies.[21]

Similarly, in the case of

> ... countries like Sierra Leone or Dahomey, with 45 percent and 68 percent of their 1967 total trade accounted for by trade with Britain and France respectively, it must indeed appear that their markets are very important to those European Powers. But for the British in 1967, Sierra Leone accounted for only .2 percent of the U.K.'s total foreign trade, while for France in that year, Dahomey accounted for only 1 percent of total trade.[22]
>
> ... the economic relationships of Britain and Sierra Leone and France and Dahomey ... are examples of "one-way" economic dependence. No economic decision in either of those African countries could have more than the most minor effect on the economies of Britain or France. In contrast, any relevant economic decision made in those European countries would have the most profound effect on the economies of those African states.[23]

Although Germany's planned economic penetration of southeastern Europe is an atypical case, it nevertheless illustrates the political and economic dangers awaiting a weak partner which conducts a high percentage of its foreign trade with one economically powerful state.

It has often been argued that small states suffer from what is called diseconomics of scale:

TABLE 5.5 Germany's percentual share
in the trade of southeastern
European countries

Country	Trade	Year 1934	Year 1938[a]
Hungary	Import	18.3	40.9
	Export	22.2	40.0
Rumania	Import	15.5	40.0
	Export	16.6	26.5
Yugoslavia	Import	13.9	39.4
	Export	15.4	42.0
Bulgaria	Import	40.2	52.0
	Export	42.8	59.0
Greece	Import	14.7	29.5
	Export	22.5	40.3
Turkey	Import	33.8	47.5
	Export	37.4	43.9

[a] Includes Austria

SOURCE: C. A. Macartney and A. W. Palmer, *Independent Eastern Europe* (London: Macmillan, 1966), p. 315.

Certain industries must operate at a minimum scale or not at all, presumably because of large indivisibilities of plant. Those countries whose markets are too small to support this "technological" minimum scale will import such products from larger countries. It is contended that nations below a critical size seldom have such industries as an aircraft industry, an integrated automobile industry, or a large-scale chemical industry.[24]

If weak states do succeed in developing large mass-producing industries, they must be export-oriented and hence more dependent on foreign markets.

. . . in a small country, a specialized enterprise, if large, is likely to be large because it is international; and its domestic segment is likely to be a small part of its total size.[25]

For the same reasons, weak states are presumably at a disadvantage in research and development of new industrial products.

The large country has more funds for research, a field for experiment wide enough to try a greater number of new proposals, and more trained people who may develop new ideas. The statistical probability of a flash of genius is presumably no greater per thousand of population in a big country than in a small one, but there are not only more people to have flashes; there are also the technicians to carry out a systematic programme of research large enough to explore all the variant possibilities implicit in a particular bright idea.[26]

Moreover, because the volume of their exports and imports is small, weak states are of necessity "price-takers." The prices they demand and pay are set entirely by the world market, independent of their domestic conditions of supply and demand.[27]

The major problems of weak states in international trade can be summarized as follows:

(a) They produce a much narrower range of products than the larger states and hence are less likely to achieve autarky. As a result they depend to a larger extent on foreign trade.

(b) They have a much higher ratio of exports (and imports) in relation to their GNP than the economically strong states.

(c) They often tend to conduct their foreign trade with fewer trading partners than do the great powers.

(d) They are relatively disadvantaged with respect to large-scale industries based on mass-production techniques. If they do develop mass-production industries, they are more dependent on external markets. Also, they usually have little to invest (in absolute terms) in research and development.

The foregoing suggests that since economically weak states depend heavily on external market conditions, they are more sensitive to foreign developments beyond their control; their economic dependence on others could easily lead to political dependence as well.

MODIFICATIONS, QUALIFICATIONS, AND CAVEATS

While many sources of weakness of the economically small and less developed states which are prescribed by traditional economic theory can be accepted as valid, the economic predicament of the weak states may not be so severe as that theory would suggest. In the first place, some empirical evidence runs counter to the general rules to which, in any case, there are many exceptions. Secondly, the economically weak states can reduce their vulnerability by taking precautionary measures. Thirdly, the political environment that has prevailed since the 1950s tends to work in favor of the economically weak states by restraining the great powers.

It is true that economically weak states, especially the LDCs, tend to produce a limited assortment of products. However, some economically small but *highly developed* states can produce a large and well-balanced variety of commodities (e.g., Switzerland,[28] Sweden, the Netherlands, and Czechoslovakia). Although the production of a small range of goods can be considered a serious disadvantage, the economic position of a country depends also on the nature of the products it exports and the markets in which they are sold.

Saudi Arabia, Kuwait, and Libya, whose single export is oil, operate in a seller's market. The demand for oil is highly inflexible, the great powers compete for the right to purchase oil, there are no effective substitutes for oil, and the number of large oil-producing countries is relatively small. The oligopolistic conditions in the oil market work to the benefit of the oil-producing states and put them in a unique position vis-à-vis consumer states. And they certainly have taken advantage of their newly acquired power. As long as these conditions exist in the oil market,[29] and as long as the OPEC countries can effectively cooperate among themselves, they are in an exceptionally strong position, despite the single-commodity nature of their production.

Similar conditions exist in other markets for primary commodities, or can be created through the cooperation among weak states which are leading producers. In the copper market,

> Four countries control more than 80 percent of the exportable supply of world copper, have already organized, and have already begun to use their oligopoly power. Two countries account for more than 70 percent of world tin exports, and four countries raise the total close to 95 percent. Four countries combine for more than 50 percent of the world supply of natural rubber. Four countries possess over one-half the world supply of bauxite, and the inclusion of Australia . . . brings the total above 90 percent. In coffee, the four major suppliers have begun to collude to boost prices.[30]

Nevertheless, there are limits to the ability of countries producing commodities other than oil to collaborate in order to improve their terms of trade and also their political position.[31] Products such as tin and copper often have substitutes, and the demand for them is not as unvarying as the demand for oil. In the case of coffee, cocoa, and sugar, the number of producing countries is relatively large, which makes cooperation more difficult.[32]

Nevertheless, by improving their own coordination, allocating quotas, regulating production, and taking advantage of the growing demand for both food and raw materials, the weak states can improve their terms of trade and, in some markets of great strategic and industrial importance, can even improve their political standing. Although weak states should try to diversify their products, a limited variety does not necessarily mean greater vulnerability.

There is also evidence to indicate that despite their potential vulnerability to external pressures and their sensitivity to fluctuations in the world markets, the weak, less developed states have received a fairly stable income from their export of primary commodities.

> . . . probably the importance of short-term export instability to underdeveloped countries has been exaggerated. There is little evidence to show that in general their economies have been damaged. In most cases fluctuations in income do not appear to be at all closely related to fluctuations in export earnings. Many countries with highly unstable exports have relatively stable incomes.[33]

> Commonly accepted explanations of the extra instability of exports of underdeveloped countries—such as specialization in primary products, commodity concentration, geographical concentration—are found to miss the mark. . . . For most underdeveloped countries, variations in the supply of exports seem to have been more important than fluctuations in demand.[34]

Similarly, the common-sense notion that the economically small states tend to have, in absolute terms, only a small share of the primary-commodity market and hence tend to be "price-takers" is not substantiated by empirical evidence. In the oil, copper, tin, rubber, and bauxite markets, they have a very substantial share and hence a substantial impact. This has been found to be true for other markets as well:

> The larger trading countries have, on the average, practically the same commodity-weighted share in world trade as all the rest, save the smallest trading countries . . . many of the smaller economies have a stronger monopolistic position, in this sense, than most of the large countries.[35]

... statistics conclusively refute the notion that the export sales of small countries comprise a small share of foreign markets and that therefore small countries are price-takers in their export markets.[36]

Although most weak states have not developed heavy industries—with the notable exceptions of Sweden, Belgium, Czechoslovakia, and Luxembourg—some have developed other types of mass-production industries.

In the first place, as Jewkes has shown, it is not clear that large mass-production industries are always more efficient; in some industries small- or medium-sized firms have proved to be just as efficient or more so.[37]

"Outside a few exceptional industries most technical economies are exhausted by firms of quite moderate size. Even relatively small and poor countries can have a number of firms of the minimum size to give full, or almost full, technical efficiency." At the outset one should note that there are certain industries whose unit costs are not likely to be affected by the scale of output. One category is the extractive industries located near raw materials; another category includes some products of superior technical quality that require skilled workmanship. Switzerland provides the classical example in the watch and precision instrument and machinery industries that are carried on by small firms, mass production methods being almost totally absent.[38]

Also, there is no positive evidence to indicate that new inventions and research have been more successful in large than in small- and medium-sized firms, though there is some evidence that once a new invention has been made it can be developed more quickly by large firms.[39]

Secondly, small states can compensate for their limited domestic markets by producing for much larger export markets. Countries such as Taiwan, Singapore, Malaysia, Hong Kong, Lebanon, Cyprus, and the Central American countries have grown at rates equal or superior to those of larger countries such as India, Indonesia, and Egypt.[40]

It was once assumed that small states were less likely to develop efficient economies, and that labor and capital were less mobile within them. The fragmentation of a large state into smaller states—smaller economic units—was supposed to be an economic disaster, of which the classic example is the dissolution of the Habsburg Empire.[41] However, as Leff has convincingly shown, fragmentation can sometimes work to the advantage of the small state that has broken away.

Surely Lebanon would not have done as well economically if the country were part of Syria. And if Pakistan had remained joined to India, its development, too, would only have been retarded by the weaknesses of Indian economic policy-making.[42]

It would certainly not be in the economic interest of affluent Libya to merge with impoverished Egypt.

Small, autonomous economic units included within a larger political framework can sometimes become the victims of the so-called "internal colonialism" practiced by the dominant region.[43] This was the problem faced by East Pakistan (Bangladesh) within Pakistan. By breaking away, the new small states can benefit economically through becoming eligible for foreign aid. "In terms of aid per capita, the smaller countries have done much better than large ones."[44] Had Lebanon been part of Syria, or Bangladesh remained an integral part of Pakistan, they would not have been able to attract as much aid as they can now, and their regional economic achievements might have been swallowed up in the large, less developed area.

When exporting countries reach an agreement among themselves to sell certain primary commodities at a fixed price, and decide to allocate export quotas to each exporting state, as was the case in the International Coffee Agreement of 1962, the small exporting states enjoy a collective good. The larger producers, such as Brazil and Colombia in the coffee agreement, who have the greatest interest in coordinating their efforts and trying to control the market prices, "will accept a greater burden in providing a collective good—in this case a higher world price for coffee."[45]

Such agreements benefit the smaller producers. The larger producers avoid price competition among themselves, and thus prices do not fall below the profit price of the smaller producers.[46] As has been the case with the International Coffee Agreement, the larger producers may even agree to reduce their own quotas rather than those of the smaller states.[47] OPEC's decision to raise oil prices well above the extraction prices benefited the less efficient and smaller producers, such as Indonesia and Venezuela, which were formerly undersold in the oil market by Saudi Arabia, Kuwait, and Iran.

All these qualifications and exceptions warn against over-stressing the connection between size and economic performance.

Many small countries [especially the developed ones] do not in fact have the characteristics that have often been ascribed to them, because the significance which country size may have is swamped by the influence of location, market access, historical ties, the level of the exchange rates, and many other factors. This also means that the group of small developed countries to which most of our attention is confined . . . does not generally have all the trade characteristics which the builders of models believed small countries to have.[48]

One notable feature of the scattered literature on the international trade of small countries is the preponderance of pessimistic arguments. It has been repeatedly suggested that small countries will be particularly unstable and dependent in various senses, that income adjustments will easily overflow into balance of payments problems, and that membership in regional trade groupings may have dire consequences for the industries of small countries. Admittedly some counter advantages of smallness have been put forward, notably that devaluation will readily correct a balance of payments disequilibrium of a small country. . . .

This "size pessimism" is difficult to understand in view of the outstanding stability of export receipts in many small countries and the relatively high rates of economic growth which many of them have had. . . . One explanation may be that most of the small developed countries do have large foreign trade sectors in relation to the aggregate sizes of their economies and may therefore be more aware of actual and possible disturbances in this sector, even though the historical experience of most of these countries in the postwar period gives no cause for their being more concerned over international trade difficulties than other countries.[49]

While economically developed small states have generally done better than abstract models would indicate, the situation of the LDCs is more difficult to evaluate. Lacking enough solid data to analyze the economic position in these countries, economists have focused their attention mainly on the developed small states. They also tend to overlook the political price paid by the LDCs for the stability of their foreign trade.[50]

The former British and, more particularly, the former French colonies in Africa have established stable relations with their one-time masters, and on occasion have even secured higher payments than in the free markets.[51] But stability of income from exports is often achieved at the expense of political concessions to and cooperation with the great powers, which continue their political presence in the African capitals.[52]

It must also be remembered that stability of income from exports can be misleading. Many LDCs would prefer to see an increase in income and an improvement in the terms of trade.

What are some of the precautionary measures the economically weak states can take to reduce their vulnerability to economic pressures and to minimize the risks involved in foreign trade? The following may be suggested:

1. They should diversify their domestic production and try to export a larger variety of products. By following such a strategy they can (a) become less dependent on the income from only a few export items; (b) become more self-sufficient;[53] (c) reduce their dependence on foreign trade in general.[54]

2. They should try to "distribute their foreign trade over many countries differing in political alignments"[55] and seek "many markets of about equal size."[56]

3. They should try to direct their trade to smaller (weaker) trading partners. It is ". . . an elementary principle of the power policy of a state to *direct its trade away from the large to the smaller trading states . . .* trade should be directed toward the poorer countries."[57]

4. They should try not to conduct their trade with only one state, especially not with a great power.

> . . . it will be an elementary defensive principle of the smaller trading countries not to have too large a share of their trade with any single great trading country, so that the integration of their economies with those of the great countries (for which no reciprocal integration is forthcoming) may be kept at a minimum compatible with their economic well-being.[58]

It is not easy for economically weak states to follow these suggestions. They must usually be willing to sacrifice some of their political security and their future economic well-being to achieve a short-term, immediate improvement in their economic position. After the long economic crisis experienced by the Balkan and Danubian states in the 1930s, they were happy to accept the possibility of future political dependence on Germany in return for immediate economic relief. Conversely, Cuba under Castro was ready to sacrifice its economic independence in order to be free to determine its form of government. Facing an urgent problem with only a limited freedom of choice, weak states often choose to solve the immediate problem, leaving the new problems thereby created to be coped with somehow in the future.

THE APPLICATION OF ECONOMIC
PRESSURE AGAINST ECONOMICALLY WEAK STATES

Weak states have sometimes been the victims of economic pressures or sanctions imposed on them by the great powers. They have suffered severe economic setbacks and dislocation as a result, but as long as the great

TABLE 5.6 Serbian exports
in 1906 and 1907 (valued in dinars)

Country	1906	1907
Austria-Hungary	30,032,477	12,932,380
Germany	19,053,882	32,925,623
Italy	572,319	4,898,867
Russia	151,650	3,133,719
Belgium	6,259,929	13,010,853

SOURCE: Wayne S. Vucinich, *Serbia between East and West* (Stanford: Stanford University Press, 1954), p. 206.

powers have not combined economic pressure with military action, the weak states have survived. The so-called "Pigs' War" between Austria and Serbia is a good example.[59]

In April 1906, the Austro-Hungarian government closed its frontiers to Serbian transit trade and imposed high tariffs on Serbian exports to the Habsburg Empire. For Serbia, whose main products were agricultural, Austria was not only its major trading partner but the only outlet (through ports and railways) for its transit trade. For thirty years it "had traded almost exclusively with Austria-Hungary. For the five-year period preceding 1906 Austria-Hungary had supplied 53.35 percent of Serbia's imports and absorbed 83.66 percent of Serbia's exports."[60]

Prior to the tariff crisis of 1906 the Serbians had attempted to diversify their trade in order to lessen their dependence on Austria-Hungary by forming a Customs Union with Bulgaria and seeking new trade partners and alternative transit routes through Bulgaria and Salonika. But Austria interfered, putting economic pressure on Serbia in order to maintain its dependence. The Serbian government had also refused to buy heavy guns and ammunition from Austria (Skoda), and instead turned to France and Germany for military supplies; an inevitable decision, since Serbia's enemy would otherwise control spare parts and ammunition in wartime. A final reason for the tariff war was that "Magyar landlords found that Serbian products came into competition with their own."[61]

Both the Austrians and Serbians were convinced that Austrian markets were indispensable to Serbia's foreign trade, which would not be able to find new markets for its products. Thus Serbia could either bow to pressure and be reduced to the status of a mere puppet, or it could rebuff Austria and assert its independence. The latter alternative was obviously more costly

TABLE 5.7 Decline in U.S.-Cuban trade
after Castro's rise to power (January 1, 1959)

Year	US Exports to Cuba	US Imports from Cuba
1958	$546,947,000	$527,831,000
1959	438,593,000	474,663,000
1960	223,726,000	357,306,000
1961	13,716,000	35,125,000
1962	13,398,000	6,808,000
1963	36,475,000	55,000

SOURCE: Anna P. Schreiber, World Politics, 25 (1973), 395.

in the short-run, but would be economically and politically advantageous in the long-run.

The tariff war which began in April 1906 lasted for nearly two years. Serbia succeeded in obtaining railway transit to Salonika (then under Turkish control) as well as a loading zone in its harbor, despite Austrian protests to Turkey. It also succeeded in finding new markets as a substitute for its lost trade with Austria. As Table 5.6 indicates, these "proved very satisfactory and accounted in no small part for Serbia's ability to endure the hardships caused by the tariff war with Austria-Hungary."[62] Among the states supporting Serbia was Austria's ally Germany, a fact that "caused not a little hard feeling between Vienna and Berlin which persisted for years."[63]

By the time the "Pigs' War" was over, Serbia had considerably improved its position vis-à-vis Austria and had consolidated its economic independence.

The customs war caused a complete change in the ratio of trade with individual foreign powers. Instead of controlling 90 percent of Serbia's trade, Austria now enjoyed but 30 percent, and trade with other states increased proportionately.

The customs war forced Serbia to improve her export products both in quality and quantity. The length of export routes necessitated, for example, a transformation in the articles of commerce; raw materials were replaced by semi-manufactured goods; live cattle were replaced by fresh and salted meats and animal products of various sorts. . . . In this way Serbia avoided "gravitating exclusively towards the Austro-Hungarian markets, for the transformed products could choose longer ways towards distant markets."[64]

Another case is the economic war waged on Cuba by the United States, which in July 1960 canceled sugar purchases from Cuba for the remainder of the year. In October there followed an embargo on all exports to Cuba except for medicine and some food products. Finally in 1962, the importation of any products of all or partial Cuban origin was banned.[65]

In 1958, 67 percent of Cuban exports went to the United States, and 70 percent of her imports originated there. Most of the equipment in the island's industries was from the United States. Under the Costigan Act of 1934, the United States bought the bulk of Cuban sugar exports at an artificial price substantially above world market prices. In 1958, the bonus resulting from this preferential treatment alone amounted to about $150 million.[66]

The objectives of the American embargo were:

To reduce Castro's will and ability to export subversion and violence to other American states; to make plain to the people of Cuba that Castro's regime cannot serve their interests; to demonstrate to the peoples of the American Republics that communism has no future in the Western Hemisphere; and to increase the cost to the Soviets of maintaining a Communist outpost in the Western Hemisphere.[67]

Had the United States been able to prevent Cuba from trading with other countries, the Cuban economy might have totally collapsed, and the country might have been coerced into accepting U.S. political demands. But Cuba succeeded, though not without enormous difficulties, in diverting its trade to the Eastern Bloc and also enlarging its market in many Western countries. In 1961 the Communist bloc was already taking 75 percent of Cuban exports, while 86 percent of its imports were coming from Communist states,[68] as can be seen from the following table:

TABLE 5.8 Geographic distribution of Cuban
exports (in percentage by groups of countries)

Group of Countries	1959	1960	1961	1962	1963	1964*
Socialist countries	2.2	24.2	74.7	82.0	67.4	59.0
Other countries	97.8	75.6	25.3	18.0	32.6	41.0

*Percentage based on the first six months of the year.
SOURCE: K. S. Karol, *Guerrillas in Power* (New York: Hill and Wang, 1970), p. 587.

Canada, Spain, Sweden, Japan, Yugoslavia, and other countries considerably expanded their dealings with Cuba despite heavy U.S. pressure,[69] which included blacklisting ships unloading cargoes in Cuba and suspension of foreign aid to countries trading with Cuba.

By mid-1961, Cuba's industrial equipment started to break down. While some spare parts were "cannibalized" from other local factories, thus accelerating the industrial breakdown, and others could be obtained in the black market, the damage to the economy was considerable.[70] The United States embargo, combined with Cuban mismanagement, affected the economy most adversely between 1961 and 1964. Between 1961 and 1968 the total Cuban per capita production dropped by 29 percent.[71] The standard of living declined and there were serious shortages of food and other consumer goods.[72]

At a very high cost to themselves, the Cubans succeeded in maintaining their political freedom and their chosen course of action. In the process, however, they seem to have traded masters, becoming as economically dependent upon the Soviet Union as they had been on the United States. In 1974 the Cubans conducted most of their foreign trade with the USSR and Soviet bloc countries, obtaining Russian instead of American spare parts for their industrial and military equipment.[73] The Russians, like the Americans before them, have pressured Cuba economically in order to achieve their political ends. In December 1967 and January 1968, after expressing displeasure with Cuba's stand on certain international issues, the Soviet Union froze the level of petroleum deliveries to the island and delayed signing the annual trade protocol.[74] In the summer of 1968 Cuba was the only state outside the Soviet bloc to give public support to the Russian invasion of Czechoslovakia; in 1974 they paid for Russian support by sending troops to Syria.[75] Cuba's dependency on Russian aid has gradually turned it into a Russian client state.

The United States caused severe economic deprivations in Cuba but did not achieve its goals. It has lost all its investments there, the balance of its Cuban trade, as well as some respect and good will in Latin America and the underdeveloped world. "As an exercise in economic warfare, United States policy hardly rates as a success."[76]

In its relations with other weak states, the USSR has also used the economic weapon quite frequently. It applied an economic embargo of its own (and on behalf of the Soviet bloc) against Yugoslavia in 1948 and again in 1957;[77] against Australia in 1954;[78] against Finland in 1959;[79] and against Albania in 1961.[80] In none of these cases has it succeeded in effecting a favorable change in the policies of the weak country. After short periods, each of the weak states hit by Soviet economic reprisals successfully directed its trade to other countries, received credits from Russia's political competitors, and finally overcame the effects of Russian economic warfare.

Turning to Rhodesia, the economic sanctions imposed after its unilateral declaration of independence in 1966 caused some initial economic difficulties, but did not undermine Rhodesia's will to continue its existing policies.[81] Rhodesia controls 75 percent of its own energy resources and continues to receive petroleum through South Africa. After facing some serious trade problems with intermediaries, Rhodesia, until recently, restored its trade to an almost normal level, while the sale of chromium ores (a strategic commodity) to the United States continued. Rhodesia's weaker neighbors, Malawi and Zambia, have had no choice but to continue economic relations.

The Arab League boycott on Israel has been a dismal failure so far. It has encouraged Israel to produce as many of its own products as possible and has led it to diversify domestic production, thus having an opposite effect from that which was intended.[82]

Economic warfare is supposed to be a weapon favoring the economically great powers:

> [economic] vulnerability should be seen more as a property of the small power than as a property of the poor nation. Thus, the general picture is that economic sanctions as a source of power tend to preserve existing power structures.[83]

In actual fact, as long as the imposition of economic sanctions is not accompanied by military action, weak states can usually withstand the pressure by contriving alternative policies.

This leads to conclusions similar to those reached in earlier chapters. Even if weak states are economically weak, they are not helpless. As in the case of political and military weakness, they compensate for *internal* weakness by adding the strength of foreign states. They can take advantage of the competition between great powers, who are ready to offer them economic support in the face of rivalry from another great power. Weak states can usually maneuver easily and change their trade partners quickly.

Another conclusion is that it usually pays to fight back. By resisting economic pressures a weak state can maintain its political integrity and exact a high price from the great power: not only an economic price but a loss of prestige resulting from the appearance of "bullying" a weak state[84] and failing to achieve political ends. The weak states need to prepare themselves for economic warfare as much as for military conflict. By adopting the four precautions suggested above, they should be able to withstand the economic pressure of the great powers. Moreover, the success that weak states have already achieved in resisting economic pressure may eventually deter the great powers from using that weapon against them.

While it is easy to find examples of successful resistance by weak states, there are many types of subtle economic pressures which they have decided not to resist. They have quietly accommodated their positions to the implicit or explicit wishes of the great powers, as has been the case between Cuba and the USSR since 1968.

> Tariff wars and interruptions of trade rarely occur, but the awareness of their possibility is sufficient to test the influence of the stronger country and to shape the policy of the weaker.[85]

Although the application of economic sanctions against weak states has not always been effective, it has nevertheless been one more weapon in the arsenal of the great powers, not available to the weak states. However, in the 1970s for the first time, economic pressure has been applied against the great powers by militarily weak and dependent states. The Arab oil-producing countries placed an oil embargo on the Western great powers and industrialized states in the aftermath of the October 1973 Arab-Israeli war. This action prompts the question: Is this embargo the product of unique circumstances favoring oil-producing countries alone, or is it a sign of the growing economic power and leverage of the economically weak and less developed countries?

The changing norms in the conduct of international relations, the mutual neutralization of the super powers, and the reality and mythology of guerrilla warfare have all led to the so-called depreciation of military coercive power possessed by the great Western powers. These inhibitions on the use of force act as intervening variables explaining why militarily weak and vulnerable states (such as the Arab oil-producing countries) can blackmail the great powers economically without being punished. Similar action by weak states only a decade ago would have been highly improbable.

Yet if the economic pressure against the Western powers and industrialized world were to become too severe, it could lead to an economic disaster or even to the extinction of the industrial civilization. In other words, there is a threshold beyond which the great powers will not hesitate to make use of their military might.[86] (Otherwise the term "great power" would have no meaning). Although this threshold is not clearly delineated, it is nevertheless real, so that the leaders of the weak and less developed states employing the economic weapon must plan their steps with caution.

The economic wealth of the Arab oil-producing countries has created a situation which is unprecedented in many ways. Controlling both vital energy resources crucial for the industrial world and a huge surplus of capital, these countries have a strength, at least on the political-economic level, that has never before been held by militarily weak states. For the first time, they can exert an influence far beyond their own territory and region.

Long before the October 1973 Arab-Israeli War, the Arab oil-producing countries had started to translate their economic wealth into political influence, beginning with the Arab world itself. Immediately after the Six Days War, at the meeting of Arab governments in Khartoum in August 1967, the oil-producing countries (especially Kuwait, Libya, and Saudi Arabia) decided to give financial support to the so-called confrontation countries (Egypt, Syria, and Jordan), to help them purchase weapons, support their war economies, and compensate for their war losses.[87] But those who have the power to grant also have the power to withhold. Indeed, after the campaign of the Jordanian government against the Palestinian guerrillas in its territory in September 1970, the Arab oil-producing countries abruptly cut back their financial aid to Jordan.

After the October 1973 war, the governments of the Arab oil-producing countries pledged financial aid of over $2 billion to the confrontation countries, of which $1,150 million was promised to Syria and $900 million to Egypt.[88] During and after the war, the oil-producing countries also helped the combatants by financing part of the weapon purchases from Russia, and they themselves bought large quantities of weapons which were made available to the confrontation countries. The large sums of money offered by the oil-producing countries give them greater influence on the receiving governments and can be used to pressure them. For example, Libya (under Qaddafi) stopped financial aid to Egypt in order to demonstrate its displeasure with the Egyptian government's decision to sign the disengagement agreement with Israel.[89]

During the summer of 1971, when the government of Malta was bargaining with Britain for higher payments for the use of bases and naval facilities, the Libyan government urged Malta to expel the British from the island, promising financial and military support. On 17 August 1971 Libya actually lent the Maltese government $12 million,[90] which undoubtedly helped it to obtain a better bargain from the British government and NATO.[91]

Before the October 1973 war, Arab pressure on African states to break off diplomatic relations with Israel finally bore fruit, partly because of promises of future financial aid and economic support. Soon after breaking with Israel, some African countries did receive soft loans from Arab countries, notably from Libya and Saudi Arabia.[92]

During and after the October War, Arab oil-producing countries decided to cut oil production to all industrialized nations by 5 percent a month, whether or not a given country had directly supported Israel; and they tried to impose a total embargo on oil exports to states supporting Israel. Not all countries are equally sensitive to the oil weapon. The United States, then importing between 5 and 10 percent of its oil from the Arabs, was much less vulnerable than others. Likewise in Sweden and Norway 70 percent or more of the energy consumed is generated domestically by hydroelectric power.[93] But Japan and the countries of the European Common Market depend more heavily on oil as their major source of energy, and so were much more open to Arab blackmail. In Japan, for example, 70 percent of all energy produced originates from oil, of which 85 percent is imported from Arab states.[94] Under this pressure, the EEC countries and Japan changed positions and made statements favorable to the Arab cause.[95]

Robert Dahl defines influence as "a relation among actors in which one actor induces other actors to act in some way they would not otherwise act,"[96] power as "a special case of influence involving *severe losses* for noncompliance,"[97] and coercion as "a form of power that exists whenever A compels B to comply by confronting him *only* with alternatives involving severe deprivation."[98] According to these definitions the Arab governments successfully *coerced* the EEC countries and Japan by means of the October 1973 oil embargo. During this crisis economic power was translated into political power. For the first time the Arabs managed to coordinate their actions, creating a united front based on both economic and political interests.[99]

The EEC countries, on the other hand, failed to cooperate with one another. Each one confronted the Arab governments separately, a process instigated and encouraged by Arab bargaining tactics. In concluding separate bilateral treaties with the EEC countries, the Arabs followed the favorite tactic of the Germans in the Balkans prior to the Second World War.[100] The Europeans suddenly found themselves more dependent on Arab oil than the Arabs were on European goods and industrial products. The terms of trade were reversed, as were political influence and strength. The weak states do not appear to be so weak anymore. Over the short range, or perhaps the medium range, the international hierarchy of power seems to have been transformed.

It is very difficult at this stage to evaluate the real power relations involved, to ascertain whether or not the Arab (and other oil-producing) countries can maintain their strength, or to know if the implications of the new power relations are relevant for other weak and less developed states.

Continuation of new power relations depends on many variables. The development of new oil fields in the United States, Europe (the North Sea and the Aegean), and other areas may gradually make the industrialized world less dependent on Arab oil, particularly if reserves prove to be available in larger quantities than expected.[101] The development of new sources of energy would weaken the bargaining power of all the oil-producing states. Also, much of the oil-producing countries' leverage is a function of their ability to cooperate among themselves. Cooperation is easy in a sellers' market. But if over the next decade new and rich oil fields are discovered, or if the oil-producing countries find it more difficult to cooperate for political reasons while consumer countries improve their own cooperation, then the oil-producing states, including the Arabs, will lose a considerable amount of their present leverage.[102]

In the final analysis the oil-producing countries are also dependent on the industrialized world. While they can accumulate a large surplus of capital and can manipulate and damage the currency of any country they choose, they are also dependent on the economic and financial situation within the countries whose economies they can destroy. The two types of economies are interlocked. Because the oil-producing countries cannot invest or spend even a small fraction of their newly acquired capital at home, they have to invest in the industrialized world in order to maintain the value of their assets and maximize their income. Once they do so, their property may be nationalized and their liquid assets frozen; and thus they would become vulnerable to counter pressures and would be less free to employ the oil weapon.[103] On the other hand, it is possible that they might acquire greater influence in Western Europe and the United States by controlling large economic empires and having an impact on employment. If that seemed likely, though, the industrialized countries might pass special legislation in order to retain full control of their economies.

If the oil-producers should invest in the industrialization of their *own* countries, they would become dependent on the technology, machinery, and spare parts of the Western industrialized countries supplying those capital goods.[104]

A similar situation exists in the military sphere. Although the Arab countries and other large oil-producing states spend more money on military hardware than Great Britain, France, or Germany, they do not manufacture weapons themselves and cannot be expected to do so in the foreseeable future.[105] The more they buy Western weapons systems, the more dependent they become on the supply of spare parts, military instruction, and military help from these countries. The greater the sophistication of the weapons they purchase, the greater their dependence. If they should decide to blackmail the Western countries in the future, they could expect to be pressured by the withholding of instruction, spare parts, and military aid. It would therefore be rational for the oil-producing countries to diversify their weapons acquisition by obtaining weapons from countries they do not intend to blackmail or that would support them in the future. It might therefore make more sense for Saudi Arabia and Iran to buy weapons from the Eastern bloc.

Thus, although the oil-producing states are becoming stronger economically and have improved their political bargaining position, they are not and cannot be in full control of their own security and defense, which is a major criterion for classifying a state as a great power. Their military capacity, and hence their security, are derivative, not original. They depend on external military help and the unwillingness of the great powers to use force against them.

For militarily weak but economically rich states, such as Kuwait or even Saudi Arabia or Libya, to say nothing of Abu Dhabi and Qatar, there is a paradoxical danger in becoming richer. Such states may attract the attention of poorer but militarily stronger neighbors and may find themselves in a weaker position than before. As a desert country, Kuwait is unattractive. As a rich but militarily weak country (a power vacuum), it may invite occupation. It required British intervention to save it from occupation by Iraq in June 1961.[106] Not only Iraq but also Iran and Saudi Arabia might like to take over Kuwait. It might even become the target of terrorist blackmail. The great discrepancy between its economic richness and its military weakness makes it very vulnerable.

The position of the Arab oil-producing countries (or of other economically strong but militarily weak states) is in accordance with the ideal type of the weak state. Although they score high in one or two dimensions of strength, they remain weak in others and therefore cannot be considered great powers.

The success of the oil-producing countries in improving their terms of trade and of the Arab governments by using oil as an economic weapon to achieve their political ends is bound to encourage other weak countries that produce primary commodities to strive for the same success vis-à-vis the industrialized states. Even without coordinated effort on their part, such a process has already begun with the growing demand for all types of raw materials. The terms of trade in the last few years have gradually "shifted in favor of the primary-producing nations. . . . The third world has actually notched up a balance of trade surplus, and its reserves have almost doubled in the past two years."[107] Recently, though, it has become evident that much if not all of the additional revenue obtained from the improvement of the terms of trade in the primary commodities markets will disappear because of the higher prices for oil.[108]

One thing, however, is clear: No other commodity is in such great demand as oil. Although the industrial world does depend on imported raw materials,[109] many of these have effective substitutes and the demand for them is more flexible. Cooperation among the exporters of raw materials would therefore be more difficult. Not only would they have to coordinate their efforts to create an oligopoly and assign quotas in one market—for copper, bauxite, tin, and so on—but they would also have to coordinate their efforts between different markets so that when the quotas for bauxite were reduced or even completely cut, the countries producing tin would not take advantage of the situation. To reach effective agreements under such conditions would be extremely difficult both politically and economically. Also, unlike the oil-producing countries, the countries producing other primary commodities have much smaller financial reserves and therefore could not afford to stop or considerably reduce their exports.[110] For the same reason, they would not be able to manipulate other currencies and economies, and thereby gain political strength.

Although the countries that produce primary commodities can expect to improve their economic position (their terms of trade) and can move toward coordinating their marketing efforts, they will find the way much more difficult than the oil-producing countries have.[111] They will not experience the "economic miracle" that some of the Arab and other oil-producing countries have managed to bring about.[112]

The economic position of weak states, like their political position, is not simply one of weakness. Historical evidence tends to confirm that despite their smaller economic size, and hence frequent economic weakness, they have succeeded in stabilizing their incomes and, with external help, have been able to resist economic pressures from much stronger states.

In the past the terms of trade tended to work against the LDCs, and they seem to have received less than a fair share for their resources. For economic, political, and moral reasons, this situation is changing. Some of the weak states have become economically strong. Economic strength, however, is not a panacea for lack of strength on the military and industrial levels. Though some weak states have acquired enormous economic wealth, they still score low on other criteria, and while they have climbed upward in the international hierarchy, they cannot yet be considered great or even middle powers.

Notes

1. There are some exceptions, such as Gustav Lagos, *International Stratification and Underdeveloped Countries*; Singer, *Weak States in a World of Powers*; and R. P. Barston (ed.), *The Other Powers: Studies in the Foreign Policies of Small States* (New York: Barnes and Noble, 1974). All three devote considerable attention to economic relations between the great powers and the weak states, but none is completely satisfactory. Singer, who devotes a long chapter (6) to "economic ties" between the great powers and the weak states, makes no reference at all to the basic literature on the subject of economics. This makes a large part of his work superfluous and sometimes inaccurate. He also seems to write in a vacuum, for he does not refer to earlier books on weak state-great power relations, such as Robinson (ed.), *Economic Consequences of the Size of Nations*; Peter Lloyd, *International Trade Problems of Small Nations*; Michael Michaely, *Concentration in International Trade* (Amsterdam: North Holland Publishing Co., 1962); Albert O. Hirschman, *National Power and the Structure of Foreign Trade*.

2. See, for example, Theodore H. Moran, "New Deal or Raw Deal in Raw Materials," *Foreign Policy*, No. 5 (Winter 1971–1972), pp. 119–134; C. Fred Bergsten, "The Threat from the Third World," *Foreign Policy*, No. 11 (Summer 1973), pp. 103–124; Zuhayr Mikdashi, "Collusion Could Work," *Foreign Policy*, No. 14 (Spring 1974), pp. 57–68; Stephen D. Krasner, "Oil is the Exception," ibid., pp. 68–84; C. Fred Bergsten, "The Threat Is Real," ibid., pp. 84–90.

3. As Albert O. Hirschman has said, the absence of war or its elimination would not lead to the elimination of economic conflict and dependence relations among states. See *National Power and the Structure of Foreign Trade*, p. 15.

4. The capability to manipulate, induce or seduce, bribe, and aid other countries with positive rewards had previously been confined to the great powers, but now the situation has changed. See Singer, *Weak States in a World of Powers*, p. 60. See also David A. Baldwin, "The Power of Positive Sanctions," *World Politics*, 24 (1971), pp. 19–38.

5. C. N. Vakil and P. R. Brahmananda, in Robinson (ed.), *Economic Consequences of the Size of Nations*, p. 134.

6. Ibid., p. 135. See also Kuznets, ibid., pp. 14, 16, 31, and Edwards, ibid., p. 128.

7. See Benjamin J. Cohen, *The Question of Imperialism* (New York: Basic Books, 1973), p. 155.

8. Nadim G. Khalaf, *Economic Implications of the Size of Nations, with special reference to Lebanon* (Leiden: E. J. Brill, 1971), p. 10.

9. *Stabilization of Prices of Primary Products, Part II: Report of the Executive Directors of the International Bank for Reconstruction and Development IBRD*, Washington, D.C., 1969, p. 11, as quoted in Alton D. Law, "Stabilization of Prices of Primary Products: A Review Article," in *Inter-American Economic Affairs*, 24 (Winter 1970), pp. 28–29.

10. See Rothschild in Robinson (ed.), *Economic Consequences of the Size of Nations*, pp. 176–177.

11. Alfred Marshall, quoted in Hirschman, *National Power and the Structure of Foreign Trade*, p. 24.

12. Tarshis in Robinson (ed.), *Economic Consequences of the Size of Nations*, p. 197; also Marcy, ibid., pp. 267, 268. See also Lloyd, *International Trade Problems of Small Nations*, p. 55.

13. Khalaf, pp. 9, 10.

14. Marcy in Robinson (ed.), *Economic Consequences of the Size of Nations*, p. 268.

15. Singer, *Weak States in a World of Powers*, p. 238. According to Singer, "Only the U.S. and the U.S.S.R. have less than 10 percent of their G.D.P. accounted for by foreign trade and hence are relatively invulnerable to outside foreign trade decisions" (p. 238). See also Johan Galtung, "On the Effects of International Economic Sanctions," *World Politics*, 19 (April 1967), pp. 386–387.

16. Singer, *Weak States in a World of Powers*, p. 328. Economic dependence is related to two separate and quite distinct aspects. First, it implies a high measure of sensitivity to external forces: dependent economies are unable to avoid being influenced by events elsewhere. Second, it involves a high measure of irreversibility of impact: dependent economies are unable to override the influence of events elsewhere. Both aspects are essential to the notion of dependence. Together they mean that foreign economies have an implicit veto power over the capability of domestic decision-makers (private or official) to direct the development of the local economy. What happens at home depends on what happens abroad. (Cohen, *The Question of Imperialism*, p. 190.)

Singer also suggests "that when as much as 10 percent of a country's G.D.P. depends on aid from a specific foreign Power, the receiving country is highly dependent economically on that donor" (p. 256).

17. See, for example, Osvaldo Sunkel, "Big Business and 'Dependencia'," *Foreign Affairs*, 50 (April 1972), pp. 517–531; and John Gerassi, *The Great Fear in Latin America*, rev. ed. (New York: Collier Books, 1973), esp. parts I, V, and VI. See also James D. Cockcraft, Andre Gunder Frank, and Dale L. Johnson, *Dependence and Underdevelopment* (Garden City, NY: Anchor Books, 1972).

18. See Basch, *Danube Basin and the German Economic Sphere*, esp. chaps. 10, 11, 15, 16. See also Hirschman, *National Power and the Structure of Foreign Trade*, pp. 34–40. Hirschman (p. 36) has summarized Germany's policy as follows:

Germany's attempt to concentrate on exports of finished products, on the one hand, and on exports to agricultural countries, on the other, had obviously the result of giving her exports a quasi-monopolistic position so far as the productive system of her trading partner was concerned. . . . In addition, to maintain this position, it was one of the great principles of German foreign economic policy to prevent the industrialization of her agricultural trading partners. Particular insistence on this point has been noted in all the commercial negotiations of Germany with her southeastern neighbors and even, to some degree and some success, with Italy.

19. Basch, *The Danube Basin and the German Economic Sphere*, p. 225. As Palmer and Macartney put it (*Independent Eastern Europe*, p. 315):

It was precisely because the smaller countries did derive important economic benefits from Germany's system that they accepted it gladly, and even competed for admission to it, in the full knowledge of its political implications.

20. Alan Palmer, *The Lands Between*, pp. 214–215. For Hungary, see also C. A. Macartney, *October Fifteenth*, pp. 136–154; and Mario D. Fenyo, *Hitler, Horthy and Hungary* (New Haven: Yale University Press, 1972), chap. 5, pp. 79–83. For Yugoslavia, see J. B. Hoptner, *Yugoslavia in Crisis 1934–1941*, pp. 94–108; also Macartney and Palmer, *Independent Eastern Europe*, chap. 8, pp. 301–342.

21. Hirschman, *National Power and the Structure of Foreign Trade*, pp. 30–31.

22. Singer, *Weak States in a World of Powers*, p. 216.

23. Ibid., p. 222.

24. Lloyd, *International Trade Problems of Small Nations*, p. 16. See also Vakil in Robinson (ed.), *Economic Consequences of the Size of Nations*, pp. 136–137.

25. Edwards in ibid., p. 125.

26. Ibid., p. 129.

27. Lloyd, *International Trade Problems of Small Nations*, p. 40.

28. For Switzerland's diversified economy, see W. A. Johr and F. Kneschomek in Robinson (ed.), *Economic Consequences of the Size of Nations*, pp. 54–77.

29. It has frequently been claimed that the OPEC countries are riding on a temporary wave of shortage but that when more oil becomes available in the early 1980s in Alaska, the North Sea, and elsewhere, they will lose much of their monopoly power. M. A. Adelman, "Is the Oil Shortage Real?" *Foreign Policy*, No. 9 (Winter 1972–73), pp. 69–107. See also M. A. Adelman, *The World Petroleum Market* (Baltimore: Johns Hopkins Press, 1972); "Almost Anything for Oil," *The Economist*, November 10, 1973, pp. 11–13.

30. C. Fred Bergsten, "The Threat from the Third World," *Foreign Policy*, No. 11 (Summer 1973), pp. 107–108. See also Theodore H. Moran, "New Deal or Raw Deal in Raw Materials," *Foreign Policy*, No. 5 (Winter 1971–72), pp. 123–127; Zuhayr Mikdashi, "Collusion Could Work," *Foreign Policy*, No. 14 (Spring 1974), pp. 56–68; C. Fred Bergsten, "The Threat Is Real," *Foreign Policy*, No. 14 (Spring 1974), pp. 84–90; Stephen D. Krasner, "Manipulating International Commodity Markets," *Public Policy*; "Bye, Bye Bauxite," *The Economist*, March 2, 1974, p. 94.

31. See Stephen D. Krasner, "Oil Is the Exception," *Foreign Policy*, No. 14 (Spring 1974). pp. 68–84.

32. Ibid., passim.

33. Alasdair I. Macbean, *Export Instability and Economic Development* (Cambridge, MA: Harvard University Press, 1966), p. 339.

34. Ibid., p. 340. See also Lloyd, *International Trade Problems of Small Nations*,

pp. 48–49, 125. See also Nadim G. Khalaf, *Economic Implications of the Size of Nations* (Leiden: E. J. Brill, 1971), pp. 45–47; 55–57; 228–229.

... size is not a significant source of instability ... dependence on trade, commodity export concentration, and geographic export concentration are not sources of extra instability in income, exports, and imports. Even if small countries turn out to have relatively higher degree of dependence on trade and higher export concentration, small countries are not as a result of these features likely to experience extra instability in their incomes, exports, or imports. These results are contrary to plausible *a priori* reasoning, and they suggest that small countries need not be very apologetic about their dependence on trade and their export concentration. (Khalaf, p. 229.)

35. Michael Michaely, quoted in Lloyd, *International Trade Problems of Small Nations*, p. 41.

36. Ibid., p. 42.

37. Jewkes in Robinson (ed.), *Economic Consequences of the Size of Nations*, pp. 95–116.

38. Lloyd, *International Trade Problems of Small States*, p. 103. E. A. G. Robinson is quoted.

39. Robinson, *Economic Consequences of the Size of Nations*, pp. 108–113; also Lloyd, *International Trade Problems of Small States*, p. 17.

40. Nathaniel H. Leff, "Bengal, Biafra and the Bias of Bigness," *Foreign Policy*, No. 3 (Summer 1971), p. 130.

41. Ibid., pp. 133–135. See also Rothschild in Robinson (ed.), *Economic Consequences of the Size of Nations*, pp. 169–172.

42. Leff, "Bengal, Biafra and the Bias of Bigness," p. 136.

43. Ibid.

44. Ibid., p. 137.

45. Krasner, "Manipulating International Commodity Markets," p. 504, n. 12.

46. Ibid., p. 505.

47. Ibid., p. 504.

48. Lloyd, *International Trade Problems of Small Nations*, p. 35. See also Rothschild in Robinson (ed.), *Economic Consequences of the Size of Nations*, p. 177.

49. Lloyd, *International Trade Problems of Small Nations*, p. 126.

50. See a comment on this problem in Alton D. Law, "Coffee: Structure, Control and Development: A Review Article," *Inter-American Economic Affairs*, 21 (Summer 1973), p. 70.

51. Cohen, *Question of Imperialism*, pp. 218–219.

52. See Henry L. Bretton, "Patron-Client Relations: Middle Africa and the Powers," and also Robin Jenkins, *Exploitation* (London: MacGibbon and Kee, 1970), pp. 106–139.

53. For example, see Knorr, *Power and Wealth*, p. 155.

54. F. J. Wiles, *Communist International Economics* (Oxford: Basil Blackwell, 1968), p. 20; and Knorr, *Power and Wealth*, p. 155.

55. Knorr, ibid.

56. Wiles, *Communist International Economics*, p. 20; see also Cohen, *Question of Imperialism*, p. 222.

57. Hirschman, *National Power and the Structure of Foreign Trade*, p. 31.

58. Ibid.

59. On this conflict, see Sidney B. Fay, *The Origins of the World War*, 2nd rev. ed., Vol. I (New York: The Free Press, 1966), pp. 359–360; and Wayne S. Vucinich, *Serbia Between East and West* (Stanford: Stanford University Press, 1954), pp. 180–209.

60. Ibid., p. 205.

61. Fay, *Origins of the World War*, I, p. 359.

62. Vucinich, *Serbia Between East and West*, pp. 201–202.

63. Fay, *Origins of the World War*, p. 360.

64. Vucinich, *Serbia Between East and West*, p. 208.

65. Anna P. Schreiber, "Economic Coercion as an Instrument of Foreign Policy: U.S. Economic Measures Against Cuba and the Dominican Republic," *World Politics*, 25 (April 1973), p. 387; and Knorr, *Power and Wealth*, pp. 146–147.

66. See Knorr, *Power and Wealth*, p. 146.

67. Dean Rusk, quoted in ibid., p. 148.

68. Schreiber, "Economic Coercion as an Instrument of Foreign Policy," p. 395.

69. Ibid., pp. 398–399.

70. Ibid., p. 396.

71. Ibid., p. 401.

72. Ibid., p. 397. See also Jorge I. Dominguez, "Taming the Cuban Shrew," *Foreign Policy*, No. 10 (Spring 1973), pp. 111–115.

73. Dominguez, "Taming the Cuban Shrew," pp. 102–104.

74. Ibid., p. 95.

75. See *New York Times*, April 1, 1974, p. 1.

76. Knorr, *Power and Wealth*, p. 148.

77. Wiles, *Communist International Economics*, pp. 499–500.

78. Ibid., pp. 501–502.

79. Ibid., pp. 503–506.

80. Ibid., pp. 499–500. See also Griffith, *Albania and the Soviet Rift*, pp. 171–173.

81. See Johan Galtung, "On the Effects of International Economic Sanctions," pp. 378–416; *New York Times*, January 6, 1974; and Ralph Zacklin, "Challenge of Rhodesia," *International Conciliation*, No. 575 (November 1969).

82. For another appraisal, see Robert W. Macdonald, *The League of Arab States* (Princeton: Princeton University Press, 1965), pp. 118–123.

83. Galtung, "On the Effects of International Sanctions," p. 386.

84. Knorr, *Power and Wealth*, pp. 151–152.

85. Hirschman, *National Power and the Structure of Foreign Trade*, p. 16.

86. See the *Economist*, Dec. 1, 1973, pp. 76–77 ("The Arabs Reach for More"); and also the *Economist*, Jan 13, 1974, p. 80. Defense Secretary Schlesinger has hinted that contingent plans for American military intervention against Arab oil-producing countries were being prepared, though their use would be highly unlikely.

87. See, for example, E. Kanovsky, "The Economic Aftermath of the Six Days War: UAR, Jordan, Syria," part II, *The Middle East Journal*, 22, (Summer 1968), p. 282.

88. *M.I.S.* (*Middle East Intelligence Report*), vol. 1, No. 15 (Nov. 1, 1973), p. 117. (This is a fortnightly published in Tel Aviv, Israel.)

89. See the *Boston Globe*, Apr. 15, 1974, p. 8. Libya cut back its annual financial support to Egypt of £20 million sterling, as well as oil shipments to Egypt.

90. *New York Times*, Sept. 2, 1971, p. 7.

91. See *New York Times*, June 20, 1971, p. 6; June 28, 1971, p. 6; June 29, 1971, p. 6; June 30, 1971, p. 4; July 4, 1971, p. 4 (section IV); Aug. 2, 1971, p. 18; Jan. 5, 1972, p. 2. For a detailed description of the crisis see *Keesing's Contemporary Archives*, XVIII (London: Keesing's Publications, 1971–72), pp. 25151–25154.

92. See the *Economist*, Jan. 5, 1974, p. 68. African and other less-developed states may have had second thoughts since then, for they lost a good bargaining card and found themselves paying higher prices for Arab oil. See the *Economist*, "Kicking the Poor," Dec. 8, 1973, p. 80. Less developed non-oil-producing countries may find that they have a common grievance with the industrialized world.

93. For Sweden, see the *Economist*, Jan. 12. 1974, p. 99. For Norway, see the *Economist*, Dec. 29, 1973, p. 56.

94. *Economist*, Nov. 10, 1973, p. 45.

95. For the text of the European Community foreign minister's statement of 6 November 1973, see *Survival*, 16 (January-February 1974). p. 39. A similar Japanese statement was made 22 November 1973, by the secretary of the Japanese government. For the text, see *Keesing's Contemporary Archives*, 1974, p. 26323.

96. Robert A. Dahl, *Modern Political Analysis*, 2nd ed. (Englewood Cliffs, NJ: Prentice Hall, 1970), p. 17.

97. Ibid., p. 32.

98. Ibid., p. 33.

99. See Zuhayr Mikdashi, "Cooperation Among Oil Exporting Countries with Special Reference to Arab Countries: A Political Economy Analysis," in *International Organization*, 28 (Winter 1974), pp. 1–30; also Krasner, "Oil Is the Exception," pp. 72–81.

100. See the *Economist*, Jan. 12, 1974, p. 31, and Feb. 16, 1974, p. 73.

101. This is Adelman's position. See M. A. Adelman, "Is the Oil Shortage Real?" *passim* and *idem.*, *Economist*, Nov. 10, 1973, p. 11.

102. It would be difficult to predict the future relations between the industrialized world and the Arab oil-producing countries. Two scenarios can be suggested. One (A) shows the conditions under which the industrialized countries would be able to improve their bargaining position; the other (B) indicates the conditions which would favor the Arab (and other) oil-producing countries:

Scenario A	Scenario B
1. A greater measure of co-operation is reached between the industrial ized countries; they establish a united	1. Coordinated economic pressure by the Arabs continues; the industrialized states cannot improve

front to oppose economic blackmail, perhaps in cooperation with
the non-oil-producing LDC's.
At the same time, Arab cooperation
is weakened by inter-Arab conflicts.

their coordination and continue
to conclude bilateral treaties
with Arab oil-producing countries.

2. Western countries become less
reluctant to threaten with the use
of force or even to apply it. Probably
they will also threaten to use economic retaliation.

2. Industrialized states are "psycho-
logically paralyzed"; their inhibitions
against the application of force or
counter economic pressure increase.

3. New oil fields and oil reserves
outside the Arab world are discovered,
and/or new alternative sources of
energy are developed. They successfully match the growth in the consumption of energy.

3. No adequate new oil fields and
reserves are discovered, and/or no
new energy sources are successfully
developed.

Other scenarios could be suggested that would fall somewhere between these extremes.

103. Robert Mabro and Elizabeth Monroe, "Arab Wealth from Oil: Problems of Its Investment," *International Affairs*, 50 (January 1974), pp. 15–27.

104. The *Economist* (comment on Iran's investments in industry), Dec 29, 1973, p. 22.

105. For example, Iran has super-modern military equipment, part of which is not yet available to the armed forces of the producing countries. *International Defense Review*, 6 (December 1973), pp. 710–729.

106. For Britain's intervention, see James Cable, *Gunboat Diplomacy*, pp. 47–419.

107. The *Economist*, Dec. 8, 1973, p. 80.

108. Ibid.

109. The dependence of the United States on certain strategic raw materials is often mentioned. The following raw materials are almost fully imported by the United States: asbestos, 86%; bauxite, 87%; beryl, 89%; chromite, 100%; cobalt, 89%; columbium-tantalum, 100%; manganese ore, 99%; mica sheet, 94%; nickel, 91%; rubber, 100%; tin, 99%. See Hanson W. Baldwin, *Strategy for Tomorrow* (New York: Harper and Row, 1970), app. 2, pp. 342–343. See also Harry Magdoff, *The Age of Imperialism* (New York: Modern Reader, 1969), p. 52.

110. Krasner, "Oil Is the Exception," *Foreign Policy*, p. 80.

111. For a debate on the possibilities of such collusion, see "One Too Many OPEC's?" *Foreign Policy*, No. 14 (Spring 1974), pp. 56–90.

112. The GNP per capita of Qatar would reach the level of $17,400 in 1974, and that of Abu Dhabi would reach $45,000. "Arab Oil Strategy," *New York Times*, March 20, 1974, p. 59.

Conclusions

Weak states cannot easily be defined or classified. Power/weakness is a continuum, and various types of power must be evaluated (e.g., military, economic). A state may be stronger in some respects than in others. Thus a complex set of criteria is necessary to distinguish the weak states from the great powers, for the differences between them are relative rather than absolute. Above all it must be remembered that the absolute strength of states has not been of primary interest in this work, but rather their strength in relation to their specific interests and needs. The weak and powerful states have many common characteristics and problems. Any attempt to separate out the weak states as a totally different "breed" is artificial. No state is all powerful and no state is completely weak.

The existing literature on weak states in international politics often portrays them as passive pawns owing their continuing existence to the benevolence of the great powers. This has never been the case. A realistic analysis indicates that while the weak states are frequently more vulnerable than the great powers, they are not helpless. Although they cannot defend themselves by their own strength against aggression on the part of a great power, they can and do maneuver within the international system to obtain help from other states.

Unlike the great powers, much of the strength of weak states is *derivative* rather than intrinsic. The diplomatic art of the weak states is to obtain, commit, and manipulate as far as possible, the power of other, more powerful states in their own interests. Weak states can sometimes manipulate and lead a great power, almost against its own will. This has led some observers to exaggerate their real power and impact on the international system.

The most important condition for the security of the weak states, therefore, is their ability to appeal to other states for help and support. This they can do only if they are free to maneuver in the international system, to choose their allies, to take advantage of the conflicts and tensions between the powers. On the other hand, the conditions most dangerous to security and independence of the weak states are isolation from the international system, or inclusion within the sphere of influence of one of the great powers, where they are closely watched and jealously prevented from developing relations with other powers. From the viewpoint of the weak states, it is not so much the *structure* of the international system that is important, but a certain condition of tension and conflict between the powers and an absence of rigidly defined and mutually respected spheres of influence.

While the weak states usually cannot defend themselves for long against the onslaught of a great power, this does not mean that they can afford to neglect the development of their own strength. The development of their own military power enables them, under certain conditions, to improve their bargaining position, or to deter an attack by a great power which fears it might be weakened vis-à-vis another great power (finite deterrence). By developing its military force, a weak state can hold its own against a great power until external help arrives, and it can defend itself effectively against other weak states. The readiness of weak states to defend themselves and fight back (or at least to convey that impression) has, on the whole, worked in their best interests.

Often their very weakness can actually be turned into an asset. In alliance treaties, weak partners frequently enjoy the benefits of a collective (public) good. They contribute proportionately less than the more powerful members but are defended by the alliance as much as any other signatory. Under other circumstances their very weakness and vulnerability can help them to obtain additional aid from a great power which has developed an interest in or staked its prestige on their continued existence.

The development of nuclear weapons, the balance of terror, and the gradual acceptance by the international community of norms that limit and inhibit the use of brute force by the great powers among themselves as well as against the weak states have further contributed to the safety and improved standing of weak states in the international system. Weak states that have been included within a "recognized" sphere of influence of one of the great powers, however, have received much less benefit from these developments.

Nevertheless, normative constraints on the use of force have had much less effect on the weak states, especially the less developed ones, than on the great powers. In the future there might be fewer wars between the great powers and more conflicts between countries such as Iran and Iraq, India and Pakistan, Israel and the Arab states, and perhaps Turkey and Greece.

Similarly, empirical evidence indicates that most weak states are economically more viable and less vulnerable than common-sense economic theories had prophesied. The great powers, on the other hand, have not always been able to translate their economic strength into political gains. When they have tried to use economic pressure to coerce weak states to accept their political demands, they have frequently failed, again due to the external help obtained by the weak states from other weak states or great powers.

In the future many of the weak states will be able to improve their economic position vis-à-vis the great powers, due to the increasing demand for primary commodities and the growing recognition on the part of industrial countries that the position of the less developed countries needs to be upgraded.

Some weak states, notably the oil-producing countries, have already been able to gain enormous economic power and to translate it into political gains. It is not clear whether they will continue to enjoy such an impact on a long-term basis, but at least they can exercise considerable short-term political influence on international politics. Yet in spite of their great economic power, and resultant political influence, in the final analysis they are militarily dependent and vulnerable. Thus they cannot be considered as powers in the traditional sense.

In conclusion, although the weak states may not be the principal *dramatis personae* in the world power play, neither are they merely small-part actors.

6

SMALL STATES IN WORLD MARKETS

Industrial Policy in Europe

PETER J. KATZENSTEIN

In the 1970s and 1980s, it is often said, the rate of economic change is accelerating while the capacity for political adjustment is shrinking. Throughout the advanced industrial world this divergence has become both a rallying cry for conservatives demanding fewer state intrusions in the market and a challenge to liberals seeking more effective state intervention. In the case of the small European states, this book has argued, economic flexibility and political stability are mutually contingent. The corporatist strain in the evolution of modern capitalism no longer yields readily to interpretations based on such established dichotomies as market and plan, private and public, efficiency and equity, Right and Left.

Under conditions of increasing vulnerability and openness, the large industrial states are groping toward workable solutions for the economic predicaments of the 1980s. The incremental, reactive policy of the small European states and a stable politics that can adjust to economic change provide a point of orientation that is both helpful and hopeful. Students of the international political economy are undecided whether the most important development of the 1970s lay in the predictable growth or the astonishing containment of protectionism. Similarly, students of domestic politics focus their attention both on the cartelization of politics in the hands of party, group, and bureaucratic elites and on the challenge that new social movements pose to established institutions. In analyzing the democratic corporatism of the small European states this book dissents from the view that capitalism is being driven by structural crisis toward

From Peter J. Katzenstein, *Small States in World Markets* (Ithaca, NY: Cornell University Press, 1985). Reprinted with permission of Cornell University Press. Cross references to pages and notes refer to the original publication.

collapse, nor does it support the view that capitalism is being resurrected by the vigors of market competition. Contradictions are inherent in all forms of political and economic domination. But democratic corporatism has been able to tolerate contradictions because of its accommodation rather than resistance to market competition and because of its inclusion of all significant actors in the decision-making process.

Prospects

The democratic corporatism of the small European states is a response to international pressures. Its proximate historical origin lies in the economic and political crisis of the 1930s and 1940s, its enduring strength in the post-war era in the liberal international economy of the 1960s and 1970s. The fear of authoritarianism, depression, and war contributed to its emergence in the 1930s. The enjoyment of democracy, prosperity, and peace contributed to its maintenance after 1945. The factors that create political regimes are not identical with those that maintain them.

At the beginning of the 1980s, however, it was no longer far-fetched to inquire whether the small European states were, for the first time since the 1930s, confronting external pressures so serious as eventually to effect a fundamental reorganization in their corporatist arrangements. How will the small European states fare in the emerging international economy?

Béla Kádár has listed some adverse developments that are putting the small European states under increasing strain.[1] A 50 percent decline in the growth rate of world trade (from 8.6% in 1960–73 to 4.2% in 1974–80) has created a decidedly less hospitable economic setting for small countries dependent on trade with others. Nonetheless, in all of the small European states except Denmark, foreign trade in goods and services continued to increase slightly between 1973 and 1979. Furthermore, sharp increases in the price of oil and unfavorable conditions in markets within the small European states (light industrial goods, semi-finished products, and consumer durables) have caused adverse changes in relative prices. Between 1973 and 1980 the terms of trade declined by about 15 percent for Denmark, 11 percent for Belgium, and 7 percent for the Netherlands, Austria, Sweden, and Switzerland. By contrast, average terms of trade in Western Europe declined by less than 6 percent, and in West Germany they remained unchanged. Unsurprisingly, compared to 1973–78 the increase in total foreign indebtedness in 1979–82 was greater in the small European states than in the large industrial countries.[2]

The small European states are also facing entirely new problems, which stem from a doubling of the relative market share of the developing countries in less sophisticated industrial products. More poorly endowed with raw materials than large countries, the small European states have typically relied heavily on the processing and re-exporting of imported primary products, areas into which newly industrializing countries are moving very rapidly. Changes now under way in the international economy thus point to the likelihood of an increasing "small-country squeeze."[3] During the last decade large advanced industrial states have shifted their R and D emphasis away from basic research in high-technology sectors toward applied research in more traditional industrial sectors. At the same time, a small group of rapidly developing countries has begun to wage a determined and effective export offensive with competitive products in some traditional industrial sectors.[4] Both developments will make it more difficult for the small European states to maintain their long-standing comparative advantage in these sectors. Thus the five small European states (Switzerland, the Netherlands, Belgium, Sweden, and Denmark) that account for the lion's share of engineering exports from small countries have been losing market share since 1973 in computers, office machinery, electrical-power-generating equipment, telecommunications, and scientific instruments.

The general economic climate facing the small European states has become harsher. From the vantage point of the mid-1980s this turn of events looks to be structural rather than cyclical. In the long term these adverse international pressures may affect the corporatist structures of the small European states in ways that are largely unpredictable today. Should the competitive pressures of the international economy create not sector-specific crises but one crisis engulfing all of society, it is conceivable that democratic corporatism will be replaced by other political structures. The traditional advantage that corporatism enjoyed in the race for international competitiveness might turn into a severe handicap as liberal, statist, or authoritarian regimes find ways of reducing labor costs to a degree politically not feasible in corporatist systems. The pressures on business to move toward neoliberal arrangements and on the unions to favor state intervention may then become overwhelming. Once a solution to the problems of structural adjustment in a rapidly changing global economy, corporatism may then be viewed by business and labor as part of the problem. But these are speculations. Only fortune tellers claim to know when another major crisis will reshape the domestic structures of the small European states as fundamentally as did the events of half a century ago.

It is, however, important to keep in proper perspective the impact of these adverse economic changes on the small European states. Since the mid-1970s journalistic accounts of the declining fortunes of the small European states have often failed to take account of the economic and political success, measured in terms of both prosperity and legitimacy, that derive from a flexible strategy of adjustment. Eye-catching headlines portrayed, for example, Denmark as "heading for hell" and suggested that its "labor strife could bring national chaos."[5] Yet, as Andrew Boyd argued in 1978, "there is no reason that the Danes cannot look facts in the face. . . . Even in their fragmented political pattern there is a broader unity of purpose than before."[6]

In an article entitled "How Sweden's Middle Road Became a Dead End," *Forbes* magazine incredulously reported that under a conservative government Sweden's national budget deficit had increased from less than $1 billion in 1976 to $12 billion in 1981. To impress on its readers the disastrous consequences of a social welfare state run rampant, the article pointed out that "in the United States a comparable budget deficit would run $200 billion."[7] A ludicrous example in 1981 had, under a conservative Republican administration, become a political reality two years later. The borrowing record of the seven small European states in international capital markets has, moreover, been more favorable than that of the large industrial countries. Measured against the total value of international bonds issued to the five large industrial countries in 1978 and 1983, the share of the small European states declined from one-half to one-quarter.[8] The search for last month's or last year's "sick man of Europe," a favorite journalistic pastime, in the late 1970s mistook recalibration of political strategies of adjustment in a rapidly changing economic context for a crisis in the very structure of democratic corporatism.

Economic statistics measuring unemployment, growth, inflation, and the balance of payments are summarized in Table 6.1. They do not support the argument that the economic position of the small European states deteriorated in the 1970s relative to that of the large industrial countries. A rank-ordering by economic performance shows that, on average, the small European states performed better than the large industrial countries in containing inflation and unemployment, that they are holding their own in economic growth, and that they are lagging in their balance of payments. As the small European states experienced more adverse changes in the international economy in the 1970s than did the large states, the relative superiority of their economic performance is all the more noteworthy. It supports the view expressed in chapter 1, that a flexible strategy of adjustment is linked to economic and political success.[9]

	(1) Annual unemployment as a percentage of total labor force				(2) Annual increase in real gross domestic product				(3) Annual changes in the consumer price index				(4) Balance of payments on current account as percentage of GNP			
	1960–80		1974–80		1960–80		1974–80		1960–80		1973–80		1960–80		1974–80	
	Rank	%	Rank	%	Rank	%	Rank	%	Rank	%	Rank	%	Rank	%	Rank	%
Switzerland	1	0.1	1	0.4	11	3.0	12	0.3	2	4.2	1	4.0	1	1.2	1	3.5
Netherlands	7	2.1	7	4.1	6	4.0	8	2.2	6	5.6	4	7.1	2.5	0.7	2	0.8
Belgium	11	3.3	10	5.7	5	4.1	5	2.4	4	5.2	5	8.1	6	0.1	9	-1.7
Sweden	6	1.9	4.5	1.9	10	3.3	9	1.8	8	6.6	9	10.3	10	-0.5	10	-1.8
Denmark	9	2.8	12	7.1	9	3.4	10	1.6	11	7.9	10	11.0	11	-2.5	11	-3.5
Norway	5	1.8	3	1.8	4	4.4	1	4.7	7	6.4	6	9.0	12	-3.4	12	-6.4
Austria	3.5	1.7	2	1.6	4	4.2	3	3.0	3	4.9	3	6.3	9	-0.4	8	-1.6
Small states' average	6.1	2.0	5.6	3.2	6.9	3.8	6.9	2.3	5.9	5.8	5.4	8.0	7.4	-0.7	7.6	-1.5
United States	12	5.5	11	6.8	8	3.5	6.5	2.3	5	5.3	7	9.2	5	0.3	4.5	0.1
United Kingdom	9	2.8	8	4.7	12	2.3	11	0.9	12	8.8	12	16.0	8	-0.3	6.5	-0.8
West Germany	3.5	1.7	6	3.5	7	3.7	6.5	2.3	1	3.9	2	4.8	2.5	0.7	3	0.6
France	9	2.8	9	4.8	2	4.6	4	2.8	9	6.8	11	11.1	7	-0.1	6.5	-0.8
Japan	2	1.5	4.5	1.9	1	7.7	2	3.7	10	7.4	8	9.7	4	0.4	4.5	0.1
Large states' average	7.1	2.9	7.7	4.3	6	4.4	6	2.4	7.4	6.4	8	10.2	5.3	0.2	5.0	-0.2

SOURCE: OECD, *Historical Statistics, 1960–1980* (Paris, 1982), pp. 37, 40, 77; David R. Cameron, "On the Limits of the Public Economy" (paper prepared for delivery at the Annual Meeting of the American Political Science Association, New York, September 1981), Table 11. W. D. McClam and P. S. Andersen, *Adjustment Performance of Open Economies: Some International Comparisons* (Basel: Bank for International Settlements, Monetary and Economic Department, December 1983), p. 10.

Yet the new era of high interest rates, forced on the small European states by economic policy decisions in larger countries, has led to even greater difficulties than the two oil shocks of 1973 and 1979. The economic clouds over Europe have visibly darkened in recent years. Large budget deficits and high interest rates reinforced the fear that inflation is a long-term problem, and unemployment has risen to heights not seen since the 1930s. Belgium suffers from a structural crisis of industry. Denmark, like many other industrial states, is struggling to realign its generous welfare policies with projections of lower economic growth. The Netherlands and Norway—blessed by access to North Sea gas and oil—are temporarily cushioned from some of their neighbors' economic hardships, but at the risk of lagging behind their competitors in rationalizing production and consumption. Even Austria, which came through the 1970s strongly, is now being forced to put Keynesianism on ice.

Since the early 1980s all of the small European states have been tightening their belts and contemplating uneasily the prospect of stable or declining living standards in the 1980s. High levels of public consumption need to be readjusted to the requirements of smaller budget deficits and a reduced reliance on international capital markets. None of the small European states is contemplating a large-scale change in policy. Instead, these countries prefer to cut and trim as they consciously seek to improve their international competitiveness. Although social and political conflicts have increased, the inclination to seek piecemeal solutions persists. Political consensus is being strained and modified, but the small European states have resisted the temptation to discard the corporatist compromise.

One Danish banker, reflecting in the early 1980s on the economic crisis of his country in the global economy, remarked that "we have been living too well on borrowed money. We were on the way to hell, but we were doing it first class."[10] Since the mid-1970s the Conservative Peoples Party has become Denmark's second-largest. For the first time since 1901 a conservative, Poul Schlüter, became prime minister in 1982. Schlüter curtailed spending programs no longer compatible with Denmark's declining international competitiveness, and within a year the country's economic performance improved. In 1983 the inflation rate was halved to 5.5 percent, and interest rates dropped from 22 to 12.5 percent. For the first time in many years the country did not run a deficit in its balance of trade, and the unemployment rate appeared to have peaked at 11 percent. In 1984 the Danish electorate honored the conservative argument that change was in order to save the welfare state. It elected a four-party minority coalition government, still fourteen votes short of controlling Parliament. A modification of welfare policies is thus possible under conservative leadership; a dismantling of the welfare state is not.[11]

Similar political developments are also occurring in the Low Countries.[12] In both countries relatively unknown prime ministers, Ruud Lubbers in the Netherlands and Wilfried Martens in Belgium, both Christian Democrats, are fashioning economic policies designed to bring established welfare policies into line with new economic realities. In the Netherlands in 1983 Prime Minister Lubbers put into effect spending cuts, a work-sharing scheme, and a 3.5 percent reduction in public-service wages. As in Denmark, the majority of the electorate accepts the need for scaling down, but as one recent summary avers, "all large parties and leading politicians advocate the continuance of the Welfare State."[13] In Belgium the government prevailed in its confrontation with public-sector unions. There, as in the Netherlands, the growth of Social Security spending has been stopped. Even Austria's Socialists, in coalition with a small liberal party since 1983, are pruning welfare expenditures to contain a further growth in public deficits. Sweden's Social Democrats, returned to office in 1982, have emphasized the need for profitability in the public sector. In the words of a spokesman of the Department of Industry, "the state-owned companies had been saying for years that either we wanted them to operate politically or profitably, but that they could not do both. They have all been told explicitly that profitability is now the overriding aim."[14]

The calibration of welfare polices with international competitiveness has intensified political conflicts in the small European states. Prime Minister Olof Palme has called Sweden's businessmen "baboons and elephants." Nevertheless, while in Sweden "it seems clear that the old magic of the thirties won't work again," Arne Ruth writes, "there is no sign that any sizable portion of the Swedish population is seriously disaffected with the basic virtues of the welfare state, even if an increasing number complain about its cost."[15] In the autumn of 1983 Prime Minister Lubbers was jostled in public by angry protesters, an act of enormous social defiance in a country as orderly as the Netherlands. But considering the intensity and magnitude of conflict that the small European states experienced before World War II, these episodes should be viewed not as a prelude to class warfare but as part of a political struggle redefining the boundaries of legitimate expectations and demands in corporatist bargaining.

In the Netherlands, as in other small European states, "people dependent on state spending have been sheltered from changes in the world economy," the *New York Times* argued at the end of 1983, "and over the past few months what we have witnessed is social shock therapy."[16] "The

announcement of the death of Dutch corporatism in the early 1980s may
be as premature as was a similar announcement in the early 1970s. Recent
interpretations of Dutch politics, for example, emphasize that in the late
1970s extensive cooperation persisted, together with intense conflict,
encouraged by the vulnerability of the Dutch economy and concealed by
a rhetorical conflict at the national level."[17] "The rise and fall of the postwar social contract in the Netherlands," writes Steven Wolinctz, "suggests
that such corporatist arrangements can be durable but not immutable."[18]
But such a focus on the instabilities and temporary breakdowns of corporatist arrangements misses an essential point. Democratic corporatism
is not an institutional solution to the problems of economic change but
a political mechanism for coping with change.

The political staying power of corporatist structures is reflected in the
way that these structures constrain the building of political coalitions that
might fundamentally challenge existing institutions and policies. Such
coalitions are made possible by recurrent cycles of industrial innovation,
maturation, and imitation that redefine the economic and political interests which different actors have in the international economy.[19] Major firms
and industry associations react to new circumstances by fashioning new
coalitions to press for political changes that may be as specific as particular industrial adjustment politics or as general as broad regime characteristics. Because corporatist structures encourage flexibility, collaboration,
and the absorption of the political consequences of economic dislocations,
alternative political coalitions are not easily formed. The political logic
inherent in the corporatist structures of the small European states instead
enhances political predictability and incremental adjustment.[20] These structures narrow power differences and link state and society intimately. They
thus succeed in capturing potential coalitions among changing political
forces and in channeling political energies into the relegitimizing of corporatist arrangements.

More severe international constraints will make the domestic politics
of the small European states more cohesive, at least in the medium term.
The formal, "consociational" arrangements made between political parties in the 1960s in several of the small continental European states have
rapidly eroded, and Social Democratic hegemony in Scandinavia partially
decomposed in the 1970s. Both developments, however, have so far left
the democratic corporatism of these seven states remarkably unchanged.
Should economic crisis intensify, interlocking interests, political practices,
and institutions in the small European states may well yield, as Charles
Sabel argues, "to the idea of a community of the vulnerable [in] a general

commitment to share equitably the burdens of adapting social institutions to a continuously changing world."[21] In the years ahead a growing sense of vulnerability should, on questions of strategy in the international economy, unite political opponents in the small states who disagree on many other substantive issues. At the same time the policy networks of the small European states show few signs of change that would deprive policy makers of the sizable number of policy instruments that they now control. The emergence of alternative political structures of participation and representation in the 1970s, for example citizen initiatives or single-issue movements, may well complement rather than replace the corporatist arrangements that have developed since the 1930s.

Changes in the form of corporatist collaboration thus do not necessarily signify its disappearance. After 45 years Sweden decided to move to a more decentralized and possibly conflictual form of labor negotiations in 1984.[22] But this decision does not necessarily ring the death bell for democratic corporatism. In the Netherlands the move toward decentralized labor negotiations has been under way for two decades without creating noticeably higher numbers of strikes or impairing, in the 1970s and early 1980s, a voluntary incomes policy that has been remarkably successful. The Swedish decision signals instead that both unions and business are looking for new institutional ways for coping with Sweden's economic difficulties. In the optimistically sentimental words of Flora Lewis, "The vision of progress is no longer blinding, but neither is it dead . . . once again, Sweden's example can inspire confidence. It is certainly not a model. It has taken some wrong turns and it is unique in ways that others cannot and would not wish to copy. But it is a reminder that rational argument and warm-hearted resolve found ways to leave the bad old days behind, and doubtless can again."[23]

Comparisons

Small states with open and vulnerable economies can respond effectively to changes in the global economy. A fairly wide range of responses is possible, as illustrated by liberal and social variants of democratic corporatism.

As the outbreak of a bitter strike in Sweden illustrated in 1980, democratic corporatism does not magically transform social and political hostility into harmony. Instead, it offers an institutional mechanism for mobilizing the consensus necessary to live with the costs of rapid economic change. For the small European states a reactive, flexible, and incremental policy of industrial adjustment occurs together with an astonishing capacity to adjust politically to the consequences of economic change. The small European states adapt domestically to economic change imposed by an international economy that they cannot hope to control. The structure of the small European states is not well suited to a political strategy based on liberal or statist premises. The relations between business, the unions, and the state are organized in a manner that compromises the logic both of unmitigated market competition and of decisive state intervention. Elaborate institutional networks and a complex policy process yield easily to marginal compensations for affected interests but strongly resist a single-minded devotion to entrepreneurial initiative or bureaucratic leadership. In sum, the small European states embody the politics of neither liberalism nor statism, but of corporatism.

The economic openness and corporatist structures of the small European states have had a strong effect on their political strategies. Open economies inspire a fear of retaliation, foreclosing protection as a political option for coping with adverse economic change. But in facilitating the emergence of corporatist domestic structures, economic openness encourages political compensations for change, foreclosing, if indirectly, strategies of structural transformation. Thus the two strategic responses with which liberal and statist industrial countries deal with change are not open to the small European states. Instead of seeking to export or preempt the costs of change, the small European states have chosen to live with the costs of change by compensating for them, politically and economically. An open economy and a position of international marginality generate a common outlook shared across the main political divisions in domestic politics. In 1937–38 both capitalist Switzerland and socialist Sweden witnessed the signing of peace agreements between business and unions. These agreements prepared the ground for a pattern of political accommodation in the postwar period that has been responsive to the requirements of international competitiveness.

As the large, advanced industrial states grope toward more adequate ways of responding to the risks and opportunities of the international economy, the example of the small European states will vary in relevance for them. Germany provides perhaps the closest approximation to the political practices characteristic of the small states. West Germany's corporatism derives as much from openness, dependence, and a sense of vulnerability brought about by the diminished size of the Bonn Republic after 1945 as from the implantation of its political parties in fresh democratic soil.[24] Throughout the 1970s German politics fostered a consensual style of policy making among political actors who conceived of one another as social partners and controlled relatively centralized institutions, especially on questions of economic and social policy.

West Germany looms very large in the economic fortunes of its smaller neighbors. For example, political choices in Bonn and Frankfurt on questions of inflation, unemployment, and the value of the deutsche mark are of enormous consequence for Switzerland and Austria. More generally, Germany has a profound effect on the other small European states. During the interwar years and in the early 1950s Germany's most prestigious economics research institute issued a series of monographs dealing with the economic development of the small European states. These studies provide a rich source of data for tracing the economic dependence of the small European states on the German economy since the middle of the nineteenth century.[25] Marcello de Cecco has recently extended this interpretation to the 1970s. He argues that "one cannot fail to be struck by the central role these countries have played in recent years in stabilizing the international trade balance of Germany. . . . These countries play a vital role in generating demand for the German investment goods industry."[26] In 1980, for example, West Germany registered massive trade deficits with both the United States and Japan. But the small European states absorbed two-fifths of total German exports and their total trade deficit with Germany was more than $11 billion, more than twice as large as the overall trade surplus of Germany in the same year.

On the surface, the close relation between economic openness and dependence, on the one hand, and the corporatist structures of the small European states, on the other, suggests an analogy to the "dependent capitalism" in Third World countries on which much theoretical and empirical work was focused in the 1970s. Latin American authoritarianism, for example, is viewed as a concomitant, or consequence, of the penetration of relatively weak domestic structures by the forces of global capitalism, the multinational corporation its most dynamic agent. Overlooking some important qualitative differences, scholars in the small European states have pointed to similarities between the position of their states and that of many Third World countries.[27] But the small European states are not in the periphery of the world capitalist system. Their insertion into the international economy occurred at an earlier date, when political and economic conditions favored national autonomy. This early development is reflected in the structural characteristics of their foreign trade. The geographic and commodity concentration of foreign trade and the imbalance between the import of raw materials and the export of manufactured goods, as well as between the export of "traditional" as compared to "modern" manufactured products, are greater in the small European states than in the large ones; but they are smaller than in the developing countries.

Developing countries depend on the import of goods, capital, and technology. The small European states depend on exports. Their economic openness and dependence on global markets shape free-trade policies that are conducive to the international competitiveness of their export industries and a politics that is geared to contain uncompetitive wage settlements and price increases. Stephen Krasner has shown that in the small European states and in the developing countries there exists a strong statistical relationship between changes in trade and changes in government revenue. However, in 1974–75 five of the six small European states included in his analysis increased government revenues in real terms, compared to only 19 of 38 developing countries. Krasner concludes that "the revenues of small industrialized countries are susceptible to changes in their trade, but these countries appear able to at least resist an absolute decline . . . while almost half of the developing countries that experienced a decline in trade also suffered a decline in government revenues."[28] It is thus not surprising that in the 1970s the small European states (with the exception of Austria) relied less on established ways of raising tax revenues than did the large industrial countries.[29]

Furthermore, and in contrast to the developing countries, the small European states have in their service sectors a valuable set of economic activities that significantly narrow the perpetual trade deficit imposed by the structure of their economies. Although the small European states depend heavily on foreign investments both for a continuous modernization of their economies and for further reductions in the deficit of their trade balance, the constraints that derive from this dependence remain latent. Austria is one small state that relies on foreign corporations to modernize and diversify its industry, but it has succeeded in making these corporations adhere to a code of conduct, for example in the area of employment, that apparently agrees with the political objectives of the government rather than the narrower economic objectives of management. Finally, the small European states, unlike many of the developing countries, have been able, through their domestic structures, to maintain a great degree of autonomy from foreign influence. This autonomy accounts for the great differences in strategy with which Switzerland, the Netherlands, and Belgium confront the world economy, compared to Austria, Denmark, and Norway.

The pressures of world markets on the domestic structures of the small European states are less intense and less direct than on the developing countries. In the latter countries there frequently emerges an alliance between the state bureaucracy, the military, and segments of the business community. Authoritarian structures that exclude labor in time of crisis may adopt repressive strategies. None of this has occurred in the small European states since 1945. But external pressures have been greater in the small European states than in large industrial countries. The openness and dependence of their economies explains the prevalence of strong corporatist structures rather than liberal or statist forms of capitalism.

Daniel Chirot has suggested that dependence and economic backwardness have created true examples of social corporatism in small socialist countries undergoing rapid development, countries such as Romania. Chirot's argument is provocative because in the 1930s Romania produced perhaps the most important theorist of corporatism, Mihaïl Manoïlescu. His theories, Chirot argues, can be found in the development strategies of both the Left and Right throughout the advanced peripheral and semiperipheral parts of the world. In contrast to the authoritarian Romanian regime of the interwar period, this socialist variant of corporatism is freed from the shackles of traditional class structures and thus can move decisively rather than half-heartedly to new political arrangements. "Manoïlescu was correct. The twentieth century is the century of corporatism. But he was wrong to think that the weak and fraudulent steps taken by fascism in the 1920s and 1930s were significant. It is only now, outside the old capitalist centers, that societies which proudly proclaim themselves Marxist are building genuine corporatism."[30] Although Chirot is wrong to dismiss the relevance of corporatist arrangements to the political practices of capitalist states, his argument dovetails with mine. Authoritarian corporatism, he argues, can be viewed as a political formula for mobilizing resources in the name of either fascism or socialism. Social or liberal variants of corporatism, I have argued, are political formulae with which to mobilize political consensus in the name of either democratic socialism or liberal capitalism.

However, dependence on the international economy limits how far the two variants of democratic corporatism can differ. The convergence in Switzerland's and Austria's exchange-rate policies serves as a good illustration. Although the two countries differed in the methods by which they permitted a sharp appreciation of their currencies in the 1970s, the methods with which they pursued a "hard-currency option" began to converge in the late 1970s.[31] Throughout most of the 1970s Switzerland specified strict targets for monetary growth and let the Franc float autonomously upward in foreign-exchange markets. Only when in 1978–79 the rate of appreciation reached levels that threatened to price Swiss exporters out of world markets did the Swiss National Bank step in and tie the franc informally to the deutsche mark, the currency of Switzerland's most important trading partner. The director of the powerful and market-oriented Crédit Suisse concluded in his reflections on the 1970s that "the value of money, unlike almost everything else under the sun, cannot be left to the free play of market forces but needs to be regulated by the State."[32]

Austria, by way of contrast, never attempted to maintain monetary sovereignty in the 1970s. The governor of Austria's Central Bank acknowledges that "Austrian monetary policy is made in Frankfurt."[33] Market forces were never permitted to determine the value of the schilling; instead, the Central Bank intervened in foreign-exchange markets to maintain a stable exchange rate with the deutsche mark. The Austrians refer to this as a hard-currency option, misleadingly in years such as 1978–80 when the deutsche mark, and with it the schilling, depreciated against the dollar and other major currencies. When either the steadiness or the strength of the deutsche mark is in question, as respectively in early and late 1980, the debates over Austria's policy reveal the same sorts of confusions that existed in Switzerland in the late 1970s and early 1980s. Although Austria and Switzerland differed in how they pursued their foreign-exchange policies throughout most of the 1970s, in the end market pressures forced the Swiss to abandon their autonomous policy and led to a convergence in the policy of the two countries.

This book reflects on a basic theme of contemporary political analysis, the interaction of historically-shaped domestic structures with the world economy. That interaction has political consequences which are far from trivial. The political tensions and changes that the small European states experience in their relations with the world economy have led to the convergence of different forms of corporatism. Corporatism emanates both from the internal logic of the domestic structures and from the external requirements of the international economy.

Lessons

What, if any, are the lessons America can learn? The increasing openness of the economy has made American industry ever more aware of the problems of international competitiveness—problems that have long been familiar to business in the small European states. Between 1970 and 1980 the ratio of U.S. exports to final sale of goods in U.S. markets more than doubled, from 9 to 19 percent; the increase in imports was sharper still, from 9 to 22 percent. Even in product categories or industry segments covered by America's restrictive trade policies, import penetration increased sharply between 1960 and 1979: from 4 to 14 percent in steel, from 6 to 51 percent in consumer electronics, and from 2 to 10 percent in apparel.[34] These figures understate the extent to which America has become an integral part of world markets. By 1980 more than two-thirds of the industrial goods produced in America were actively competing with foreign products.[35] The growing dependence of the American economy on global markets reinforces a sense of vulnerability. Since the mid-1970s the success of Japan's export offensive on the American market has convinced a growing number of Americans that national competitiveness is determined by more than endowment with natural resources and the workings of the market. The strong position that Japanese steel, automobile, and computer industries achieved within two decades suggests that the economic security of American workers and American firms is threatened by Japan's superior ways of organizing for international competition.

Growing economic openness also marks large advanced industrial states in Europe. According to World Bank data, between 1970 and 1980 the share of manufacturing imports grew from 16 to 23 percent in France, from 19 to 31 percent in West Germany, from 16 to 28 percent in Britain, and from 9 to 15 percent in the external trade of the EEC.[36] Geoffrey Shepherd and François Duchêne show similar increases in Europe's major industrial sectors. Glenn Fong has calculated that in the 1970s the rate of change at which the economies of the five large industrial states opened to the international economy was about 50 percent faster than for the small industrial states. America is thus not alone in experiencing sharp increases in economic openness and vulnerability.[37] Under these novel conditions the notion of steering the economy (with all relevant variables under direct control) may, according to Fritz Scharpf, be less useful than the notion of small-boat sailing (in which the captain keeps the boat afloat through skillful adaptation to and exploitation of circumstances beyond control).[38] We could do worse than look to the example of the small European states for lessons in how to react politically to conditions that are new to us and old for them.

Beset by mounting economic troubles during the last decade, the United States has found foreign success stories increasingly attractive. It is evident in America's recent infatuation with and resentment of Japan. Like small boys at a local fair pressing hard against the back of the tent, curious American intellectuals and politicians are often reduced to primitive forms of political voyeurism. Confronted with the astonishing suc-

cess of the small European states in the 1950s, one economist observed rue-
fully (and unconvincingly) that "policy has been somewhat more sensi-
ble in the relatively open economies."[39]

Switzerland and Austria stand out as the two clearest examples of the
liberal and social variants of democratic corporatism to which the other
small European states approximate in different degrees. In order to
account for the exemplary success of these countries in the 1970s, some
propose explanations that reflect what a friend of mine calls the Seven
Dwarf Theory of Central Europe: the Austrians and the Swiss are both so
successful because they depart for work each morning with a happy yodel.
In one newspaper column George Will subscribed to the audaciously com-
monsensical notion that Austrians like to work and are, therefore, economically successful.[40] The explanation will no doubt please Catholics in
Austria, dismay Calvinists in Switzerland, confound faithful readers of
Weber's *Protestant Ethic* everywhere, and leave unconvinced those who
value evidence; in the mid-1970s the Austrians worked shorter hours than
the Swiss. Representative Henry Reuss, chairman of the Joint Economic
Committee, expressed this bafflement: "When you put America's economic
performance up against this country's, one is certainly compelled to seek
what there is about the Austrian structure which enables your much better performance to occur."[41]

In an article entitled "Are There Any Swiss Lessons for the U.S.?" one
of Switzerland's most powerful bankers offered scant hope. He concluded, "My country's institutions are tailor-made for a small nation with
the historical peculiarities of Switzerland."[42] Another analysis links Austria's
success to political commitments not easily transferred to other societies:
"The lesson which can be learned is that tripartite bargaining offers prospects for the attainment of some of the objectives of the working people.
The particular forms, machinery, and administrative arrangements are of
less importance than the desire to achieve certain broad policy goals in an
unstable world."[43] Without linking his prescription for America to the political experience of the small European states, Robert Reich summarizes
aptly the secret to their success in arguing that "we need political institutions that are as versatile as flexible-system enterprises—less concerned
with making 'correct' decisions than with making correctable ones; less
obsessed with avoiding error than with detecting and correcting for error;
more devoted to responding to changing conditions and encouraging
new enterprises than to stabilizing the environment for old enterprises."[44] In the political parlance of one conservative economist Reich's

prescription is nothing more than "fashionable fascism," an unfortunate oversimplification.[45]

This book offers no easy solutions to America's problems. Economic performance measures have influenced the argument at several points, but they are not the book's primary concern. I have argued, rather, that the small European states frame political choices in a distinctive way. Their choices are conditioned by two sets of forces: historically shaped domestic structures and the pressures of the world economy. These two sets of forces interact. And it is in the process of interaction—the unending and limited conflicts over economic and social issues—that the requirements of domestic and international politics converge in a flexible strategy of adjustment.

We cannot apply the "lessons" of the small European states for the simple reason that we cannot remake our history. The very attempt of a Republican president drastically to recast the shape of America in the 1980s illustrates the narrow political limits in this country of "unlimited opportunities." Yet even while writing this book, I could observe history changing America. The declining fortunes of America's steel and automobile industries, as well as the wood stoves reappearing in New England, illustrate our increasing economic openness and vulnerability. Suzanne Berger and Michael Piore have rightly pointed to the disadvantages of a narrow conception of political possibilities. This book was motivated by an idea that they have put well: the largest problem we face, they write, is "our beliefs about the limits of the possible. In order to release both imagination and will from the constraints of false necessity, we need a vision of the diverse possibilities that can be realized within industrial societies."[46]

Looking at the politics of unfamiliar countries may be confusing, but it can also be illuminating, even liberating. The small European states offer us an intriguing perspective because in an era of shrinking economic resources their political conflicts do not resemble the image, so familiar in Washington, of wrestlers in a china shop. "Bigness in a nation has certain advantages," writes Andrew Shonfield, "but it does sometimes succeed in swamping the national perception of what is obvious to smaller people."[47] That national perception is a distinctive trademark. The small European states acknowledge that policy is an essential ingredient in reaffirming and modifying an always evolving consensus, that victory in any battle must be balanced against the need to assure the loser of another round in a protracted, limited war. It is of course a sobering thought that other countries, especially small, powerless, and vulnerable ones, are better equipped than the large, powerful, and less vulnerable United States to deal politically with the economic dislocations and uncertainties of the 1980s. The record of the 1970s, however, and the argument of this book suggest that such a thought cannot be dismissed easily. But in this case the bad news brings good in its train. Our difficulty in grasping the political and economic achievements of the small European states reflects a lack of political imagination—a loss more easily remedied than many others.

This book has focused on the political consequences of economic openness and international vulnerability. "Adversarial politics" typical of the United States is constrained in the small European states by awareness of common interest and the "unitary politics" it creates.[48] Typical of small European states is decision-making by consensus, which supplements majority rule. A "unitary politics" can of course emerge, at least for a time, in large industrial states: with technocrats through a logic of things that reduces politics to administration; with Weberians through the institutionalization of charisma; with Marxists through the struggle for socialism; and with conservatives through wise statesmen determining the collective good in the realm of moral philosophy rather than individual preference. Typically, though, all such appearances are temporary; as Jane Mansbridge argues, "Like war itself, efforts to create a unitary 'moral equivalent of war' lose their glamor."[49] America provides ample illustrations. On economic questions policy initiatives are often couched in the language of national security. The National Defense Highway Act, the National Education Act, and a variety of energy programs are all described aptly by what Theodore Lowi has claimed of American foreign policy more generally: in overselling the threat it also oversells the remedy.[50]

Since the 1930s the small European states have experienced in economic openness and international vulnerability at least a partial substitute for the "moral equivalent of war" (when not experiencing war itself). A flexible economy and cooperative politics has been one consequence. A second consequence, not stressed here, is the danger inherent in corporatist arrangements. The widespread notion of a common good, suggested by international economic pressures, makes political conflicts over basic political choices illegitimate for longer periods of time than in large industrial states. It is no accident that Parliament, as the institutional arena where such choices are typically fought out in liberal democracies, has less importance in Switzerland and Austria than in any other advanced industrial state.[51] As large industrial states increasingly experience those consequences of economic openness and vulnerability to which the small European states have had decades to adapt, the trend toward democratic corporatism will undoubtedly alter the style and substance of democratic politics.

In some sectors of American society, formal or informal corporatist arrangements have appeared as a natural response to the economic crisis of the late 1970s and early 1980s. Chrysler's Loan Guarantee Board was staffed by members of the federal government, management, and the unions. New York City's fiscal crisis was managed by informal cooperation between bankers like Felix Rohatyn, trade union officials like Victor Gotbaum, and state officials. Less spectacular attempts have occurred in other situations with mixed success. Industry advisory committees, set up during the Tokyo Round of trade negotiations, collaborated successfully because of the threat posed by foreign competition. By contrast, the Steel Tripartite Commission, confronted with a severe crisis in the American steel industry, failed to overcome ideological and legal barriers to successful cooperation. Where the perception of vulnerability and crisis approaches levels considered "normal" in the small European states, corporatism has become part of America's political repertoire.

But short of a general crisis engulfing all of American society—a crisis like the Great Depression or World War II—corporatism faces substantial difficulties at the national level. In many ways corporatism is antithetical to the core of American politics. Distrust of administrative discretion has encouraged a litigational style of politics and an emphasis on procedural fairness that is at odds with the requirements of corporatist bargaining. Furthermore, American society is relatively unorganized: Peak associations that can claim broad social support are rare. For example, corporatism in America would have to include organized labor, yet the proportion of workers organized by American trade unions is only between one-half and one-third of corresponding numbers in the small European states—and the American proportion is declining. Social movements such as the civil rights movement or the women's movement effect political changes on their own in America. In the small European states they are typically captured by existing groups or political parties. In the well-organized societies of the small European states corporatism is inclusionary. Transplanted to America, corporatism tends toward exclusion.

In the case of the small European states, the interaction of national and global factors to force a flexible policy of adaptation is not new. Reflecting on the 1930s, Carol Major Wright concluded in 1939: "If it is not likely that a small country can effectively 'take arms against a sea of troubles' it is equally clear that efforts at isolation from world market changes are costly and indeed ruinous. . . . The little countries must emulate David who rejected the hampering armor that Saul pressed upon him and relied on his mobility and quick adaptability."[52] The insistence on the need for adaptability that Wright derived from the experience of the 1930s is confirmed by the 1970s and 1980s, but the prescription for a certain type of government intervention is not. Today the air resounds with calls for "positive" rather than "negative" adjustment, for policies that accelerate rather than slow the shift of factors of production from "declining" to "growth" sectors. The international bureaucrats who first coined these phrases in the mid-1970s hoped to elevate to a programmatic level the political necessity for a rapid restructuring of domestic economies. How else could one avoid a dangerous relapse into another round of protectionism, 1930s-style? The capacity to maneuver abroad and adapt at home requires a mobility of the factors of production that among the successful developing countries frequently coincides with authoritarianism and political repression.[53] This is an unlikely choice for the small European states. During the last half-century all the advanced industrial states have witnessed vast transformations in the character of their economy and politics. Calls for "positive adjustment" are surrounded by the same air of unreality as policy prescriptions derived from the venerable distinction between market and plan: Through excessive repetition they soon acquire the unenviable status of platitudes. Issued often with little understanding of the capacities of political structures and the pressures acting upon them, these exhortations represent the Peter Pan approach to public policy: One closes one's eyes and wishes really hard.

The distinctive strategy by which the small European states adjust to change derives from corporatist domestic structures that have their historical origin in the 1930s and 1940s. Crisis conditions can create domestic structures that combine democratic practices with political efficacy and economic efficiency. In the past decades the large industrial states have moved uneasily toward the conditions of economic openness and vulnerability, long characteristic of the small European states. For optimists among us, this is cause for cheer: It represents movement toward an essential condition if this decade is to deliver the promises rather than the horrors of the 1930s.

The adjustment strategy of the small European states is summed up by the story of the snake, the frog, and the owl. Fearful of being devoured by the snake, the frog asks the owl how he might survive. The owl's response is brief and cryptic: Learn how to fly. None of the small European states has learned to soar like the eagle. What they have learned to cultivate is an amazing capacity to jump. Although they appear to land on their stomachs, in fact they always land on their feet and retain the ability to jump again and again in different directions, correcting their course as they go along. In a world of great uncertainty and high-risk choices, this is an intelligent response. Frogs can escape snakes, and the small corporatist states can continue to prosper—not because they have found a solution to the problem of change but because they have found a way to live with change.

Notes

1. Béla Kádár, "Adjustment Patterns and Policies in Small Countries," in István Dobozi, Clare Keller, and Harriet Matejka, eds., *International Structural Adjustment: A Collection of Hungarian and Swiss Views* (Geneva: Graduate Institute of International Studies, 1982), pp. 93–104.

2. International Monetary Fund, *International Financial Statistics*, Supplement Series no. 6 (1983), p. 105.

3. Peer Hull Kristensen and Jørn Levinsen, *The Small Country Squeeze* (Roskilde, Denmark: Institute of Economics, Politics and Administration, 1978). See also *Wall Street Journal*, 14 December 1982, pp. 1 and 17.

4. Kristensen and Levinsen, *Small Country Squeeze*, pp. 37, 47–48, 91–98, 270–73, 316–17.

5. *Der Spiegel*, 3 November 1980, pp. 184–88; *World Business Weekly*, 11 May 1981, p. 11.

6. Andrew Boyd, "How the Storm Changed the Signs," *Economist*, 28 January 1978, Survey, p. 30.

7. "How Sweden's Middle Road Becomes a Dead End," *Forbes*, 27 April 1981, p. 35.

8. Morgan Guaranty, *World Financial Markets*, January 1984, author's calculations.

9. *University of Pennsylvania News*, 20 August 1982 (081682); *Der Österreich-Bericht*, 19 August 1982, p. 1. See also Manfred G. Schmidt, "The Welfare State and the Economy in Periods of Economic Crisis: A Comparative Study of Twenty-Three OECD Nations," *European Journal of Political Research* 11 (March 1983), 1–26; Schmidt, "Arbeitslosigkeit and Vollbeschäftigungspolitik," *Leviathan* 11, 4 (1983), 451–73.

10. Quoted in *Wall Street Journal*, 14 December 1982, p. 17, and 22 September 1983, p. 35. See also *New York Times*, 21 July 1983, p. A8; Bent Rold Andersen, "Rationality and Irrationality of the Nordic Welfare State," *Daedalus*, Winter 1984, pp. 130–34.

11. *New York Times*, 19 January, p. 2; *Der Spiegel*, 16 January 1984, pp. 97–99; and *Economist*, 30 June 1984, pp. 58–59.

12. *New York Times*, 8 December 1983, p. A2, and 3 June 1984, p. 9.

13. M. C. P. M. Van Schendelen, "Crisis of the Dutch Welfare State," *Contemporary Crises* 7 (1983), 218.

14. Quoted in *New York Times*, 21 April 1984, p. 31.

15. Arne Ruth, "The Second New Nation: The Mythology of Modern Sweden," *Daedalus*, Spring 1984, p. 56.

16. *New York Times*, 8 December 1983, p. A2.

17. Arthur F. P. Wassenberg, "Neo-Corporatism and the Quest for Control: The Cuckoo Game," in Gerhard Lehmbruch and Philippe C. Schmitter, eds., *Patterns of Corporatist Policy-Making* (Beverly Hills: Sage, 1982), pp. 83–108; Erwin Zimmermann, "Entwicklungstendenzen des Korporatismus und die Industriepolitik in den Niederlanden," in *Neokorporatistische Politik in Westeuropa*, University of Constance, Sozialwissenschaftliche Fakultät, Fachgruppe Politikwissenschaft/Verwaltungswissenschaft, Diskussionbeitrag 1 (1982), pp. 107–31.

18. Steven B. Wolinetz, "Wage Regulation in the Netherlands: The Rise and Fall of the Postwar Social Contract" (paper prepared for presentation at the Council for European Studies Conference of Europeanists, Washington, D. C., 13–15 October 1983).

19. James R. Kurth, "The Political Consequences of the Product Cycle: Industrial History and Political Outcomes," *International Organization* 33 (Winter 1979), 1–34; Peter Gourevitch, "Breaking with Orthodoxy: The Politics of Economic Policy Responses to the Depression of the 1930s," *International Organization* 38 (Winter 1984), 95–130; and Thomas Ferguson, "From Normalcy to New Deal: Industrial Structure, Party Competition, and American Public Policy in the Great Depression," *International Organization* 38 (Winter 1984), 41–94.

20. Peter J. Katzenstein, *Corporatism and Change: Austria, Switzerland, and the Politics of Industry* (Ithaca: Cornell University Press, 1984), especially chaps. 5 and 6.

21. Charles F. Sabel, "From Austro-Keynesianism to Flexible Specialization: The Political Preconditions of Industrial Redeployment in an *Astgemeinschaft*" (paper delivered at the Österreichische Nationalbank, Vienna, 20 May 1983).

22. *Wall Street Journal*, 6 September 1983, p. 38, and 13 April 1984, p. 37.

23. *New York Times*, 24 January 1984, p. A25.

24. See Peter J. Katzenstein, "Problem or Model? West Germany in the 1980s," *World Politics* 23 (July 1980), 577–98; Katzenstein, "West Germany as Number Two: Reflections on the German Model," in Andrei Markovits, ed., *The Political Economy of West Germany: Modell Deutschland* (New York: Praeger, 1982), pp. 199–215; and Katzenstein, *A Semi-Sovereign State: Policy and Politics in West Germany* (Philadelphia: Temple University Press, forthcoming).

25. Wolfgang Kohte, *Die niederländische Volkswirtschaft heute: Ihre Wandlungen seit der Vorkriegszeit* (Stuttgart: Kohlhammer, 1954); Ludwig Mülhaupt, *Strukturwandlungen und Nachkriegsprobleme der Wirtschaft Schwedens* (Kiel: Institut für Weltwirtschaft, 1952); Gerhard Pfeiffer, *Strukturwandlungen und Nachkriegsprobleme der Wirtschaft der Niederlande* (Kiel: Institute für Weltwirtschaft, 1950); Wolf von Arnim, *Strukturwandlungen und Nachkriegsprobleme der Wirtschaft Dänemarks* (Kiel: Institut für Weltwirtschaft, 1950); Hugo Heeckt, *Strukturwandlungen und Nachkriegsprobleme der Wirtschaft Norwegens* (Kield: Institut für Weltwirtschaft, 1950); Allan Lyle, *Die Industrialisierung Norwegens* (Jena: Fischer, 1939); Wilhelm Keilhau, *Volkswirtschaftspolitik und weltwirtschafl-*

iche Stellung Norwegens (Jena: Fischer, 1938); G. M. Verrijn Stuart, *Die Industrie-politik der niederländischen Regierung* (Jena: Fischer, 1936); Jens Samsöe, *Die Industrialisierung Dänemarks* (Jena: Fischer, 1926); and Sven Helander, *Schweden's Stellung in der Weltwirtschaft* (Jena: Fischer, 1922).

26. Marcello de Cecco, "Introduction," in de Cecco, ed., *International Economic Adjustment: Small Countries and the European Monetary System* (Oxford: Blackwell, 1983), p. 3.

27. See for example several contributions in *Österreichische Zeitschrift für Politikwissenschaft*, 1978/3, and Otmar Höll and Helmut Kramer, "Kleinstaaten im Internationalen System: Endbericht," unpublished manuscript, Vienna, 1977. A more sophisticated discussion can be found in Margret Sieber, *Die Abhängigkeit der Schweiz von ihrer internationalen Umwelt: Konzepte und Indikatoren* (Frauenfeld: Huber, 1979), pp. 330–46 and 386, and in Hans Vogel, *Der Kleinstaat in der Welt-politik: Aspekte der schweizerischen Aussenbeziehungen im internationalen Vergleich* (Frauenfeld: Huber, 1979). A broad range of approaches is contained in Höll, ed. *Small States in Europe and Dependence* (Vienna: Braumüller, 1983).

28. Stephen D. Krasner, *Structural Conflict: The Third World against Global Liberalism* (Berkeley: University of California Press, forthcoming), manuscript, Chapter 2, p. 17.

29. Richard Rose, *Understanding Big Government: The Programme Approach* (Beverly Hills: Sage, 1984), p. 113.

30. Daniel Chirot, "The Corporatist Model and Socialism: Notes on Romanian Development," *Theory and Society* 9, 2 (1980), 378. On the importance of Manoïlescu see also Philippe C. Schmitter, "Still the Century of Corporatism?" in Schmitter and Gerhard Lehmbruch, eds., *Trends toward Corporatist Inter-mediation* (Beverly Hills: Sage, 1979), pp. 7–52.

31. Helmut Frisch, "Stabilization Policy in Austria, 1970–80," in de Cecco, *International Economic Adjustment*, pp. 117–40; René Kästli, "The New Economic Environment in the 1970s: Market and Policy Response in Switzerland," in ibid., pp. 141–59. See also Marian E. Bond, "Exchange Rates, Inflation, and Vicious Circles," *International Monetary Fund Staff Papers* 27 (1980), 679–711; Niels Thygesen, "Exchange-Rate Experiences and Policies of Small Countries: Some European Examples of the 1970s," International Finance Section, Department of Economics, *Essays in International Finance* no. 136, (Princeton, N. J., December 1979); Eduard Hochreiter, "Theoretische und praktische Aspekte der Aussen-währungspolitik kleiner Länder," *Wirtschaftspolitische Blätter* 23, 3 (1976), 21–32; and "Tracking Europe's 'Small' Currencies," *World Business Weekly*, 2 March 1981, pp. 51–52.

32. Rainer E. Gut, "Trends in Foreign Exchange and Finance Markets as Seen from Switzerland," *Crédit Suisse Bulletin* 86 (Autumn 1980), 5–8.

33. Quoted in Paul Lewis, "The Austrian Economy Is a Strauss Waltz," *New York Times*, 22 March 1981, p. F8.

34. Ira C. Magaziner and Robert B. Reich, *Minding America's Business: The Decline and Rise of the American Economy* (New York: Harcourt Brace Jovanovich, 1982), p. 33.

35. Robert B. Reich, *The Next American Frontier* (New York: Times, 1983),

7

THE ROLE OF SMALL STATES
IN THE EUROPEAN UNION

BALDUR THORHALLSSON

The research has analyzed whether the special characteristics of smaller states (strong corporatism and concentrated economic interests, according to Katzenstein) impact their approach in the decision-making process of the EU in the areas of the CAP and the Regional Policy. The empirical evidence established in this research supports the main hypothesis. The behavior of smaller states can be distinguished from the behavior of the larger states. Smaller states have a different approach towards the Commission and their negotiating tactics differ from the negotiating tactics of the larger states in the Council of Ministers, the European Council, and in bilateral negotiations with the Commission.

This difference in behavior between the smaller and larger states can be explained by the small administrations, their characteristics and different range of interests of the smaller states. Smaller states are forced to prioritize between the sectors of these two policy areas because of their small administrations. They do not have enough staff, expertise, or other resources to follow all negotiations. As a result, they become reactive in many sectors. However, they are proactive in their most important sectors. This is because they use the special characteristics of their administrations, such as informality, flexible decision-making, greater room of maneuver for their officials, guidelines given to negotiators rather than instructions, and the greater role of Permanent Representatives in domestic policy-making to ease their workload and to operate within the decision-making process of the CAP and the Regional Policy. They can also prioritize between sectors

From Baldur Thorhallsson, *The Role of Small States in the European Union* (Burlington, VT: Ashgate, 2000). Reprinted with permission of Ashgate Publishing Limited. Cross references to pages and notes refer to the original publication.

without damaging their interests because they have a narrower range of interests in those policy areas than the larger states.[1]

A Modification of Katzenstein's Theory:
The Limited Explanatory Role of Corporatism

The special characteristics of smaller states identified by Katzenstein do not provide a satisfactory explanation for the distinguishing behavior of the smaller states in the areas of the CAP and the Regional Policy. His approach has to be widened in order to give the complete picture. A new variable, the size of the state's administration and its characteristics, should be taken into consideration when explaining the international behavior of member states. Katzenstein does briefly mention the relationship between administrations of the smaller states and their domestic economic policy-making but his approach fails to take account of the advantages and disadvantages which stem from the smallness of an administration, and how its resulting characteristics can influence a state's international behavior.

The evidence produced in this study supports Katzenstein's assertion that strong corporatism affects the international behavior of smaller states in the EU context. In addition, there are indications that their vulnerability and their open economies lead to economic specialization which also has an effect, in our case, within the CAP and the Regional Policy. However, the strong corporatism in the smaller states does not explain their different approach towards the Commission and their different negotiating tactics, compared to the larger states. This is because the larger states are just as restricted as the smaller states by their domestic interests, as sectoral corporatism has indicated. Agrarian interests, regional authorities, and other interests are involved in the domestic decision-making of the larger states, which restricts their behavior in negotiations in the CAP and the Regional Policy. They have to come from the negotiation table in Brussels with positive deals for their domestic interests just as the smaller states have to because of their corporatist framework, and as liberal intergovernmentalist theories argue.

Katzenstein distinguishes between the strong corporatism of the smaller states in Europe and the weak corporatism of the larger industrial states. Democratic corporatism in the smaller states, he claims, can be traced back to the 1930s, and he argues that their economic openness and dependency has established a compelling need for consensus. This consensus has been created between the main actors in the smaller states through complex and delicate political arrangements. There is a close relation between the eco-

nomic openness and dependency of the smaller states and their corporatist structures: "The openness and dependence of their economies
explains the prevalence of a strong corporatist structure."[2] This has "had
a strong effect on their political strategies."[3] Katzenstein further argues that
small states in Europe frame "political choices in a distinctive way."[4] These
choices are conditioned by two sets of forces which interact: "historically-
shaped domestic structures and the pressures of the world economy."[5] The
interaction between those forces alters the style and substance of the
response of smaller states.

Our findings support Hick's criticism of the approach of Katzenstein
in its virtual equation of smallness with corporatism.[6] Our case studies
illustrate that the strong corporatism, defined by Katzenstein, in the
smaller states, fails to explain their different negotiating tactics in the EU
context. Evidence indicates that the weak corporatism of the larger states
includes a close cooperation between the governments of the larger states
and their domestic interests, which we have referred to as sectoral corporatism. This relationship affects their negotiating tactics in the EU institutions and leads the larger states towards inflexibility just as the strong
corporatism of the smaller states does. Hicks argues that Katzenstein's theoretically central concept of democratic corporatism is problematic. This
is because "it produces a categorization of corporatist nations that is incon-
sistent with the categorizations of others."[7] He also argues that it is incon-
sistent with Katzenstein's own claims for superior corporatist economic
growth and with its own standards for identifying corporatism.[8]

Katzenstein's notion of the strong corporatism in the smaller states is,
for instance, blurred in practice when he tries to distinguish between it and
what he calls the weak corporatism in Germany. He argues that Germany
gets closest of the larger states to the strong corporatism of the smaller
states because its corporatism derives from openness, dependency, and a
sense of vulnerability brought about by the diminished size of the Federal
Republic of Germany, after 1945 along with the implantation of the
German political parties.[9] The style of policy-making in Germany has been
characterized by consensus among political actors,[10] but its corporatism
falls short of being the same as in the smaller states because "political parties play a greater role in the handling of conflicting objectives across
different sectors of policy."[11]

Hick concludes his criticism of Katzenstein's notion of democratic corporatism by stating that although it helps in studying the interactions of
smaller states, "it is better to view Katzenstein's democratic corporatism
as an organizational device than as a theoretical concept."[12] This is because

Katzenstein's approach identifies no single institutional complex in his six small states which enhances democratic corporatism and which consolidates understanding of the disparate strategies of the smaller states.[13]

Katzenstein's approach has also been criticized for using the economic environment to explain the political consensus of the smaller states in Europe. The approach is "weakest . . . when explaining the political consensus as a result of the economic environment."[14] Griffiths and Pharo suggest that the collective action theory should be applied if we are to understand periods of strong consensus in smaller states. This is because the nature and strength of the major interest groups, the farmers and workers, might be useful in the explanation. They further criticize Katzenstein's approach for its focus upon internal factors when explaining the behavior of smaller states. For them an analysis of factors, other than just internal economic and political factors, might be helpful. They continue: "A lot of work remains to be done in the field of how international openness reflects back on the domestic political scene."[15]

Administrative Size and Characteristics: An Important Explanatory Variable

The characteristics of the administrations of the smaller states are key factors in explaining how smaller states operate in the decision-making processes in the CAP and the Regional Policy. These features are in contrast to the characteristics of the administrations of the larger states and their EU working procedure: a hierarchical structure, formal decision-making processes, limited or no maneuver for officials, and strict instructions to negotiators in Brussels from their capitals.

The administrations of the smaller states are, of course, not all the same and the coordination of EU policy-making within them differs. Our evidence, however, indicates that all their working procedures concerning EU matters are characterized by similar features. The administration of Luxembourg must however be distinguished from the other small administrations as it has even less capacity to participate in sectors within the CAP and the Regional Policy because of its extraordinarily small size. Also, the administration of Greece has a more limited capacity than the other administrations of the smaller states, because it has been slower to develop a formal structure in handling EU issues. However, it has responded to the workload by adopting informal working methods, by being flexible in handling matters, and by giving its officials considerable scope for maneuver in sectors which are not regarded as being important domestically.

These administrative features are even more evident in the case of the administration of Greece than in other small administrations. Furthermore, Greece puts heavy emphasis on prioritization as it concentrates only on issues where it has important domestic interests. This eases the workload of the administration. The administration of Portugal also had some difficulties in handling EU matters during its first year of membership. However, these difficulties seem to be over and the Portuguese administration is characterized by the same features in handling matters within the CAP and the Regional Policy as other small administrations.

If we look at the administrations of the larger states, the administrations of Spain and Italy are weaker than the administrations of Britain, Germany, and France. The Spanish administration has made an attempt to adopt some of the characteristics of a small administration in order to overcome its weakness. It has opted for informal working methods between officials which has made them more able to cope with the wide scope of the CAP and the Regional Policy. Informal methods of communication between officials have also sped up the EU domestic decision-making process. Furthermore, the Spanish Permanent Representation's participation in EU negotiations is helped by their involvement in the domestic decision-making process. However, the Spanish administration has created these informal working methods between officials without developing a flexible decision-making structure concerning EU matters. The administration itself is characterized by the typical features of large administrations such as a formal decision-making structure and the limited scope of maneuver for its negotiators. Therefore, the administration has adopted the same approach towards the Commission as other large administrations, and its negotiating tactics in the Council of Ministers and the European Council are identical with the negotiating tactics of the other larger states.

The administration of Italy is a somewhat different case. It is considerably weaker than the administrations of Britain, Germany, France, and Spain, for a number of domestic reasons. The Italian administration has had difficulties in its EU policy coordination, in presenting a coherent policy-stand in EU negotiations, and in implementing EU legislation. The administration has not tried to overcome these weaknesses by adopting some of the characteristics of a small administrations like the Spanish administration. As a result, Italy cannot be regarded as being as active within EU policy-making, in the areas of the Regional Policy and the CAP, as the other larger states. Italy is active in pursuing its interests but it falls short of taking as predominant a role as the other larger states. However, we also have to take the pro-European attitude of Italy into consideration, as this partly explains why Italy has, on some occasions, been flexible and not taken a confrontational stand in negotiations. This has been the case for a number of negotiations in the Regional Policy. However, the main reason for the less predominant role of Italy in debates concerning the Regional Policy, is its administrative weakness in handling matters concerning this policy-area, both within the decision-making process of the EU and domestically.

The weakness of the Italian administration leads us to the question of whether the conducting of EU business within the Italian administration has more in common with the administrations of the smaller states than the administrations of the larger states. However, this is not the case. The EU working procedure of the Italian administration is characterized by centralization, a hierarchical structure, formality, and inflexible decision-making. Also, the negotiators in Brussels get instructions rather than guidelines from ministries. They have limited room for maneuver in negotiations and they do not participate in domestic EU decision-making. All this stiffness within the administration adds to the lack of domestic coordination over EU matters. Furthermore, the lack of coordination between ministries and weak working procedures between them add to the difficulties for negotiators in presenting a coherent stand within the CAP and the Regional Policy. It also makes it more difficult to adopt a confrontation stand within the Councils even though the pro-European attitude of the Italian governments plays its part in this as well. However, the Italian administration has the capacity to participate in all negotiations within the CAP and the Regional Policy, which is not the case for the small administrations. All these features of the administration of Italy distinguish it from the administrations of the smaller states. Italy plays an active role in negotiations concerning the CAP and the Regional Policy but its administrative weakness and pro-European attitude have on some occasions led it towards a more flexible and less confrontational stand in negotiations than the other larger states. The weakness of the Italian administration and its consequences further strengthens our claim that a variable "administration" has to be considered when the participation of member states in the EU decision-making is analyzed.

Administrative Size and Characteristics: The Relationship Between Smaller States and the Commission

The size and characteristics of the administrations of the smaller states provide an important insight into the approach of the smaller member states towards the Commission. Firstly, the larger states are able to exert a stronger influence upon the Commission. The smaller states compensate for this by using the special characteristics of their small administrations to develop a special relationship with officials of the Commission. Secondly, due to the limited capacity of the administrations of the smaller states, they rely more upon the Commission to get their proposals through the Council. The size and characteristics of small administrations provide an explanation for the routine working process and their increased reliance on the Commission.

All our case studies, in Chapter 6 and 7, indicate that larger states tend to have a more confrontational approach towards the Commission. Large administrations have enough information and resources available to challenge the Commission's position and they tend to do so on all occasions. On the other hand, the limited capacity of the administrations of the smaller states means that they cannot lobby the Commission to the same extent as administrations of the larger states. Smaller states try to compensate by developing a special relationship with officials of the Commission and by exercising their influence within its advisory committee system, using the restrictive comitology procedures.[16] Smaller states are active in their attempt to influence the Commission in sectors where they have important interests, but reactive in others. The officials of the smaller states are able to establish a routine working process with officials of the Commission because of their smaller number of interests, in our two policy areas, compared with the larger states, and because they have a smaller number of officials dealing with individual cases. They can offer the Commission's officials a quicker, and often, a more efficient domestic decision-making process as decisions are made by informal contacts and the decision-making process itself is flexible. They have greater room for maneuver than officials of the larger states and they often oversee the whole domestic process as they can be involved in the state's policy-formation and its implementation. They also tend to work with the Commission in order to find a common solution. This was, for instance, clear in our case studies concerning the new Cohesion Fund, the increased resources of the Regional Policy in 1992, and in the revision of Objective 1 areas in the Regional Policy reform in 1993. Officials of the smaller states of Ireland, Portugal, Greece, and Belgium, which were supposed to benefit most from these policy changes, worked with the Commission in order to find a common solution, while officials from all the larger states were more confrontational towards the Commission.

Smaller states rely on the Commission to put their views forward in sectors where they do not have important domestic interests because they depend upon its resources and information. If we look at the sectors where smaller states do have direct domestic interests, they still have a bigger need for the Commission's support. For, as Chapter 6 demonstrates, although they have the resources and information needed to take a policy-stand, they always try to avoid isolation as they are less likely to be able to block proposals on their own than the larger states. The smaller states look to the Commission for support and while they may not always receive it they demand that the Commission acts as a mediator between them and the larger states. In order to enhance the mediator role of the Commission they tend to work with it during the early stages in the decision-making process. Whereas the larger states will not hesitate to take on a whole Council meeting and the Commission, smaller states tend to move towards a compromise before they become isolated in a Council meeting.

Furthermore, "one might add that they (smaller states) sometimes use their weakness to get even more from the Council than the larger member states, for instance, by using an attitude which says: 'Don't bully me, I am so small and fragile.' When not directly opposed to larger member states' interests, it sometimes works surprisingly well."[17]

Administrative Size and Characteristics: The Negotiation Tactics of Smaller States

Our evidence indicates that the negotiation approaches of the smaller states are identical and can be distinguished by two features: Smaller states tend to be inflexible in negotiations where they have important interests, but are flexible in negotiations where they do not have specific interests. This twofold negotiation approach differs from the negotiation approach of the larger states. They tend to be inflexible in all negotiations regardless of whether they have direct domestic interests involved.

Evidence in Chapter 7 demonstrates that the effectiveness of strong corporatism as an explanation for the behavior of smaller states in the negotiation process in the CAP and the Regional Policy, is limited because of the close cooperation between governments of larger states and their domestic interests. The chapter indicates that the governments of larger states are as bound by a close cooperation with their domestic interests as the governments of the smaller states are by their corporatist structure. It is the size and characteristics of the administrations of member states and their range of domestic interests in these two policy-areas which explains their different negotiating tactics.

This research has shown that small administrations have similar characteristics and that they differ from the characteristics of the large administrations. Also the range of interests of the smaller states is different from the larger states in the CAP and the Regional Policy. As a result the approach of the smaller states towards the Commission as well as their negotiating tactics in negotiations in the Council of Ministers, the European Council, and in bilateral negotiations with the Commission, are not the same as the larger states. Katzenstein's approach is found to be correct in that the economic openness and vulnerability of smaller states affects their economic specialization, leading to a different range of interests in the CAP and the Regional Policy compared to the larger states. However, his approach carries the danger of the wrong conclusion if a new variable, the size and characteristics of an administration, is not taken into account in explaining the behavior of smaller states in the EU decision-making process, in the areas of the CAP, and the Regional Policy. The special role of small administrations in negotiations in the EU and the importance of their relationship with the Commission should not be neglected.

Notes

1. The new member states of the EU (Finland, Sweden, and Austria) seem to prioritize between sectors in the EU to the same extent as the other smaller states, according to our interviews conducted in Brussels and an article in a Norwegian journal on EU matters. It states that Finland puts emphasis upon a few issues within the EU, mainly some particular sectors within the CAP and the Regional Policy. At the same time Finland makes an effort to be pro-European on all occasions. See *Europa brevet, Uavhengig norsk perspektive på Europas utvikling* (1998), No. 137, 28 September, p. 3.

2. Katzenstein, P. (1985), op. cit., p. 203.

3. Ibid., p. 200.

4. Ibid., p. 207.

5. Ibid., p. 207.

6. Hicks, A. (1988), "National Collective Action and Economic Performance: A Review Article," in *International Studies Quarterly*, Vol. 32, No. 2, p.136.

7. Ibid., p. 137.

8. Ibid., p. 137. See a detailed criticism of Katzenstein's work, pp. 131–153.

9. Katzenstein, P. (1985), op. cit., p. 210.

10. Ibid., p. 201.

11. Griffiths, R. T. and Pharo, H. (1995), op. cit., p. 36.

12. Hicks (1988), op. cit., p. 145.

13. Ibid., p. 145.

14. Griffiths, R. T. and Pharo, H. (1995), op. cit., p. 36.

15. Ibid., p. 36.

16. Phillips, K. (1993), *Comitology, a study*, an unpublished internal study conducted on the behalf of the Council to: ". . . unravel the mystery surrounding comitology—what is it exactly, how does it work, and why has it become a source of friction between the institutions of the Community? . . . (and to) . . . examine the role it (comitology) plays in the legislative process. . . ."

17. An interview with an official in the General Secretariat of the Council.

PART III

Small State Capacity
in International Relations

8

LEARNING, REALISM, AND ALLIANCES

The Weight of the Shadow of the Past

DAN REITER

Alliances are central to international relations: they are the primary foreign policy means by which states increase their security, and they are crucial determinants of the outbreak, spread, and outcome of wars. The dominant theory in international relations scholarship—realism—because of its focus on power and security also places a great emphasis on alliances. This article tests realist predictions for alliance behavior against those of learning theory, which is emerging as an alternative conceptual framework to traditional realism. Whereas realism proposes that states ally in response to changes in the level of external threat, the learning theory advanced here proposes that states make alliance policy in accordance with lessons drawn from formative historical experiences. The empirical test in this article uses quantitative methods of analysis to compare the predictions of realism and learning for the alliance choices of minor powers in the twentieth century. The evidence clearly points to learning as the dominant explanation of states' alliance choices, and it shows that variations in the levels of external threat have only marginal effects on alliance behavior.

Significantly, these strong empirical results were achieved using a relatively simple conception of learning. The basic learning proposition is that lessons are drawn from significant foreign policy experiences: continuity of policy follows success, while innovation follows failure. Some scholars have built relatively sophisticated models of learning that incorporate microeconomic concepts of incomplete information to forecast how decision makers use new information to change their beliefs. Unfortunately,

From Dan Reiter (1994), "Learning, Realism, and Alliances: The Weight of the Shadow of the Past." *World Politics* 46(4): 490–526. Reprinted with permission of Johns Hopkins University Press.

the sophistication of these models comes at the expense of constraining the degree to which they can be tested empirically. This article relies on a model of learning derived deductively from decision-making theories, yet simple enough to permit rigorous empirical testing.

The first section of this paper draws on principles of social psychology and organization theory to build a general theory of learning in international politics, before drawing out learning hypotheses specific to the question of how states choose between alliances and neutrality. The second section presents realist ideas about how alliance choices are made, as well as specific realist hypotheses. The following sections present the data set, minor power alliance choices in the twentieth century, and a discussion of how the variables are operationalized. Empirical results are then presented and discussed, followed by conclusions.

A Theory of Learning in International Politics

Leaders often face considerable uncertainty when trying to predict the effects of foreign policy actions. In order to understand the world politics question of how foreign policy is made, it is necessary to ask the broader social science question, how do decision makers cope with uncertainty? One answer is that decision makers draw decisions from past experiences to help cope with difficult choices. In international relations scholarship, there have been a number of theoretical and empirical works that address the question of learning in international politics. Many of these works have drawn on ideas from two different fields of decision analysis: social psychology and organization theory.[1] This article draws on these two fields to build a theory that predicts that state behavior is determined by experiential learning.[2] Since state action is the product both of individuals acting on the basis of their own beliefs and of organizations acting within the larger framework of the state and society, decision theories from both of these fields are necessary to provide a complete understanding of the learning process.

Decision Theory Foundations

Social psychology portrays the human individual less as obeying the dictates and logic of the scientific method, and more as seeking explanations using less reliable analytical techniques. This is a vision of the individual as a "naive scientist"; people are seen as using the imprecise tools of human intuition to seek knowledge. Richard Nisbett and Lee Ross described two sets of tools used by the naive scientist: knowledge structures and judgmental heuristics.[3] Knowledge structures, or schemata, are mental frameworks within which data are organized for storage and retrieval. Schemata serve a number of functions: they lend structure to experience, determine what information will be encoded or retrieved from memory, affect the speed of cognition, and facilitate problem solving.[4] Such knowledge structures are used for the attribution of causation—if an individual attempting to attribute causation perceives in the environment a cue for a particular schema, then this schema is recalled to present an explanation for the phenomenon in question.[5]

The second set of tools—judgmental heuristics—are strategies used for the execution of certain inferential tasks.[6] The social psychology literature outlines three such heuristics: the representativeness heuristic, which guides individuals to associate an event with a causative explanation that has some similar characteristics; second, availability, which proposes that information more available in memory storage is more likely to be accessed than information that is less available, so that information perceptually salient to the observer often attracts causal attribution; finally, anchoring and adjustment, or that which impedes individuals to make insufficient adjustments from an initial judgment as more information is received.

One theory of learning that combines the ideas of knowledge structures and judgmental heuristics is analogical reasoning. Individual reasoning on the basis of analogies draws parallels with past events to provide guidance for the problem at hand.[7] This idea fits in well with the basic principles of knowledge structures laid out above, in that individuals reason by drawing on schemata/analogies in order to facilitate data storage and retrieval. Experimental studies have found subjects prone to reasoning on the basis of a single instance, confirming that schemata are used to cope with situations requiring great cognitive effort,[8] and that subjects who were given descriptions that included irrelevant items that were intended to cue them to certain analogies made judgments in accordance with the intended analogies more than subjects who read descriptions without such cues.[9]

Organization theorists have also placed great emphasis on the topic of learning. Three central principles of organizational behavior relevant to organizational learning have emerged from the last several decades of research: organizations are oriented toward targets, organizational behav-

ior is driven by routines, and organizational behavior is history dependent.[10] In assessing how organizations learn from experience, some scholars have found that organizations are most likely to change old ways of
thinking and behaving after failures, which both spur action and provide
a rich source of information for determining how to improve operations.
Successes, on the other hand, provide information and often the resources
necessary to conduct searches for improvements in strategy, but also tend
to produce complacency and stifle the drive to innovate.[11]

Both the social psychology and organization theory views of learning
predict that the inertia acquired by belief systems ought to make learning relatively infrequent. Individuals' knowledge structures tend to acquire
inertia, such that beliefs tend to persevere through reception of new, dis-
crepant information.[12] Similarly, organizations tend to develop collective
interpretations of history, which acquire the status of myth within the
organization and can be very resistant to change.[13] For both individuals
and organizations, often only a crisis or significant experience can overcome this inertia and form a new belief. From a social psychological point
of view, there are two (nonexclusive) ways of thinking about what makes
an event formative: that the nature of an event makes it more available
to memory, and that an event actually creates a new schema. Social psychology predicts that events that are vivid to the perceiver are more likely
both to be more available to memory and to form a new schema. Information has been described by social psychologists as vivid "to the extent
that it is (a) emotionally interesting, (b) concrete and imagery-provoking,
and (c) proximate in a sensory, temporal, or spatial way."[14] These sorts
of ideas are easily applied to international politics: one can distinguish
between events with more or less emotional or physical impact (such as
wars causing either many or few casualties), and between events directly
experienced (and therefore vivid) versus events that happen to another
state (and are therefore experienced only vicariously). Vivid information
is theorized to be easier to recall, because of emotional affect and the greater
amount of sensorily interesting detail associated with vivid information.
Further, a vivid event is more likely to engender the recruitment of entirely
new schemata, thereby providing analogies for future application. Despite
the strong theoretical support for the vividness effect, the experimental
evidence from social psychology is mixed, though some studies of learning in world politics have observed learning in accordance with the vividness effect.[15] Organization theory categorizes events along similar lines.
A significant crisis threatening organizational goals is often necessary to
dislodge beliefs and encourage new thinking. Similarly, direct experience

can be more likely to stimulate organizational learning than events experienced vicariously.[16]

Learning Hypotheses

The empirical question of this paper is: what are the causes of states' preferences for alliance or neutrality? An alliance is defined as *a formulated mutual commitment to contribute military assistance in the event one of the alliance partners is attacked*.[17] When deciding whether to enter an alliance or remain neutral, a nation must consider that entering an alliance in peacetime provides the benefits of extended deterrence and military assistance in the event of war, at the expense of raising the risks of being involved in wars of no direct interest to the nation. Neutrality offers the benefit of decreasing the chances of involvement in the wars of other nations, with the cost that the nation has no allies to help deter potential aggressors or defend against attacks.[18] This is a choice for which there is no universal, indisputable answer; neither neutrality nor alliance is a logically dominant strategy for all nations at all times. Therefore, whether a state chooses alliance or neutrality is likely to depend on whether it believes that alliance poses too great a risk of involvement or if it believes that international cooperation is necessary to protect its security.

Of course, characterizing a state's alliance policy as either allied or neutral is something of a simplification. Rather than as a dichotomy, the choice of neutrality or alliance can be conceptualized as a continuum along which there are different forces of neutrality and alliance. However, the act of signing a mutual defense treaty is a unique dividing place along the spectrum, as relations between states that have such a treaty are qualitatively different than they are when no such treaty exists. Empirical research confirms that a state is more likely to go to war to aid another state if there is a mutual defense pact between them.[19] The significance of these agreements makes the decision of whether or not to become party to one the most important choice a state will make in fashioning its alliance policy.

In terms of learning theory itself, the tendency for decision makers to learn simple lessons argues for keeping the set of possible lessons limited. Learners tend to keep analogies simple; the more complex the analogy, the more difficult is its application in a different context. For example, if the lesson from the appeasement at Munich in 1938 was, "When faced with a German threat to annex an ethnically similar piece of territory from a neighbor, the British and French should not give in," it could not have been applied by American decision makers to the contextually different decision to defend South Korea in 1950. Instead, the lesson taken from Munich was kept broad and simple—"aggressors must be opposed to prevent future aggression"—so that it could be applied to other circumstances. Additionally, a less cognitive effort is required both to construct and to apply lessons that are simple, because there are fewer historical idiosyncrasies that have to be matched between the past event and the current context. Of course, relying on overly simple lessons and neglecting important historical details can often lead to inappropriate analogizing and misguided choices.[20] In sum, this model assumes that nations can draw one of two lessons from a formative event: either that neutrality best protects national security or that alliance best protects national security.

The empirical analysis in this paper is limited to the alliance choices of minor powers. Great and minor powers need to be considered separately because they have fundamentally different security needs: a minor power is concerned mostly with direct threats to its security, whereas a great power must also consider the security of those proximate and overseas territories and countries instrumental to the security of its homeland and national interests.[21] This greater simplicity of minor powers' foreign interests means that experiences can be more easily coded as successes or failures, as a minor power focuses mostly on the question of how its choice of alliance or neutrality affected the national security and territorial integrity of the homeland. A great power, on the other hand, must assess the effects of an experience—such as a major war or diplomatic crisis—along a number of dimensions because of its extended foreign policy interests. Limiting the data set to minor powers makes it easier to compose a complete list of possible lessons a state might garner from a formative experience, increasing confidence that the learning hypotheses are a valid test of learning theory. This maintenance of internal validity comes at the expense of diminishing the external validity of the test, since if minor and great powers draw different kinds of lessons from systemic wars, then the minor power learning hypotheses are not easily applied to the behavior of great powers. However, if the empirical tests reveal that these learning hypotheses are powerful explanations of minor power behavior, then we can suspect that learning theory might also change our understanding of great power behavior, given that organization theory and social psychology principles ought to apply to great power decision processes, too.

Since a peacetime military alliance explicitly addresses the possibility of war, experiences in wars ought to be formative of beliefs about alliances. Indeed, social psychology would predict that since alliance policy is the centerpiece of a minor power's wartime foreign policy, it will be assigned responsibility for success or failure in the war, perhaps even if the minor's alliance choice was irrelevant to its eventual fate. Systemic wars in which great powers fight each other for very high political stakes are the most likely of wars to be formative because they are generally the most earth-shaking events in world politics, providing "the punctuation marks of history, primarily because they force drastic realignments in the relationships among states."[22] Further, in systemic wars more than in other wars minor powers are more likely to attribute dire fortunes to their alliances, because in a systemic war the minor power's relative weakness makes its alliance choice crucial to determining whether or not it is involved in a war and, if involved, how it will fare. Since systemic wars are used as formative events, the model focuses on the preference of minor powers for alliance with great powers only, as a minor power's alliances with other minor powers are generally not meant as a solution to the problem of such a systemic war, but rather for smaller scale threats. Therefore, the general proposition (discussed in more detail below) is that systemic wars are formative events that determine minor powers' beliefs concerning whether neutrality or alliance with great powers is preferable. Some nonsystemic wars may be significant enough to form a minor power's beliefs about alliances; but the majority of these conflicts are not likely to be, especially given that alliances generally play a lesser role in nonsystemic wars because of their smaller scale. In other words, internal validity is better maintained by excluding all nonsystemic wars in this study, thereby risking the exclusion of a few formative events, than by including all nonsystemic wars and including several events that are not likely to be formative of beliefs about alliances.

World Wars I and II were the systemic wars of the modern era for which the choice of alliance or neutrality was most important for minor powers.[23] In a systemic war, a minor power attempts to be either allied or neutral. A minor power is defined as attempting to be allied if it has a mutual defense treaty with one or more of the belligerent great powers when war breaks out, or if it is a neutral at the start of the war but eventually joins one of the warring coalitions without being attacked first. Otherwise, it is attempting neutrality. Organization theory predicts that whether the outcome was failure or success dominates the drawing of lessons, and that failure encourages innovation while success promotes continuance. Success and failure are defined as follows:

—If a minor power attempted neutrality in a systemic war and was not invaded during the war, the experience is considered a success; otherwise, it is a failure.[24]

—If a minor power attempted being allied, was on the winning side, and was not invaded, the experience was a success. If it was allied and invaded but acquired more population in postwar territorial settlement than it lost in the war, the experience was a success. The experience was a failure if a nation was allied and on the losing side, or if it was on the winning side and was invaded and did not recover as much population in postwar territorial settlements as it lost during the war.[25]

Two different propositions of how formative events drive behavior were tested. The first proposition assumes that the vividness of a state's *individual* experiences dominates belief formation, so that its individual, national experience in a systemic war determines what lessons are drawn and how it behaves after the war.[26] The systemic war is clearly formative for all states who were belligerents in the war; a nearby state that escapes participation by remaining neutral has also had a formative experience, in the same way that an individual who escapes injury in a severe car accident because she wore her seatbelt is likely to become an ardent supporter of seatbelt use.

> Hypothesis 1. A minor power can attempt either alliance or neutrality with a great power in a systemic war. If it experiences failure, it will switch policies following that war; if it experiences success, it will continue that policy.[27]

A different learning hypothesis assumes that a state does not focus solely on its own experience, believing instead that a lesson should incorporate the formative event experiences of all states. The implication is that all states garner the same lesson from a systemwide, formative event, regardless of individual experience.[28] According to this latter proposition, a minor power would weigh the formative event experiences of all minor powers equally in order to determine a composite lesson about the relative merits of alliance and neutrality. A single systemwide lesson produced by a formative event is learned by all minor powers, and can range from strongly advocating alliance, to indifference between neutrality and alliance, to strongly advocating neutrality.

> Hypothesis 2. A systemic war will produce a systemwide lesson on the effectiveness of alliance with a great power based on the sum of experiences of minor powers in the war. All minor powers will adopt policies in congruence with the systemwide lesson in the years following the war.

REALISM AND ALLIANCES

The dominant theory of international relations is realism. Kenneth Waltz's neorealism is the definitive, modern statement of the realist emphasis on national power, the importance of security concerns, and the focus on the state as the important actor in international politics. Significantly, its structural emphasis centers on the behavior of great powers, and offers few answers to the question of how minor powers behave.[29] However, Waltz's description of two alliance behaviors for great powers in the face of threat—*buck-passing* (loosening alliance commitments) and *chain-ganging* (tightening alliance commitments)—closely reflects the decisions faced by minor powers. Like neutrality, buck-passing entails decreasing the chances of successful deterrence and defense in order to decrease the chance of entanglement; and, as with alliance, chain-ganging entails increasing the chances of successful deterrence and defense at the expense of increasing the chances of entanglement. Thomas Christensen and Jack Snyder argued that Waltz's structural realism is insufficiently specified to predict whether buck-passing or chain-ganging is more likely. They add a new variable to structural realism, proposing that when the global power structure is multi-polar, buck-passing is more likely if the defense is perceived to have an advantage on the battlefield, while chain-ganging is more likely if the offense is perceived to have the advantage. Significantly, these latter authors concede that it is *beliefs* about the offense/defense balance, a parameter clearly outside the sparse theoretical structure of structural realism, that determine whether chain-ganging or buck-passing prevails, as opposed to the objective state of the offense/defense balance.[30]

A variant of realism that avoids reliance on beliefs to make predictions about the alliance choices of minor powers is Stephen Walt's balance of threat theory.[31] Walt explored the question of whether a state, when faced with an external threat, would ally against the source of threat (*balance*) or with the source of the threat (*bandwagon*). Walt outlined a number of hypotheses predicting when states would be more likely to balance and when they would be more likely to bandwagon, and found that balancing is more prevalent than bandwagoning. Walt also provided an answer to the question of why states seek to join alliances at all: they do so as a response to a perceived threat, since, as threat increases, the probability of alliance (whether it be with or against the source of the threat) increases; and as threat decreases, the probability that new alliances will form decreases and the probability that existing alliances will break apart increases.[32] He has executed case studies of his theory for alliance behavior in the Middle East and Southwest Asia.[33]

Significantly, Walt defines bandwagoning in such a way that true neutrality is not an option for a threatened state. If, when faced with a threat, a state signs no formal alliance with the source of threat, then Walt considers this to be accommodation and, therefore, bandwagoning with the source of threat. For example, he views Belgium's formal declaration of neutrality in the late 1930s as bandwagoning with Germany, though Belgium signed no alliance or nonaggression pact with Germany.[34]

This conflation of three categories—bandwagoning, balancing, and neutrality—into two—bandwagoning and balancing—is unjustified, as there are genuinely different consequences for a state that opts for formal neutrality than there are for one that bandwagons. A formal alliance is a very good indicator of the likelihood that one state will agree to defend another state if attacked: in a military crisis, a formal alliance may be necessary to ensure the participation of an otherwise uninvolved participant because of the implications that breaking an alliance would have for that state's international reputation.[35] The international arena is not as zero-sum as Walt would imply; not every state need be classified as either with one side or with the other in a conflict. Some states may attempt to avoid becoming embroiled in future military conflict by not taking sides. As Robert Osgood put it, "Every state must have an alliance policy, even if its purpose is only to avoid alliances."[36] Additionally, if neutrality can be defined as alliance, then balance of threat theory has made one of its principal claims—that the probability of alliance is positively correlated with the perceived level of threat—quite difficult to falsify. In a threatening environment, every state, even those that have formally declared neutrality, could be coded as having allied with some side; this makes it far too easy to find that there are no states that do not enter alliances in the face of threat, seriously undermining the falsifiability of the threat-alliance proposition.

As applied to the structural realist dichotomy of buck-passing and chain-ganging, Walt's argument that threats motivate alliances implies that chain-ganging dominates buck-passing. Of course, it is possible that, in the face of a general threat posed to the international system, such as the Nazi German threat in the late 1930s, minor powers might follow the basic logic of buck-passing and seek neutrality to avoid the risks of entanglement, rather than follow the logic of balancing or bandwagoning by entering an alliance. Extending Christensen's and Snyder's argument, I propose that there is not theoretical space in traditional realism to predict whether minor powers are likely to prefer neutrality or alliance in the face of a systemic threat. Realism provides the theoretical structure to support predictions opposite one another that, when facing a systemic threat, the affected minor powers could enter alliances to either balance against or bandwagon with the threat, or they could seek neutrality in order to pass the buck of defending the status quo to other countries. The argument of this paper, parallel to that of Christensen and Snyder, is that a minor power's formative experiences in wartime determine whether it will subscribe to the logic of neutrality or alliance, and therefore whether it will choose alliance or neutrality in the years after the war. To provide a comparative test of the argument that experiences determine alliance policy, this paper will test a simple balance of threat prediction, that the probability of alliance is positively correlated with the presence of external threat.

While learning predicts that formative experiences determine whether or not a minor power will prefer alliance with a great power, balance of threat theory predicts that a minor power is more likely to prefer alliance with a great power—whether it be a revisionist or status quo great power—when the prospect of such a systemic war appears imminent. The prospect of such a great power war concerns all minor powers in the region because their geographic proximity risks their involvement. A revisionist great power may invade a neutral minor power in order to take advantage of the minor power's geographical location in its struggle with other great powers, even if the neutral power has no specific dispute with the revisionist. For example, Germany invaded neutral Belgium in 1914 and 1940 even though Germany had no disputes with Belgium—each time it needed to move through Belgian territory in order to improve its chances of inflicting military defeat on France. Balance of threat theory would predict that if systemic war appears to be impending, a minor power would join either with the revisionist power in order to avoid being overrun or with the defending powers in an attempt to balance against the revisionist threat. Even though a specific threat may not be posed to the minor power in question, it ought to perceive a threat to its security coming from potential involvement in a systemwide conflict. The logic of balance of threat theory predicts that the minor power would prefer alliance in the face of such a peril, which I will refer to as "systemic threat."

> Hypothesis 3. A minor power is more likely to prefer alliance with a great power if it perceives that a systemic war in its region is imminent.

The relative military status of the minor power is also likely to affect its perception of threat and therefore the likelihood of its willingness to prefer alliance. Realism predicts that a relatively strong minor power may feel that it will be left alone in a major war; even if its military capabilities are not large enough to prevent conquest by a great power, they may be sufficient to inflict high enough costs on the great power to dissuade it from attacking.[37] Conversely, a very small minor power will probably not feel that it can inflict enough costs on a great power invader to discourage it from attacking.

> Hypothesis 3a. If a minor power perceives that a systemic war is imminent, the greater the military disadvantage it faces concerning the potential great power revisionist, the more likely it will be to prefer great power alliance.

Balance of threat theory predicts that geography plays an important role in mediating threat.[38] If a minor power is geographically exposed to a potential great power revisionist, it is more likely to think that it will be drawn into a systemic war than if it rests at the geographic perimeter of the system. The exposed minor power, therefore, perceives a greater threat and is more likely to prefer alliance.

> Hypothesis 3b. If a minor power perceives that a systemic war is imminent, it is more likely to prefer great power alliance if it is geographically exposed to the potential revisionist than if it is not.

The dependent variable is limited to one form of third-party assistance, mutual defense alliances with great powers. If a minor power can count on one-way defense commitments made to it by one or more great powers, it will be less likely to prefer a mutually committing alliance with a great power. In such a case, the minor power has acquired great power extended deterrence without increasing the chances of its entanglement in a war.

> Hypothesis 3c. If a minor power perceives that a systemic war is imminent, it is more likely to prefer great power alliance if one or more great powers have made nonalliance defense commitments to it than if no such commitments have been made.

A minor power can also be threatened (and therefore prefer alliance) if it perceives the possibility of being attacked based on a more specific, local issue, such as a demand for the revision of a territorial border. Such a threat could come from one or more states, great or minor. Balance of threat theory predicts that the presence of such a threat would increase the probability that the threatened minor would prefer an alliance with a great power, though it also allows for the possibility that the threatened minor would seek alliance with one or more other minor powers (a dependent variable not examined in this article), given that such a threat, which I will call "direct threat," would often be more limited than a systemic threat.

> Hypothesis 4. The level of perceived direct threat is positively correlated with the probability that a minor power will prefer alliance with a great power.

Balance of threat theory also predicts that if the minor power in question has alliances with other minor powers or nonalliance defense commitments from great powers, the external threat is effectively lessened, so the need to ally with a great power to deal with the direct threat is diminished.

> Hypothesis 4a. The more a minor power can count on minor power alliances or nonalliance great power commitments, the less likely it will be to seek alliance in the face of a direct-level threat.

A vigorous balance of threat advocate might argue that learning is just a special application of balance of threat theory, in that learning theory proposes that a state adopts a policy of neutrality or alliance based on its belief about which one more effectively deals with threats. Strictly speaking, this is partly true: the learning theory outlined here maintains that the problem to which a policy of neutrality or alliance is addressed is threat from the international environment. However, while balance of threat theory assumes that the universal response to threat is either to ally with or against it, learning theory proposes that a state can follow either buck-passing/neutrality logic or balance/bandwagon logic to address an emerging threat. Also, balance of threat theory focuses on short-term reactions to changes in the international environment, while learning theory explains how long-term ideas about grand strategy are formulated. After a formative event, learning theory predicts that a state that has learned a lesson favoring alliance would prefer alliance with a great power even if there is no current threat in the international environment, because such an orientation is in accord with a broad belief in the utility of alliance in dealing with threats when they arrive. A balance of threat advocate might contend that this is a case of a state balancing against a possible future threat, therefore validating her theory. However, if this were true, then all states would always prefer alliance, since the international anarchy assumed by realism means that a future threat is always possible. If she argued that some states do not always prefer alliance because different states have different views on how to address possible future threats, then this would beg the question of where these different views come from, which learning theory answers by proposing that past experiences determine how states come to view the best way of dealing with future threats.

DATA

Cases.   The objective of the empirical test was to build a data set large enough to permit generalization of the results based on the application of quantitative methods of analysis.[39] Cases in the data set are observations of peacetime behavior of minor powers, specifically whether or not the minor power preferred alliance with a great power or not at a given time (as distinct from the question of whether or not a minor power was actually a member of an alliance) following two formative events in the twentieth century, World Wars I and II. To be included, a country must be a member of the Correlates of War data set as a non-great power member of the nation-state system during the formative event, and must be located in a primary theater of conflict during the formative event (Europe for World War I; Europe, the Middle East, or Southeast Asia for World War II). Additionally, the government must not be a puppet controlled by an outside power. This excludes a number of East European nations after World War II because of Soviet military domination; Greece after World War I because of the 1917 Allied-sponsored coup there; and Greece in the late 1940s because of the extensive American control of politics in Greece until elections were held in 1950. For the post-World War I period, the data set included Albania, Belgium, Bulgaria, Denmark, the Netherlands, Norway, Portugal, Romania, Spain, Sweden, Switzerland, and Turkey. For the post-World War II period, the data set included Australia, Belgium, Denmark, Egypt, Finland, Greece, Iran, Iraq, Ireland, Luxembourg, the Netherlands, New Zealand, Norway, Portugal, Spain, Sweden, Switzerland, Thailand, Turkey, and Yugoslavia.

The learning hypotheses make simple predictions: alliance preferences for a state for all years following a formative event will be in accordance with the lesson of the formative event. It is necessary, however, to collect more than one observation per minor power per formative event, in order to test for the possibility of variation in alliance policies across time during a postevent period, as well as for variation in the level of threat across time (implying varying balance of threat predictions). The modeling question, then, is: in which years of the post-formative event period should observations be made? The general guideline used for selecting the years of observation was to include years with different levels and sources of threat to provide a richer test of the balance of threat hypotheses. Observation years were spaced apart evenly, and the starting year for each was a few years after the end of the formative event in order to allow for the staggered emergence of the postwar order. For each case, behavior was coded for about the length of a generation, twenty years, at four points in time: in the post-World War I period, 1921, 1927, 1933, and 1939; in the post-World War II period, 1949, 1955, 1961, and 1967. These years reflect different conditions in the international environment. For the interwar period, 1921 represents both the nadir of German economic and military power and Italy before the rise of Mussolini; 1927 reflects substantial turmoil and instability in the Balkans and the first years of Mussolini's rule; 1933 represents new conditions in the Balkans; and 1939 contains the months before the outbreak of world war. For the postwar period, 1949 represents a Stalinist Soviet Union overshadowing a frantically rebuilding Europe; 1955, a relaxation of the U.S.-Soviet conflict of 1961, increased tensions between the superpowers due to a number of international crises; and 1967, the start of another thaw in the cold war.

Making observations only for every sixth year might attract the criticism that the validity of the empirical results has been seriously degraded. Given the need to collect data to catch variations in the level of threat, there is an argument for collecting data for every time period for which data is available. For this model, that would be yearly, as the threat hypotheses are operationalized using annual defense spending figures. Observations were taken several years apart, however, because there are good reasons to suspect positive autocorrelation, due to institutional inertia, in codings of alliance preferences for successive years; putting gaps between observation years ought to diminish substantially the distortional effects of such autocorrelation.[40] Left unaddressed, this autocorrelation might artificially inflate the apparent power of learning theory, because the continuity in alliance preferences predicted by learning theory might be boosted by the autocorrelation. Additionally, inclusion of more and more observation years per country diminishes the credibility of the claim that each of the observation years is a separate case, as the observation years would be so close together in time that they would become less and less separate phenomena, thereby artificially increasing the size of the data set and potentially distorting empirical results. Significantly, reducing the amount of time between observation years (and thereby increasing the number of observations) would not introduce much new information to the analysis, as the observation years chosen catch all of the direct and systemic threats as well as all of the minor power preferences for great power alliances that occur during the time period under examination—there are no one-year blips of threat or alliance preference that fall between observation years. Given that the degree of the autocorrelation can only be guessed at and is likely to vary from case to case, I preferred to forgo a formal test of the hypothesis that the dependent variable is autocorrelated (such as putting a lagged dependent variable on the right-hand side of the equation); instead I space out the observation years to reduce the distorting effects of auto-correlation and improve confidence in the model's estimates. In any event, discovering autocorrelation would not have clear implications, since the learning hypotheses themselves predict very high autocorrelation; as lessons are drawn only from formative events, states follow the same lesson in the years following the formative event—meaning that learning would predict that the dependent variable should not change across time for a single country. Therefore, if autocorrelation in the dependent variable was found, it would be very difficult to know whether it was due to institutional inertia or because states were acting in accordance with the learning hypothesis and therefore were learning only infrequently. As a check on the possibility that an interval of six years between observations diminishes inertia insufficiently to leave the empirical results undistorted, analysis will also be performed on versions of the data set that put more time between observations, so as to reduce further the effects of possible institutional inertia. In sum, though the model does not provide a test of the hypothesis that the dependent variable is autocorrelated, it provides rigorous tests of the realist and learning hypotheses that were reasonably unbiased from autocorrelation and that extract as much information as possible from the records of history without distorting conclusions by sub-stantially inflating the data set.[41]

Operationalization of the hypotheses. This section lays out the equa-tion and its components, explaining the operationalizations and coding rules for the variables. The dependent variable is dichotomous, coded 1 if the minor power preferred a mutual alliance with a great power (follow-ing the Correlates of War list of great powers) that committed the parties to military action (as opposed to nonaggression treaties or agreements to consult in the event of war) during the year in question, and coded 0 if not.[42] Since the dependent variable is dichotomous, a logit method of esti-mation is used. The logit equation to be estimated is presented first to give the reader something to refer to in the explanations of the specific vari-ables that follow.

$$\text{Pr(prefer alliance)} = 1/(1 + e^{-X\beta}) \quad (1)$$

$$X\beta = K + \beta_1(\text{INDL}) + \beta_2(\text{SYSL}) + \beta_3(\text{DTMB}) + \beta_4(\text{DCOM}) + \beta_5(\text{STRS}) + \beta_6(\text{STRS})(\text{GEOG}) + \beta_7(\text{STMB}) + \beta_8(\text{STMB})(\text{GEOG}) + \beta_9(\text{SCOM})$$

The abbreviations for the equations and the ensuing Tables are as follows:

Pr (prefer alliance) is bounded at 0 and 1, though the actual codings are either 0 or 1

K = constant

INDL = individual learning variable (dichotomous)

SYSL = system learning variable (continuous, bounded at 0 and 1)

DTMB = direct threat military balance (continuous, with a lower bound of 0)

DCOM = amelioration of direct threat military balance from commitments other than great power alliances (continuous, with a lower bound of 0)

STRS = for systemic threat, revisionist share of great power resources (continuous bounded between 0 and 100)

STMB = systemic threat military balance between revisionist and minor powers (continuous, with a lower bound of 0)

GEOG = geographical exposure variable (dichotomous)

SCOM = amelioration of systemic threat military balance from nonalliance great power commitments (continuous, with a lower bound of 0)

Hypothesis 1—the individual learning hypothesis—was expressed as a dichotomous variable, INDL, and coded 1 if the lesson advocated alliance (if the country was allied and succeeded, or was neutral and failed) it was coded 0 if the lesson advocated neutrality (if the country was allied and failed, or if it was neutral and succeeded). Hypothesis 1 proposes that ß1 will be positive. Hypothesis 2 posits that each formative event provides one systemwide lesson on great power alliances that is followed by each minor power. The content of the lesson is determined by the collective experiences of all the relevant minor powers in that formative event. This variable, SYSL, is a number from 0 to 1 that indicates the content of the lesson—the extent to which it advocates neutrality or alliance. A value of 0 would be the strongest lesson for neutrality, a value of .5 would indicate a lesson favoring neither, and a value of 1 would indicate the strongest advocacy for great power alliance. The fraction is constructed as follows:

$$SYSL = \frac{(\text{sum of failed neutral and successful allied minors for that event})}{(\text{number of minors for that event})} \quad (2)$$

For World War I, there were two failed neutrals and two successful allied nations out of a total of twelve nations, producing a systemwide learning fraction of .33 for interwar cases. This is a lesson moderately favoring neutrality. For World War II, there were nine failed neutrals and four successful allied states out of a total of twenty nations, producing a value of .65 for post-World War II cases. This is a lesson moderately favoring great power alliance. Hypothesis 2 proposes that ß2 will be positive.

The realist hypotheses are more difficult to operationalize. Since the hypotheses are to test the validity of the balance of threat variety of realism, the basic objective is to construct acceptable measurements of threat. Generally speaking, both intentions and capability are necessary components of a threat; a simple relation might be that intentions and capabilities are multiplied together to construct composite threat, expressing the notion that a very powerful but friendly country poses no threat (as a large capability index times an aggressive intentions index of zero equals a composite threat of zero), and that a fiercely aggressive but small country poses little threat (a high aggressive intentions index times a low capabilities index equals a low composite threat).[43]

Of these two components of threat, the presence of a threatening intent is more difficult to measure. Concerning direct threats, a minor power was considered threatened if one or more other powers (minor or great) presented demands for the revision of territorial borders or challenges to the sovereignty of the ruling government of the target in the year in question or in the previous year, and if the target perceived these demands to carry the risk of military conflict in the near future. Lesser threats to sovereignty, such as economic penetration, are excluded, as responses other than military alliance are more appropriate. One way to capture this balance is to use the ratio of military spending of the threatener(s) to the threatened, where the ratio is 0 if there is no threat.[44] However, there is probably a diminishing return to increases in fear from increases in capability; for example, the level of fear may double as the ratio increases from 2:1 to 4:1, but it is not likely to double as the ratio increases from 100:1 to 200:1. A simple transformation indicating diminishing marginal returns but retaining monotonicity is to take the square root of this military spending ratio. This square root is DTMB, and Hypothesis 4 predicts that ß3 will be positive. A separate value for the testing of Hypothesis 4a, DCOM, consists of the amelioration of the direct threat military balance offered by minor power alliances and nonalliance commitments from great powers. The amelioration of this threat is also calculated using defense spending data. Hypothesis 4a predicts that this coefficient, ß4, will be negative.[45]

A systemic threat is posed to the international system by a revisionist great power. The first task in building a measure of systemic threat is to assess the perceived likelihood of imminent great power war. This was coded as a dichotomous variable: if a great power initiated a militarized crisis with another great power or with a regional ally of another great power in the year of observation or the previous year, then all minor powers in that region during the observation year will be considered to perceive that this is a potentially revisionist great power, and that the possibility of an imminent great power war is high. For the post-World War I years, Germany qualifies as a perceived potential revisionist in 1939 because of its annexation of the Sudetenland in 1938 and its invasion of Czechoslovakia in 1939. The Soviet Union qualifies as a perceived potential revisionist in Europe in 1949 because of the Berlin blockade, and in 1961 because of the Berlin deadline crisis. China counts as a potential revisionist in East Asia in 1955 because of its actions and threats against the American ally Taiwan. If a great power war is perceived as imminent because of such a militarized crisis, then it is assumed that minor powers will perceive the probability of an actual outbreak of war to depend on the relative share of great power capabilities held by the potential revisionist, since a greater share of great power resources gives the revisionist a better chance of winning, hence increasing the chances that systemic war will break out. For each of the potential great power revisionists, the average of the revisionist's share of each of the Correlates of War's six measures of material capabilities among the great powers—military spending, military troop levels, total population, urban population, energy consumption, and iron and steel consumption[46]—was recorded as STRS. Hypothesis 3 proposes that this measure is positively correlated with the probability that the minor power will prefer alliance, predicting therefore that ß5 will be positive. Hypothesis 3a predicts that the weaker the minor power feels relative to the revisionist, the more likely the minor is to seek alliance with a great power. Relative strength was measured by taking the square root of the ratio of the revisionist's military spending to that of the minor power to create STMB. Hypothesis 3a predicts that ß7 will be positive. Hypothesis 3b predicts that geographic exposure to a systemic threat increases the probability of preferring alliance. This idea is operationalized as a dummy variable. If a great power lies between the minor power and the potential revisionist, then the minor is coded as unexposed, and the exposure variable, GEOG, is coded as 0; otherwise, the minor power is exposed, and GEOG is coded as 1. GEOG is included as an interactive term with the resource share and revisionist military balance variables, as realism would predict that if a minor power is geographically exposed, it will feel more threatened by a more powerful revisionist. Therefore, Hypothesis 3b predicts that ß6 and ß8 will be positive. Nonalliance great power defense commitments to the minor power that ameliorate the systemic threat are reflected in SCOM, which is measured using the same method as DCOM, only in reference to systemic threats. Hypothesis 3c predicts that SCOM will be negative.

Empirical results. The results of the logit analysis of equation 1 are shown in Table 8.1. Overall the equation does quite well in predicting the alliance choices of states. In 90 percent of the cases, the model correctly predicted alliance choices. More specifically, Table 8.1 indicates that both the individual and the systemic learning variables, INDL and SYSL, have statistically significant impacts on the dependent variable. Discerning the individual effects of these two variables is a slightly more difficult task, however. The apparent substantive and statistical significance of the systemic variable can be misleading, since, if decision makers learned only according to their own lessons and not at all by systemic lessons, then the empirical results would still show the predictions of the systemic learning variables as doing well, because a systemic lesson is composed of individual lessons. For example, if systemic learning had no real effect and half of the individual lessons were for neutrality, it would appear that systemic learning would be having some effect because half of the sample was, as predicted, preferring neutrality, though systemic experiences had been irrelevant to the forming of preferences. Such a phenomenon is not inconceivable with this data set: for post–World War I cases, 23 percent of the nations preferred alliance, and the systemic learning variable was coded as .33; for post–World War II cases, 68 percent of the nations preferred alliance, and the systemic learning variable was coded as .65.

One way to separate out the effects is to see if the individual learning hypothesis is successful at predicting individual cases, particularly for those nations that had preferences in opposition to the systemic lesson derived from the formative experience. The empirical results point to individual learning as a powerful explanation of the dependent variable—by itself, the individual learning variable correctly predicts 111 out of 127 cases, as compared with the entire model correctly predicting 114 correctly, and the systemic learning variable alone predicting 89 cases correctly. Further, of the cases for which the predictions of individual learning were at odds with those of systemic learning (40 cases), the individual learning variable cor-

TABLE 8.1[a] Logit estimation of the causes
of minor power alliance after World Wars I and II

Variable Name	Estimated Coefficient	Standard Error	Significant Level
Learning			
INDL	4.80	0.796	<0.0005
SYSL	5.78	2.37	0.008
Direct threat			
DTMB	-0.0119	0.155	—
DCOM	-0.111	0.189	—
Systemic threat			
STRS	0.0784	0.0496	0.06
STRS*GEOG	-0.192	0.0725	0.01[b]
STMB	-0.0467	0.0395	—
STMB*GEOG	0.227	0.112	0.02
SCOM	-0.659	1.23	
Constant	-5.07	1.42	<0.0005
n=127			
Log-likelihood (0)	-87.387		
Log-likelihood function	-36.102		
Likelihood ratio test	103.470 with 9 D.F.		

	Actual Number of Cases	Prediction Success Correctly Predicted	Percentage
Outcome 0 (preferred not to ally)	60	53	88
Outcome 1 (preferred to ally)	67	61	91
Total	127	114	90

[a] Abbreviations used in this table can be found on page 247.

[b] The sign of the estimate is not in the predicted direction, but is statistically significant at the .01 level for a two-tailed significance test. All other significance tests are one-tailed.

rectly predicted 80 percent of these cases against 20 percent for the systemic learning variable. Therefore, individual learning appears to be more dominant than systemic learning in decision makers' thinking about the costs and benefits of neutrality and alliance, meaning that the data provides strong empirical support for Hypothesis 1 and more qualified support for Hypothesis 2.

The estimates for the direct threat variables (DTMB and DCOM) are clearly not statistically significant, leading to the conclusion that Hypotheses 4 and 4a ought to be rejected. Of the systemic threat variables, the military balance variables appear to have little substantive if limited statistical significance; likelihood ratio tests reveal that the two systemic threat military balance variables (STMB and GEOG*STMB) and the direct threat variables add so little to explaining the dependent variable that they can be justifiably excluded.[47] Another such test reveals that inclusion of the systemic threat resource share (STRS and GEOG*STRS) and strategic threat commitment (SCOM) variables is justified.[48] As displayed in Table 8.2, logit analysis of a model excluding these four variables offers essentially similar results as the logit analysis of equation 1. The high standard error for the estimate of SCOM offers evidence against Hypothesis 3c. As predicted, states that are geographically unexposed to a systemic threat are more likely to prefer alliance with a great power than if there was no systemic threat, and the greater the resource share of the revisionist power, the greater the likelihood that they will prefer such an alliance (a caveat to this finding is that the estimate has only moderate statistical significance, at the .06 level). However, if the threatened minor power is geographically exposed to the systemic threat (74 percent of those states facing a systemic threat were coded as being geographically exposed), then the net effect (.0422 - .0736 = -.0314) is for the threatened minor power to be *less* likely to prefer alliance with the great power than if there is no systemic threat. This is strong evidence against Hypothesis 3b, and in opposition to the predictions of balance of threat theory. Further, as the revisionist's share of great power resources increases, the chances of the minor power preferring neutrality increase even further, again in opposition to the predictions of balance of threat theory. These findings are not dismissible as stochastic hiccups—again, a likelihood ratio test supports the inclusion of the strategic threat resource share and commitment variables, STRS, GEOG*STRS, and SCOM. The real effect in this sample, then, is that for geographically exposed states, the presence of a systemic threat decreases the likelihood that a minor power will prefer alliance. Certainly, this is a finding at odds with the predictions of balance of threat theory, which proposes that status quo states will tend to

TABLE 8.2[a] Logit analysis of alliance choice
excluding strategic threat military balance variables

Variable Name	Estimated Coefficient	Standard Error	Significance Level
Learning			
INDL	4.29	.650	<.005
SYSL	4.72	2.12	.02
Systemic threat			
STRS	.0422	.0327	.10
STRS*GEOG	-.0736	.0385	.06[b]
SCOM	-.542	.747	—
Constant	-4.39	1.23	<.0005
n=127			
Log-likelihood(0)	-87.387		
Log-likelihood function	-38.797		
Likelihood ratio test	98.0798 with 5 D.F.		

| | | Prediction Success | |
	Actual Number of Cases	Correctly Predicted	Percentage
Outcome 0 (preferred not to ally)	60	53	88
Outcome 1 (preferred to ally)	67	60	89.5
Total	127	113	89

[a] Abbreviations used in this table can be found on page 247.

[b] The sign of the estimate is not in the predicted direction, but is statistically significant at the .06 level for a two-tailed significance test. All other significance tests are one-tailed.

ally together to balance against a state bent on systemic hegemony or territorial expansion. It would seem to offer support to the argument that, ceteris paribus, minor powers are more likely to follow the logic of buckpassing than that of balancing or bandwagoning.

The next task is the determination of the relative magnitudes of the effects of learning and threat. Direct comparison of coefficient estimates as a means of assessing explanatory power is difficult in this case, given the logit form of the model and the variety of units used in measurement. A more fruitful approach is to think specifically about the predictions of the two theories under examination. Balance of threat theory predicts that in a high-threat environment, a state will be more likely to choose alliance rather than neutrality regardless of its lesson, and in a low-threat environment, a state will be more likely to choose neutrality rather than alliance regardless of its lesson. Buck-passing logic agrees that the presence of threat is the key external variable determining alliance choices, but proposes that alliances are likely to break apart as threats appear. Learning theory, on the other hand, predicts that regardless of the level of external threat, a state is likely to choose alliance if its lesson advocates alliance and likely to choose neutrality if its lesson advocates neutrality. These propositions can be tested by comparing the predicted values for the dependent variable at high and low levels of threat and for lessons of alliance and neutrality. The focus here will be on individual learning, since that appears to be the more powerful of the two learning explanations, and on systemic threat, as the direct threat variables have no statistically significant effect. Only the systemic threat resource share variable will be examined, as the systemic direct military balance variable was found to be not systematically related to the dependent variable. In order to assess how predictions for the dependent variable change as the values for individual learning and systemic threat resource share change, the other independent variables need to be held constant. The comparison will assume that there is no direct threat, and the systemic learning value will be set at .5, the indifference point (again, a value of 1 would mean that the systemic lesson strongly favors alliance, whereas a value of 0 would mean that the systemic lesson strongly favors neutrality). The analysis compares five different systemic threat environments, in all of which the minor power is assumed to have been geographically exposed: the 1939 Nazi German threat, the 1949 Soviet threat, the 1955 Chinese threat, the 1961 Soviet threat, and an environment of no threat. For each of these environments, the predictions for the dependent variables are compared for the case of an individual lesson favoring neutrality and an individual lesson favoring alliance. These predictions are presented in Table 8.3.

As predicted by learning theory, the likelihood of a state choosing alliance or neutrality is strongly determined by the nature of the individual lesson, and the level of systemic threat has only marginal effects on this variable. Confidence that formative experiences determine how minor powers come to decide between alliance and neutrality is bolstered by the high rate of accuracy of the individual learning hypothesis in predicting the dependent variable for the entire data set (87 percent). The realist prediction that the level of threat alone strongly determines the alliance/neutrality choice of a state is not confirmed by the data. The individual learning variable, there-

TABLE 8.3 Predictions of minor powers' alliance choices given
different levels of systematic threat and different individual lessons[a]

Year	Systemic Threatener (Resource Share)		Predicted probability of choosing alliance with an individual lesson of neutrality (INDL = 0)	Predicted probability of choosing alliance with an individual lesson of alliance (INDL = 1)
1939	Germany	(23.4)	.060	.816
1949	USSR	(34.9)	.042	.754
1955	PRC	(20.4)	.065	.829
1961	USSR	(28.3)	.051	.791
—	No Systemic Threat	(0)	.117	.902

[a] Table entries are predicted values for y, calculated based on coefficient estimates in Table 8.2.

fore, has a high degree of substantive significance in relation to balance of threat theory, as well as a high level of statistical significance. This comparison illustrates that the data indicate high empirical support for Hypothesis 1 and no empirical support for Hypothesis 3, as the observed, marginal effect is not in the predicted direction. The result does point to a small tendency for minor powers to follow buck-passing logic rather than to balance or bandwagon in the face of threat, formative experiences aside.

A possible criticism of the data set discussed earlier is that by taking a number of observations for the period following each formative event, the estimated strength of individual learning is inflated. If decisions about whether to be allied or remain neutral are not taken as frequently as every six years, this might mean that inertia rather than adherence to a lesson was causing the continuity in a state's alliance choices. One way to test for this possibility is to split up the data set: if there is such inflation when observations are made for behavior at six year intervals, then breaking up the data set so as to increase the span of time between observations ought to deflate the estimated strength of the individual learning variable. Table 8.4 compares the coefficient estimates and standard errors for regressions of the full data set (for observations taken in the years 1921, 1927, 1933, 1939,

TABLE 8.4[a] Sensitivity analyses of logit estimates
for alliance choices varying the time between observations[b]

Variable	(1)[c]	(2)[d]	(3)[e]	(4)[f]	(5)[g]	(6)[h]	(7)[i]
Learning							
INDL	4.80^n	9.45^l	4.28^n	4.19^l	4.07^m	5.82^m	4.47^m
	(.796)	(4.22)	(.952)	(1.78)	(1.35)	(1.97)	(1.52)
SYSL	5.78^m	23.0^j	4.31	11.77^j	4.78	2.39	-.169
	(2.37)	(13.8)	(3.91)	(6.08)	(4.32)	(7.26)	(10.9)
Direct threat							
DTMB	.0119	-.233	.440	-.258	.437	1.10	.170
	(.155)	(.412)	(1.07)	(.202)	(1.27)	(6.01)	(.944)
DCOM	-.111	-.037	-.166	-.434	.0305	-.788	—
	(.189)	(.439)	(1.44)	(2.02)	(2.05)	(6.75)	—
Systemic threat							
STRS	$.0784^j$	.0837	-.067	—	—	—	—
	(.04%)	(.0755)	(.127)				
G*STRS	$-.192^n$	$-.399^n$	—	—	—	—	—
	(.0725)	(.219)					
STMB	-.047	-.109	-.0265	-.0547	8.74	.0648	.00575
	(.0395)	(.0727)	(.178)	(.0951)	61200	(.0751)	(.285)
G*STMB	$.227^l$	.411	—	.0151	—	-.131	-.00714
	(.112)	(.324)		(.0959)		(-141)	(.196)
SCOM	-.659	—	-.862	—	—	—	-.780
	(1.23)		(2.02)				(1.23)
Constant	-5.07^n	-15.0^k	-4.39^k	-7.62^l	-4.40^m	-4.42	-1.80
	(1.42)	(8.84)	(2.41)	(3.70)	(2.57)	(3.76)	(6.67)
n	127	63	64	31	32	32	32
Log-likelihood (0)	-87.8	-43.6	-22.2	-21.5	-21.9	-22.1	-22.2
Percentage correct for model	88	90	88	90	91	94	91
Percentage correct for INDL	87	87	88	81	91	94	84

[a] Abbreviations used in this table can be found on page 247.

[b] Entries in rows with equation terms are coefficient estimates; numbers in parentheses are standard errors.

[c] Years of observation: 1921, 1927, 1933, 1939, 1949, 1955, 1961, 1967.

[d] Years of observation: 1921, 1933, 1949, 1961.

[e] Years of observation: 1927, 1939, 1955, 1967.

[f] Years of observation: 1921, 1949.

[g] Years of observation: 1927, 1955.

[h] Years of observation: 1933, 1961.

[i] Years of observation: 1939, 1967.

[j] Significant at the .10 level.

[k] Significant at the .05 level.

[l] Significant at the .025 level.

[m] Significant at the .01 level.

[n] Significant at the .0005 level.

[o] The sign of the estimate is not in the predicted direction, but estimate is statistically significant at the .10 level or higher for a two-tailed significance test. All other significance tests are one-tailed.

1949, 1955, 1961, and 1967) with separate regressions for each half or quarter of the data set. In one half, observations were taken for 1921, 1933, 1949, and 1961; and in the other they were taken for 1927, 1939, 1955, and 1967. For quarters of the data set, separate analyses were conducted on observations for the years 1921–49, 1927–55, 1933–61, and 1933–67. This last test on quarters of the data set is an especially good one for the hypothesis that institutional inertia may be inflating the results, since it examines only one observation per country per formative event, removing completely the possible effects of institutional inertia.

As Table 8.4 clearly indicates, similar empirical conclusions as to the importance of the learning variables and the insignificance of the threat variables can be drawn when the data set is split into halves or quarters. The individual learning hypothesis is the only variable whose coefficient estimate remains relatively stable and retains a very high degree of substantive and statistical significance across all permutations of the data set, including all four runs in which only one observation was made per country per formative event. Institutional inertia, then, is not artificially inflating the estimated importance of the individual learning variable.

Another possible criticism of the data set is that the Soviet Union actually posed a systemic threat to Europe throughout the Cold War, and that by counting only the late 1940s and early 1960s as years of Soviet threat, an artificially low estimate of the effect of systemic threat is produced. One way to explore this possibility is to reconfigure the data set with the assumption that the Soviet Union posed a systemic threat to Europe in each of

TABLE 8.5[a] Sensitivity analysis of logit estimates for alliance
choices using different assumption about the level of Soviet threat[b]

	Variables			
	Standard Data Sets[c]		Modified Data Sets[d]	
Learning				
INDL	4.80	(.796)[j]	4.66	(.770)[j]
SYSL	5.78	(2.37)[h]	6.93	(2.62)[i]
Direct threat				
DTMB	0.012	(.155)	-0.0307	(.159)
DCOM	-0.111	(.189)	-0.114	(.193)
Systemic threat				
STRS	0.078	(.050)[c]	-0.0174	(.0389)
STRS*GEOG	-0.192	(.072)[k]	-0.111	(.0577)[k]
STMB	-0.047	(.040)	-0.0040	(.0383)
STMB*GEOG	0.227	(.112)[g]	0.182	(.109)[f]
SCOM	-0.659	(1.23)	0.638	(1.23)
Constant	-5.07	(1.42)[j]	-5.20	(1.42)[j]
Percentage of				
correct predictions	90		89	
n=127				

[a] Abbreviations used in this table can be found on page 247.
[b] Table entries are coefficient estimates, with standard errors in parentheses.
[c] Systemic Soviet threat coded as present in 1949 and 1961.
[d] Systemic Soviet threat coded as present in 1949, 1955, 1961, and 1967.
[e] Significant at the .10 level.
[f] Significant at the .05 level.
[g] Significant at the .025 level.
[h] Significant at the .01 level.
[i] Significant at the .005 level.
[j] Significant at the .0005 level.
[k] Sign of the estimate is not in the predicted direction but estimate is statistically significant at the .06 level or higher for a two-tailed significance test. All other significance tests are one-tailed.

the post-World War II observation years. Table 8.5 presents the results of such an analysis, comparing these results to those reached with the assumption that there was a Soviet threat only in the late 1940s and early 1960s. As is evident in Table 8.5, coding the USSR as a threat to Europe from the late 1940s through the late 1960s does not alter the conclusions that learning is still the dominant explanation of the dependent variable, that external threat has only marginal effects on the dependent variable, and that those effects may in fact be in the opposite direction to that predicted by balance of threat theory.

DISCUSSION

The strong conclusion of the empirical tests is that individual experiences are powerful determinants of alliance preferences, and that variations in external threat, in contrast to the predictions of balance of threat realism, have very little effect. Further, the marginal effect observed is opposite to that predicted by balance of threat theory, suggesting that minor powers tend to follow buck-passing/neutrality logic more frequently than balance/bandwagon logic. These findings are in contrast to those of some other quantitative works on alliances that emphasize the strong effects of changes in the international environment on alliance policy.[49] There are a number of possible explanations for this discrepancy in results. First, many of these studies used a different coding scheme for evaluating international threats, often relying on Bruce Bueno de Mesquita's model, which equates security with a nation's utility for war.[50] Second, this is the first quantitative analysis to compare the predictions of realism with learning—many of the other studies tested only realist hypotheses. Last, other alliance research has executed tests that are less direct than those in this article, meaning that their dependent variables were slightly different.

An important caveat to this finding is that this paper presents only a limited test of balance of threat theory. The dependent variable is a major shift in foreign policy toward or away from formal military alliance; it is limited to minor-great power alliances; and the independent variables for threat measure only relatively high threats, the appearance of imminent great power war, or an intense local conflict threatening international war. Threats, balancing, and bandwagoning may occur in smaller increments, as states worry about and react to lesser threats, and may take steps short of entering a defense pact in order to address an emerging threat. However, a danger attending the coding of small changes in threat and alliance policy is that it can make balance of threat theory difficult to falsify. There is always threat to be found if one looks hard enough, and most diplomatic actions are in some sense balancing or bandwagoning, as they either strengthen or weaken ties with other nations. Therefore, though the test of balance of threat theory in this paper is limited, this limitation is necessary to keep the hypotheses easily falsifiable.

Learning and Regional Alliance Patterns

Individual learning correctly predicts many regional patterns of alliance and neutrality. All three of the Southeast Asian nations in the data set—Australia, New Zealand, and Thailand—preferred alliance after World War II, though China did not pose a real threat to any of them at that time, with the exception of China's direct confrontations with the United States in the 1950s. These commitments to alliance were driven directly by the nations' formative World War II experiences. To take one example, the 1941 Japanese invasion had a great impact on Thai foreign policy after the war:

> The crisis of 1941 is the key to understanding Thai attitudes towards SEATO. Thailand entered SEATO in order to avoid being left once more at the mercy of an overpowering enemy, defenceless and without allies. Thailand entered SEATO, too, in order to reaffirm and reinforce its links with the United States and the United Kingdom, the two great powers which, despite their interest in the country's independence, did at the crucial moment shrink from entering an all-out war on Thailand's behalf because they had assumed no prior commitments to come to its assistance. And the continuing aim of Thai diplomacy is to secure a situation in which the intervention of the Western great powers on its side is never left in doubt. On its own side, Thailand had to learn that the policy of neutrality has proved unsuccessful and that a policy of playing with both sides was not ultimately satisfactory. To expect reliable assistance, one has to be reliable oneself.[51]

In Europe, individual learning explains the peculiar checkerboard patterns of neutrality and alliance since World War I. Consider Switzerland, the Netherlands, and Belgium: these three West European countries were quintessential nineteenth-century neutrals, and all of them attempted neutrality in World War I. Neutral Belgium was invaded in 1914, an experience that played a key role in causing it to revamp its foreign policy toward alliance and away from neutrality after the war. Switzerland and the Netherlands emerged from the war unscathed, reinforcing their neutral orientations. All three again attempted neutrality in World War II, and the two that were invaded, Belgium and the Netherlands, joined NATO after the war; while Switzerland, which had successfully avoided involvement in the war, remained neutral. Historians point to the various individual experiences in the two world wars as central in driving each state's alliance preferences.[52] Balance of threat theory, on the other hand, would predict that the three states would seek alliance in the late 1930s, since all lay on potential invasion routes between Germany and France and would balance against or bandwagon with the provocative Soviet Union of the late 1940s and early 1960s.

Another interesting checkerboard of alliances and neutrality is Scandinavia. Experiences of successful neutrality for Denmark, Sweden, and Norway in World War I reinforced their traditional adherence to neutrality, a commitment that lasted through the late 1930s in the midst of a mounting German threat.[53] However, the two nations that experienced failed neutrality in World War II, Denmark and Norway, abandoned their long traditions of neutrality to join NATO. One historian argued that the strong impacts of these divergent experiences determined the eventual collapse of the negotiations for a Scandinavian Defense Union (SDU) as well as the Norwegian and Danish decisions to join NATO and the Swedish decision to remain neutral:

> Divergent wartime experiences played a significant role in the SDU negotiations and clearly affected the outcome of the negotiations between Sweden and Denmark. For Sweden there was little reason to change a successful foreign policy that had served her well through the Napoleonic wars. Danish and Norwegian neutrality, however, was shattered by the German attack on 9 April 1940, and the event raised serious doubts as to the desirability of continuing the old policy. Oslo and Copenhagen feared a repetition of April 1940, this time with the Soviet Union as aggressor. The Swedish political scientist Krister Wahlbäck addresses much attention to what he calls the 9 April syndrome.[54]

Conversely, escaping involvement in World War II cemented Sweden's commitment to neutrality after 1945, in spite of the failed neutrality of its two Nordic neighbors:

> Again, this rejection [of alliance] was neither due to any doctrinaire belief in neutrality, nor to a lack of sympathy with the West, but was based on historical experience and an evaluation of the situation prevailing within the country at the time. . . . Whether or not her neutrality was the sole reason Sweden was spared during two world wars or was merely incidental, it has nevertheless exerted a powerful influence on the Swedish people. Public opinion and all the country's democratic parties regard it as self-evident that this historically proven concept should continue as a fundamental national policy.[55]

Additionally, the single Scandinavian nation that was allied during World War II, Finland, experienced failure and opted for neutrality after the war. Realism does not successfully predict the Scandinavian checkerboard of alliances, since the geographic similarity of the locations of these four nations (all are exposed to Soviet military might and would be located on the northern front of a European conflict) would lead to a balance of threat hypothesis prediction that all four would either balance against or bandwagon with the Soviet threat. Only the individual learning hypothesis successfully explains the variety of individual decisions made by the Scandinavian nations.

These cases also reveal that states learn about an aspect of foreign policy not included as a dependent variable in the quantitative analysis—the level of domestic armament. Norway's belief that a large military was not necessary to ensure the country's security was confirmed by its successful World War I experience and was reversed (along with its faith in neutrality) by its World War II experience. Sweden and Switzerland, on the other hand, drew the lesson from World War II that neutrality is only effective if it is coupled with high levels of domestic armament. Though this model did not provide a quantitative test for learning about domestic armament, these observations may offer a useful elaboration of James Morrow's expected utility model of alliances, which sees both arms and alliances as means to increase security, and proposes that the choice of arms or alliances depends on nonsecurity components of the state's utility.[56] The analysis here suggests that a state's choice of its arms/alliance mix is also dependent on its beliefs about the relative contributions of arms and alliances to security, beliefs that emerge from formative experiences.

It is interesting to note that alliance preferences are not well explained by the systemic learning predictions expressed in Hypothesis 2. As the alliance checkerboards in Northern and Western Europe demonstrate, minor powers tend to act in accordance with the lessons offered by their own experiences, rather than to look to the experiences of all states in order to draw wider lessons. This empirical finding adds support to the proposition that states focus on their own national experiences and not on those of other countries.

One set of cases for which the individual learning predictions do not do well is the post-World War II Middle East, in which only some of the individual learning predictions are correct. As predicted, Iraq and Egypt, as failed allies, eventually steer toward neutrality in the 1950s, but they maintain their preference for alliance in the late 1940s. Walt claimed to find evidence of balancing and bandwagoning behavior in the post-World War II Middle East; this study's coding of threats, though, indicated that in that region preferences for alliance with a great power were not systematically related to the level of external threat. One possible explanation is that since these states are Third World nations, their relative political underdevelopment means that leaders pay especially great attention to domestic political threats and coalitions, implying that a complete model of Third World alliance preference must take account of such factors.[57] Other cases in which individual learning failed as an explanation are post-war Yugoslavia, post-war Spain, Albania in the early 1920s, Turkey just before World War II, Belgium in the late 1930s, and Romania in the early 1920s and late 1930s.[58]

Forming Beliefs About Specific Allies

This article tests the proposition that minor powers draw general lessons about neutrality and alliance. Another possibility is that minor powers instead learn about specific nations as allies. If minor powers did learn about nations, then we would expect that from a formative experience they would draw lessons about which nations are the most valuable allies. Presumably they would want to ally with the victors, would shun alliance with the losers, and would prefer alliance with the victors to neutrality. There are likely to be few lessons about nations from a world war in the sense described above; after a world war the defeated nations are much less powerful than the victors for at least several years, so it would be uninteresting to predict that minor powers would not ally with the defeated great powers, as alliance with a defeated great power after a world war would run counter to both the learning proposition and realism. Additionally, the historical record indicates that not all minor powers tend to ally with the victor after a world war; some prefer to remain neutral.

A different way to conceptualize learning about specific allies is to examine a different class of formative events, great power militarized crises. If minor powers draw lessons about the resolve of specific, great power allies, often we would expect that after a great power crisis, the allies of the (diplomatically) defeated great power would tend toward neutrality, neutrals would tend toward alliance with the victorious great power, and allies of the victor would not tend toward neutrality or alliance with the defeated power. This argument is most often applied to the reactions following the string of British and French diplomatic defeats in the middle and late 1930s, which included the ineffectually contested Italian invasion of Ethiopia, the German remilitarization of the Rhineland, the German annexation of Austria, the appeasement of Germany at the 1938 Munich conference, and the 1939 invasion of Czechoslovakia. These diplomatic defeats did have some effects on minor power behavior, most notably the crumbling of the Little Entente between France and the East European powers,[59] and the shift from some faith in the League of Nations as an effective guarantor of collective security toward more unilateral neutrality on the part of several neutrals.[60] Elsewhere in Europe, however, the predicted effects did not materialize. Historical research points to a complex array of domestic political factors driving the break in the Franco-Belgian alliance rather than to a loss of faith in French resolve over the German remilitarization of the Rhineland.[61] Additionally, the British-Portuguese alliance remained intact, and the predicted bandwagon effects did not appear, as neutral nations refrained from flocking to the German camp. Turkey even began negotiating an alliance with Britain and France in mid-1939.

There appears to be even less crisis-driven learning in the post-World War II period. In 1949 the U.S. had demonstrated its resolve to defend its extended foreign policy interests in Europe by standing with West Berlin through the Soviet blockade in the first major showdown between East and West. This resolve was further demonstrated in its strong response to the invasion of South Korea. These events occurred after the signing of the Brussels Treaty and the expression of interest in forming an Atlantic security structure, so they cannot be attributed to lessons learned from the Berlin crisis or the invasion of Korea. Though it might be too much to expect the communist-dominated East European nations to flee the Soviet camp, what is missing is any movement on the part of Yugoslavia, Finland, Sweden, Ireland, or Switzerland toward joining NATO after the Soviets lifted the blockade on Berlin in 1949. Similarly, the U.S. victories over the Soviet Union in the Berlin deadline crisis of 1961 and the Cuban Missile Crisis of 1962 failed to move any European neutrals into NATO (or Warsaw Pact nations into neutrality, for that matter) or Cuba away from Soviet influence. In short, then, there is some limited support for the proposition that great power crises can serve as formative events for minor powers, but the effect is not nearly as large as it is for world wars as formative events.

Conclusions

This article presents striking empirical results: the alliance choices of minor powers in the twentieth century were determined mainly by lessons drawn from formative national experiences, and only marginally by variations in the levels of external threat. Also striking is that these states learned in quite a simple fashion: success promoted continuity and failure stimulated innovation. This is an encouraging finding for the exploration of the role of beliefs in international relations, as it points to the broader conclusion that the construction of elaborate models of incomplete information is not the only path to understanding the role of beliefs. The significance of this alternate, simple model path is that it lends itself much more easily to the application of more rigorous, quantitative empirical tests than do sophisticated formal models of learning. The finding of the virtual irrelevance of variations in the level of threat to states' decisions is a serious blow to the balance of threat variant of realism. In a more limited way, it also strikes at traditional realism in general, given the acceptance of balance of threat theory among realists and the importance of alliances to realism. Indeed, the accurate prediction of alliance behavior is virtually a sine qua non of realism, and failure to do so ought to encourage reconsideration of traditional concepts of realism.

While this successful empirical challenge to traditional realism might point in the direction of the construction of an entirely new framework of international politics, a more fruitful path might be to put these findings in the context of a more extensively specified version of realism. The empirical results of this paper do not challenge the realist assumptions that states act in their self-interest or that state behavior is dominated by concerns over security issues. The divergence from traditional realism emerges from the learning proposition that some states react differently than others to the same set of circumstances. Similar to the point made by Christensen and Snyder, these results encourage the conclusion that to understand how decision makers cope with the uncertainty intrinsic to world politics, it is necessary to account for beliefs. An enlightened version of realism, then, would recognize the important role decision-makers' beliefs play in forming foreign policy and would acknowledge that exploring the origins of these beliefs can substantially improve our understanding of world politics.

Notes

A version of this paper was presented at the October 1993 Midwest meeting of the International Studies Association in Chicago. This article is based upon work supported under a National Science Foundation Graduate Fellowship. I am also grateful for support from the MacArthur Foundation. I would like to thank Robert Axelrod, Nancy Burns, Paul Diehl, Paul Huth, Ted Hopf, Scott Gartner, Karl Mueller, and Jennifer Shulman for their comments on various drafts, though I alone am responsible for any errors.

1. For works drawing on ideas from social psychology, see Robert Jervis, *Perceptions and Misperceptions in International Politics* (Princeton: Princeton University Press, 1976); Jack Snyder, *Ideology of the Offensive* (Ithaca, NY: Cornell University Press, 1984); Deborah Welch Larson, *Origins of Containment* (Prince-

ton: Princeton University Press, 1985); Yaacov Y. I. Vertzberger, "Foreign Policy Decisionmakers as Practical-Intuitive Historians: Applied History and Its Short-comings," *International Studies Quarterly* 30 (June 1986); Jack Snyder, *Myths of Empire: Domestic Politics and International Ambition* (Ithaca, NY: Cornell University Press, 1991); Yuen Foong Khong, *Analogies at War* (Princeton: Princeton University Press, 1992). For works drawing on ideas from organization theory, see John D. Steinbrunner, *The Cybernetic Theory of Decision* (Princeton: Princeton University Press, 1974); John P. Lovell, "Lessons of U.S. Military Involvement: Preliminary Conceptualization," in Donald A. Sylvan and Steve Chan, eds., *Foreign Policy Decision Making* (New York: Praeger, 1984); Barry Posen, *Sources of Military Doctrine* (Ithaca, NY: Cornell University Press, 1984); Matthew Evangelista, *Innovation and the Arms Race* (Ithaca, NY: Cornell University Press, 1988); Scott D. Sagan, *The Limits of Safety: Organizations, Accidents, and Nuclear Weapons* (Princeton: Princeton University Press, 1993). Ideas from information economics have been applied to this question as well. See, for example, Robert Powell, "Nuclear Brinksmanship with Two-Sided Incomplete Information," *American Political Science Review* 82 (March 1988), and R. Harrison Wagner, "Uncertainty, Rational Learning, and Bargaining in the Cuban Missile Crisis," in Peter C. Ordesbook, ed., *Models of Strategic Choice in Politics* (Ann Arbor: University of Michigan Press, 1989). For a review of different ideas about learning in international relations scholarship, see Jack S. Levy, "Learning and Foreign Policy: Sweeping a Conceptual Minefield," *International Organization* 48 (Spring 1994), and William W. Jarosz with Joseph S. Nye, Jr., "The Shadow of the Past: Learning from History in National Security Decision Making," in Philip E. Tetlock et al., eds., *Behavior, Society, and International Conflict*, vol. 3 (New York: Oxford University Press, 1993).

2. For this study, learning is broadly conceptualized as the application of information derived from past experiences to acquire understanding of a particular policy question. This is distinct from what has been called "corrective" learning, in which experience necessarily improves performance over time. For a discussion of different definitions of learning, see Philip E. Tetlock, "Learning in U.S. and Soviet Foreign Policy: In Search of an Elusive Concept," in George W. Breslauer and Philip E. Tetlock, eds., *Learning in U.S. and Soviet Foreign Policy* (Boulder, CO: Westview Press, 1991).

3. Richard Nisbett and Lee Ross, *Human Inference: Strategies and Shortcomings of Social Judgment* (Englewood Cliffs, NJ: Prentice-Hall, 1980).

4. Shelley E. Taylor and Jennifer Crocker, "Schematic Bases of Social Information Processing," in E. Tory Higgins, C. Peter Herman, and Mark P. Zanna, eds., *Social Cognition: The Ontario Symposium*, vol. 1 (Hillsdale, NJ: Lawrence Erlbaum Associates, 1981); Roger Schank and Robert P. Abelson, *Scripts, Plans, Goals and Understanding* (Hillsdale, NJ: Lawrence Erlbaum Associates, 1977).

5. Robert P. Abelson, "Script Processing in Attitude Formation and Decision Making," in *Cognition and Social Behavior* (Hillsdale, NJ: Lawrence Erlbaum Associates, 1976); Abelson and Mansur Lalljee, "Knowledge Structures and Causal Explanation," in Denis J. Hilton, ed., *Contemporary Science and Natural Explanation* (New York: New York University Press, 1988). For a discussion of schemata as applied to international relations, see Larson (note 1).

6. Daniel Kahneman, Paul Slovic, and Amos Tversky, eds., *Judgment under Uncertainty: Heuristics and Biases* (Cambridge: Cambridge University Press, 1982); Nisbett and Ross (note 3).

7. Stella Vosniadu and Andrew Ortony, eds., *Similarity and Analogical Reasoning* (Cambridge: Cambridge University Press, 1989); Khong (note 1).

8. Stephen J. Read, "Once Is Enough: Causal Reasoning from a Single Instance," *Journal of Personality and Social Psychology* 45, no. 2 (1983).

9. Thomas Gilovich, "Seeing the Past in the Present: The Effect of Associations to Familiar Events on Judgments and Decisions," *Journal of Personality and Social Psychology* 40, no. 5 (1981).

10. Barbara Levitt and James G. March, "Organizational Learning," *Annual Review of Sociology* 14 (1988). See also Chris Argyris, *On Organizational Learning* (Cambridge, MA: Blackwell, 1993).

11. Sim B. Sitkin, "Learning through Failure: The Strategy of Small Losses," in Barry M. Staw and L. L. Cummings, eds., *Research in Organizational Behavior* 14 (Greenwich, CT: JAI Press, 1992); Bo Hedberg, "How Organizations Learn and Unlearn," in Paul C. Nystrom and William H. Starbuck, eds., *Handbook of Organizational Design* (London: Oxford University Press, 1981), 1:17–18; Philip Mirvis and David Berg, eds., *Failures in Organization Development and Change* (New York: Wiley, 1977).

12. Nisbett and Ross (note 3).

13. Paul C. Nystrom and William H. Starbuck, "Managing Beliefs in Organizations," *Journal of Applied Behavioral Science* 20, no. 3 (1984); Hedberg (note 11), 6; Levitt and March (note 10), 324; Sten A. Jönsson and Rolf A. Lundin, "Myths and Wishful Thinking as Management Tools," in Paul C. Nystrom and William H. Starbuck, eds., *Prescriptive Models of Organizations* (Amsterdam: North-Holland, 1977).

14. Nisbett and Ross (note 3), 45. On schemata and belief changes, see Jennifer Crocker, Susan T. Fiske, and Shelley E. Taylor, "Schematic Bases of Belief Change," in J. Richard Eiser, ed., *Attitudinal Judgment* (New York: Springer-Verlag, 1984).

15. A number of studies have failed to find that vivid events are more persuasive. See Shelley E. Taylor and Suzanne C. Thompson, "Stalking the Elusive 'Vividness' Effect," *Psychological Review* 89 (1982); Shelley E. Taylor and Joanne V. Wood, "The Vividness Effect: Making a Mountain out of a Molehill?" in Richard P. Bogozzi and Alice M. Tybout, eds., *Advances in Consumer Research* 10 (Ann Arbor, MI: Association of Consumer Research, 1983); Rebecca L. Collins et al., "The Vividness Effect: Elusive or Illusory?" *Journal of Experimental Social Psychology* 24 (January 1988); Susan T. Fiske and Shelley Taylor, *Social Cognition* 2d ed. (New York: McGraw-Hill, 1991). However, Collins et al. found that vivid events are *believed* to be more persuasive, raising the possibility that vivid events are more persuasive by self-fulfilling prophecy. Additionally, some studies have found that events experienced firsthand have a greater impact on behavior than those experienced vicariously. See Fiske and Taylor, 520–21, and Sanford L. Braver and Van Rohrer, "Superiority of Vicarious over Direct Experience in Interpersonal Conflict Resolution," *Journal of Conflict Resolution* 22, no. 1 (1978). For examples of international relations research that found that events experienced firsthand were formative of beliefs, see Jervis (note 1) and Khong (note 1).

16. Sitkin (note 11), 238; Levitt and March (note 10), 329–31; Viday Mahajan, Subhash Sharma, and Richard Bettis, "Adoption of the M-Form Organizational Structure: A Test of Imitation Hypothesis," *Management Science* 34 (October 1988).

17. The formality of an alliance declaration is not a diplomatic triviality. Morgenthau has remarked, "When the common interests are inchoate in terms of policy and action, a treaty of alliance is required to make them explicit and operative." Hans Morgenthau, "Alliances in Theory and Practice," in Arnold Wolfers, ed., *Alliance Policy in the Cold War* (Baltimore: Johns Hopkins University Press, 1959), 188.

18. Alliances with great powers are distinguished here from one-way commitments by a great power to defend the minor power, because mutual alliances increase the minor power's risk of entanglement far more than one-way commitments.

19. J. David Singer and Melvin Small, "Formal Alliances, 1815–1939," *Journal of Peace Research* 3, no. 1 (1966); and Paul Huth and Bruce Russett, "Deterrence Failure and Crisis Escalation," *International Studies Quarterly* 32 (March 1988).

20. Ernest R. May, *"Lessons" of the Past* (New York: Oxford University Press, 1973); Richard E. Neustadt and Ernest R. May, *Thinking in Time: The Uses of History for Decision-Makers* (New York: Free Press, 1986); Khong (note 1).

21. George Liska, *International Equilibrium* (Cambridge, MA: Harvard University Press, 1957), 25; Raymond Aron, *Peace and War: A Theory of International Relations*, trans. Richard Howard and Annette Baker Fox (Garden City, NY: Doubleday, 1966), 58; Kenneth Waltz, *Theory of International Politics* (New York: Random House, 1979), 72.

22. Sally Marks, *The Illusion of Peace: International Relations in Europe, 1918–1933* (New York: St. Martin's Press, 1976), 1. See also Robert Gilpin, *War and Change in World Politics* (Cambridge: Cambridge University Press, 1981); Jack S. Levy, *War in the Modern Great Power System, 1495–1975* (Lexington: University Press of Kentucky, 1983); William R. Thompson, *On Global War: Historical-Structural Approaches to World Politics* (Columbia: University of South Carolina Press, 1988); and George Modeski, *Long Cycles in World Politics* (Seattle: University of Washington Press, 1987). A leading proponent of the argument that systemic wars do not have unique causes agrees that systemic wars do have unique effects. Bruce Bueno de Mesquita, "Big Wars, Little Wars: Avoiding Selection Bias," *International Interactions* 16, no. 3 (1990), 159–60.

23. Neutrality and alliance were not important policy categories for most minor powers after either the Wars of Louis XIV, when the concepts of sovereignty and independence were not as widely applicable as in the twentieth century, or the Napoleonic Wars, when the great powers imposed order via the Concert of Europe.

24. Invasion constitutes the failure of neutrality since the primary reason neutrality is chosen is to avoid participation in war.

25. This is admittedly a crude measure for alliance failure, but population is a good index with which to compare wartime losses with gains made in postwar settlements.

26. It is also assumed that a formative event (systemic war, in this application) has a watershed effect, such that previous formative events are dominated by the

most recent formative event in terms of belief formation. This watershed assumption is necessary to avoid infinite regress in determining which event is formative. For 1994 France, for example, there are a number of events that one could deem to be the "primary" event in French learning about international affairs, such as World War II, World War I, the Napoleonic Wars, and so forth. The organization theory proposition that crises create new myths that replace old ones supports the watershed assumption.

27. A similar argument was made by Donald E. Nuechterlein, "Small States in Alliances: Iceland, Thailand, Australia," *Orbis* 13 (Summer 1969). This paper builds on this past work by constructing a theory of learning, testing its predictions on a broader set of data, and comparing these predictions to those of realism.

28. If a state thinks that its own experience is not idiosyncratic and that the experiences of other nations are relevant, then learning from the experience of all minor powers in a formative event would be more unbiased than learning just from one's own experience.

29. Waltz (note 21), is quite blunt on this point (pp. 72–73). There is, however, a considerable literature on the foreign policy problems of non-great powers— termed variously as middle powers, small powers, weak states, and the like—though it is often descriptive rather than predictive. See Annette Baker Fox, *The Power of Small States: Diplomacy in World War II* (Chicago: University of Chicago Press, 1959); Robert L. Rothstein, *Alliances and Small Powers* (New York: Columbia University Press, 1968); Jerry Wilson Ralston, *The Defense of Small States in the Nuclear Age: The Case of Sweden and Switzerland* (Neuchâtel: La Baconnière, 1969); Robert O. Keohane, "Lilliputians' Dilemmas: Small States in International Politics," *International Organization* 23 (Spring 1969); Peter J. Katzenstein, *Small States in World Markets* (Ithaca, NY: Cornell University Press, 1985); Efraim Karsh, *Neutrality and Small States* (London: Routledge, 1988); and Karl Mueller, "Strategy, Asymmetric Deterrence, and Accommodation: Middle Powers and Security in Modern Europe" (Ph.D. diss., Princeton University, 1991).

30. Thomas J. Christensen and Jack L. Snyder, "Chain Gangs and Passed Bucks: Predicting Alliance Patterns in Multipolarity," *International Organization* 44 (Spring 1990). Interestingly, they note that experiences often drive beliefs about the offense-defense balance. For a diverse list of propositions concerning alliances, see Ole Holsti, P. Terrence Hopmann, and John D. Sullivan, *Unity and Disintegration in International Alliances: Comparative Studies* (New York: John Wiley, 1973).

31. Stephen M. Walt, *The Origins of Alliances* (Ithaca, NY: Cornell University Press, 1987).

32. This last point, that alliances are likely to break up as the threat recedes or disappears (such as after an aggressor is defeated in war), was made by Walt (note 31), 29–30; and Morgenthau (note 17), 191–92.

33. Walt (note 31); and idem, "Testing Theories of Alliance Formation: The Case of Southwest Asia," *International Organization* 42 (Spring 1988). A number of quantitative studies using an expected utility approach has found varying empirical support for the general proposition that threats play a part in driving alliance choices, though most of these works have tested models of decision that are more sophisticated than Walt's. See Bruce D. Berkowitz, "Realignment in International

Treaty Organizations," *International Studies Quarterly* 27 (March 1983); Michael T. Altfeld, "The Decision to Ally," *Western Political Quarterly* 37 (December 1984); David Lalman and David Newman, "Alliance Formation and National Security," *International Interactions* 16, no. 4 (1991); Thomas R. Cusack and Richard J. Stoll, "Balancing Behavior in the Interstate System, 1816–1976," *International Interactions* 16, no. 4 (1991). For an expected utility model that emphasizes the importance of domestic as well as international factors in shaping alliance behavior, see James D. Morrow, "Alliances and Asymmetry: An Alternative to the Capability Model of Alliances," *American Journal of Political Science* 47 (November 1991); and idem, "Arms versus Allies: Trade-Offs in the Search for Security," *International Organization* 47 (Spring 1993).

34. Walt (note 31), 31n.

35. See the works cited in note 19.

36. Robert E. Osgood, *Alliances and American Foreign Policy* (Baltimore: Johns Hopkins University Press, 1968), 19–20.

37. Mueller (note 29).

38. Walt (note 31), 23–24.

39. Most empirical research in learning focuses on a small group of cases, including May (note 20); Snyder (note 1, 1984 and 1991); Posen (note 1); Evangelista (note 1); and Khong (note 1). In particular, the cases of American and Soviet learning during the Cold War are receiving increasing attention. See Breslauer and Tetlock (note 2); Michael G. Fry, ed., *History, the White House and the Kremlin* (London: Pinter Publishers, 1991); Manus I. Midlarsky, John A. Vasquez, and Peter V. Gladkov, eds., *From Rivalry to Cooperation: Russian and American Perspectives on the Post Cold War Era* (New York: HarperCollins, 1994). Two studies of learning in world politics using larger samples are Russell Leng, "When Will They Ever Learn?" *Journal of Conflict Resolution* 27 (September 1983); and Paul K. Huth, *Extended Deterrence and the Prevention of War* (New Haven: Yale University Press, 1988).

40. Autocorrelation means that there is a systematic relationship between the dependent variable at time t and the dependent variable at time t-1.

41. This technique is know as systematic sampling. John R. Freeman, "Systematic Sampling, Temporal Aggregation, and the Study of Political Relationships," in J. A. Stimson, ed., *Political Analysis* (Ann Arbor: University of Michigan Press, 1990).

42. Coding for the dependent variable was made on the basis of primary and secondary historical sources. The absence of alliance between a minor power and any great power does not necessarily indicate the preference on the part of the minor power for neutrality; the minor power may prefer great power alliance, but there is no willing great power. In such a case, the dependent variable was coded as 1.

43. Walt (note 31), 21–26.

44. Correlates of War data on military spending were used. Using troop levels is problematic for small powers, as some countries rely on reserve or militia forces for defense. It is difficult to assess the contribution of these forces except on a case by case basis, because the quality of these forces and the speed with which they could be committed to the national defense vary widely.

45. The military forces from other countries committed to the security of the defender need to be considered separately from the defender's own military

forces, because the ally cannot commit all of its forces to help the defender since it has to defend its own territory as well as that of the defender.

46. On these measures, see J. David Singer, S. Bremer, and J. Stuckey in Bruce Russett, ed., *Peace, War, and Numbers* (Beverly Hills, CA: Sage, 1972).

47. The likelihood ratio test statistic (LRTS) is twice the difference of the log likelihood values for the restricted and unrestricted model specifications. In this case, that value is 5.39, which is greater than the critical value for .20 in a chi-squared distribution, meaning that we can conclude with confidence that there is little systematic relationship between these four variables (STMB, GEOG*STMB, DTMB, and DCOM) and the dependent variable. On this test, see Gary King, *Unifying Political Methodology* (Cambridge: Cambridge University Press, 1989).

48. The LRTS for comparing the model in equation (1) with a model including just the two learning variables in 14.8, which is significant at the .05 level with 7 degrees of freedom.

49. See Altfeld (note 33); Lalman and Newman (note 33); Berkowitz (note 33. Lalman and Newman propose that a different global distribution of power encouraged a greater propensity to ally after World War II than after World War I. The learning hypothesis argues that this greater tendency was due to the individual experiences of states in wartime and is preferable to the distribution of global power explanation because it accounts for decisions of individual states for alliance or neutrality as well as for systemwide patterns.

50. Bruce Bueno de Mesquita, *The War Trap* (New Haven: Yale University Press, 1981). This paper used an alternative method of directly measuring external threats for two reasons. First, utility for war is an imprecise conceptual proxy for security, partly because it implies that a state is more secure the more it stands to gain from the prosecution of war. Second, Bueno de Mesquita's method uses alliances to predict foreign policy preferences, raising falsifiability concerns for an application here, given that alliances would be used as both dependent and independent variables.

51. George Modelski, "The Asian States' Participation in SEATO," in George Modelski, ed., SEATO: *Six Studies* (Melbourne: F. W. Cheshire, 1962), 90–91.

52. On Belgium, see Jonathan Helmreich, "The Negotiation of the Franco-Belgian Military Accord of 1920," *French Historical Studies* 3 (Spring 1964); and Paul-F. Smets, ed., *La pensée européene et atlantique de Paul-Henri Spaak (1942–1972)*, 2 vols. (Brussels: J. Goemere, 1980). Belgium broke off its alliance with France in 1936 due primarily to an array of domestic political factors. Of course, this case constitutes a failure for both learning hypotheses. On the 1936 break, see David O. Kieft, *Belgium's Return to Neutrality* (Oxford: Clarendon Press, 1972). On Switzerland, see Jacques Freymond, "The Foreign Policy of Switzerland," in *Foreign Policy in a World of Change* (New York: Harper and Row, 1963), 151–52. On the Netherlands, see Amry Vandenbosch, *Dutch Foreign Policy since 1815* (The Hague: Martinus Nijhoff, 1959), 289. A more extensive discussion of these and other cases is presented in Dan Reiter, "Learning, Realism, and Alliances: An Empirical Examination of the Causes of Alliances" (Ph.D. diss. University of Michigan, 1994).

53. F. A. Abadie-Maumert, "Le pacifisme norvégien entre 1919 et 1940 et ses conséquences," *Guerres mondiales et conflits contemporains* 40 (October 1990); Fox (note

29), 81, 111–12; T. K. Derry, *A History of Modern Norway, 1814–1972* (Oxford: Clarendon Press, 1973), 415; Nils Ørvik, *Trends in Norwegian Foreign Policy* (Oslo: Norwegian Institute of International Affairs, 1962), 6, 12; Samuel Abrahamsen, *Sweden's Foreign Policy* (Washington, DC: Public Affairs Press, 1957), 14.

54. Gerald Aalders, "The Failure of the Scandinavian Defence Union, 1948–1949," *Scandinavian Journal of History* 15 (1990), 133–34. Nazi Germany invaded Norway and Denmark on April 9, 1940.

55. Ralston (note 29), 209.

56. Morrow (note 33, 1991, 1993).

57. Steven R. David, "Explaining Third World Alignment," *World Politics* 43 (January 1991); Michael N. Barnett and Jack S. Levy, "Domestic Sources of Alliances and Alignments: The Case of Egypt, 1962–73," *International Organization* 45 (Summer 1991); and idem, "Alliance Formation, Domestic Political Economy, and Third World Security," *Jerusalem Journal of International Relations* 14 (December 1992).

58. Curiously, being a nondemocracy seems to be nearly a necessary condition for not behaving as the individual learning hypothesis predicts. For more on this pattern, see Reiter (note 52).

59. Rothstein (note 29).

60. Nils Ørvik, *The Decline of Neutrality, 1914–41* (Oslo: Tanum, 1953), 177–90.

61. Kieft (note 52).

9

NORM ENTREPRENEURS

Scandinavia's Role in World Politics

CHRISTINE INGEBRITSEN

Introduction

Challenging the commonly held view that "the powerful do as they will, and the weak do as they must," this article analyzes how a group of small states in northern Europe play a role in strengthening global codes of appropriate behavior referred to as "norms." Scandinavian contributions to international society vary from institutionalizing norms of "sustainable development' in global environmental policy, to the creation of a common security institution (the Conference on Security Cooperation in Europe, CSCE or OSCE), to providing a model of generous and consistent aid to the poor. Scandinavia has consistently and actively sought to influence more powerful states in establishing and strengthening global norms of cooperation. These themes are explored on the basis of case studies and sources from Scandinavia.[1]

Classic approaches to the study of international politics give priority to the material power, or capabilities, of states relative to other states in the world. In these analyses, scholars have tended to understate the independent influence of smaller states, such as the five northern European states of Norway, Sweden, Denmark, Finland, and Iceland.[2]

The end of the Cold War provided an opportunity to critically evaluate how we think about power in global politics because so many of our theoretical frameworks were brought into question. In recent years, scholars in international relations have been re-examining the definition of power, and have begun to focus on how states exercise influence in ways that do not conform to strictly economic and military capabilities.[3] Instead

Christine Ingebritsen (2002), "Norm Entrepreneurs: Scandinavia's Role in World Politics." *Cooperation and Conflict: Journal of the Nordic International Studies Association* 37(1): 11–23. Reprinted with permission of Sage Publications Ltd.

of viewing the international system as fragmented and anarchic, a new wave of scholarship examines how states become socialized into an international community or society. Within this community, there are established practices, codes of conduct, and standards of acceptable behavior, referred to as "norms," that influence state interests and identity. More theorists have begun studying the interactions between states and non-state actors, understood to comprise a global civil society (Clark et al., 1998: 1–35). Thus, ideational and normative conceptions of politics have been receiving more attention, i.e., there is a recognition of how states are not only pursuing territorial expansion, material wealth, and the maximization of power on a global scale, but are also concerned with reputation, identity, and community (Klotz, 1995; Finnemore, 1996; Katzenstein, 1996).

The Role of Norms in International Politics

International relations theorists have examined how norms become salient, when norms become institutionalized, and how norms shape or define state interests and identity. Not all norms are influential, or hegemonic, in international politics. Norms may co-exist, conflict, or fail to be recognized by the majority of states in the international community. Yet tracing why states ought to pursue a particular policy, or participate in international cooperation has introduced new and exciting areas for research—as long as scholars acknowledge variance in the strength, legitimacy, and salience of international norms (Cortell and Davis, 1996: 2).

In a review of the norms literature published in *International Organization* (1998), Martha Finnemore and Kathryn Sikkink specify three stages in the life-cycle of norms. The first phase is norm emergence, the second is norm acceptance, and the final stage is norm internalization. "Norms do not emerge out of thin air: they are actively built by agents having strong opinions about appropriate or desirable behavior in their community" (1998: 896). For norms to emerge, agents (individuals, states, or societal actors) act as "norm entrepreneurs," mobilizing support for particular standards of appropriateness and persuading states to adopt new norms (pp. 897–901).

For norms to "take" (phase two of the norm life-cycle), there must be evidence of a contagion or socialization effect: states conform to the norm in the absence of domestic pressure. And finally, norms become internalized so that "conformance with the norm becomes almost automatic" or unquestioned (p. 904).

This analysis extends the study of norms and traces how and why a particular group of states have emerged as "norm entrepreneurs" in international politics.[4] Not only have international norms been perpetuated and enforced by those with a preponderance of power, they also originate in a group of states that share distinct ideas about appropriate forms of domestic and international intervention. Thus, Scandinavia, a group of militarily weak, economically dependent small states, pursues "social power" by acting as a norm entrepreneur in the international community.[5] In three policy areas (the environment, international security, and global welfare), Scandinavia has acted to promote a particular view of the good society.

While some critics may view the role of norm entrepreneur as strategic action by a small state, this does not discount the effects of Scandinavia's pursuit of different models of interaction, models that structure the choices available to states in international politics.[6]

Why Scandinavia?

Scandinavia became a norm entrepreneur in contemporary international politics precisely because of its remote geographic position, limited material capabilities, and unique domestic institutions. As argued by Peter Lawler, "there is inscribed upon the collective identities of the Scandinavian states decades of innovative domestic reformism and multifaceted internationalism" (1997: 567).

With the consistent efforts of Scandinavia to promote its views and strengthen particular international norms, states of the sub-region have earned a global reputation as trustworthy and effective negotiating partners. This reputation is consciously cultivated and deepened as a cornerstone of Scandinavian diplomatic relations.[7]

Scandinavia's peripheral position in relation to Europe has historically permitted these states to remain aloof from international engagement. The decision to enter into militant alliances has been a post-Second World War development, and these states have been among the last to consider joining the European Union (Ingebritsen, 1998). The prominence of neutrality and non-alignment as preferred foreign policy strategies distinguishes the Scandinavian states from other, larger, European powers. Instead of adopting a passive role in foreign policy-making, however, the two states that have had the longest tradition of neutrality (Sweden and Finland) have actively brokered negotiations between East and West since 1945; and have played a role in building new security institutions in Europe—from the OSCE to the Petersberg Tasks outlined in the Amsterdam Treaty.

Scandinavia's dependence on natural resources for economic survival has led these states to adopt pragmatic development philosophies as a matter of necessity. To sustain the economy, social regulations were adopted by the governments to conserve common resources earlier than in other societies. In contrast to elsewhere in Europe, late industrialization meant that these states avoided the ecological consequences of rapid growth and urbanization.

Finally, the prominence of social democratic institutions with ideologies of social partnership (Katzenstein, 1985) and a preference for consensus in policy-making enables these states to maintain consistency as they seek to export their model abroad—in environmental policy-making, peace-keeping, and international aid policy. The following discussion traces how Scandinavian states have influenced internationally accepted codes of conduct in world politics.

SCANDINAVIA AND ENVIRONMENTAL NORMS

For the last century, the Scandinavian states have protected the environment and sought to preserve the integrity of rural areas. As early as 1803, large parts of forests in eastern Scandinavia were declared nature reserves, and the precedent established for the regulation of resource-dependent economies. The idea of setting aside parks and nature reserves was pioneered in the twentieth century throughout the Scandinavian area by national associations advocating conservation (Hermanson, 1997).

As Scandinavian economies industrialized, these governments adopted elaborate land-use policies at the local, national, and regional levels, policies designed to minimize the effects of industrialization on society and the environment. These policies restricted the location of manufacturing facilities and were intended to reduce the harmful effects of pollution.

Culturally, Scandinavia shares a well-institutionalized tradition of respecting common property. "Allmansrätt" is Swedish for "everyone's right," and refers to the relationship between individual rights and land use. From a young age, Scandinavians are socialized into looking after and maintaining nature as they find it—on hikes, camping trips, and when passing through a neighboring farm. This has institutionalized a set of norms just as strict as any legal definition of property rights and which is socially enforced. Comparative studies have shown that there is widespread public concern about the environment and a "green consciousness" in the Scandinavian societies (Hermanson, 1997).

As in other industrialized nations, the 1970s was a decisive era for environmental action. In Scandinavia, however, governments were particularly active. For example, Sweden hosted the UN Conference on the Environment in Stockholm in 1972; ministries of the environment were established in Norway and Denmark; and social movements encouraged citizen responsibility and environmental education. Throughout Scandinavia, consumer producers have been labeled in accordance with environmental standards. These eco-friendly products are indicated by the symbol of a swan or a seal (Hermanson, 1997).

Norwegian leadership in promoting norms of "sustainable development" through the United Nations is another example of Scandinavian norm entrepreneurship. In 1983, the United Nations created the World Commission on Environment and Development to examine the relationship between people, resources, the environment, and development on a global scale. In 1987, under the leadership of Dr. Gro Harlem Brundtland (a Norwegian), the World Commission on Environment and Development presented its report, *Our Common Future*, and so launched an international debate around the concept of "sustainable development." The Brundtland Commission's report outlines a new agenda for managing the combined challenges of global economic development and environmental management:

> We are now forced to concern ourselves with the impacts of ecological stress—degradation of soils, water regimes, atmosphere, and forests—upon our economic prospects. We have in the recent past been forced to face up to a sharp increase in economic interdependence among nations. We are now forced to accustom ourselves to an accelerating ecological interdependence among nations. (World Commission on Environment and Development, 1987: 5)

The Brundtland report emphasizes a balanced approach to developing the global economy in an age of limited resources.

> Humanity has the ability to make development sustainable—to ensure that it meets the needs of the present without compromising the ability of future generations to meet their own needs. The concept of sustainable development does imply limits—not absolute limits but limitations imposed by the present state of technology and social organization on environmental resources and by the ability of the biosphere to absorb the effects of human activities. (p. 8)

While some analysts criticize use of the term as a "slogan so frequently used that it has lost most of its sense and power," the integration of ecological considerations with development priorities has become a shared goal of global development policy (Sverdrup, 1997: 55).

The sustainable development norm has taken hold—so much so that some are hesitant to use the term because it has become a label for "good practices," and has given rise to global discussions on sustainable industry, sustainable energy, sustainable transport, and sustainable land use (van den Bergh and van der Straaten, 1994). Thus, in international environmental meetings, sustainable development has been accepted as the starting point for discussions—the disputes center around what standards should be adopted, who should pay for the costs associated with meeting these criteria, and what kinds of enforcement mechanisms are appropriate.

The salience of the sustainable development norms is visible at the national, local, and regional levels of governance. In European states, environmental legislation, targets, and new methods of data-gathering have been adopted to enhance sustainability. The European Commission interprets "sustainable development" as an environmental quality objective, and has sought to establish this norm in the European Union (O'Riordan and Voisey, 1997: 15). The concept is the focus of international development activity coordinated through the United Nations, and the focus of the Conference on Environment and Development in Rio de Janeiro (1992). National governments (particularly the member-states of the OECD) have, to varying degrees, initiated action programs designed to meet the recommendations of the Brundtland Commission Report (Angell et al., 1991: 123–34).

Since the end of the Cold War, the Swedish government has initiated sustainable development projects in the Baltic Sea. The environmental legacy of the Soviet empire has devastated the Baltic Sea region. According to a statement made by the Prime Minister of Sweden from the Parliament on 6 October 1998:

> Sweden will show the way in the transition to sustainable development. The work of protecting the environment, stimulating local initiative and encouraging the ecocycle approach will continue. An Agenda 21 for the Baltic Sea region will be coordinated in preparation for EU enlargement. (Swedish Ministry of Foreign Affairs, 1998: 4)

Some of the most impressive efforts in Sweden's commitment to sustainable development are visible at the municipal level, where localities have adopted goals for reducing carbon dioxide emissions and energy consumption, promoting biodiversity and otherwise promoting an environmentalist agenda (Forsberg, 1997: 10–11).

Thus, sustainable development has taken hold throughout Europe, and has become the dominant organizing principle in global development policy. The norm of sustainable development has survived the first two phases of the norm life-cycle: emergence and internalization. Scandinavia has played a comparable role as norm entrepreneur in securing the peace.

MULTILATERAL SECURITY

As foreign and security policy analyst Johan Jørgen Holst argued, the Scandinavian states played a critical "bridge-building" function between the two blocs during the Cold War period.[8] Conflict avoidance and prevention, confidence-building measures, and reassurance strategies were implemented to dissipate the prospect of war in Europe—and the threat to Scandinavian territory, airspace, and surrounding seas. The role of neutral and non-aligned states proved critical in establishing a cooperative framework and in stabilizing the transformation of Eastern Europe.

Janie Leatherman and Dan Thomas are among the numerous international relations scholars who have examined the peaceful transformation of the Cold War system of opposing military blocs. Leatherman and Thomas each conducted separate investigations into the effects of the Conference on Security Cooperation in Europe (CSCE) had on conflict prevention (Leatherman, 1993; Thomas, 1991). According to their findings, the CSCE contributed to altering the East-West conflict by redefining the rules of the game.

The meetings in Finland that led to the conclusion of the Helsinki Final Act (1975) established the basis for East-West cooperation prior to the end of the Cold War based on universal principles of human rights. Framed as a means of bringing adversaries to the negotiating table, the Helsinki Act proved to be a "catalyst for change in Eastern Europe" (Leatherman, 1993: 404). Transitional social movements in Hungary, Poland, East Germany, Czechoslovakia, Bulgaria, and Romania were strengthened, to varying degrees, by the normative effects of the Helsinki Final Act. The Act established the CSCE, a multilateral institution that "altered the institutional opportunity structure for opposition groups and provided them with alternative resources" (p. 405).

In the process of establishing the principles for cooperation, a tense solution occurred when the Soviet delegation reacted against the language adopted. The 10 principles outlined in the negotiations went further than the Soviets had anticipated (see Table 9.1). In particular, the right of states to determine their own laws and regulations came under attack. The so-

TABLE 9.1 Ten principles of the Helsinki Final Act

1. Sovereign equality
2. Refraining from the threat or use of force
3. Inviolability of frontiers
4. Territorial integrity of states
5. Peaceful settlement of disputes
6. Non-intervention in internal affairs
7. Respect for human rights and fundamental freedoms
8. Equal rights and self-determination of peoples
9. Cooperation among states
10. Fulfillment in good faith of obligations under international law

SOURCE: Heraclides (1993: 22).

called "Finnish compromise" averted a weakening of the principles, with the Finns insisting on the original principles being modified to include a clause acceptable to both East and West (Heraclides, 1993: 22).

Within the structure of the CSCE itself, neutral and non-aligned nations (Finland, Sweden, Austria, and Switzerland) were designated to serve in the office of chairman, to oversee the drafting of texts, and to offer suggestions for compromise (Heraclides, 1993: 48, 72–3, 141). As Alexis Heraclides argues:

> The CSCE always had more to it than was apparent. Compared to other world bodies with superpower participation it was probably most effective in the period from 1975 until 1991. During the cold war, in particular, the CSCE can be registered as a qualified success of the quiet approach, by which means it also played a role in bring about the end of the world (the Eastern European world) not with a bang, to use T. S. Eliot's words, but a whimper. (p. 172)

It should be noted, however, that the CSCE/OSCE has not been able to prevent the ethnic conflict and state disintegration we have witnessed in Europe since the transformation of East-West relations. However, as NATO redefines its role in Europe, the northern neutrals (Finland and Sweden) have remained important partners in transforming the capacities of NATO, and in promoting alternative means of conflict prevention.

In addition to the Finnish role in implementing the CSCE progress, the Scandinavian states collectively strengthen norms of conflict mediation and peaceful resolution of conflict. Norway has established an international reputation as third party mediator with the conclusion of the Oslo Accords. Even though the conflict persists, the Oslo Accords have established an important framework (a reliance on informal, behind-the-scenes negotiations) and guide further cooperation in the Middle East region. In awarding the Nobel Peace Prize each year, Scandinavia focuses international attention on the peaceful resolution of conflict and strengthens its role as a norm entrepreneur.

In securing the peace, northern Europeans have a comparative advantage. Strategic considerations guide US policy-makers, yet are less of a constraint on Scandinavian leaders. As a large, federal state with a divided government, the United States has domestic institutions that impede coherent and decisive action in international politics. Scandinavian states, on the other hand, have a relatively small group of makers of foreign policy-makers and a tradition of consensus-building, enabling more consistent policy-making.[9] Prominent Scandinavians are often asked to mediate in international conflicts. The Finnish President, for example, was the preferred broker in reaching a peaceful settlement in the Kosovo crisis.

The influence of Scandinavians in global norm entrepreneurship is also visible in a third issue-area: the provision of foreign aid.

SCANDINAVIA AND GLOBAL WELFARE

Prior to the Second World War, there was a distinct absence of a "norm" for global welfare improvement. It was not considered a responsibility of rich nations to assist poor nations—nor did national governments devote resources to the provision of foreign aid. The adoption of the welfare state became an important catalyst for the establishment of foreign aid policies. As domestic institutions took responsibility for impoverished groups *within* society, and perpetuated a norm of social solidarity, the logical extension of this commitment was a global one. However, this burden was not shared equally.

As argued by David Lumsdaine in *Moral Vision in International Politics*, developed democracies typically provide aid for humane purposes. "The strongest source of support for promoting the economic development of the poor countries has been a sense of justice and compassion" (Lumsdaine, 1993: 283). Yet the extent of a domestic, institutionalized commitment to alleviating poverty varies extensively—from a minimalist social insurance system (US, UK), to a universal, comprehensive system of "cradle to grave" benefits.

In international comparisons of foreign aid contributions, the Scandina-

TABLE 9.2 Foreign aid expenditure: National patterns

High	*High*	*Low*
	Belgium, Denmark	Australia
	France, Sweden	Canada
	Norway, The Netherlands	
Government foreign	Germany	
aid (ODA/GNP)		
Low	Finland, Italy	Austria, Japan
		New Zealand, USA
		Switzerland, UK

SOURCE: Compiled from Lumsdaine (1993: 122).

vian states have consistently given a higher percentage of their gross national product (GNP) than other states during the post-war period (see Table 9.2). The most recent United Nations comparison of Official Development Assistance (ODA) shows Denmark to be the leading donor country, followed by Norway and Sweden (see Table 9.3).

Not only has Scandinavia given more aid relative to national wealth, it also differs from larger states in the motivation for providing assistance. In contrast to the United States, aid is not provided for strategic purposes, although some groups or industries may benefit from national patterns of foreign aid. Historically, Scandinavian states have given aid for ideological purposes and distributed aid to states in greatest need.

Although a recent study has revealed how Sweden has reformed its aid policy, the amount of Swedish aid as a percentage of GNP remains high. Because of economic constraints, the principled position of the Swedish government not to seek benefits from aid has been modified. "The previously scorned practice of tying Swedish aid to the purchase of Swedish goods and services or to prescribed financing arrangements became more acceptable as an element of aid policy" (Schraeder et al., 1998: 316–17). Nonetheless, Scandinavian states are advocates for development-giving—in international institutions, and in their past performance as generous welfare providers.

I believe that the Scandinavian model (commitment to achieving social solidarity at home) has contributed to a logical extension of this philosophy on global welfare—even though this norm has not been widely internalized in the international community, as Martha Finnemore has persuasively argued.

TABLE 9.3 Scandinavian norm entrepreneurship
official development assistance flows in 1996

Country	ODA ($m)	ODA/GNP (%)
Australia	1,121	0.30
Austria	557	0.24
Belgium	913	0.34
Canada	1,795	0.32
Denmark	1,772	1.04
Finland	408	0.34
France	7,451	0.48
Germany	7,601	0.33
Ireland	179	0.31
Italy	2,416	0.20
Japan	9,439	0.20
Luxembourg	82	0.44
The Netherlands	3,246	0.81
New Zealand	122	0.21
Norway	1,311	0.85
Portugal	218	0.21
Spain	1,251	0.22
Sweden	1,999	0.84
Switzerland	1,026	0.34
United Kingdom	3,199	0.27
United States	9,377	0.12

SOURCE: Compiled from OECD (1998: 76).

Conclusion

This analysis has identified three issue-areas in which Scandinavia acts as a norm entrepreneur in international politics. Sustainable development practices, the peaceful resolution of conflict, and the norm of transferring resources from rich to poor have been strengthened by Scandinavia's demonstrated leadership, and through Scandinavian participation in international institutions.

In an age of multilateral governance, the United States' government has repeatedly confronted alternative paradigms, or norms, promoted by Scandinavia. However, these norms have not been internalized equally—

nor have they displaced competing paradigms of development, conflict management, or aid provision. Industrialization is still a priority—with minimal attention given to the environment in some parts of the world. Nations continue to rely on weapons of mass destruction, and practice deterrence when other means of conflict prevention fail. Although governments are rhetorically committed to humanitarian aid, contributions to foreign aid by states outside Scandinavia have not increased substantially. Instead, Scandinavia has consistently presented competing norms to the international community. One such norm (sustainable development) has come the farthest in the norm life-cycle, and has been internalized by development agencies, NGOs, the United Nations, the European Union, and the scholarly community. These institutions are adopting practices designed to improve the quality of human life according to ecological criteria.

The previous discussion examined how Scandinavian states have developed and strengthened global norms. However, in other issue areas, Scandinavia has been unable to play the role of norm entrepreneur. As the populations of northern European states have become more diversified, Scandinavian governments have confronted an internal conflict over cultural preservation versus multiculturalism. Even though government goals promote equality, many citizens are skeptical about the effects of immigration on Scandinavian societies. How will Scandinavian welfare systems survive with a new class of participants who do not share a common religion, language, or understanding of widely held social norms?

Nor does Scandinavia consistently act with one voice in its role. For example, some states in Scandinavia (Iceland and Norway) pursue policies that directly conflict with prominent environmental norms by hunting whales, seals, and wolves. Within Scandinavia there are prominent differences between preservationists and conservationists—both view themselves as "norm entrepreneurs" yet they strengthen different models of the good society.

This article defines Scandinavia as a group of states with a distinct role in international society. Scandinavia consistently provides standards—from models of global environmental management and alternative means of conflict resolution to models of global giving.

Scholars are invited to "test" the argument put forward here (relying on separate issue-areas and other like-minded states), and to explore the limits and possibilities of "social power" in international relations.

Notes

I thank William Fischer, Morten Hein, Peter Katzenstein, Iver Neumann, Mette Lykkebo, Andrew Nestingen, Sabrina Ramet, Ketil Thorvik, and two anonymous reviewers for their comments on a previous draft of this article.

1. "Scandinavia" as used in this discussion refers to the five northern European states—Denmark, Norway, Sweden, Finland, and Iceland. Other small states (such as Belgium, The Netherlands, and Luxembourg) may practice like-minded politics in their international relations, yet are outside the scope of this analysis.

2. For a discussion of Norway and Iceland's resistance to membership in the European Union, even though Denmark, Sweden, and Finland have all joined, see Ingebritsen (1998).

3. See the works of Iver Neumann, Jon Mercer, Elizabeth Kier, and Thomas Risse as examples of new thinking in international relations theorizing.

4. Kathryn Sikkink used the term "norm leaders" in referring to Scandinavia's role in international relations (informal discussion at the annual meeting of the International Studies Association, Minneapolis, Minnesota, 1998).

5. "Social power" was adopted in a discussion between the author and Audie Klotz in 1995.

6. Discussions with Morten Hein, Visiting Scholar, University of Aarhus, February 1999, Seattle, Washington.

7. Scandinavian embassies and consulates actively promote shared norms bilaterally, and through participation in multilateral institutions. Numerous conferences, publications, and scholarly research are devoted to exporting Scandinavian norms to the international community.

8. For a discussion on "bridge-building," see Holst (1985) and Udgaard (1973: 125–30, 177).

9. For an in-depth discussion of important differences between Scandinavian (relying on examples from Norway) and U.S. foreign policy-making, see Egeland (1988).

CONCLUSION

Learning from Lilliput

CHRISTINE INGEBRITSEN

The study of small states in international relations has evolved from explaining anomalies, puzzles, and residual activity in the international system of states, to engaging some of the most important issues in the study of international political economy, international security, and international society. From the postwar contributions of Annette Baker Fox, and the paradoxes of small state power identified by Peter Katzenstein, Robert Keohane, and David Vital; the effects on international agenda-setting of coalitions of small states; and the capacity for small states to play a role in regional governance structures, to the "social power" of small states seeking to influence international norm selection and recent studies of identity and reputation by Iver Neumann and Jon Mercer, the literature on small states offers valuable insights to the study of power in international politics. The lessons from Lilliput, as the scholars assembled in this volume attest to, have moved the study of the small from the periphery to the center in the study of international relations.

First wave theorists established why it is relevant to shift attention away from large states to other less prominent areas of the international system. These scholars were less concerned with how small states defy expectations of great power theories than with getting these states on the intellectual map of international relations theorizing. Once on the map, second-wave theorists put forward alternative theoretical arguments for small state agency. Third- and fourth-wave theorists no longer question the relevance of small states in the international system and are further refining arguments concerning relative capacities of small states, reputation and image in international relations, and the role of small states as global agenda-setters. The classic contributions to these waves of theorizing are reviewed in this chapter as a reminder of how far small state theorizing has come, and where it is headed.

For many scholars, *The Power of Small States* (1959) is the classic comparison of small states, and one of the early contributions to what we now refer to as the international relations literature on small states. Although the starting point of the study is the explanation of how a group of five small states (Turkey, Finland, Norway, Switzerland, and Spain) resisted great power belligerence, the underlying assumptions of the study are pessimistic: small states *should not* be able to resist more powerful states. The study, which focuses on the decision-making of small state leaders and the pressures of great power politics, is informed by the principles of the Realist School of International Relations. The author does, however, open the possibility of opportune moments in great power politics when small states can exploit the structure of the system, and/or influence the calculations of larger powers. And even if they fail to play this role, the idea of the relative capacity of the small state is introduced in the European context. According to Annette Baker Fox, "the continued existence and, indeed, startling increase in the number of small states may seem paradoxical in the age of superpowers and the drastically altered ratio of military strength between them and the rest of the world. It is well known that the ability to use violence does not alone determine the course of world politics. Some of the other determinants can be observed with exceptional clarity in the diplomacy of the small powers which were striving to stay out of World War II."[1]

Subsequent comparisons shifted away from the diplomatic maneuvers of small state leaders against superior military might, to the paradox of how small states succeed in the international political economy. Again, the assumption is pessimistic: small states are "price takers" and inherit the rules of the game. The odds are against smaller economies, yet economic performance indicators are impressive. In some contributions, small states outperform larger states; whereas in other contributions, small states are embedded in hierarchies within which few options exist.

The larger, more powerful states in the international system increasingly share the global challenges of "smallness" as suggested in Peter Katzenstein's 1985 volume, *Small States in World Markets*. Although Katzenstein's analysis focused on how governments develop strategies to cope with enhanced market competition, the rapid revival of European integration engages both small and large states in the EU, and in the international political economy. International terrorist threats have elevated the successes of some small states (i.e., Iceland) in developing technological solutions to monitoring criminal activity at airports and border crossings. New security threats, such as threats to human security associated with an environmental catastrophe, require learning from societies where a concerted commitment to environmentalism is in place. In many issue areas following the end of the Cold War, hegemons are responding to a global agenda, as opposed to establishing the rules of the game, as we witnessed in the establishment of the post-World War II regimes governing the world economy—from Bretton Woods to GATT. Some small states become the "tail that wags the dog," in issue-areas such as global whaling policy.

Not all small states are perceived as important to the study of international relations. In fact, the field is "Euro-centric," reflecting the path-dependent development of a unique group of well-situated states in the international division of labor.[2] Yet even within the periphery, some small states can and do "break out" of the cycle of dependence and provide examples of Lilliputian success. Learning from the capacity to influence even when the odds are against another party is an enduring lesson for students of international relations. As are the limits of the most powerful actors of the system, who are constrained by their size, institutions, or policy legacies in intervening abroad; or tracking down terrorists who threaten the security of U.S. airspace. The inversion of power (strong is weak; weak becomes strong) is a fascinating dimension of international study.

This book compiles some of the major scholarly contributions to the study of small states in world politics. Inevitably, important voices have not been heard, and authors who have written on the role of small states have received only a footnote. It is not the intent of the editors of this collection to provide an overview of every word written on the subject, but rather to share with our students and colleagues those contributions we have found to be compelling in our study and teaching of alternative approaches to international relations. Two Europeans and two Americans edited this collection, with an effort to incorporate both sides of the Atlantic in developing our list.

Theoretical developments in the field of international relations provide new opportunities for small state theorizing. For example, constructivist approaches to international relations encourage a broader conception of power to include what a state perceives its power to be. By incorporating non-objective measures of power, this approach (not by intent, but by effect) expands the scope of legitimate topics for investigation in international relations. Recognizing how and why states pursue national interest and national identity in world politics, and the role of reputation in international society, has engaged scholars researching both small and large states.[3]

What are the enduring lessons from the small state literature? In conclusion, we outline a few of the important insights suggested by this burgeoning literature.

Five Lessons from Lilliput

From the perspective of smaller powers in the international system, there is greater freedom of maneuver than classic international relations theorizing suggests. Small states are not merely pawns in a world structured around a narrow definition of state interests. Keohane argues, "possession of superior military and economic force cannot guarantee small power compliance with big power interests. . . . it is evident that small states on the rim of the alliance wheel can pursue active, forceful and even obstreperous policies of their own."[4] As the European Union's history suggests, and as smaller powers engage international institutions, agenda-setting is not only possible, but is a likely outcome, when domestic institutions permit consistent, focused interest articulation. Even as "price takers" in international markets, small states can outperform larger states in the international political economy in comparative measures of economic success.[5]

Societal forces in small states may, on occasion, outsmart the strong. The resistance movements during Germany's occupation of Denmark and Norway during WWII, and the triumph of weak states against superior forces (from Finland to Vietnam), are enduring examples of how the smaller players in the international system defy our expectations. Prominent individuals, referred to as "norm entrepreneurs" or "rooted cosmopolitans," can bring parties to the table in new and innovative ways—as demonstrated by Norwegian activism in working behind the scenes to negotiate the Oslo Accords, an internationally recognized benchmark in achieving trust between opposing parties in the Middle East conflict—and as transnational actors in international society.[6]

Small states in international relations may serve as examples to others in the international system. Precisely because particular small states are outside the formal corridors of power, they may serve as examples of how to organize society, and/or exercise influence in world politics. Scandinavia has cultivated a niche in international society as a social laboratory for innovative solutions—from the provision of welfare benefits according to principles of universalism, to the awarding of the Nobel Peace Prize.[7] Iceland, the smallest of the Nordics, invests heavily in new environmental technologies in order to be the first country in the world to become completely independent of fossil fuels. As argued by Alan Milward, the three Benelux states (Belgium, the Netherlands, and Luxembourg) established path-setting ways of collaboration important to the eventual adoption of the Treaty of Rome.[8] Smallness may also be an advantage to policy entrepreneurship, as Clive Archer, Neill Nugent, and Baldur Thorhallsson argue in their analyses of small states and European integration.[9]

Small states are players in the international system—even though they do not structure the rules of engagement. Small state theorizing has commonalities with the study of gender in international relations. Many of the activities of small states are not detected on the radar screen, and fall out of the analyses of contemporary theories of international relations. Yet many small states and members of these societies are working diligently, behind the scenes, to articulate a different vision of how the system can and should be governed. Some of these visions (such as the New International Economic Order, or NIEO) fail to take hold, and yet raise issues of economic justice on the global agenda. Other measures, such as treaties on human rights and environmental codes of conduct, are adopted by international institutions and require larger states to comply with (or justify divergence from) a particular set of norms.

Might does not make right. Small states are in the position to protest the actions of more powerful states precisely because of their relative capacities. Small powers can provide a moral balance of power in the international system. Hans Blix, the Swedish weapons inspector, has played a critical role in protesting American intervention in Iraq, similar to the role defined by Olof Palme during the Vietnam War. America's treatment of prisoners during wartime has also led to widespread criticism throughout the globe, with small powers playing a leading role.

As new states join the European Union, their voices will not be lost in a system of regional governance based on principles of federalism. Pressures to conform to a common currency and common defense policy place particular demands on small states who have defined their role differently in the system. Yet the capacity to export ideas to the EU level of governance is an important aspect of regional politics.[10]

Students of international relations benefit from an "inside-out" study of the foreign policy making of smaller powers in the system. Field research outside the major power centers reveals interesting, unexplored dimensions of the complexities of world politics. And supplementing our reading lists with examples of anomalies in power relations more effectively captures the day-to-day politics in our global world. This volume brings together important contributions that seek to balance the disparity between the small and larger states in the study of international relations, and bridges the divide between European and American approaches to the field. We invite the next generation of scholars to amend this volume, as the theories and evidence of the role of small states in international relations continues to evolve.

Notes

1. Annette Baker Fox, *The Power of Small States: Diplomacy in World War II* (Chicago: University of Chicago Press, 1959), vii.

2. Immanuel Wallerstein, *The Modern World System I* (Orlando, Florida: Academic Press, 1974).

3. See Jonathan Mercer, *Reputation in International Politics* (Ithaca, NY: Cornell University Press, 1996); and Peter J. Katzenstein, ed., *The Culture of National Security: Norms and Identity in World Politics* (New York: Columbia University Press, 1996).

4. Robert Keohane, "The Big Influence of Small Allies," *Foreign Policy* no. 2, (1971): 161–162.

5. Peter Katzenstein, *Small States in World Markets* (Ithaca, NY: Cornell University Press, 1985).

6. See Christine Ingebritsen, "Norm Entrepreneurs: Scandinavia's Role in World Politics," *Cooperation and Conflict*, 37, no. 1, (March 2002): 11–23; and Sidney Tarrow, *Rooted Cosmopolitans*, book manuscript.

7. Christine Ingebritsen, *Scandinavia in World Politics* (Boulder, CO: Rowman and Littlefield Publishers, 2006).

8. Alan Milward, *The European Rescue of the Nation-State* (London: Routledge, 1992).

9. *Current Politics and Economics of Europe,* Guest Editors Clive Archer and Neill Nugent, "Small States and the European Union," 11, no. 1, (2002).

10. "The Scandinavian Way to Europe," special issue of *Scandinavian Studies* ed. Christine Ingebritsen, 74, no. 3, (Fall 2002).

ANNOTATED BIBLIOGRAPHY

JESSICA BEYER

Ahnlid, A. (1992). "Free Riders or Forced Riders? Small States in the International Political Economy: The Example of Sweden." *Cooperation and Conflict: Journal of the Nordic International Studies Association* 27(3): 241–276. This article analyzes the trade policies of small industrialized states using the example of Sweden. Ahnlid argues that, against the expectations of hegemonic stability theory, small states are not free riding (i.e., implementing protection at home, while enjoying free trade abroad) but are forced to pursue liberal policies mainly by systemic constraints. Small developed states contribute to an open international economic order, while larger actors and developing countries—at least before the establishment of the World Trade Organization—could sometimes act against the trade regime.

Alapuro, R., M. Alestalo, E. Haavio-Mannila, R. Väyrynen, eds. (1985). *Small States in Comparative Perspectives: Essays for Erik Allardt.* Oslo: Norwegian University Press. This volume is a tribute to Erik Allardt, a Finnish sociologist. To that end, it is an eclectic collection, roughly grouped in the three categories of "Comparing States in Europe," "Inter-Nordic Comparisons," and "Finland in Comparative Perspective." The chapters cover a wide range of topics, including issues affecting the daily lives of Finns, inter-Nordic differences in corporatist structures, center-periphery relations, and small European states. Chapters largely focus on Scandinavia and are generally comparative. Further, many deal with state-society relations. Contributors include: Dag Anckar, Shmuel N. Eisenstadt, Robert Erikson, Peter Flora, Johan Galtung, Ilkka Heiskanen, Voitto Helander, Ulf Himmelstrand, Pekka Kosonen, Rita Liljeström, Pertti Pesonen, Seppo Pöntinen, Onni Rantala, Paavo Seppänen, Magdalena Sokolowska, Veronica Stolte-Heiskanen, Hannu Uusitalo, Tapani Valkonen.

Amstrup, N. (1976). "The Perennial Problem of Small States: A Survey of Research Efforts." *Cooperation and Conflict: Journal of the Nordic International Studies Association* 11(3): 163–182. Amstrup offers a survey of research on small states, with a particular focus on defining a small state. He breaks small state literature into six different approaches. First, scholars such as Annette Baker Fox and David Vital avoid the problem of definition, often considering it irrelevant. Second, scholars such as R. P. Barston link "smallness" to a measurable characteristic, such as population size. Third, Amstrup presents the argument that the relationship between large and small states cannot be explained by size alone, but is dependent on other variables, such as the structure of the international system, states' geographical positions, and domestic political systems. Scholars in this area would further argue that size is relative and relational; therefore, what counts as a small state depends on the question being asked. Fourth, scholars such as Robert Rothstein and Wilhelm Christmas-Møller consider size to be best defined by self-perception. In other words, states that *think* they are small *are* small. Fifth, some scholars analyze small state behavior by looking at specific situations, which are selected because they show essential characteristics of small state behavior. Sixth, scholars such as Raimo Väyrynen argue that it is necessary to differentiate size. Väyrynen suggests a five-piece definition that includes rank, degree of external penetration, type of behavior, interests in competition, and decision-makers conceptualization of the role of their states. Amstrup concludes by arguing that there are two large issues in the small state literature. The first is the lack of an accumulation of research efforts. He says that studies on small states largely ignore each other. The second is the elusiveness of the concept of small states.

Archer, C., N. Nugent (2002). "Introduction: Small States and the European Union." *Current Politics and Economics of Europe* 11(1): 1–10. In the introduction to a special issue of Current Politics and Economics of Europe titled "Small States and the European Union," Archer and Nugent frame the special journal issue by examining difficulties in defining small states. They also discuss the contributions of small states to the Europeanization project and offer suggestions for future research.

Armstrong, H. W., R. Read (1995). "Western European Microstates and European Union Autonomous Regions: The Advantage of Size and Sovereignty." *World Development* 23(7): 1229–1245. Armstrong and Read examine the economic success of microstates and some European regions with high levels of autonomy. By comparing GDP per capita and unemployment, they find that success seems to be highly related to activity in the financial services sector, tourism, and, at times, natural resources. They find that microstates and regions within Europe do better than regions adjacent to the EU, which is contrary to literature that stresses the disadvantages of microstates. However, they are unable to explain why microstates and regions within Europe do better, as their data are limited.

Armstrong, H. W., R. Read (1998). "Trade and Growth in Small States: The Impact of Global Trade Liberalization." *The World Economy* 21(4): 563–585. Armstrong and Read assert that there is a trend toward disintegration of pre-existing states, and that now more than 45 percent of all countries have populations of less than three million people. In this article, they address the impact of global trade liberalization on small countries. They argue that small country economies are characterized by small domestic markets, limited resource bases, narrowness of output and exports, openness to trade, vulnerability, and greater social cohesion, identity, and social capital. The structural openness of these economies makes it necessary for them to be highly integrated into the global economy. This high level of integration means that while they may be the greatest beneficiaries of global trade liberalization, they are also the most vulnerable to its effects. Armstrong and Read argue that small states are vulnerable for two reasons. First, often their niche trading strategy is reliant on bilateral trading agreements rather than multilateral agreements. Second, narrow economic structures limit small state ability to react to changes in global economy, particularly because they cannot compete with larger economies. Therefore, while global trading liberalization is believed to increase well-being globally, it could ultimately harm small states.

Armstrong, H. W., R. Read (2002). "Small States and the European Union: Issues in the Political Economy of International Integration." *Current Politics and Economics of Europe* 11(1): 31–48. Armstrong and Read use the accession of Cyprus, Malta, Slovenia, Estonia, Latvia, and Lithuania to the EU as a way to understand the implications for small states entering regional trade agreements. They argue that traditional frameworks for understanding integration are not appropriate because of the distinctive characteristics of small state economics. They assert that EU membership may have negative effects on small economies and, consequently, political strategies must compensate for these effects.

Azar, E. E. (1973). *Probe for Peace: Small-State Hostilities*. Minneapolis: Burgess Publishing Company. Azar presents a clear outline of anthropological, psychological, economical, ecological, and interaction-based theories and the causes they offer for war. Azar focuses on small states, asserting that there are far more armed conflicts between small states than between large ones. Because their behavior is different from that of the great powers, understanding the constraints on the behavior of the great powers furthers understanding of conflict between small states. Azar uses the Arab-Israeli conflict as a case study to illustrate his point. He concludes with policy suggestions for reducing hostilities in the Middle East. Broadly, he wants to convey to the reader that war is a complex phenomenon with multiple, interlocked causes, as is peace.

Baehr, P. R. (1975). "Small States: A Tool for Analysis?" *World Politics* 27(3): 456–466. This article is a book review of Edward E. Azar's *Probe for Peace: Small State Hostilities* and Marshall R. Singer's *Weak States in a World of Powers*, which both attempt to explain small state behavior in international relations. Baehr begins his review by discussing the idea that fewer, bigger states could lead to a more peaceful world. He argues that although there was a movement in this direction, the decrease in the number of states in the world did not lead to change. He criticizes Azar and Singer's definitions of a small state, preferring the definitions offered by Keohane or Rothstein. Baehr is equally unimpressed with Singer's work. According to Baehr, Singer looks at the U.S., the Soviet Union, Japan, the UK, and France and the "weaker" states associated with them. He argues that most of Singer's book deals with the ties that bind individuals and groups across state boundaries. Baehr questions Singer's data, and suggests that Singer is biased because he appears to be in favor of a world of strong states. Baehr concludes with the assertion that the literature on the role of small states in international relations brings the relativity inherent in the notion of "independence" into focus. But he argues that inquiry into small states in IR is still in a very elementary stage, and he asserts that the concept as an analytical tool is insufficient as it is too broad. He finishes by raising the question of whether smallness is a useful mode of analysis if nearly all states are small.

Baille, S. (1998). "A Theory of Small State Influence in the European Union." *Journal of International Relations and Development* 1(3–4): 195–219. Baille aims to create a model of small state influence in the European Union (EU), using Luxembourg as a model. Baille's approach argues that there are three explanatory variables for small state influence in the EU. First, Baille argues that small state influence is directly related to its particular historical context. Second, Baille asserts that the level of small state influence depends on institutional frameworks, in other words, the rules, procedures, norms, and principles that facilitate the defense of small state interests. Third, Baille argues that the negotiation behavior of small states, which is geared towards conflict-avoidance, has an impact on their influence.

Baker Fox, A. (1959). *The Power of Small States: Diplomacy in World War II.* Chicago: Chicago University Press. Baker Fox argues that though a state's ability to get what it wants through violence is a type of political power generally reserved for large states, both large and small states can use economy, ideology, and diplomatic methods to achieve their goals as well. In order to understand the influence of small powers, Baker Fox examines the cases of five neutral states—Turkey, Finland, Norway, Sweden, and Spain—during WWII. She argues that the main objective of the governments of these states was to wait out WWII while convincing the combatants that neutrality was beneficial to all. In other words, these neutral states had to convince the combatants that the cost of using force against them would outweigh any gains. Baker Fox discovered that the small states were likely to remain free of pressure if one or more of the following were true: the demanding great power would be deprived of necessary goods and services that the neutral country controlled; the opposing enemy would retaliate for the invasion of the neutral country; or the neutral country would join the other enemy's cause. She believes that the war would have been different without efforts by small states to remain neutral.

Barston, R. P. (1973). *The Other Powers: Studies in the Foreign Policies of Small States.* London: George Allen & Unwin Ltd. The contributors to this volume examine the foreign policies of nine small states—Norway, the Netherlands, Switzerland, Zambia, Israel, Cyprus, Cuba, Singapore, and New Zealand. Specifically, they analyze how foreign policy objectives are framed, organizational structures that create and implement foreign policy, available choices, interest areas, and the ways in which the nine small states deal with the results of foreign policy. Barston argues that great powers are distinguished from small states by resources, economic development, military capability, and success of their foreign policies. Ultimately, Barston offers six general situations when a small state may have disproportionate influence over what might be imagined. First, a state's weakness can be a bargaining source if a great power perceives the state's territory to be strategically important enough to provide military assistance. Second, small state bargaining power will increase if there is a clear threat to both great powers. Third, when coalitions of small states are weakly organized, have disputed leadership, and include members with differing political and value systems, the coalitions will have difficulty implementing common objectives. Fourth, in certain circumstances a small state can sometimes act against a great power. Fifth, small states can use international organizations to generate support for their policies. Sixth, small states can resist non-military sanctions if they are not universally applied and if they receive support from border states. Contributors include: Peter R. Baehr, Ronald P. Barston, Marion Bone, Jacques Freymond, Reg Harrison, Frank H. H. King, Nils Ørvik, Jacob Reuveny, David Stansfield.

Bauwens, W., A. Clesse, O. F. Knudsen, eds. (1996). *Small States and the Security Challenge in the New Europe.* London: Brassey's. Bauwens, Knudsen, and Clesse examine the long-term security of small states in post-1989 Europe. For the editors, not only are great powers increasingly reluctant to assert their will, but, in contrast to the past, the roles of great powers and small states in the international system is no longer clear. Further, they argue that consequences of the transition from a policed bi-polar world to an unstructured system are still unclear.

Benedict, B. (1967). *Problems of Smaller Territories.* London: The Athlone Press. The chapters of this book are the papers from a two-year seminar by the Institute of Commonwealth Studies of the University of London that aimed to discover if there were problems common to all small territories. First, the authors discuss the demographic characteristics of smallness. Second, the authors deal with the political considerations of smaller territories, focusing largely on the enormous administrative costs small territories must bear to be independent, as well as the security risk. Third, the authors focus on the economic problems of small countries, in particular small home markets and a lack of diverse resources. Fourth, they engage in a discussion of the sociology of small territories. Finally, they present a series of case studies of British Honduras, Luxembourg, Polynesia, the High Commission Territories such as Swaziland, and the Tory Islands. Strategically, the authors argue that a political solution seems to lie in integration within a larger territory and economical integration with neighbors. Contributors include: B. Benedict, K. C. Edwards, A. D. Knox, A. W. Singham, T. E. Smith, J. E. Spence, D. A. G. Waddell, R. G. Ward, D. P. J. Wood.

Bjøl, E. (1968). "The Power of the Weak." *Cooperation and Conflict: Journal of the Nordic International Studies Association* 3(2): 157–168. Bjøl argues that small states have played prominent roles in international relations, often successfully defending their interests. He wants to reintroduce an old analytic category into the study of small states—geography. He asserts that examining security geography is necessary if researchers want to elaborate a conceptual framework for the analysis of the role of small states in international relations. For example, both Switzerland and Albania are difficult to invade because they are so mountainous. Bjøl argues that the power approach is of limited utility when looking at small states. Rather, he believes that it is better to think in terms of the intensity of interest a state has in an area. This is important because while large states have many things occupying their attention at any given time, small states are able to focus on a few or single issues. He also believes that questions of prestige and provocation should be introduced into the study of small states, as well as examinations of the psychology of negotiations. Bjøl largely draws on examples from Scandinavia to support his argument.

Blair, P. W. (1967). *The Ministate Dilemma*. New York: Carnegie Endowment for International Peace, Occasional Paper 6. Blair addresses the issue of ministates in the United Nations, namely the implications of large numbers of very small, financially limited states joining the UN. Blair argues that the ministates could have a large impact on the UN because each state has a vote in the General Assembly. Blair entertains various options for the inclusion of ministates in the UN, including intermediate membership status.

Crowards, T. (2002). "Defining the Category of 'Small States'." *Journal of International Development* 14(2): 143–179. In light of previous studies that used a single parameter to define state size—usually population—Crowards combines population, land area, and income to categorize countries. His method is quantitative and he concludes that there are 79 states that could be classified as small.

Dommen, E., P. Hein, eds. (1985). *States, Microstates, and Islands*. London: Croom Helm. Dommen and Hein begin their book with a definition of a microstate. They do not believe that one can look at a list of members of the United Nations as a starting point. They look at territory, population, and government as necessary attributes of "state," as well as the ability to entertain relations with other states. The authors argue that it is possible that entirely different approaches to the problems of societal, environmental, political, and economic management are necessary for microstates than approaches useful to understanding and solving problems in large states. Further, to properly understand microstates, the authors advocate leaving traditional theories and forging new concepts. Contributors include: Antony Dolman, Edward Dommen, Francois Doumenge, Philippe Hein, David Murray, David Pitt, UNCTAD Secretariat.

Duursma, J. (1996). *Fragmentation and the International Relations of Micro-states: Self-determination and Statehood*. Cambridge: Cambridge University Press. In this book, Duursma presents an international legal analysis of European microstates. In particular, Duursma is curious about what lessons can be learned from existing microstates that have been successful in the international system. She outlines their general international legal context, in particular the right to self-determination, legal criteria for statehood, and microstates in international organizations. Duursma focuses on the European microstates of Liechtenstein, San Marino, Monaco, Andorra, and the Vatican City. She concludes that microstates are some of the largest beneficiaries of international law and its enforcement, particularly because of their inability to defend themselves militarily.

Duval, R. D., W. R. Thompson (1980). "Reconsidering the Aggregate Relationships Between Size, Economic Development, and Some Types of Foreign Policy Behavior." *American Journal of Political Science* 24(3): 511–525. Duval and Thompson's study unsuccessfully attempts to reproduce the results of Maurice East's 1973 study of small state behavior. They assert that East's sample is unrepresentative of the international nation-state population. According to Duvall and Thompson, East used a non-random and incrementally designed sample of countries. Specifically, they believe the sample set is skewed toward countries that have more experience in the international system as well as encompassing 10 of the top 15 military spenders in 1970, two of which are small states. Duval and Thompson retest East's hypotheses with a more representative sample, and they are unable to reproduce his results. In Duvall and Thompson's test, they find no support for either of the models East considered. They conclude by saying that East's operationalization procedures cast doubt on the validity of his outcomes. They further point out that studies on the relationship between size and types of foreign policy rarely agree completely, and they locate this problem in the lack of a definition of size.

East, M. (1973). "Size and Foreign Policy Behavior: A Test of Two Models." *World Politics* 25(4): 556–576. East tests two competing models of foreign policy using a data set of 4,448 foreign policy events initiated by 32 nation-states between 1959 and 1968. He gathers support for a model that predicts the following:

> Large states initiate more foreign policy events alone, while small states initiate more joint behavior.
>
> The targets of small state action will be groups of states or intergovernmental organizations.
>
> Small states will engage in more high-risk behavior than large states.
>
> Small states are unambiguous in foreign policy.
>
> Economic issues are of more importance to small states.

Further, East finds little difference in the behavior of developing small states and developed small states.

Eide, E. B. (1996). "Adjustment Strategy of a Non-Member: Norwegian Foreign and Security Policy in the Shadow of the European Union." *Cooperation and Conflict: Journal of the Nordic International Studies Association* 31(1): 69–104. Eide argues that Norway's role in the international system changed fundamentally with the end of the Cold War. The disappearance of the Soviet Union, the decline of NATO, and the rise of the European Union means that Norway has lost much of its influence over Western European security policy. Eide discusses the future of Norwegian foreign and security policy as a non-EU member, particularly in relation to Sweden and Finland. He finds that though Finland and Sweden's membership will have repercussions for Norway, Nordic cooperation will not disappear. Further, Eide notes that there are deep divides within Norwegian society over Norway's membership in the European Union, which can be viewed as a split between the Norwegian state and nation. Eide argues that this division will continue to shape Norway's policy toward Europe.

Elman, M. F. (1995). "The Foreign Policies of Small States: Challenging Neorealism in Its Own Backyard." *British Journal of Political Science* 25(2): 171–217. Though neorealist theory would argue that structural factors determine the foreign policies of small states, Elman argues that, while the system influences the decisions of emerging states, subsequent choices are more likely to be the result of domestic institutional choices. She examines pre-1900 U.S. domestic regime change and its foreign security policy. Elman asserts that the U.S. case offers a starting point for study of the emerging states in Eastern Europe.

Galloway, D. (2002). "The Treaty of Nice and 'Small' Member States." *Current Politics and Economics of Europe* 11(1): 11–30. Galloway argues that the negotiations at the Nice Intergovernmental Conference offer an important lens for examining the competing interests of "small" and "large" member states. Even though the conference was focused on negotiating the enlargement of the EU, small states were preoccupied with maintaining their power in the EU. According to Galloway, taking both informal and institutional factors into account, Nice did not erode the power of small states.

Goetschel, L., ed. (1998). *Small States Inside and Outside the European Union: Interests and Policies.* Boston/Dordrecht/London: Kluwer Academic Publishers. The contributors to this volume identify the main interests of Europe's small states and outline the different strategies that these states employ in foreign and security policy. The first portion of the book examines the concept of the small state. The second portion highlights the consequences of regional integration for small states. The third portion of the book looks at security policy and small states. Finally, the authors examine the future of small states within the European Union. The authors find that small states gain from institutionalism, comprehensive security issues, quasi-federalism, country weighting in institutions, enlargement of the EU, cooperative and non-competitive negotiation behavior, their role as "honest brokers," national decision-making processes, and the identity of each state. However, the contributors argue that in spite of these gains, small states do not always act in their own self-interests and that large states can still act unilaterally to great effect, while small states cannot. Contributors include: Wilhelm Agrell, Günther Baechler, Sasha Baillie, Uffe Balslev, Anton Bebler, Tony Brown, Franz von Däniken, Anton Egger, Charles-Michel Geurts, Laurent Goetschel, Heiner Hänggi, Antti Kuosmanen, Andreas Norkus, Andreas Rendl, Fritz R. Staehelin, Teija Tiilikainen, Daniel Thürer, Martin Zbinden.

Griffin, C. (1995). "Confronting Power Asymmetry: Small States, Strategic Behavior, and National Interest." *Social and Economic Studies* 44(2/3): 259–286. Griffin focuses on the Caribbean Common Market countries, offering policy options, most of which center around increased ability to operate in Washington, D.C. He argues that the transforming global order has created new opportunities for interaction between countries at a non-governmental level. At the same time, the Western hemisphere is characterized by an asymmetrical power structure. Though there is leveling of security interests between large and small states, there has been no leveling for weak and resource-deficient microstates in the Caribbean.

Gstöhl, S. (2002). *Reluctant Europeans: Norway, Sweden, and Switzerland in the Process of Integration.* Boulder, CO: Lynne Rienner Publishers. Gstöhl addresses the puzzle of why Norway, Sweden, and Switzerland have been so reluctant to join the European Community. Economic theory would predict that such small, wealthy, open economies, which trade heavily with the European Community, would want to join; however, the opposite has been the case. Gstöhl argues that economic interests alone do not explain the integration preferences of these three countries, but rather these economic concerns coexist and are often dominated by political constraints, such as domestic institutions, social cleavages, and foreign policy traditions. Examining Norway, Sweden, and Switzerland over five decades Gstöhl finds that the less important market access is, and the stronger domestic and geo-historical constraints are, the lower the level of integration.

Gunter, M. M. (1977). "What Happened to the United Nations Ministate Problem?" *American Journal of International Law* 71: 110–124. Gunter seeks to explain the "ministate problem" discussed in the United Nations (UN) in the 1960s and 1970s. After the Ministate Committee reached an impasse on the issue of ministate membership, the Legal Council opened the door to ministate membership. The bulk of the United Nations ministate problem is centered on how to align voting power with the realities of the international system. Gunter traces the process to the point where the United Nations agrees that it will not take any steps to limit the membership of ministates.

Handel, M. (1985). *Weak States in the International System*. London: Frank Cass. Handel asserts that the literature, prior to his contribution, had focused on small states as the passive pawns of great powers; however, he argues that this has never been the case. According to Handel, while small states are frequently more vulnerable than larger ones, they are never helpless. Their strength is different from that of a great power, as it is derivative rather than intrinsic. They can obtain, commit, and manipulate the power of more powerful states. For Handel, the condition of tension and spheres of influence in the international system is important for small states. Finally, and something of a foreshadowing of Katzenstein's later argument, Handel argues that weak states are more economically viable than economic theories would predict. Handel concludes that though weak states are not the main actors in the international system, their roles are not peripheral.

Hanf, B., K. Soetendorp, eds. (1998). *Adapting to European Integration: Small States and the European Union*. London: Longman. The authors attempt to measure whether there has been a reorientation of the organization of national politics and policy-making as a result of Europeanization and EU membership. In other words, they focus on the impact of membership on the domestic policies of small states. They choose to examine small states not only because the majority of the integration literature deals with the larger states, but also because one would expect that small states, because of past necessity, would be highly organized and experienced at pursuing their interests at the international level. Focusing on Belgium, the Netherlands, Denmark, Ireland, Greece, Spain, Austria, Sweden, Norway, and Switzerland, the authors discover that governmental adaptation has been incremental, and that there is a great diversity of political and strategic adaptation. Contributors include: Jan Beyers, Michael Christakis, Soren Z. von Dosenrode, Magnus Ekengren, Kenneth Hanf, Bart Kerremans, Stephan Kux, Brigid Laffan, Paul Luif, Francesc Morata, Ben Soetendorp, Bengt Sundelius, Ulf Sverdrup, Etain Tannam.

Hansen, P. (1974). "Adaptive Behavior of Small States: The Case of Denmark and the European Community." P. J. McGowan, ed. *Sage International Yearbook of Foreign Policy Studies, 2.* London: Sage: 143–174. Hansen attempts to answer the question of why Denmark, Norway, Sweden, the Netherlands, and Austria, all small and structurally similar states, would have such different positions on the foreign policy decision to join the European Community. He asserts that the central issue for Denmark in the 15 years prior to 1973 has been how to cope effectively with changes in the external environment. He discerns two competing views within Denmark. First, some Danes argued that the effects of boundary exchanges could best be controlled through autonomous regulation. All necessary adaptation could be made through domestic structures without compromising national sovereignty. Second, in contrast, some argued that Danish structures were not capable of coping with changes in the external environment and change could best be dealt with by trying to use available opportunities to influence the environment. Proponents of the second perspective ultimately won, but there is still a strong voice advocating the first. Therefore, though Denmark joined the European Community, its orientation towards the EU is more like that of Britain.

Harbert, J. R. (1976). "The Behavior of the Ministates in the United Nations, 1971–1972." *International Organization* 30: 109–127. Harbert examines the voting pattern of states with populations of fewer than one million in the UN General Assembly. He measures the cohesiveness of 23 ministates in four issue areas: political, colonial, economic, and social/humanitarian/cultural issues. Harbert finds that the greatest ministate cohesion centers on colonial and economic issues, and that there is less cohesion on social/humanitarian/cultural issues. Further, Harbert finds that ministates and the USSR vote similarly on colonial and economic issues, while ministates and the U.S. and the colonial powers vote similarly on social/humanitarian/cultural issues. Also, Harbert notes that the ministate voting pattern and the African-Asian group in the United Nations are similar. Therefore, Harbert believes that size alone is not sufficient to differentiate one state from another.

Harden, S., ed. (1985). *Small Is Dangerous: Microstates in a Macro World.* London: Frances Pinter Publishers. The contributors to this volume assert that the 1982 Falklands War shows how the vulnerability of very small states to external attack, as well as internal destabilization, can lead to serious repercussions. These very small states are mostly the legacies of European colonial empires, and most of their problems come from their small economic and human resource base. The contributors to this volume largely focus on security problems, but they also discuss the role of various institutions; the legal framework that small territories find themselves in, with particular attention paid to international intervention; issues related to policing the Exclusive Economic Zones surrounding small islands; factors which contribute to political stability, especially economic factors; and steps to increase economic and political stability. They conclude with a draft declaration on microstates for the General Assembly of the United Nations. Contributors closely examine the cases of the Southern African, Caribbean, and Pacific states. Contributors include: Donald Anderson, Peter Blaker,

Hugh Hanning, Rosalyn Higgins, David Jessop, Patrick Keatley, Peter Lyon, Lord Mayhew, Malcolm Shaw, Jack Spence, Donald Cameron Watt.

Harris, W. L. (1970). "Microstates in the United Nations: A Broader Purpose." *Columbia Journal of Transnational Law* 9: 23–53. Harris attempts to address the question of whether it would be possible to incorporate the increasing number of microstates into the United Nations. Harris notes that one of the most preoccupying concerns is what the microstates could do with their combined voting powers. Harris considers the problems with microstate membership in the UN and concludes with policy recommendations. Harris believes that it would be difficult to keep microstates out or to allow them in with limited rights. Rather, though including microstates may cause unpredictable outcomes, he believes that it will ultimately be beneficial.

Hey, J. A. K., ed. (2003). *Small States in World Politics: Explaining Foreign Policy Behavior.* Boulder, CO: Lynne Rienner Publishers. This book attempts to move toward a conceptual framework for examining small state behavior in the global arena. By using an inductive approach, the contributors hope to avoid the two major issues of small state literature. Hey identifies these in the introduction as arguments with little evidence that attempt to disprove the widely held belief that small states are passive actors at the mercy of the international system and as arguments with an outdated focus on state security. In the conclusion of the book, Hey draws four conclusions from this collection of studies. First, the system level is the key explanatory factor in small state policy. Second, small states engage in international organizations and draw on international laws and norms to enhance their leverage and independence in the world system. Third, Hey argues that the domestic level of analysis appears to have less impact than other factors, though the regime type and the level of development are important. Finally, for a small state, the individual leader can exert enormous influence, particularly in developing states. The book's case selection includes Paraguay, the English-speaking Caribbean states, Panama, Luxembourg, Austria, Gambia, Jordan, and Laos. Contributors include: Zachary Abuza, Jacqueline Anne Braveboy-Wagner, Jeanne A. K. Hey, Paul Luif, Frank O. Mora, Curtis R. Ryan, Abdoulaye Saine, Peter M. Sanchez.

Höll, O., ed. (1983). *Small States in Europe and Dependence.* Boulder, CO: Westview Press. The chapters of this book discuss various social science approaches to the small Western European states in the international environment. The book begins with small state theories and then turns to case studies of Switzerland, Luxembourg, Finland, Ireland, and Austria. Contributors examine the strategies for small states to reduce dependence on large states and conclude with a case study of Sweden. Contributors include: Wilhelm Christmas-Møller, Charles Doerner, Ole Elgström, Hans Heinz Fabris, Mario Hirsch, Otmar Höll, Kimmo Kiljunen, Helmut Kramer, Hans Mouritzen, Manfred Rotter, Margret Sieber, Benno Signitzer, Anselm Skuhra, Bengt Sundelius, Sven Tägil, Raimo Väyrynen, Hans Vogel, James Wickham.

Hong, M. (1995). "Small States in the United Nations." *International Social Science Journal* 47(2): 277–287. Hong argues that the end of the Cold War offers a special opportunity for small states to cause systematic change in international organizations, such as reorganizing and reforming the United Nations Security Council, as well as the relationship between the General Assembly and the Security Council. Hong asserts that because all states are considered equal in accordance with the principle of sovereign equality in most international organizations, small states can use their larger numbers to cause change. For example, two-thirds of the UN members, or 120 states, could be considered small states because they have populations of 10 million or fewer. Hong argues that though realists would not predict that small states matter, within the UN's institutional framework they have weight for three reasons. First, they can cause change with their larger numbers by working together. Second, they are a constant reminder of the principle of sovereign equality regardless of state size. Third, the United Nations is structured in such a way that small states can prevent major powers from using the organization for their own interests.

Ingebritsen, C. (1998). *The Nordic States and European Unity*. Ithaca, NY: Cornell University Press. Ingebritsen addresses the question of why Norway, Denmark, and Iceland have been more resistant to European policy coordination than Sweden and Finland. She argues that because the Nordic states have strong, centralized economic interest organizations, the leading sectors in each country, combined with political coalitions that organized for and against accession, shaped each country's response to European policy coordination. Ingebritsen argues that states dependent on manufacturing were under more pressure to join the European Commission than states reliant on the export of raw materials.

Ingebritsen, C. (2002). "Norm Entrepreneurs: Scandinavia's Role in World Politics." *Cooperation and Conflict: Journal of the Nordic International Studies Association* 37(1): 11–23. Ingebritsen makes the argument that the Scandinavian countries exert influence in the international system by serving as "norm entrepreneurs." She asserts that arguments that focus on security, adaptation to changes in the political system, and ways in which small states use international organizations or legal solutions to further agendas ignore the possibility of less materially-based influence. Though Scandinavia does not consistently speak with one voice and has not always been successful, in some issue areas it has been effective in exporting different ways of conceptualizing international relations. Ingebritsen focuses on environmental norms, multilateral security, and global welfare.

Ingebritsen, C. (2006). *Scandinavia in World Politics*. Lanham, MD: Rowman and Littlefield Publishers. Ingebritsen argues that Scandinavians—Denmark, Finland, Iceland, Norway, Sweden—have developed a particular niche in international relations due to their particular history and culture, often serving as a leader where larger more powerful states do not. In particular, the Scandinavian states have promoted a vision of how states should behave in world politics. Ingebritsen focuses on the origins of Scandinavian global agenda-setting; the impact of Sweden, Finland, and Denmark on the European Union; Norway's prominent role as a peace-builder; and Finnish and Icelandic innovations.

Karsh, E. (1988). *Neutrality and Small States*. New York: Routledge. Karsh explores neutrality, an important foreign policy tool for both large and small states. He examines Spain, Sweden, Switzerland, Ireland, Norway, and Finland during the Second World War and argues that the failure of Norway and Finland's neutrality was largely due to miscalculation. Karsh also examines post-World War II neutrals, and offers a theoretical perspective to understand neutrality in Europe.

Katzenstein, P. J. (1985). *Small States in World Markets: Industrial Policy in Europe.* Ithaca, NY: Cornell University Press. Katzenstein examines the cases of Sweden, Norway, Denmark, the Netherlands, Belgium, Austria, and Switzerland. Presented with a situation that is something of an anomaly—the success of these states in the world system—he sets out to identify what is distinct about these states that would allow their success. Katzenstein asserts that the small European states are exposed to a world market over which they can never hope to exert influence, but they have adapted by compensating for changes, as well as using the power of the state. The strategy of these small states in dealing with the world system both responds to and reinforces domestic structures. Katzenstein argues that this model arises out of the distinctive history of these states.

Katzenstein, P. J. (2003). "Small States and Small States Revisited." *New Political Economy* 8(1): 9–30. Katzenstein reconsiders his groundbreaking book *Small States in World Markets: Industrial Policy in Europe* 18 years after its publication. He argues that none of his reviewers identified his first and most important explanatory variable—a small state's perception of vulnerability, which generates an ideology of social partnership in the small states he examined. He also addresses the reviews of the book, pointing out that though his methodology was critiqued, as well as the change that happened in Sweden, Norway, Denmark, the Netherlands, Belgium, Austria, and Switzerland after the book was published, none of his reviewers questioned his argument. Finally, he examines the prospects for these seven states.

Katzenstein, P. J., ed. (1997). *Tamed Power: Germany in Europe.* Ithaca, NY: Cornell University Press. The central arguments of this book are, first, that the "Germanization" of Europe is linked to the "Europeanization" of Germany, and second, that smaller European states have more power within the European framework than would be expected. The intention of the volume is to examine the institutionalization of power, and, thereby, the role of Germany in Europe. Ultimately, the same structures that restrict Germany's power grant power to the smaller European states. Authors examine the Low Countries, Spain, Greece, Scandinavia, and Central Europe. Contributors include: Jeffrey J. Anderson, Wlodek Aniol, Danes Brzica, Simon J. Bulmer, Timothy A. Byrnes, Péter Gedeon, Christine Ingebritsen, Hynek Jerábek, Peter J. Katzenstein, Paulette Kurzer, Michael P. Marks, Zuzana Poláčková, Ivo Samson, Frantisek Zich.

Keohane, R. O. (1969). "Lilliputians' Dilemmas: Small States in International Politics." *International Organization* 23(2): 291–310. In this article, Keohane reviews the following books:

> George Liska (1968), *Alliances and the Third World.* Studies in International Affairs, No. 5. Baltimore, MD: Johns Hopkins Press.

Robert E. Osgood (1968), *Alliances and American Foreign Policy.* Baltimore: Johns Hopkins Press.

Robert L. Rothstein (1968), *Alliances and Small Powers.* New York: Columbia University Press.

David Vital (1967), *The Inequality of States.* New York: Oxford University Press.

Keohane outlines the perspectives of each of these books, comparing their definitions of small states and their approaches to describing the place of the small state in the world system, with particular attention to their descriptions of alliances, the ways in which each deals with nuclear weapons, and any recommendations the authors might have for large states involved in conflicts with small states. Throughout, Keohane highlights the strengths and weaknesses of each author, ultimately judging Rothstein's to be the most important of the four.

Keohane, R. O. (1971). "The Big Influence of Small Allies." *Foreign Policy* 2: 161–183. Keohane argues that though there are many examples of the limits placed by large states on smaller states, the reverse is also true. Because of the American worldview and specific foreign interests of domestic groups, there is a rise in bargaining power and influence of small allies. The U.S. is linked to numerous smaller allies through extensive bilateral and multilateral agreements. To fix American over-response to small allies would be difficult; therefore, it is important for policymakers to remember that when institutional alliances are formed, changes take place in the ways American decisions are made.

Kindley, R., D. Good (1997). *The Challenge of Globalization and Institution Building: Lessons from Small European States.* Boulder, CO: Westview Press. The essays in this book arose from a conference entitled "The End of the Cold War and Small European States" held by the Center for Austrian Studies at the University of Minnesota in 1993. The conference focused on how globalization affects institutional change. Contributors argue that in the face of globalization societies seek out and implement strategies for survival and adaptation. They also assert that the uniformity predicted by convergence theorists only marginally applies to the experiences of the European small states. Globalization not only constrains policymakers, but it creates opportunities for policy maneuvering and encourages institutional adaptation. The contributors focus on European small states, because these states have weathered globalization with reasonable success and center attention on two groups of small states: the successful Northern states of Finland, Denmark, Austria, Sweden, and Norway, and five post-Communist small states—Hungary, Bulgaria, Estonia, Latvia, and Lithuania. The general conclusion of the book is that though there is a diversity of responses to globalization, these small states show that they have considerable room to maneuver and a capacity to adapt economic institutions. The contributors argue that small European states have relied successfully on two approaches to economic policy. On the one hand, they have manipulated exchange rates to lower the international price of exports and have implemented corporatist income policies to limit production costs. On the other hand, institutionalized class compromises have ensured social peace, which has led to a favorable business climate. These strategies offer a lesson for regions within larger states that must respond to globalization with little assistance from central governments. Contributors include: Robert Holzman, Randall W. Kindley, Tibor Kuczi, Seija Lainela, Csaba Makó, Pekka Sutela, Niels Thygesen, Gunther Tichy, Franz Traxler, Juhana Vartiainen.

Krasner, S. (1981). "Transforming International Regimes: What the Third World Wants and Why." *International Studies Quarterly* 25(1): 119–148. Stephan Krasner's article is focused on the impact of the Third World on the United Nations. According to Krasner, the demands of these nations are a function of their domestic and international weaknesses. In his examination of the impact of the Third World nations on the United Nations, he asserts that the South has been able to alter principles, norms, rules, and procedures in the international system. He argues that because the Third World cannot hope to control the international system, they instead press for international arrangements that offer them some control. One of the principal ways they press for these arrangements is to take advantage of regimes created for other purposes. Krasner states that one of the distinguishing features of Third World countries has been their unity in pushing their demands.

Kurzer, P. (2001). *Markets and Moral Regulation: Cultural Change in the European Union.* Cambridge: Cambridge University Press. Kurzer is attempting to explain change in culturally valued policies in three of the small European Union member states. These policies are alcohol policy in Sweden and Finland, which is less tolerant than that of other member states; drug policy in the Netherlands, which is more tolerant than that of other member states; and abortion policy in Ireland, which is less tolerant than that of other member states. Kurzer says that each of these policies reflects deeply held cultural values. However, in each case there has been convergence with broader European values that can be seen in legal and institutional changes. Kurzer finds that the formal aspects of European integration have caused a series of changes in the way ordinary people live, which then causes a change in values. Freer travel and exchange of goods and services has led to a change in popular preference. Only in the case of alcohol policy did the European Union directly intervene, challenging government monopolies over alcohol sales. Governments are now forced to address the issue of a policy mismatch with popular preference.

Lindell, U., S. Persson (1986). "The Paradox of Weak State Power: A Research and Literature Overview." *Cooperation and Conflict: Journal of the Nordic International Studies Association* 21(2): 79–97. Lindell and Persson offer an "inventory" of the research and literature concerning the ways in which small states can exercise influence over great powers. First, they group literature that looks at power bases of small states and assert that the nature of the system—be it hierarchical, hegemonical, or based on a balance of power—is important. Second, they focus on literature about alternative courses of action that small states can take in the international system. The propositions they discuss mainly concern small states in a bipolar system. In their conclusion, Lindell and Persson acknowledge that they have made a number of assumptions in grouping concepts and definitions, in particular that it is possible to distinguish between the exercise of influence and the creation of security, active influence and passive deterrence, and the influence due to certain qualities of states or actions due to an adversary's shortcomings.

Liska, G. (1957). *International Equilibrium: A Theoretical Essay on the Politics and Organization of Security*. Cambridge, MA: Harvard University Press. Liska proposes an equilibrium theory of the organization of security and international relations. The central concept of institutional equilibrium is applied to international organizations with respect to structure, the commitment of its members, and its functional and geographic scope. A successful organization on a national, regional, or global scale requires that institutional, military-political, and socio-economic factors and pressures for and against stability be equilibrated. Liska argues that once the balance of power among states is controlled by an international institution, the distribution of security, welfare, and prestige ceases to be the result of conflict. Conflict is supplanted by the norms and sanctions of the institutional design. Liska does not explicitly challenge the more traditional arguments about the international system, but rather he discusses how that system changes when states are a part of international organizations. Though Liska largely accepts the idea that small states are at the mercy of larger states in the international system, it is apparent that he sees the situation of small states as more nuanced than purely a question of absolute power, because his discussion centers around the change that institutionalization can have on international relations. He asserts that a state that is low on the hierarchy of power but strategically located in the network of interdependence has the ability to wield influence, particularly if other states are dependent on its resources. Though he does not think that smaller states have had much success in shaping international relations, he offers examples of attempts by small states to shape international organizations. He also introduces the idea that small states consider themselves a moral factor in world affairs, stressing ideals of sovereignty and independence, and he briefly mentions the role that small states may play in mediating between large powers.

Liska, G. (1968). *Alliances and the Third World*. Baltimore: Johns Hopkins Press. Liska approaches the subject of alliances between industrialized powers and less developed states. Liska describes the international system and then examines the functions, causes, and dynamics of alliances between lesser and greater powers. He argues that alliances are an important mode of analysis because their role in international relations is extremely important, both as an institutional stabilizer of political behavior, as well as helping create conventions while reducing the role of coercion.

Lloyd, P. (1968). *International Trade Problems of Small Nations*. Durham, NC: Duke University Press. Lloyd's purpose is to ascertain whether it is possible to develop a theory of small nation trading. He uses national income to determine which states are small states and finds that the size of the country is not a major determinate of trade ratios or a factor in the determination of commodity concentration of exports.

Luif, P. (1995). *On the Road to Brussels: The Political Dimension of Austria's, Finland's, and Sweden's Accession to the European Union.* Vienna: Braumüller. Luif examines why Austria, Finland, and Sweden, all successful European Free Trade Association countries, finally applied for European Community membership. He tracks their approach to the European Community over time and finds that the elites in these countries saw application as a way to solve economic problems. Further, he argues that the significant barrier of neutrality policy ceased to be an impediment with the end of the Cold War.

Männik, E. (2002). "EU and the Aspirations of Applicant Small States: Estonia and the Evolving CESDP." *Current Politics and Economics of Europe* 11(1): 77–90. Männik outlines Estonia's involvement in the development of Common European Security and Defense Policy (CESDP). Estonia's integration into the CESDP can be characterized by its effort to improve its security in a region dominated by Russia. However, Männik asserts that in the future this behavior may change as Estonia willingly accepts the new threats associated with membership.

Mathisen, T. (1971). *The Functions of Small States in the Strategies of the Great Powers.* Oslo: Universitetsforlaget. Mathisen examines the environment and characteristics of small states in an effort to understand the relationship between great and small powers. To this end, Mathisen analyzes the political structures of small states, structures of international power, and small states' range of possible choices.

McIntyre, W. D. (1996). "The Admission of Small States to the Commonwealth." *Journal of Imperial and Commonwealth History* 24(2): 244–277. McIntyre traces the transformation of the British Commonwealth of Nations. As late as 1960, membership was confined to states that could be expected to exercise political and economic influence in the world system. However, by 1995, the British Commonwealth of Nations was almost entirely made up of small, mini, and microstates. McIntyre describes this change.

Mendelson, M. H. (1972). "Diminutive States in the United Nations." *International and Comparative Law Quarterly* 21: 609–630. Mendelson focuses on the dual criteria for membership in the United Nations: statehood and the ability to fulfill Charter obligations. He questions whether small states really are states in the eyes of international law, whether they are able to fulfill the obligations of UN membership, and whether their membership will benefit the UN. He concludes by entertaining alternatives to full membership. Mendelson argues that it is not necessarily bad that the UN is the one place in the international system in which the weak are equal to the strong.

Miles, L. (2002). "Small States and the European Union: Reflections." *Current Politics and Economics of Europe* 11(1): 91–98. Miles concludes "Small States and the European Union," a special issue of *Current Politics and Economics of Europe,* with the lessons learned from the study of small states. Miles asserts that small states have been important policy shapers in the EU. He also argues that domestic factors shape national attitudes towards integration, and offers suggestions for future research, highlighting the number of small states in the EU.

Moses, J. W. (2000). *Open States in the Global Economy: The Political Economy of Small-State Macroeconomic Management.* New York: St. Martin's Press. Moses begins his book by saying that small states are a good case to examine globalization because they have experience with vulnerability to the external environment. His argument is threefold. First, he argues that increased capital mobility forces small states to seek out and use new macroeconomic instruments to maintain full employment. Second, the general consensus that postwar economic policies in small states relied on deficit-financed, or Keynesian economic policy, is incorrect. Rather, he argues that such policies were rarely needed as the postwar period was characterized by even economic growth. Third, methodologically speaking, Moses argues that scholars need to return to a more inductive approach to avoid misunderstanding the nature of economic policy choices. He focuses on Norway, treating it as an Ecksteinian "plausibility probe" intended to test hypotheses on a single case before extending study to a larger sample. He chooses Norway because it is dominated politically by its labor party; its political system is characterized by corporatism; it has consistently maintained full employment; and it maintains policy autonomy.

Nansen, F. (1918). "The Mission of the Small States." *The American-Scandinavian Review* 6(1): 9–13. Writing during World War I when Norway's neutrality had been violated, Nansen argues that Norway has a right to exist. He asserts that it is the duty and mission of small states to keep peace, and that it is the small neutral states that will tie the world back together again after it has been destroyed. He says that it is the job of the neutral countries to keep "the chain of human development unbroken." Nansen, the Norwegian Minister on Special Mission to the United States, says that the future may show a return to small states as the map dissolves and the pieces that were welded together fall apart. He argues that large states are by their nature imperialistic because they put their ultimate reliance in force, which small states cannot do. He concludes confidently that Scandinavia will be free again.

Neuman, S. G., ed. (1976). *Small States and Segmented Societies: National Political Integration in a Global Environment*. New York: Praeger Publishers. In attempting to solve the puzzle of how and why societies succeed or fail at regulating themselves, contributors to this volume believe that the answer lies in the effects international environmental factors have upon internal domestic politics of cohesion. Their argument is twofold. First, that the extent of cohesion within a state is likely a product of domestic institutional relationships or international pressures, most likely a complex interaction between the two. Second, the authors argue that internal cohesion is related to external pressures rather than to pre-existing ethno-cultural or political divisions. The authors investigate the experiences of Cyprus, Pakistan, Zaire, Yugoslavia, East Germany, the Philippines, and Guyana, all small states that suffered insurgency movements. With the exception of the GDR, which serves as a control case, all of these states were attempting to govern more than one ethnic group. In each of these cases, the authors find evidence that supports their claims. Contributors include: Arthur M. Hanhardt, Inayatullah, Lyman H. Legters, Wyatt Macgaffey, Stephanie G. Neuman, Lela Garner Noble, Adamantia Pollis, William Sharp, Raymond T. Smith.

Neumann, I. (1992). "Poland as a Regional Great Power: The Inter-war Heritage."

I. Neumann, ed. *Regional Great Powers in International Politics.* London: St. Martin's Press. The major theoretical aim of the book is to find out how the position of regional great powers causes policy issues and choices that can be seen across regions. Along these lines, Neumann argues that the Poles thought of themselves as a great power and paints a mixed picture of Poland's status. Though some of its very small neighbors, such as Lithuania, fell under its influence, Poland, with large territory and population, had economic issues that complicated its ability to act as a power. It also was sandwiched between two great powers, and, according to Neumann, unfortunately attracted the attention of both.

Nuechterlein, D. E. (1969). "Small States in Alliances: Iceland, Thailand, and Australia." *Orbis* 13: 600–623. Nuechterlein is dealing with the question of why certain small states join great powers instead of adopting non-alignment policies, and why, once in alliances, they remain in them over time. He analyzes three small allies of the United States: Iceland, Thailand, and Australia. He argues that there are seven major factors that influence foreign policy decisions: historical, geographical, and economic factors, external threats, internal security, military capability, and receptivity to foreign bases. Nuechterlein draws four conclusions. First, Iceland and Thailand´s alliance with the U.S. was largely the result of a failure of neutrality policy. Second, an absence of a colonial tradition enhances a state's willingness to accept an alliance without great power. Third, Nuechterlein argues that there was a general agreement on the principal security threat between the countries. Fourth, he discusses the willingness of the protector to employ military power to deter an attack. However, Nuechterlein asserts that alliances can change if the benefits diminish.

Ólafsson, B. G. (1998). *Small States in the Global System: Analysis and Illustration from the Case of Iceland.* Brookfield, VT: Ashgate. Ólafsson engages in a study of the economic and political status of small states using Iceland as a case. His broad conclusion is that traditional assumptions about the minimum size of states is not justified in economic or political terms, and he argues that there are no serious disadvantages resulting from small state size. And, even if there are disadvantages, Ólafsson argues that states such as Iceland and Luxembourg have successfully overcome these disadvantages. He asserts that other small states can obtain standards of living similar to that of Iceland if they invest in education and human capital. Ólafsson also asserts that geographical factors can play a role in the success of a small state. In the case of Iceland, as a small island state its Exclusive Economic Zone essentially extends its geographic area. Further, because of their military vulnerability, small states benefit from a stable global system and should be active in international organizations such as the United Nations. Ólafsson does not believe that regional integration increases the political and economic power of small states, though he concludes by saying that international cooperation between small states is beneficial.

Osgood, Robert E. (1968). *Alliances and American Foreign Policy.* Baltimore: Johns Hopkins Press. Osgood argues that alliances are an important mode of analysis because they are an integral part of world politics. Osgood asserts that alliances are one of the primary tools of states to cooperate with other states to protect and advance their interests. Osgood points out that every state must have an alliance policy, even if it is to avoid all alliances. Osgood's book centers on the United States, but ponders the nature of alliances between a super power and weaker states.

Papadakis, M., H. Starr (1987). "Opportunity, Willingness, and Small States: The Relationship Between Environment and Foreign Policy." C. F. Hermann, C. W. Kegley, J. Rosenau, eds. *New Directions in the Study of Foreign Policy*. Boston: Allen & Unwin: 409–432. Papadakis and Starr's intention in this chapter is to develop and apply a comparative foreign policy model based on conceptions of environment, willingness, and opportunity. They apply their model to the case of small states because, according to the authors, size is consistently a variable in distinguishing differences in foreign policy behavior. Further, they assert that it is easier to control for other determining factors because small states have the most constrained opportunity sets. Papadakis and Starr argue that though a state's environment defines the situation in which that state can act, how the state actually acts is dependent on a list of factors, including opportunity sets at each level of a state's environment, the state's perception of its environment, and the state's willingness to take any given course of action. Papadakis and Starr state that conventional wisdom says that small states have limited resources, which are the determinants of state capacity; however, they think a more nuanced view of power than these traditional assumptions suggest is needed. The authors argue that state power can emerge from factors other than material resources, that the size of states makes a difference in their power capacity, and that power and influence can be exercised on less than a system level.

Paterson, W. E. (1969). "Small States in International Politics." *Cooperation and Conflict: Journal of the Nordic International Studies Association* 2: 119–123. Paterson critiques David Vital's approach to the study of small states in *The Inequality of States*. In particular, Paterson says that Vital never defines "small power." He also problematizes Vital's comparison, as well as his case selection, and raises some measurement issues. Though he thinks that Vital's analysis should be modified, he does not dispute his argument that there are large constraints on small state foreign policy choices.

Plischke, E. (1977). *Microstates in World Affairs: Policy Problems and Options*. Washington, D.C.: American Enterprise Institute for Public Policy Research. In this book, Plischke explores the expansion of the global community and possible future growth. He is interested in the growing diplomatic "problem" of small states, particularly microstates, questioning whether all small states (in terms of population) be given the same weight in international affairs as the large states. Plischke uses population to define size. He addresses the issue of equal voting in the UN, and discusses the "legal fiction" that a new state becomes the legal equal of all others. He says that this poses some difficulties—as the U.S. is twice as populous as all the small states combined, and yet small states control the majority of voting power. Plischke urges the U.S. and other large states to think about the impact these small states are going to have as their numbers increase—particularly because many of them are former colonies, which have what he names "post-colonialist" suspicion of the larger states. He says that small states are going to transform the international system and that we need to think about what this means, because the longer the large states wait to think about this, the fewer the options. He concludes with policy suggestions: restricting statehood; abstention, dissuasion, and exclusion; institutional reorganization and alignment; weighted representation and voting; and special forms of membership.

Rapaport, J., E. Muteba, J. Therattil (1971). *Small States and Territories: Status and Problems.* New York: United Nations Institute for Training and Research. Rapaport, Muteba, and Therattil's objective is to examine the role of very small states and territories in international affairs. The study examines states with a population of less than one million that have some degree of international individuality—even if it is tenuous. The authors address the issue of why these states have managed independence and find that the largest factor is geographic isolation, though other historical factors, such as colonialism, can also have an impact. The study is divided into four broad pieces. First, it deals with the historical background and the issues raised by the participation of small states in international organizations. Second, it analyzes the status of these states in terms ·of their political evolution and international relations. Third, it examines the practical problems of small states, such as small territory and limited resources. Finally, the authors suggest options for international action. Dealing with the problems of small states and territories, they assert that most small state problems are related to underdevelopment in general, such as lack of resources.

Rees, N., M. Holmes (2002). "Capacity, Perceptions, and Principles: Ireland's Changing Place in Europe." *Current Politics and Economics of Europe* 11(1): 49–60. Rees and Holmes consider the impact of EU membership on Ireland's capacity, perceptions, and principles. For Rees and Holmes, membership has had a positive impact on Ireland by moving it from the periphery. However, they argue that membership has also had negative impact by placing it in a larger entity that, at times, has differing interests. The rejection of the Nice Treaty is an example.

Reid, G. L. (1974). *The Impact of Very Small Size on the International Relations Behavior of Microstates.* London: Sage. Reid focuses on the international behavior of very small states. He argues that the political independence of many small states since 1960 indicates that there have been changes in norms of statehood and in beliefs about the viability of statehood. This process is occurring at the same time that many large states are moving toward regional integration. Reid asserts that size is a major determining factor of behavior. Therefore, he argues that size should be treated as the independent variable, while foreign policy behavior should be the dependent variable. In light of this, the extent to which a state can participate in external affairs will be dictated by the size of its surplus capabilities.

Reiter, D. (1994). "Learning, Realism, and Alliances: The Weight of the Shadow of the Past." *World Politics* 46(4): 490–526. Reiter tests the idea that small powers learn about neutrality and alliance, as well as change strategies. He finds that the alliance choices of small powers in the twentieth century were largely shaped by lessons from national experiences rather than by variations in levels of external threat. When a national policy was successful, it was continued; when it was not, it was discontinued.

Reiter, E., H. Gärtner, eds. (2001). *Small States and Alliances*. Heidelberg: Physica-Verlag. Reiter and Gärtner want to understand the conditions that lead states to engage in alliances by focusing on small states. To this end they bring together scholars and policy-makers to discuss small states and alliances. They conclude with policy recommendations.

Risse-Kappen, T. (1995). *Cooperation Among Democracies: The European Influence on U.S. Foreign Policy*. Princeton, NJ: Princeton University Press. After observing what he perceived to be a disproportionate European, and particularly German, influence on American nuclear decisions, Risse-Kappen set out to answer the question of whether West Europeans had a significant impact on American foreign policy, and if so, what the extent of this impact was. He argues that the West Europeans and the Canadians did exert a greater influence on American foreign policy during the Cold War than most have believed, and that traditional alliance theories, which largely focus on power and strategic interactions, cannot explain the impact Europeans had on American policy. Beginning with the Realist idea of the "big influence of small allies," Risse-Kappen ultimately argues that such influence was, because of the transatlantic alliance system, made up of liberal democracies, and has affected the collective identity of all of its members, including the U.S. Employing Putnam's argument about two-level games, Risse-Kappen further argues that domestic pressures were used to increase leverage in transatlantic bargaining, which is important because use of material power was considered inappropriate. Finally, he contends that transnational and transgovernmental coalitions among bureaucratic and societal actors put pressure on the U.S. to accept allies' demands. He examines the moderation of U.S. policies during the Korean War, the Suez Crisis (a case when the U.S. severely violated the norms of consultation), the 1958–1963 test ban negotiations, the Cuban missile crisis, and NATO's nuclear decisions. Therefore, Risse-Kappen argues, it is not useful to conceptualize NATO as simply another military alliance; instead, NATO is an important framework for Europeans to shape American policy.

Robinson, E. A. G., ed. (1960). *Economic Consequences of the Size of Nations (Proceedings of a Conference Held by the International Economic Association)*. New York: St. Martin's Press. E. A. G. Robinson's edited volume is a series of conference papers, which attempt to return to Adam Smith's question of the relationship between the size of nations and their economic prosperity. Contributors to this volume, all economists, entertain questions about the economic advantages of nations with large populations versus the advantages of those with small populations. Because many of the arguments for establishing common markets and free trade areas are based on assumptions about economies of scale, contributors address the question of the market size necessary to exhaust the principles of economies of scale. The contributors look at the handicaps and advantages of some of the bigger and smaller countries, focusing specifically on the United States, Switzerland, and Belgium, with some reference to Sweden. They conclude that it is easy to exaggerate the importance of scale among the many factors that influence productivity. They are reluctant to speak of an optimal size, but they conclude that even small countries can have a number of firms of the minimum size to give full, or almost full, technical efficiency. Further, they find that there are certain industries or groups of industries that are ordinarily found in larger countries but not in smaller ones. There also appear to be differences in diversification of industries, as the firms in smaller countries tend to be less specialized and more diversified. Additionally, there appear to be differences in the character of competition, as it is easier to develop a monopoly in small countries than in large countries. Finally, contributors argue that in larger economies, the specialization of firms extends to the service industry. Contributors found the question of adaptability difficult to address. Specifically, they wondered whether small nations have an advantage because of homogeneous populations, closely integrated systems, and flexibility in political and economic organization. Contributors generally found that if small states do have an advantage in adaptability, it is a precarious one. Contributors include: P. R. Brahmananda, L. Duquesne de la Vainelle, C. D. Edwards, S. Fabricants, D. Hague, J. Jewkes, W. A. Jöhr, F. Kneschaurek, S. Kuznets, G. Leduc, G. Marcy, V. A. Marsan, L. T. Pinto, W. Prest, E. A. G. Robinson, K. W. Rothschild, T. Scitovsky, I. Svennilson, L. Tarshis, R. Triffen, C. N. Vakil, P. J. Verdoorn, J. Weiller.

Rothstein, R. L. (1968). *Alliances and Small Powers*. New York and London: Columbia University Press. Traditional international relations literature assumes that small powers are essentially big powers writ small. If this view is correct, then there is no real reason to study small powers as separate entities. However, Rothstein believes that small powers are something more, or are different from, great powers, and the central purpose of this book is to establish this point. Rothstein argues that small powers think and act differently from large powers, and failure to acknowledge these differences will make any analysis simplistic. To make this argument, Rothstein largely focuses on the security problem that faces most small powers in the post-1815 world, specifically on the problem of achieving security through alliance policy. Rothstein defines a small power as one that realizes that it cannot obtain security by the use of its own capabilities and therefore must rely on the aid of other states, institutions, and other processes for its own security. Rothstein's analysis covers history since 1815, focusing on small European powers, and he hopes to offer a starting point for future investigations.

Sharp, G. P. (1987). "Small State Foreign Policy and International Regimes: The Case of Ireland and the European Monetary System and the Common Fisheries Policy." *Millennium: Journal of International Studies* 16(1): 55–72. Sharp is concerned with two predictions regarding international relations. First, governments are less concerned with emphasizing national identity and independence when there are obstacles to gain through intergovernmental cooperation. Second, because small states will succeed disproportionate to size in a regime, their commitment to independent foreign policy will decline. Sharp examines what he believes to be the two main strategies of the Irish government in response to the European Community by looking at the cases of the European Monetary System and the Common Fisheries Policy. These strategies are a community identity and an attempt to exploit the rules through demands. Over time the Irish policy shifts to favor integration and supranational decision-making because it is beneficial to Ireland.

Schou, A., A. O. Brundtland, eds. (1971). *Small States in International Relations.* Uppsala: Almqvist & Wiksell. The chapters included in this volume are the papers from the Nobel Symposium 17. The chapters examine a range of small state behaviors and roles in international relations including neutrality and work in international organizations. It includes reflections by A. Baker Fox, R. Barston, K. Birnbaum, E. Bjøl, A. O. Brundtland, E. Coppieters, H. Eek, J. Freymond, J. J. Holst, R. Hyvärinen, L. G. M. Jaquet, P. Muñoz Ledo, S. Lemass, I. Nicolae, J. Okumu, S. Poplai, L. Reczei, J. Sanness, A. Schou, G. Schram, G. Stourzh, J. Sverdrup, K. Törnudd, D. Vital, and R. Vukadinovic.

Singer, M. (1972). *Weak States in a World of Powers: The Dynamics of International Relations.* New York: The Free Press. Singer crosses levels of analysis to understand power relations, the nature of the ties between strong and weak states, and the interaction between elites in different states. Singer focuses on post-WWII relations between the U.S., the Soviet Union, Japan, Great Britain, France, and the weak states that are associated with them.

Sisay, H. B. (1985). *Big Powers and Small Nations: A Case Study of United States-Liberian Relations.* Landham, MD: University Press of America Inc. Sisay's book describes U.S.-Liberian relations to 1980. Sisay is interested in U.S. policy in Liberia, particularly in whether the U.S. behaved imperialistically. He asserts that the U.S. State Department actively intervened in Liberian affairs for a variety of reasons. First, Sisay argues that because Liberia was founded by the U.S., the State Department felt morally obligated to lend assistance. Second, he asserts that following Britain's Stevenson Restriction Act, which significantly raised the price of rubber, there was pressure to find a cheap source of rubber. Firestone Tires opened huge rubber plantations in Liberia, which ultimately caused big changes in Liberian internal and external relations. Ultimately Sisay asserts that U.S. policy toward Liberia was largely marked by caution, apathy, paternalism, and non-intervention.

Sutton, P., A. Payne (1993). "Lilliput Under Threat: The Security Problems of Small Island and Enclave Developing States." *Political Studies* 41: 579–593. Sutton and Payne call the reader's attention to the fact that there are 45 states in the world with a population of less than one million. Of these 45, 36 are developing states. They assert that there are five characteristics of a small developing state: openness, islandness or enclaveness, resilience, weakness, and dependence. They argue that these states are exposed to other predatory states, organizations, and individuals. However, Sutton and Payne find that in the face of these obstacles, these states are remarkably resilient, and make use of strategies that differ in each regional context.

Thorhallsson, B. (2000). *The Role of Small States in the European Union.* Burlington, VT: Ashgate. Thorhallsson analyzes whether small states have a different range of interests in the European Union and if their policy-making differs from that of the larger states. Thorhallsson asserts that size is a significant factor in determining the behavior of the smaller states in the EU decision-making process. He compares seven small states—Luxembourg, the Netherlands, Denmark, Ireland, Belgium, Portugal, and Greece—to five larger states—Germany, France, the United Kingdom, Spain, and Italy. He focuses on the Common Agricultural Policy and Regional Policy, areas where the degree of difference between member state preferences is large. Thorhallsson concludes that the behavior of smaller states can be distinguished from that of larger states in that small states have a different approach to the Commission and they exhibit different negotiating tactics. He argues that because small states do not have sufficient resources to follow all negotiations, they become reactive in some sectors while being proactive in the most important sectors. Thorhallsson argues that small states use the informality, flexible decision-making, the greater maneuvering room of their officials, and the greater role of Permanent Representatives in domestic policy-making—all distinctive administrative features—to operate within European decision-making processes. Ultimately, Thorhallsson asserts that Peter Katzenstein's widely accepted theoretical framework on small states in the international system must be modified because it fails to provide an explanation for the ability to distinguish between small and large states in the Common Agriculture Policy and Regional Policy. Though his findings support Katzenstein's argument about the effects of strong corporatist arrangements on small state behavior in international affairs, Thorhallsson believes that the size of state administration and its characteristics should be taken into consideration.

Thorhallsson, B. (2002). "Consequences of a Small Administration: The Case of Iceland." *Current Politics and Economics of Europe* 11(1): 61–76. Thorhallsson argues that small size and the distinct characteristics of the Icelandic administration have impacted Iceland's relationship with the EU. Further, Thorhallsson contends that the EU has "Europeanized" ministries, most notably the Ministry of Foreign Affairs, which has gained prominence and has increased its role in policy-making. He asserts that the new status of the Ministry of Foreign Affairs has allowed the last two foreign ministers to adopt a more pro-EU stance.

Väyrynen, R. (1971). "On the Definition and Measurement of Small Power Status." *Cooperation and Conflict: Journal of the Nordic International Studies Association* 2: 91–102. Väyrynen divides possible definitions of small power status into four categories: the rank of a country, the nature of the behavior of small powers, the distinct interests of small powers versus those of the great powers, and the use of concepts from role theory. He argues that a rank analysis serves as the best foundation, but that looking at behaviors and concepts from role theory is also fruitful. In addition, he argues that the ways in which leaders of small powers perceive the role expected of them by the public are important, as are contextual effects, such as the region and the state of the international political economy.

Vital, D. (1967). *The Inequality of States: A Study of the Small Power in International Relations.* Oxford: Clarendon Press. Vital attempts to analyze the political options of small states, which are acting alone, in other words, a non-aligned small state acting on the basis of its own resources. His conclusions are not optimistic. He argues that it is materially and humanly costly for a non-aligned small state to maintain independence and sovereignty and that the cost of independence is only rising. However, despite these findings, he does not believe that small non-aligned states are an endangered species. Though small states might find themselves in a precarious situation at the time Vital was writing, he believed that because the international system was divided between great nuclear powers, states were cautious in conflict, making small non-aligned states more secure. Therefore, with differing success, Vital concludes that small states can enjoy some autonomy.

Vital, D. (1971). *The Survival of Small States: Studies in Small Power/Great Power Conflict*. London: Oxford University Press. Vital states that in a nuclear world of a "balance of terror," there is a class system of states. The first class is made up of states with extensive militaries and nuclear arsenals, and force cannot be directly applied against members of this first class. However, Vital argues that force can be used against all other members of different classes. He believes that the advent of nuclear weapons created a situation in which a conflict between a weak and a strong country needed to be redressed by a powerful third country. He draws upon three cases, Czechoslovakia, Israel, and Finland, to illustrate the limitations of a small power to operate independently in the face of opposition from a strong power. These cases are not entirely pessimistic as they also reveal some of the options available to these small powers. Ultimately, however, as in his book *The Inequality of States*, his view of prospects for these states is pessimistic—in his words, "tragic."

CONTRIBUTORS

ANNETTE BAKER FOX is a senior research scholar at the Saltzman Institute of War and Peace Studies, Columbia University, New York.

JESSICA BEYER is a doctoral candidate at the University of Washington.

JORRI DUURSMA is adjunct faculty at the International University of Monaco and University of Leiden, Netherlands.

SIEGLINDE GSTÖHL is professor of European Politics and Administration at the College of Europe, Bruges, Belgium.

MICHAEL HANDEL is research associate at the Harvard Center for International Affairs and the Hebrew University, Jerusalem, Israel.

CHRISTINE INGEBRITSEN is associate professor of Scandinavian Studies and Associate Dean of Undergraduate Education, University of Washington, Seattle.

PETER J. KATZENSTEIN is Walter S. Carpenter Jr. Professor of International Studies, Cornell University, Ithaca, New York.

ROBERT O. KEOHANE is James B. Duke Professor of Political Science at Duke University, Durham, North Carolina.

IVER B. NEUMANN is Director of Research at the Norwegian Institute of International Affairs, Oslo, Norway.

DAN REITER is Director of Graduate Studies, Department of Political Science, Emory University, Atlanta, Georgia.

BALDUR THORHALLSSON is associate professor of Political Science at the University of Iceland

DAVID VITAL is professor emeritus of Political Science, Tel Aviv University, Israel.

INDEX